OS/2 Programmer's Desk Reference

OS/2 Programmer's Desk Reference

V. Mitra Gopaul

McGraw-Hill, Inc.

New York San Francisco Washington, D.C. Auckland Bogotá
Caracas Lisbon London Madrid Mexico City Milan
Montreal New Delhi San Juan Singapore
Sydney Tokyo Toronto

Library of Congress Cataloging-in-Publication Data

Gopaul, V. Mitra
    OS/2 programmer's desk reference / V. Mitra Gopaul.
        p.   cm.
    Includes index.
    ISBN 0-07-023748-4
    1. Operating systems (Computers)   2. OS/2 (Computer file)
I. Title.
    QA76.76.063G668   1995
    005.265—dc20   94-44828
                                                     CIP

1 2 3 4 5 6 7 8 9 0   AGM/AGM   9 0 0 9 8 7 6 5

ISBN 0-07-023748-4

The sponsoring editor for this book was Jerry Papke, the editing supervisor was David E. Fogarty, and the production supervisor was Donald Schmidt.

Printed and bound by Quebecor/Martinsburg.

McGraw-Hill books are avaiable at special quantity discounts to use as premiums and sales promotions, or for use in corporate training programs. For more information, please write to the Director of Special Sales, McGraw-Hill, Inc., 11 West 19th Street, New York, NY 10011. Or contact your local bookstore.

To my mother, Saimawantee,
for her love and self-sacrifice

Contents

Preface

As an OS/2 programmer, I have come to realize that long gone are the days when applications were developed with an editor and a language. Nowadays, given the complexity of operating systems and demands for intuitive and user-friendly applications, developing software is becoming a rigorous task.

To write a simple Presentation Manager (PM) application with a main window, a menu bar, few pull-downs, online help, and a dialog box, you will need the following software tools:

- C/C++ compiler
- Linker
- NMAKE utility program
- Resource compiler
- Dialog editor
- Icon editor
- Information Processing Facility (IPF) compiler
- Tag language
- Editor
- Integrated development environment

Now, if you add another dimension to this application, such as access to DB2/2 or the use of COBOL or REXX, program development becomes more complicated. It is impossible to remember the syntax of commands or statements for all these software tools. With the software tools listed above, you will need a dozen reference manuals and books on these subjects. Often, when you desperately need to know the correct ways of coding a statement or command, you reach for the manual, but it's not available. Someone has borrowed it.

For many years I yearned for *one* book, right on my desk, like a dictionary, containing all the information commonly used by most programmers. I know that many of my colleagues also need such a book; therefore, I wrote *OS/2 Programmer's Desk Reference.*

About This Book

This book is an attempt to provide information about tools commonly used by OS/2 programmers. The topics covered are sufficiently varied to be useful in most of your development and maintenance work. The subjects are C and C++, compiling and linking programs, COBOL, DB2/2, SQL (IBM Structured Query Language), Toolkit, IPF, preprocessor directives, OS/2 commands, and REXX.

As you probably know, computers must be fed with precise information; for instance, a missing comma or variables with incorrect data can make utility programs unpredictable. When writing this book, I focused on giving the reader the kind of information that is essential in making work more productive. This book is a repository of syntax, commands, and keywords of the most widely used tools by OS/2 programmers. The illustrations and examples, included wherever possible, should make your coding task a little bit easier.

I assumed that the reader has a basic knowledge of the subjects covered here. Although it is useful for learning programming concepts and practices, the material is presented in such a way as to benefit both experienced and novice programmers. It should refresh your memory if you have forgotten something, and the easy-to-understand descriptions and examples should enrich your understanding if you are exploring new areas.

How This Book Is Organized

There are 11 chapters, each dealing with subjects such as database, language, utility programs and software products. The subject matter is organized to be both practical and useful. Assuming that the book will be used primarily as a desk reference, I have arranged the information in either alphabetical or hierachical order depending on the nature of the subject matter. Also, you may notice as you go through this book that the chapters are developed in a consistent way, with the same conventions used throughout.

Chapter 1 is a reference for programmers using C language. Chapter 2 discusses the syntax and examples that are specific to C++ language. Chapter 3, on compiling and linking C and C++ programs, contains useful information about the compiler options and linker libraries and how to invoke them. In Chapter 4, a comprehensive review of the COBOL language, you will find explanations and examples of divisions, sections, paragraphs, statements, verbs, and other COBOL elements. Chapter 5 gives all the syntax of DB2/2 commands and explains DB2/2 functions and parameters. Chapter 6 discusses all the SQL statements and functions. Chapter 7 describes all the utility programs that accompany the OS/2 Toolkit. Chapter 8 is a reference for programmers using IPF. Chapter 9 explains how to use the preprocessor directives for C/C++. Chapter 10, which presents all the commands of OS/2, is a quick reference for syntax, usage, and return codes. Finally, in Chapter 11, which is a reference for REXX programmers, descriptions of instructions and examples are presented to enhance the reader's understanding.

Notational Convention

In the general format of the commands and statements used in this book, a few symbols are not part of the syntax and must *not* be included when you code your program. These symbols and their meanings are as follows:

Symbol   **Meaning**

[ ]   The option enclosed by the brackets ([ ]) is not required but can be included, for example, [and] are not part of the following command,

```
IQC [filename]
```

< >   Only one of the alternatives enclosed by the angle brackets (< >) must be chosen, for example,

```
ICC </S or /T>
```

or   The alternatives enclosed by the brackets (< > or [ ]) are separated by "or", for example,

```
ICC </S or /T> [/W or /R]
```

_____   The underlined word is the default value.

...   The horizontal or vertical ellipses indicates that the preceding parameter(s) can be coded more than once. This applies to variables, filenames, options, keywords, and so on, that are enclosed in brackets.

All keywords of the command syntax are written in uppercase or lowercase characters; they must be coded as shown.

All strings in italic lowercase characters are variables that can be changed to any other strings to suit your programming style. In your code they represent values that you supply to the commands.

Conclusion

OS/2 Programmer's Desk Reference is unique. In the published literature, there are numerous books and manuals on each subject discussed here or on combinations of these subjects; however, to this author's knowledge, this is first time that all these programmers can find all these diverse and sought-after subjects in one place.

This book is written with the needs of the programmer in mind. I am certain that it will replace many of the books and manuals on your desk. It should serve you for a long time in your demanding task of software development and maintenance.

Acknowledgments

First, I must thank Jay Ranade for his technical guidance for this book. After spending many months writing this book I am very grateful to Gerald Papke, senior editor, for supplying me with the research materials promptly and for his encouragement. Many thanks to the editing staff of McGraw-Hill, namely David Fogarty, Cathy Hertz, and Donald Schmidt, for their meticulous work to ensure that the information given here is accurate, clear, and useful.

I am grateful to Gail Ostrow, Melissa Robertson, and Mark Nunn of IBM for supplying me with software and reference materials related to OS/2. Thanks to many of my friends and colleagues, especially Maddie and Ray Wingett, Abby Micheles, and Cedric Debbo, for their encouragement, positive thoughts, and great interest in the progress of this work.

Finally, my special gratitude to my wife, Gaye; my daughter, Laiia; and my son, Sanjiv for their unfailing support and encouragement throughout this project; also for their understanding when I took time away from them.

V. Mitra Gopaul

C Language

This chapter is a reference guide for programmers using C language. For the reader's convenience, discussion of C and C++ has been divided into two seperate chapters. This chapter deals primarily with C; and Chapter 2, with C++. As C is a subset of C++—and thus all operations performed in C can be performed in C++ (but not vice versa)—it is assumed that C++ programmers will be conversant with all syntax and other aspects of C and might want to skip Chapter 1 and that C programmers, who may not be concerned with object-oriented programming and other C++-specific concepts and methodology, might want to skip Chapter 2. In this chapter, we'll discuss topics common to both C and C++ such as:

Elements of C
Declarations and Definitions
Expressions and Operators
Precedence and associativity
Statements

1.1 Elements of C

As does any language, C has a few basic elements that programmers must be aware of:

- Characters and tokens
- Trigraphs
- Escape sequences
- Comments
- Language keywords

This section briefly describes these elements.

◘ Characters and tokens

A program consists of a series of tokens. A *token* is simply a sequence of characters. Many such tokens, separated by spaces, must follow the syntax rules of the language. For example, the following is a short program made up of many tokens.

```
/* to illustrate data declaration */
#include <stdio.h>

main()
{
  int x, y, z; /* data declaration of
            variables x, y, z */

  x = 10, y =20; /* initialize x with
            value 10 and y with 20 */
  z = x + y ; /* add variables x and y and
            place the result in variable z */
  /* print the value of z */
  printf( " x + y = %d \n", z );
}
```

The following is a list of characters recognized by C language.

- Lower- and uppercase letters:
  a to z and A to Z

- Decimal digits:
  0 to 9

- Graphic characters:

```
! " # % & ' ( ) * + , - . / :
; < = > ? [ \ ] _ { } ~ ^ |
```

- Space character

- Control sequence characters for horizontal tab(tabulator), vertical tab, formfeed, and end of string. These characters are treated as spaces.

Trigraphs

Not all the characters used in C language, as listed previously, are available on all keyboards. It is possible to code a program using a sequence of three characters, called a *trigraph*, to represent the missing character. During the compilation of the program, the compiler makes the translation from the trigraph sequence to the missing character. The following is a list of all the trigraph sequences and the characters represented.

Trigraph sequence	Character represented
??=	#
??(	[
??)	]
??<	{
??>	}
??/	\
??'	^
??!	|
??-	~

Escape sequences

In a program you can code special control characters, such as alert, backspace, and a new line. These control characters are also known as *escape sequences* and each escape sequence has two characters. The first character is always a backslash '\', followed by a control character.

Escape Sequence	Character Represented
\a	Alert
\b	Backspace
\f	New page
\n	New-line
\r	Carriage return
\t	Horizontal tab
\v	Vertical tab
\\	Backslash
\'	Single quotation
\"	Double quotation
\0	Null character (end of string)

◘ Comments

A comment starts with characters /* and ends with characters */; for example,

```
/* This is a comment */
```

A comment can occupy more than one line. The compiler treats comments as white spaces; they are ignored. Some compilers allow comments in a nested manner; for example,

```
/* /* This is a wrong comment */ */
```

◘ Identifiers or names

Identifiers are simply names given to functions, data objects, and labels. A *name* is a token made up of a sequence of letters, digits, and underscore (_). If names of these items are chosen with care, they may contribute to readability and documentation and may also help remove any confusion. There are some limitations on the length and significance of identifiers; ANSI C allows up to 32 characters.

All internal names are case sensitive. In other words, the compiler recognizes the difference between upper- and lowercase characters. In external names, upper- and lowercase characters are treated the same way.

◻ Language keywords

There are many reserved words in C language (see examples in Fig. 1.1). They have special meanings in the context of programming; these keywords should not be used in any other way or be redefined.

auto	break	case	char	const	continue
default	do	double	else	enum	extern
float	for	goto	if	int	long
register	return	short	signed	sizeof	static
struct	switch	typedef	union	unsigned	void
volatile	while				

Figure 1.1 C language keywords.

When writing a program you should also keep in mind names that have been used for system calls and library functions. These names are not C language reserved words, but using them out of context may result in unpredictable results.

◻ Constants

A constant is a data object that does not change during the execution of a program. There are five types of constants:

- Integer
- Floating-point number
- Character
- String
- Enumeration

1.2 Data Declarations

In a C program, data storage, also known as *variables*, must be first declared before being used. *Data declaration* simply means to tell the compiler to reserve a specific amount of memory space associated with that variable and to give a name or identifier (or name) to the variable.

After a variable is declared, a program is able to manipulate the content of the variable already declared as a data object with a specific memory location.

The general form of a declaration is

```
storage-specifier type-specifier variable-list;
```

storage-specifier tells the compiler how to store the variables that follow.

type-specifier describes the type of the data object.

variable-list assigns a name to the data object, which can be used in a program.

● Example

To illustrate these aspects of data declaration, let's look at a simple example.

```
/* to illustrate data declaration */
#include <stdio.h>

main()
{
  int x, y, z; /* data declaration of
            variables x, y, z */

  x = 10, y =20; /* initialize x with
            value 10 and y with 20 */
  z = x + y ; /* add variables x and y and
            place the result in variable z */
  /* print the value of z */
  printf( " x + y = %d \n", z );
}
```

The statement

```
static int x, y, z ;
```

specifies to the compiler to allocate memory space for three variables and give them the name **x, y** and **z**. The keyword *int* (discussed in the next section) indicates that each variable must be large enough to hold an integer value. The storage specifier is **static**.

In the next statement,

```
x = 10, y = 20;
```

the program assigns 10 and 20 to **x** and **y**, respectively. This is an example of a program making use of a variable; this is an instruction to the compiler to place values in the memory space already reserved.

Next we have the expression

```
z = x + y ;
```

Again this statement instructs the compiler to calculate **x + y** and to place the result in memory occupied by variable **z**. Finally, we print the result value **z** using the **print** function.

1.3 Data Types

Earlier we considered how to give reserve memory and give it a name so that it can be referenced in a program. Now, let's look at variables that can be declared with different data types. There are several data types, which can be grouped into two categories: scalar and complex. The scalar data types are

    Characters
    Floating-point numbers
    Integers
    Pointers
    Enumeration

From these data types, you can build more complex data arrangements such as:

    Arrays
    Structures
    Unions

This section describes how to use variables with all these data types, and also shows how to define your own data type names which are derived from the basic types.

◧ Character data types

There are three basic character data type—char, unsigned char, and signed char—differentiated with respect to the ranges of values each type can hold. A character variable occupies one byte. The following shows the different types and the range of values in the OS/2 environment.

Type	Range
char	0 to 255
unsigned char	0 to 255
signed char	-128 to 127

A character variable can be used in the same way as an integer variable. If it is declared as *signed*, the high-order bit determines whether the value is negative or positive. If the character variable has an *unsigned* data type, the compiler treats all values as positive. A variable with any of these character data types will hold a single character. A *char* variable is initialized with a character constant, which is formed by enclosing a character with a pair of single quotes (not to be confused with double quotes used for enclosing string constants).

● Example

In the following statement, the **char_var** variable is initialized to character 'w'.

```
char char_var = 'w' ;
```

You can also initialize a character variable with a nonprintable character constant. In the next example, the **newline** variable is first defined as **char** datatype and its initial value is '\n' escape sequence (new line).

```
char newline = '\n';
```

In the following example, the **number_of_books** variable, defined as **unsigned char**, has an initial value of 20.

```
unsigned char number_of_books = 20 ;
```

The type specifier **char** can also be used to define an array of characters. In the following example, the **city** variable is declared as a character array, and each element of the array is initialized with a character ('N', 'e', 'w', etc.).

The statement

```c
for( i = 0; i < 8; ++i )
  printf( "%c", city[i] );
```

loops eight times, starting with i = 0 to i = 7, and prints each element of **city** array. The statement

```c
printf( "\n" );
```

prints a new line after printing all the elements of **city** array.

```c
/*******************************************
This program illustrates the character array.
*******************************************/
#include <stdio.h>

static char city[] = { 'N','e','w',' ','Y','o','r','k' };

main()
{
    int i;

    for ( i = 0; i < 8; ++i )
      printf( "%c", city[i] );
    printf( "\n" );
}
```

C does not have a string data type; the **char** data type is used to make an array of characters into a string variable. In fact, a string is made up of individual characters and terminates with a NULL character ('\0').

In the following example, the **city** variable is defined as an array of characters and is initialized with a string constant rather than by setting individual cells to a character constant as in the previous example. This time double quotes are used; the compiler automatically adds a NULL character after the last character of the string. In contrast, the string is printed using the format specifier '%s', which prints the string. In the previous example we printed individual characters of the **city** array.

```c
/*******************************************
This program illustrates character string
*******************************************/
#include <stdio.h>
static char city[] =  "New York";
```

```
main()
{
    printf( "%s\n", city );
}
```

The main difference between an array of characters and a string is that the latter has a NULL character ('\0') at the end string, namely, 'New York', placed by the compiler. In an array, the compiler does not have a NULL charater; however, you may place one, if you wish.

◘ Floating-point variables

Floating-point variables are declared with three different data type specifiers: **float, double,** and **long double.** These data types are needed if a variable is to hold a fractional component or very large numbers.

● Example

In the following program, the **float_var** variable is defined as **float, double_var** as **double,** and **long_var** as **long double.** Each is initialized with a floating-point number and then printed with the **printf** function.

```
/**********************************************
This program illustrates floating-point variables.
**********************************************/

#include <stdio.h>

main()
{
    float float_var   = 441.22 ;
    double double_var = 9.44E+11 ;
    long double long_var = 8.55E+55 ;

    printf( "float variable  = %f \n", float_var );
    printf( "double variable  = %E \n", double_var );
    printf( "double long variable  = %E \n", long_var );
}
```

◘ Integers

Variables that hold integer values must be declared as one of the following six datatypes:

short or **short int**

int or **signed int**
long or **long int**
unsigned short or **unsigned short int**
unsigned or **unsigned int**
unsigned or **unsigned int**
unsigned long or **unsigned long int**

● Example

In the following example, the **short_num** variable is defined as an array of integers with **short** data type. The elements of the array are initialized to the values -127, 0, 10, and 128. Variable **i** is declared as an **int** data type; **unsigned_num** is defined as an **unsigned** datatype and initialized with 65000; the **long_num** variable is defined with the *long* specifier with the initial value set to -80000.

```
/************************************************************
This program illustrates integer variables
************************************************************/

#include <stdio.h>

main()
{
  short   short_num[] = { -127, 0, 10, 128 } ;
  int     i ;
  unsigned   unsigned_num = 65000 ;
  long    long_num = -80000 ;

  for ( i = 0 ; i < 4 ; ++i )
    printf( "short integer number = %d \n",
                   short_num[i] );
  printf( "unsigned integer = %d \n", unsigned_num );
  printf( "long integer = %ld \n", long_num );
}
```

◻ Void Type

Variables can be declared to hold no value with the specifier *void*. The *void* data type is used mainly to declare functions that do not return a value.

◻ Single-dimension arrays

An *array* is made of two or more data objects occupying contiguous memory space. The data types of all the data objects in an array are the same. Each data object is called an *element*, which is accessed by an index. All the elements are referenced by the same identifier found in the array declaration. An array can have one or more dimensions.

A single-dimension array declaration has the following general form:

```
storage-specifier type-specifier variable-name [size];
```

storage-specifier denotes whether an array is a local or a global variable.

type-specifier establishes the data type of all the elements of the array.

variable-name identifies the array and all its elements.

size indicates to the compiler the number of elements the array will hold.

● Example

In the following example, the **number**, a **static** variable, is defined as an array of four integers. Each element of this one-dimensional array is set to an initial value: -127, 0, 10, and 128.

```
int number[4] = { -127, 0, 10, 128 } ;
```

The values of each element of **number** look like this:

Element	Value
number[0]	-127
number[1]	0
number[2]	10
number[3]	128

In the following program, the index and the value of each element of **number** array are printed.

```
/*********************************************
This program illustrates the integer array.
**********************************************/

#include <stdio.h>

static int    number[4] = { -127, 0, 10, 128 } ;
```

```
main()
{
  int i;

  for ( i = 0 ; i < 4 ; ++i )
    printf( "Index is %d, value is = %d \n",
                  i, number[i] );
}
```

In the following statements, character arrays are declared and initialized: **month1** array, with characters; **month2** array, with a string with double quotes; and **month3** array, with string enclosed within double quotes only.

```
static char month1[] = { 'F', 'e','b' } ;
static char month2[] = { "Feb" } ;
static char month3[3] = { "Feb" } ;
```

If you omit the dimension of the array and set a string constant as an initial value, as was done for the **month2** variable, then the compiler terminates the array with a character constant '\0' (NULL). But for the **month3** variable only 3 bytes are allocated and initialized. The following table shows how the compiler initializes elements of these three arrays.

Element	Value	Element	Value	Element	Value
month1[0]	F	month2[0]	F	month3[0]	F
month1[1]	e	month2[1]	e	month3[1]	e
month1[2]	b	month2[3]	b	month3[2]	b
		month2[4]	\0		

◘ Multidimensioned arrays

The general form of a multidimensional array definition is

```
type-specifier variable-name [size1][size2]...[sizen];
```

This is similar to the one-dimensional array definition, except that there are multiple size values.

● Example

The following declaration of an array **points** variable has two dimensions containing 12 elements; all elements are of integer data type.

```
int points[3][4];
```

The compiler always finds contiguous space for an array of any dimension. For the sake of convenience, let's look at this two-dimensional array as a rectangular format with rows and columns. Therefore, the **points[3][4]** array has three rows and four columns, arranged as follows:

Row	Column 1	Column 2	Column 3	Column 4
1	points[0][0]	points[0][1]	points[0][2]	points[0][3]
2	points[1][0]	points[1][1]	points[1][2]	points[1][3]
3	points[2][0]	points[2][1]	points[2][2]	points[2][3]

The next example shows how to initialize each element of points array.

```
int points[3][4] = { 1,2,4,8,
             2,4,8,16
               3,6,12,24
          };
```

The following program shows how to access the content of each element of an array.

```
/*****************************************************
This program illustrates multidimensional array variables.
*****************************************************/

#include <stdio.h>

static points[3][4] = { 1,2,4,8
                2,4,8,16
                3,6,12,24
              };

main()
{

int i,j;

for (j = 0; j < 3; j++ )

   for ( i = 0 ; i < 4 ; i++ )

     printf( "points[%d][%d] = % d\n",
             j, i, points[j][i] );
}
```

The output of the program looks like this:

```
points[0][0] = 1
points[0][1] = 2
points[0][2] = 4
points[0][3] = 8
points[1][0] = 2
points[1][1] = 4
points[1][2] = 8
points[1][3] = 1
points[2][0] = 3
points[2][1] = 6
points[2][2] = 12
points[2][3] = 24
```

◘ Enumeration

An *enumeration* is a data type used to represent a set of integer values. After defining an enumeration, you can declare a variable using that enumeration data type. Such a definition specifies all the valid values of that data type.

The general definition form of an enumeration is

```
enum identifier { enum1, enum2, ... } variable-list ;
```

enum is the keyword defining an enumeration data type.

identifier is the name you give to such a data type. The list of enumerators (*enum1, enum2*, etc.) gives the data type a set of constant integer values.

variable-list is an option for declaring variables of the enumeration data type.

The main point regarding enumeration is that each enumerator is a symbol representing an **integer** value. There are three ways of assigning the values. First, by default, the compiler sets the value of the first enumerator to 0, the second enumerator to 1, the third to 3, and so on. For example, a declaration

```
enum fruit { orange, peach, apple, mango };
```

will assign 0 to **orange**, 1 to **peach**, 2 to **apple**, and 3 to **mango**. Second, you can explicitly give an enumerator a value by placing an equal sign (=) and an integer after the enumerator. In a declaration

```
enum fruit { orange = 5, peach, apple, mango };
```

orange has value 5 and **peach**, **apple**, and **mango** will have 6, 7, and 8 repectively. Third, an enumerator will always have one value greater than the previous one. Of course, if it is the first unassigned enumerator, its value is always zero.

● Example

The following statements declare an enumeration called **coins** and variable **money** of that data type.

```
enum coins ( penny, nickel, dime );
coins money;
```

In the following program, **flag** is defined as an enumeration data type. The variable **sw** is declared to be of enumeration data type **flag** and initialized to **off**, one of the enumerators. The statement

```
if ( sw == off )
   printf( "The switch is off\n");
```

tests whether **sw** is enumerator **off**; if it is true then the **printf** function is executed. Next, **sw** is assigned the value represented by enumerator **on**.

```
/****************************************
This program illustrates enumeration.
****************************************/

#include <stdio.h>

main()
{
  enum flag ( on, off ) sw = off ;

  if ( sw == off)
    printf ( "The switch is off\n" );

  sw = on ;

  if ( sw == on )
    printf ( "The switch is on\n" );
}
```

◘ Pointer

Pointers are addresses to data objects. A variable declared as a pointer is used as a memory address of a data object. The general form a of pointer declaration is

```
type-specifier *variable-list;
```

type-specifier can be any data type.

variable-list consists of one or more variables of the data type.

◘ Structure

A **structure** is a collection of variables or data objects. It is a convenient way to keep and manage related data. Unlike the array—requiring all elements to have the same data type—the variables of a structure can be of different data types. Each data object of a structure is called a *member* (also known as a *field* or *element*). The name of each field must be unique within a given structure. But you can use the same member name in more than one structure.

The general form of defining a structure is

```
struct [identifier]{
       type-specifier variable-name;
       type-specifier variable-name;
       .
       .
       .
       } [variable-list];
```

struct is the keyword to defining a structure. It is placed at the beginning of the definition.

identifier is the name you give to the structure.

type-specifier is the data type of a member.

variable-name is the name of the member.

variable-list contains one or more variables as part of the structure declaration.

The *identifier* and *variable-list* are optional; however, you cannot omit both of them. In a structure declaration, the compiler does not allocate any memory space unless a *variable-list* is included in the declaration.

● Example

In the following definition of an **employee** structure there are seven fields, each with different data characteristics but part of an **employee** record. Each elememt is a variable, declared with a data type and an indentifier, and terminated with a semicolon (;). The **temp_employee** and **perm_employee** variables are also part of the **employee** structure definition. The **retired_employee** variable is defined as the same structure data type but on a separate statement.

```
struct employee {
        char name[30];
        int  street_num;
        char street[40];
        char city[20];
        char prov[3];
        char postal_code[6];
        unsigned long int salary;
        } temp_employee, perm_employee;

struct employee retired_employee;
```

A structure definition cannot have itself as a member. However, it is valid to include a member as being a pointer to the structure. For example, in the following structure **address**, a member **next_rec** is a pointer to the structure **address**.

```
struct address   {
        char name[30];
        char street[40];
        char city[20];
        char state[3];
        struct address *next_rec;
        };
```

It is possible to initialize all or some members of the structure during the declaration; for example,

```
struct address new_address =
  { 1233, "Belle View Lane", "New York","NY", 10003 };
```

The next program illustrates how to use a structure. It prints each element of the structure using the **printf** function.

```
/********************************************
This program illustrates structure variables.
********************************************/

#include <stdio.h>

struct address   {
        int  street_num;
        char *street;
        char *city;
        char *state;
        unsigned long zip;
        };

struct address new_address =
   { 1233, "Belle View Lane", "New York","NY", 10003 };

main()
{
printf("%d %s\n", new_address.street_num,
          new_address.street );
printf("%s, %s %ld\n", new_address.city,
          new_address.state,
          new_address.zip );
}
```

◘ Bitfield structure

With C, it is possible to store and access information as bits within a byte. To do so, you declare a member of a structure as an integer with a specific length of bits. Such a member is called a *bitfield*. There are many reasons for using bits as fields of data. Some of these are

1. Bits can be **boolean** variables, especially when storage is limited.
2. You may want to interface with devices that encode information in bit strings.
3. You may want to access any bit within a byte.

Although these operations can be achieved with the bitwise operators of C, **bitfield** adds structure, efficiency and readability to your programs.

A bitfield is declared as a special kind of structure. The data type of the elements can only be **int**, **unsigned** or **signed**. The declaration of each bitfield contains a *type-specifier*, a *variable-name*, and a colon (:) and is followed by the length of the field.

The general form of a bitfield structure is

struct [*identifier*] {
      type-specifier variable-name : length;
      type-specifier variable-name : length;
      .
      .
      .
      } [*variable-list*];

struct is the the keyword to define a structure. It is placed at the beginning of the definition.

identifier is the name you give to the structure.

type-specifier is the data type of a member.

variable-name is the name of the member.

variable-list contains one or more variables as part of the structure declaration.

If *length* is zero (0), it causes the next field to be aligned on the next integer boundary. A structure variable with bitfield elements cannot be an array; nor can you declare a pointer to such a variable.

The *identifier* and *variable-list* are optional; however, you cannot omit both of them. In a structure declaration, the compiler does not allocate any memory space unless a *variable-list* is included in the declaration.

● Example

The following program defines a structure called **flags** and declares a **comm** variable of type **flags**. The structure has seven elements, but the storage of **comm** requires only four integers.

```
/******************************************
This program illustrates bitfield variables
*******************************************/

#include <stdio.h>

struct flags {
        unsigned active : 2 ;
        unsigned ready  : 1 ;
        unsigned error  : 1 ;
```

```
        int counter ;
        unsigned receive : 10 ;
        unsigned 0 ;
        unsigned xmit     : 10 ;
        } comm ;
main()
{
   comm.error = 0;
   comm.ready = 1;
   comm.receive = 999;

   if ( comm.error )
     printf( "Error\n" );
   else if ( comm.ready )
     printf( "Received data is %d \n", comm.receive );

}
```

Each element occupies memory as follows:

Member	Storage
Integer 1	
active	2 bit
ready	1 bit
error	1 bit
Integer 2	
counter	integer
Integer 3	
receive	10 bits
Integer 4	
xmit	10 bits

Since the fourth element *counter* requires a full integer for storage, the compiler gives the first three elements a full integer. Now, the fifth and seventh elements get one integer each because they are separated by the sixth element which has length zero. Note that to access a structure member you need the structure name and member name separated by dot (.), for example, **comm.error**.

◼ Union

A *union* provides a way of having two or more variables share storage. A union declaration is similar to that of a structure, with elements having different data types. In a structure each element has its own memory space; in a union all elemets occupy the same memory location.

The general form of a union declaration is

```
union identifier {
       type-specifier variable-name;
       type-specifier variable-name;
         .
         .
         .
       } [variable-list];
```

union is the keyword to define a union. It is placed at the beginning of the definition.

identifier is the name you give to the union.

type-specifier is the data type of a member.

variable-name is the name of the member.

variable-list is one or more variables as part of the union declaration.

● Example

In the following example, the **wt_code** is defined as a union type. In the next statement, the *convert* is a union and defined as **wt_code** data type. The compiler allocates sufficient memory to hold the largest member; therefore, 2 bytes are allocated to the **convert** variable. In this case **short int** type requires 2 bytes and **char** occupies only 1 byte. These 2 bytes are allocated to the **convert** variable.

```
union wt_code    {
       short int weight ; /* requires 2 bytes */
       char code  ; /* requires 1 byte */
       };
union wt_code convert ; /* maximum bytes        */
                    /* reserved is 2 bytes */
```

Now, let's see how both members, **weight** and **code**, share the same storage. The **weight** variable takes 2 bytes; the first of these bytes is also used by the **code** variable.

```
        |<--    weight   -->|
        .....................
        | byte 0 | byte 1 |
        .....................
        |<-code->|
```

In the following program, the **profile** union and the **employee** variable are declared in the same statement. The **profile** union has four elements. The first three variables are **name, birthday,** and **age,** and their basic data types are **char** and **int.** The fourth element is a **convert** union variable. The compiler gives the **employee** variable 20 bytes of storage, and all its members share the same memory location.

```
/****************************************
 This program illustrates union variables.
 ***************************************/

#include <stdio.h>

 union wt_code   {
        int weight ;
        char code  ;
        };

 union profile   {
        char name[20];
        char birthday[9];
        int age;
        union wt_code convert ;
        } employee = "John Smith" ;

 main()
 {
   union info *recp = &employee;

   printf("Name is %s.\n", employee.name );

   recp->age = 30 ;

   printf("Age is %d.\n", employee.age );
 }
```

The **employee** variable is initialized with a string constant "John Smith." Only the values of the first member of a **union** variable may be initialized.

To access a union member, use the same notation as that used to access a member of a structure. The three statements in the body of the preceding program illustrate how to access union members. The first one prints the field name, the second assigns value 30 to **age,** and the last prints the value of **age.**

▣ Typedef-name

By using the keyword **typedef** you create a new name with existing data types. In effect, you are defining your own data type name. A **typedef** does not create a new data class; nor does it reserve any storage. It allows creation of a user qualified data type. The new data type can be used to declare a variable.

The general form of a **typedef** definition is

> **typedef** *type-specifier identifier*;

type-specifier can be any data type such as **int, char**, and **float**.

identifier is the new name you give to the new type.

● Example

To create a new data type name **DOLLAR** having the same characteristics as type **float**, you would use

```
typedef float DOLLAR;
```

Now, you can use this new type **DOLLAR** to declare a variable, say, **rent**.

```
DOLLAR rent;
```

The compiler recognizes **rent** as a **float** variable.

What is the advantage of creating a new data type based on an existing one? It allows the programmer to define types that reflect the intended use. Previously, we defined a type **DOLLAR** and used it to declare a **rent** variable. This approach adds to the self-documentation of your code and facilitates maintenance efforts later on.

The next program illustrates further the definitions and use of user-defined data types. At the top you will see three statements with the keyword **typedef**. The first defines the new type **DOLLAR** as float; the second defines type **NAME** as an array of 30 characters; the third one, **EMP_REC**, uses a structure construct in its definition. This structure has three fields, where the first two variables, **surname** and **salary**, use previously defined data types **NAME** and **DOLLAR**. The third, **age**, variable is of **int** type.

The statement

```
EMP_REC employee[ EMP_NUM ];
```

is a declaration of the array called **employee** with **EMP_NUM** (100) elements of type **EMP_REC**. Assuming the array has been initialized, the body of the program shows how to access each element and field of the **employee** array. The variable **i** indexes through the **employee** array, and the dot operator (.) is used to access each field.

```
/*******************************
This program illustrates typedef.
*******************************/

#include <stdio.h>

#define EMP_NUM 100
typedef float DOLLAR;
typedef char NAME[30];
typedef struct   {
      NAME surname;
      int age;
      DOLLAR salary;
      } EMP_REC;

EMP_REC employee[ EMP_NUM ];

main()
{
int i;

for ( i = 0 ; i < EMP_NUM ; i++ )
   printf( "Name is %s, Age is %d, Salary is %f \n",
      employee[i].surname, employee[i].age,
      employee[i].salary (;
}
```

1.4 Storage Specifiers

There are four ways to tell the compiler how the memory should be allocated for a variable. You can specify the storage with one of the following classes:

- Automatic
- Static
- External
- Register

These class-specifiers are discussed in the following paragraphs. In using them, it is important to note whether a variable is local and global in relation to a function where it is used. A *local* variable, when declared within the body of a function, is local to the function. Variables declared outside a function are called *global* variables. The time of memory allocation and duration of the variable depends on whether it is local or global.

◙ Automatic class

When storage class is not specified, the default is the **auto** class. This storage class is most commonly used. All local variables in a function are declared as **automatic** local variables. They are of transient duration, "created" at the time the function is called, and last as long as the function is being executed. Such a variable *cannot* be accessed by other functions.

When declaring a local variable within a function it is more precise to declare it with the **auto** specifier; however, it is rarely used explicitly.

● Example

In the following example, the **n** and **limit** variables in the **count** function are declared as **auto** storage class. Both of them are local to the **count** function and last as long as this function is executed. The **for** loop,

```
for ( n=0; n < limit ; n++ );
```

simply increments **n** from 0 to 10.

```
count ()
{
    auto int n;
    int limit = 10;
    for ( n=0; n < limit ; n++ );
}
```

◙ Static class

A variable defined with a **static** specifier is permanently established. There are two ways of using the **static** storage class: local and global.

The static local variables: When you use a static specifier to define a variable within a function or block of code, the compiler creates a local but permanent data object. It is known to the function only where it is defined. Therefore, a static local variable cannot be referenced outside the function where it is declared. Such a variable retains its value from one execution of the function to the next.

● Example

The following example shows how a local static variable is used. In the **print_num** function the local **number** variable is defined as a local static variable and initialized to value zero. When the **print_num** function is first called in the **main** function, a value 10 is added to zero (0) and printed. The next time, value 10 is added to 10 and printed.

```
/***********************************************
 This Program illustrates a local static variable.
 **********************************************/
# include <stdio.h>
void prt_num();
main()
{
   print_num();
   print_num();
}

void print_num()
{
   static int number = 0;
   number = number + 10 ;
   printf( "Number is %d \n" , number );
}
```

The static global variables: When you use a static class specifier to declare a variable outside a function, the compiler creates a global and permanent data object. Such a variable is known to function(s) only below the variable declaration within the file. It is different from global variables with **extern** storage class discussed later. Static global variables are not accessible to functions in another file.

● Example

The following example shows how a static global variable is used. In file 1 the **number** variable is declared as a global variable, initialized to zero. In the same file, the **print_num1** funtion prints the **number** variable after adding value 10 to it. In file 2 the **number** variable is defined again as a global variable, but initialized to the value 100. The function **print_num2** also prints the **number** variable after adding value

10 to it. In **main**, both **print_num1** and **print_num2** are called, but the results are different. In **print_num1** function, 10 is added to 0, while in **print_num2** function 10 is added to 100.

File 1

```
/************************************************
    This program illustrates static global variables.
*************************************************/
#include <stdio.h>
static int number = 0;
void print_num1();
void print_num2();
main()
{
   print_num1();
   print_num2();
}

void print_num1()
{
   number = number + 10 ;
   printf( "Number is %d \n" , number );
}
```

File 2

```
static int number = 100;
void print_num2()
{
   number = number + 10 ;
   printf( "Number is %d \n" , number );
}
```

◘ External class

Generally a C program can be divided into several parts. Each part resides in a separate file. Each part, called a *source module*, is made up of many functions which are compiled separately. During link time, all the modules are pulled together into an executable program.

It is possible for variables to be declared in one module but accessed by functions in another module. To allow global access to a data object, you use the **extern** storage class. A global variable is declared outside a function using the keyword **extern**. If a declaration is found in a module without a specifier but it is outside a function, the default is *always* a global variable.

The compiler allocates memory for all **extern** storage classes just before program execution begins. This memory is freed after the program terminates.

If a variable with **extern** is declared in one file, this variable is available to all functions after it is declared within that file. However, if you want to access the same variable from a function in another file, you have to declare the variable with the extern specifier again in that file.

● Example

In the following example, there is a **main** function in file 1 and a **counter** function in file 2. The global variable called **first** is defined in file 1 without any storage-class specifier.

The **main** function and **first**, which is a global variable, are found in the same file; therefore, **main** can access **first** without a declaration. However, the **counter** function, found in another file, also references the **first** variable but needs a declaration with the **extern** specifier.

File 1

```
/*****************************************
This program illustrates extern variables.
******************************************/

#include <stdio.h>
int first; /* global definition of first */

main()
{
    int count, last;
    first = 10 ;
    last  = 20 ;
    count = counter( last );
    printf( "First = %d, last = %d and count = %d \n",
       first, last, count );
}
```

File 2

```
/*****************************************
This program counts from first to last
*****************************************/
counter( last )
int last;
{
    int i, count;
    extern int first; /* declaration of variable first */
    count = 1;
    for ( i = first; i < last; i++ )
      count++;
    return ( count );
}
```

A declaration can appear at the beginning of a block (as in **counter** of the preceding example) or outside a function (only once in one file). In the **counter** function, the **for** loop is used to count from the value of **first** to the parameter **last**. The count is returned to the calling function.

◘ Register class

The **register** class applies only to variables of type **int**, **char**, and **float**. The **register** specifier requests that the compiler stores the declared variables in the register of the CPU (central processing unit), rather than memory, where variables are normally stored. This kind of storage expedites operation on a variable. It is useful to maximize the speed in a critical part of a program, where a variable is heavily used (e.g., to control a loop). It is used as a local variable; therefore, it is transient. It cannot be used as a global variable, but can be passed as a parameter to a function.

If the **register** storage class is properly used, it can significantly enhance the performance of a function. There are only a few general purpose registers available to the compiler. Therefore, the number of **register** class variables at any given time is limited. This number depends on the compiler you are using.

● Example

In the next example, **l** and **n** variables in the **count1** function are declared with the **register** specifier. The **for** loop

```
for ( n=0; n < l ; n++ );
```

is to count from 0 to the value of **l**, which is 10,000. And in **count2** the **n** variable is declared as **auto** storage class.

```
/*********************************************************
This program illustrates the register storage class.
*********************************************************/

main()
{
int limit = 10000;
count1 ( limit );
count2 ( limit );
}

count1 ( register int l )
{
    register int n;
```

```
    for ( n=0; n < l ; n++ );
}

count2 ( l )
int l;
{
    int n;
    for ( n=0; n < l ; n++ );
}
```

◻ Volatile

By using the attribute **volatile** in a definition or declaration, you are telling the compiler that this variable's value may be changed by ways not explicitly specified in the program. For this reason, the compiler will not optimize the portion of the code where the variable is used, leaving the original intent inact.

The general form of *volatile* definition is

```
volatile storage-specifier variable-list;
```

● Example

One illustration of its use is where a variable holding real-time data is updated by a subroutine of the operating system. In the following example, the **clock** variable is defined as a **volatile** data object. It is assumed that the variable **clock** is updated every tenth of a second by a routine outside this program. This program prints in tenths of seconds the elapsed time needed to increment **i** 10,000 times.

```
/*************************************************
   This program illustrates the volatile variable.
 *************************************************/

# include <stdio.h>

volatile int clock;

main()
{
    int time,i;
    time = clock;
    for( i = 0; i < 10000 ; i++ );
    printf( "Elapsed time is %d \n", clock - time );
}
```

◘ Const

In certain situations you would not want the content of a variable to change. Such a change could inadvertently, however, causing a programming error. To avoid any unintentional alteration of a variable, you can declare a variable with the **const** attribute.

The general form of the **const** definition is

```
const storage-specifier variable-list;
```

Such a definition will explicitly declare the variable as a constant. The compiler will flag any attempts to modify a variable declared as **const**. In the following statements, the **version** and **name** variables are defined as **const**.

```
const float version = 1.20 ;
const char name[] = "Softek International";
```

1.5 Expressions

This section explains the use of expressions and operators in C. An expression is a sequence of operators, constants, function names, function calls, and any objects and pointers of any type. Any combination of these various pieces can be a valid part of an expression. The general classes of expressions are

- Constant expression
- Primary expression

During the course of the discussion of expressions, references will be made to data types or groups of data types. The following lists the types that collectively belong to a group.

Groups	Types
Integral	Character
	Enumeration
	Integer
Arithmetic	Integral
	Floating-point number

Groups	Types
Scalar	Arithmetic
	Pointers
Aggregate	Arrays
	Structures
	Unions

◘ Precedence and associativity

The *precedence* determines the order in which operations are performed; the contents of Figure 1.2 are arranged from highest to lowest precedence. At the top are primary operators, which have the highest priority; the comma operator, at the bottom of the list, has the lowest precedence. Within a given group, such as a group of multiplicative operators (*, /, and %), all operators have the same priority. Now, let's see how the compiler applies the built-in precedence rule. In the expression

```
a - b * x / y
```

the multiplication and division operators have higher precedence than does substraction. Therefore, the expression **b * x / y** is calculated first and the result is substracted from **x**. However, you can change the precedence by explicitly stating the grouping of the operands within parentheses. The previous expression is rearranged to

```
( a - b ) * ( x / y )
```

Then the subtraction and division have the same precedence and are evaluated before the multiplication. The associativity rule establishes how an operation is evaluated. If it is "left to right" the operators are evaluated from left to right. The rule "right to left" rule implies that the operators are performed from right to left.

Precedence	Operators	Associativity
Primary	. -> ( ) [ ]	left-to-right
Unary	-+ ! - ++ -- (typename) & * sizeof	right-to-left
Multiplcative	* / %	left-to-right
Additive	+ -	left-to-right
Bitwise shift	<< >>	left-to-right
Relational	<= >= < >	left-to-right
Equality	!= ==	left-to-right
Bitwise AND	&	left-to-right
Bitwise XOR	^	left-to-right
Bitwise OR	|	left-to-right
Logical AND	&&	left-to-right
Logical OR	||	left-to-right
Conditional	?:	right-to-left
Assignment	= += -= *= /= <<= >>= %= &= ^= |=	right-to-left
Comma	,	left-to-right

Figure 1. 2 Precedence and association of operators.

◘ Constant expression

A *constant expression* is made up of one or many constants, such as

- Integer constants
- Character constants
- Floating-point constants
- Enumeration constants
- Other constant expressions

The value of the constant expression is evaluated at the time of compilation of a program. While the program is being executed, this value cannot be changed.

A constant expression is required in the following cases:

- The **case** keyword must be followed by a constant expression in a **switch** statement.
- To specify the size of an array.
- An enumeration identifier must be assigned a constant expression.
- To assign initial values to external or static variables.
- In the **#if** preprocessor statement.

In the first three situations, the constant expression must be one of the following:

- Integer constants
- Character constants
- Enumeration constants
- Casts to integral types
- **sizeof** expression

In the same situations, you can use only the following operators:

- Arithmetic operators
- Bitwise operators
- Relational operators
- Conditional expression operators

In the fourth case, all the above rules of constants and operators are valid.

◘ Primary expression

There are six types of primary expressions:

- Indentifier
- Constant expression
- Parenthesized expression
- Function call
- Array element specification
- Structure and union specification

The primary operators are grouped from left to right, and all of them have the same precedence.

◘ Indentifier

An *identifier* is a primary expression. It is declared as a *name* for a data object or function. If an identifier is declared as an array, the value of the identifier is the address of the first object of the array.

Constant

A *constant* is a primary expression, and its type may be **int, long,** or **double** depending on the form.

Parenthesized expression ( )

As seen earlier, the precedence rule forces execution of certain operations before others. Parenthesized expressions are used to explicitly state how operands and operators are grouped together. This allows you to change the order in which the compiler will evaluate an expression.

● Example

In the example

```
x - y * z ; /* multiply first */
```

the multiplication of **y** and **z** will be done before the subtraction. You can change the order of the operation with parentheses. If you want the subtraction done first, you can force the compiler to do so by enclosing the subtraction in parentheses; for example,

```
( x - y ) * z ; /* subtract first */
```

If you parenthesize the multiplication,

```
x - ( y * z );
```

it will not change the normal order of calculation, which is multiplication first and subtration next.

◘ Function call ( )

A *function call* is a primary expression followed by a list of arguments enclosed in parentheses. The list may be empty or may contain one or more expressions. Multiple expressions are separated by commas. If you wish to change the value of the parameter within a function, you would pass a pointer to the variable rather than the value.

Arrays and functions are always converted to pointers before they are passed as parameters to a function.

If a function call is defined as a function returning type **int**, then in an expression the value returned by such a function is of **int** data type. Similarly, a primary expression defined to return **float** type, will result in **float** type.

● Example

The following are examples of function calls:

```
sort()
counts( x+y, y+10 )
read( buffer, length )
```

Before any function is executed, an expression of the argument list, if any, is evaluated and becomes the argument of the function. For example, **x+y** and **y+10** will be first calculated and passed as values to the **counts** function. The values of actual parameters, such as **x** and **y**, are never changed, but assigning the value to the parameter changes the value within the function.

◘ Array element specification [ ]

An *array subscript* is a primary expression when it is followed by an expression enclosed by a pair of square brackets ([ ]). This value of expression after it is evaluated refers to an element of an array. If the array is declared as a **char** data type, it is a pointer to the first character of the string.

The primary expression is a pointer, and the type subscript must be an integer value. The compiler converts the expression within the brackets into an address of the array element.

● Example

In the example

```
horses[ y + 2 ]
```

the expression **y+2** is first evaluated, yielding an integer value. This value is then used to calculate the memory location of element **y+2**.

◘ Structure and union specifications (. or ->)

A primary expression followed by a dot (.) followed by an identifier is an expression. The primary expression must be a variable name defined as **structure** or **union** type. The identifier must be a member within the **structure** or **union**. The following is a dot expression:

```
employee.name
```

A primary expression followed by an arrow operator (->) followed by an identifier is an expression. The primary expression must be defined as a pointer to **structure** or **union** type. The identifier must be a member within the **structure** or **union**. The following is an arrow operator expression.

```
employee->name
```

1.6 Operators

C language is rich in built-in operators. Each operator is a symbolic character telling the compiler to execute certain mathematical or logical tasks. There are five general classes of operators.

● Unary operators
● Binary operators
● Conditional operators
● Assignment operators
● Comma operators

While discussing operators, we will refer to data types or groups of data types. The types that collectively belong to a group are listed as follows:

Groups	Types
Integral	Character
	Enumeration
	Integer
Arithmetic	Integral
	Floating-point numbers
Scalar	Arithmetic
	Pointers
Aggregate	Arrays
	Structures
	Unions

1.6.1 Unary operators

A unary operator acts on only one value. The following are unary operators:

Increment ++	Bitwise negation ~
Decrement --	Address &
Unary plus +	Indirection *
Unary minus -	Cast
Logical negation !	**sizeof**

All these unary operators have the same precedence. In an expression with many unary operators, the compiler groups them in right-to-left order.

◘ Increment ++

The *increment* operator (++) simply adds one (1) to the operand. After the following statement is executed

```
y++;
```

the value of **y** is incremented by one.

But if the operand is a pointer, the increment depends on the size of the object it is pointing to. Let's say **intp** is an integer pointer variable. The statement

```
intp++;
```

will increase the value of **intp** by 4 since an integer occupies 4 bytes. Or, if **structp**, a pointer variable, is defined as a pointer to a structure of size 20 bytes, the example

```
structp++;
```

will add value 20 to **structp**.

The increment operator can be placed before or after an operand. In an expression with several operands, the position of ++ is significant. If you place ++ before the operand, the operand is first incremented and then used in the expression.

In the example

```
y =   ++x + z;
```

value 1 is first added to variable **x**; then the result is added to **z**, and the final sum is placed in **y**.

If you place ++ after the operand, the current value of the operand is first used in the expression, and then its value is incremented.

In the example

```
y = x++ + z;
```

the current value of **x** is added to **z**, the result is placed in **y**, and then **x** is incremented by one.

◘ Decrement --

The *decrement* operator (--) simply substracts one (1) from the operand. After the statement

```
y--;
```

is executed, the value of **y** is decremented by one.

But if the operand is a pointer, the decrement depends on the size of the object it is pointing to. Let's say **intp** is an integer pointer variable. The statement

```
intp--;
```

will decrease the value of **intp** by 4 since an integer occupies 4 bytes. Or, if the pointer variable **structp** is defined as a pointer to a structure of size 20 bytes, the example

```
structp--;
```

will decrease the value of **structp** by 20.

The decrement operator can be placed before or after an operand. In an expression with several operands, the position of -- is significant. If you place -- before the operand, the operand is first incremented and then used in the expression.

In the example

```
y =   --x + z;
```

value 1 is first subtracted from the **x** variable, then the result is added to **z**, and the final result is placed in **y**.

If you place -- after the operand, the current value of the operand is first used in the expression, and then its value is decremented. In the example

```
y = x-- + z;
```

the current value of **x** is added to **z**, the result is placed in **y**, and then **x** is decremented by one.

◼ Unary plus +

The *unary plus* operator (+) does not change the value of the operand. In fact, this operator is seldom used. The operation of the statement

```
+x;
```

will not change the value of **x**.

◨ Unary minus -

The *unary minus* operator (-) multiplies the value of the operand by -1. When the unary minus is applied to an operand, the sign of the value is switched. For example, if the **number** variable has value 10, then

```
-number;
```

will change the value to -10. If **number** has value -10, then

```
-number;
```

will change the value to 10.

◨ Logical negation !

The logical negation operator (!) is used to test whether the value of an expression is false. The expression is first evaluated, and if it is zero (0), the logical negation operator yields a one (1). If the result of the negation is nonzero, then the negation operator returns a zero (0). The result of the logical negation operator is always of **int** type. In the following statements, the variable **flag** is tested for a zero or nonzero value.

```
if ( !flag )

  printf( "flag is zero" );
else

  printf( "flag is non-zero" );
```

If the result of operation **!flag** is 0, then

```
printf( "flag is zero" );
```

is executed. Otherwise, this segment of thr program executes

```
printf( "flag is nonzero" );
```

Another use of the logical negation operator is to easily "flip" the value of a flag between one and zero; for example,

```
flag =  !flag ;
```

will switch the value of **flag** to one or zero depending on whether its value before the operation is zero or nonzero.

◘ Bitwise negation ~

The bitwise negation operator (~) changes the content of every bit of the operand. All the bits that are 1s are changed to 0s and vice versa; all bits that are 0s are switched to 1s. The bitwise negation operator therefore produces the one's complement of the operand. Let's say **y** is defined as an **unsigned char** variable and has a value 10. The 8-bit binary representation of **y** is 00001010. Now, the expression

```
~y;
```

will produce the binary value   11110101.

◘ Address &

The *address* operator (&) produces the memory address of the operand, for example,

```
py = &y;
```

assigns the memory location of the **y** variable to **py**. It is assumed that **py** is declared as a pointer variable to the same type as **y**.

The operands of the & operator can be variables or array elements. But it is illegal to have **bitfield** or **register** variables as operands of an address operator.

◘ Indirection *

The *indirection* operator (*) uses as its operand the address to data object. The operand must be a pointer variable, and the result depends on the data type. The following statements first declare **a** and **b** as **int** variables and then **pa** as an integer pointer variable.

```
int a,b;
int *pa;
```

The statement

```
b = *pa;
```

assigns the value pointed to by **pa** to **b**. In this case, the result of the operator * is an integer value. The following sequence of statements

```
pa = &a;  /* assign address of a to pa */
b  = *pa; /* assign content of pa to b */
```

demonstrates how to assign the address and contents of **a** variable, which is the same as

```
b = a;
```

◙ Cast

The *cast* operator converts the value of an expression to a specific data type. To do so, you place the parenthesized name of the data type before the operand. For example, you define **z** as an integer and you want the result of expression **z/5** to be a **float** type. To guarantee that the compiler yields a fractional component, you use the **cast** operator. In the statement

```
price = (float) z/5 ;
```

the value **z/5** is assigned to the **price** variable, which is defined as a **float** type.

◙ sizeof

The **sizeof** operator gives the size of an operand in the number of bytes. The operand can be a variable or type, but it cannot be a bitfield or a function. In the following program, **sizeof** determines the size of **x** and **city**, which are variables. It also calculates the number of bytes occupied by an **int** data type.

```
/***********************************************
This program illustrates the use of sizeof operator.
***********************************************/

#include <stdio.h>

int x;

char city[] = "New York";

main()
{
   printf("Size of x is %d \n", sizeof(x));
   printf("Size of city is %d \n", sizeof(city));
   printf("Size of int is %d \n", sizeof(int));
}
```

After this program is run, it shows

```
Size of x is 4
Size of city is 9
Size of int is 4
```

1.6.2 Binary operators

A *binary operation* requires two operands which are separated by a *binary* operator. They are not of the same precedence. The evaluation of binary expressions is done according to the precedence rule listed in the Fig. 1.2. However, if an expression has many operators of the same precedence, the compiler will evaluate them in left-to-right order.

The following sections describe each binary operator and its operation.

◼ Multiplication *

The multiplication operator (*) calculates the product of two operands. In the statement

```
   result = x * y ;
```

x is multiplied by **y** and the result is placed in the **result** variable.

The * operator is treated as associative. An expression with several multiplications may be rearranged by the compiler, although subexpressions are enclosed in parentheses. The expression

```
result = x * y * z ;
```

can be interpreted in three different ways:

```
result = ( x * y ) * z ;
result = x * ( y * z ) ;
result = ( x * z ) * y ;
```

◘ Division /

The *division* operator (/) calculates the quotient of two operands. In the statement

```
result = x / y;
```

x is divided by **y** and the result is placed in the **result** variable.

If you use two positive integers as operands, the compiler will ignore any remainder produced by the division operation. For example, in the expression 9/4 the result is 2, discarding the remainder .25.

But if one operand has a negative value, then truncation will occur in the result.

◘ Remainder %

The *remainder* operator (%) produces the remainder when two operators are divided. For example, the result of expression

```
9 % 4
```

is 1.

The type of both operands must be integer. The usual arithmetic conversions on operands are performed by the compiler.

◘ Addition +

The *addition* operator (+) produces the sum of the operands. For example, in the expression

```
a + b
```

the value of **a** is added to **b**. If there are many addition operators in an expression, the operators are grouped in left-to-right order.

The operands can be integers, floating-point numbers or pointers. If one operator is an integer and the other is a pointer, the compiler first converts the integer operand to an address offset and then does the addition. The result is an address of a data object.

◘ Subtraction -

The *subtraction* operator (-) produces the difference between the operands. In the expression

```
a - b
```

the value of **b** is subtracted from **a**. If there are many subtraction operators in an expression, the operators are grouped in left-to-right order.

The operands can be integers, floating-point numbers, or pointers. In case an integer is subtracted from a pointer, the compiler computes the operation in the following steps:

- The integer type operand is converted to an address offset.
- After the subtraction is done, the result is an address of the same type as the pointer operand.

◘ Bitwise left and right shift << >>

The shift operators (<< and >>) literally shift the bits of the left operand. The right operand is the number of places (bits) that the left operand is to be shifted.

The left shift operator << moves bits toward the left, while the right shift operator >> moves bits toward the right. The shift operators are grouped in left-to-right order.

The operands must be integer values. The right operand is always converted to an integer value, while the type of the result is the same as that of the left operand.

In the expression

```
x << 2;
```

the **x** variable, declared as **short** type, is shifted left by two positions.

The following shows the content of **x** in binary and decimal representations before and after the left shift operation.

```
0000 0000 0000 0011        3      (before)
0000 0000 0000 1100        12     (after)
```

Every shift to the left has the same effect as multiplying the value by 2. The right end of **x** is filled with zeros (0s). In the expression

```
y >> 2;
```

y, declared as **short** type, is shifted by 2.

The following shows the content of **y** in binary and decimal representations before and after the right shift operation.

```
1100 0000 0000 0000        49152 (before)
0011 0000 0000 0000        12288 (after)
```

Every shift to the right has the same effect as dividing the value by 2. The left end of **y** is filled with zeros (0s).

The results of a shift operator are undefined if the right operand is a negative value or is greater than or equal to the number of bits of the left operands. If the right operand is a zero (0), the left operand is unchanged.

◖ Relational < > <= >=

The *relational* operators (<>, <=, and >=) compare two operands for a valid relationship. The result of the relational operators is either one (1) if the relationship is true; otherwise, it is zero (0). The operands can be of arithmetic type, or pointers of the same type.

If the operands are of arithmetic type, the usual arithmetic conversion (discussed later) on operands are performed by the compiler. The relational operators are grouped in left-to-right order.

The following shows the result of each relational expression:

x < y   evaluates to the value 1 if **x** is less than **y**, otherwise 0.

x <= y   evaluates to the value 1 if **x** is less than or equal to **y**, otherwise 0.

x > y   evaluates to the value 1 if **x** is greater than **y**, otherwise 0.

x >= y   evaluates to the value 1 if **x** is greater than or equal to **y**, otherwise 0.

◻ Equality == !=

The *equality* operators (== and !=) compare two operands for equality. The result of the equality operators is either one (1) if the relationship is true; otherwise, the result is zero (0). The operands can be arithmetic type or pointers of the same type. It is also legal to have one operand as a pointer and the other as a null pointer or an integer with value zero (0).

If the operands are of arithmetic type, the usual arithmetic conversion on operands are performed by the compiler. The equality operators are grouped in left-to-right order.

The following shows the result of each equality expression:

x == y   evaluates to the value 1 if **x** is equal to **y**, otherwise 0.

x != y   evaluates the value 1 if **x** is not equal to **y**, otherwise 0.

◻ Bitwise AND &

The *bitwise AND* operator (&) compares the values of the operand bit by bit. If the bit of the first value is 1, and the corresponding bit of the second value is also 1, the result is 1. Otherwise, it is set to 0.

In the statement

```
z = x & y;
```

a bitwise comparison of **y** and **x** is done, and the result is placed in **z**. If **x** and **y** had values 16,645 and 51,850, repectively, the 16-bit binary representations after the operation would be

```
x          0100  0001  0000  0110
y          1100  1010  1000  1010
z          0100  0000  0000  0010
```

If the corresponding bits of **x** and **y** are 1, the bit in the same position of **y** is 1; otherwise, it is 0. In an AND operation, both operands must be of integral type.

◘ Bitwise exclusive OR ^

The *bitwise exclusive OR* (^) operator compares the values of the operand bit by bit. If the bit of both values is 1 or 0, then the corresponding bit of the result is 0. Otherwise, it is set to 1.

In the statement

```
z = x ^ y;
```

a bitwise comparison of **y** and **x** is done, and the result is placed in **z**. If the **x** and **y** had the values 16,645 and 51,880, repectively, the 16-bit binary representations of **x**, **y**, and **z** after the operation would be

```
x          0100  0001  0000  0110
y          1100  1010  1000  1010
z          1000  1011  1000  1100
```

If the corresponding bits of **x** and **y** are not the same, the bit in the same position of **z** is 1; otherwise, it is 0. In an OR operation, both operands must be of integral type.

◘ Bitwise Inclusive OR |

The *bitwise inclusive OR* (|) operator works in the following ways. For corresponding bits of both operands, if one or both bits are 1s, the corresponding result bit is a 1. Otherwise, it is set to 0.

In the following statement a bitwise comparison of **y** and **x** is done, and the result is placed in **z**.

```
z = x | y;
```

If **x** and **y** had values 16,645 and 51,880, respectively, the 16-bit binary representations of **x**, **y**, and **z** would be

```
x        0100 0001 0000 0110
y        1100 1010 1000 1010
z        1100 1011 1000 1110
```

In an inclusive OR operation, both operands must be of integral type.

◘ Logical AND &&

The *logical AND* operator (&&) checks two operators for nonzero values. If both have nonzero values, the result of the AND operation is 1; otherwise, it is 0.

Both operands must be scalar types. In an expression, the AND operators are grouped in the left-to-right order. The usual arithmetic conversion on operands is performed by the compiler.

For the logical expression

```
x && y
```

the following gives the result of three different pairs of **x** and **y**:

```
result          x       y

   0            0  &&    0
   0            0  &&    3
   1            5  &&    2
```

In the first two cases, the result is zero because **x** is zero in both cases. In the third case, the result is 1 because both **x** and **y** have nonzero value.

◘ Logical OR ||

The logical OR operator (||) checks two operators for nonzero value. If either has a nonzero value, then the result of an OR operation is one (1); otherwise, it is zero (0).

Both operands must be scalar types. The AND operators are grouped in the left-to-right order. For the logical expression

```
x || y
```

the following shows the results for three pairs of **x** and **y** values.

```
result      x      y
  0      0  &&   0
  1      5  &&   2
  1      0  &&   3
```

The first result is zero because both **x** and **y** are zeros. The last two results are ones because either one or both **x** and **y** are nonzeros.

◘ Conditional operator ?:

The *conditional* operator (?:) is the most unique among operators in the C language. It requires three operands and two symbols. The first operand is placed before the question mark (?), followed by the second operand and the colon (:), and the third operand after the colon.

The general form of a conditional expression is

```
condition ? expression1 : expression2
```

condition is usually a relational expression, which is evaluated by the compiler.

If the result from the evaluation of the *condition* is nonzero, then *expression1* is evaluated, and the result is the value of the condition expression. If *condition* is zero, then *expression2* is evaluated and the result is the value of the conditional expression.

The conditional operator is best understood by an example to determine the maximum of two values: **x** and **y**. This function is usually programmed as follows:

```
int max( int x, int y )
{
    int z;

    if ( x > y )

        z = x ;
    else
```

```
    z = y ;

  return ( z );
}
```

The same logic can be programmed by using the conditional operator. For example, the following statement accomplishes the same task as the above **max** function.

```
    z = ( x > y ) ? x : y ; /* z = max(x,y) */
```

The conditional expression can be any expression, and it is enclosed in parentheses only for the sake of readability. First the expression **(x > y)** is calculated. If it is true (i.e., nonzero), the **x** is assigned to **z**; otherwise, **y** is assigned to **z**.

The conditional expression works according to the following rules:

- The conditional operand must have scalar type.
- The second and third operands can be any of these types:

    - Arithmetic type
    - Same structure type
    - Same union type
    - Same pointer type

- The result of the conditional operator has the same type as the second and third operands.
- If the second and third operands are arithmetic types, then the usual arithmetic conversion on operands are performed by the compiler.

1.6.3 Assignment operator =

The *assignment* operator (=) gives a value to the left operand after evaluating the right operand. In an expression with many assignment operators, the operators are grouped in right-to-left order. There are two kinds of assignment operators:

- Simple assignment
- Compound assignment

◻ Simple assignment

The *simple assignment* operator simply takes the value of the right operand and gives it to the left operand. Both operands must be of:

- Arithmetic type
- Same structure type
- Same union type
- Pointers to same type

If both operands are arithmetic types then the usual arithmetic conversion on operands is performed by the compiler.

A few examples of assignment operators are

```
employee.age = 50 ;
employee.hours = regular + overtime ;
ptr = &prices[10] ;
chr = name[i] ;
x = y = z = 0 ;
value = 2.55 + 10 ;
*p = 's' ;
```

◘ Compound assignment

An expression with *compound assignment* contains two operators: an assignment operator and any other binary operator. Figure 1.3 is a list of all compound assignment operators.

Operator	Example	Equivalent Expression
+=	x += y	x = x + y
-=	x -= y	x = x - y
*=	x *= y	x = x * y
/=	x /= y	x = x / y
%=	x %= y	x = x % y
<<=	x <<= y	x = x << y
>>=	x >>= y	x = x >> y
&=	x &= y	x = x & y
^=	x ^= y	x = x ^ y
|=	x |= y	x = x | y

Figure 1.3 Assignment operators.

1.7 Statements

It is the *program-control statements* of any language that give power and flexibility to a computer. In essence, the control statements are the strength of a language; they dictate the flow of a program execution. They are powerful building blocks of programs.

Both C and C++ have a rich and diverse set of control statements. This section explains the basics of the control flow of these statements and also shows how you can use them effectively to produce versatile and robust programs.

The following is a list of statements types:

- Expression statement
- **label** statement
- **if** statement
- **if-else-if** statement
- **switch** statement
- **for** loop statement
- **while** loop statement
- **do/while** loop statement
- **break** statement
- **continue** statement
- **goto** statement
- null statement

These statements are described in the following paragraphs.

▣ Expression statement

- General form

```
expression ;
```

- Description

An *expression* statement is simply an expression followed by a semicolon (;). As seen earlier in this chapter, there are many types of expressions.

- Example

A few examples of expression statements are

```
++count;

y = y + z;

printf("Expressions");

x - ( y * z );
```

◘ Label statement

● General form

```
labeled-statement:
  label: statement

label: named-label
    case-label
    default-label
```

● Description

Before discussing statements, let's consider the label concept. A **label** is placed before a statement and is an identifier to which control is transferred. There are three kinds of labels: **plain** label, **case** label, and **default** label. The **plain** label is used with a **goto** statement, and the **case** label and the **default** label are used in a **switch** statement. These statements are discussed later.

◘ If statement

● General form

```
if ( expression )
    statement;
[else
    statement;]
```

● Description

The **if** statement allows a statement to be executed only after a condition is met.

else is an optional clause.

expression can be any valid C expression, which can include relation and logical operators, functions, and pointers. This expression is first evaluated; when the result is TRUE (nonzero), the statement associated with **if** is acted on. If the *expression* evaluates to FALSE (zero), and **else** exists, the computer will execute the statement or the block of statements forming part of the **else**. In other words, only statements associated with either **if** or **else** are executed, never with both **if** and **else**.

● Example

In the next example, **if** statement is used to check whether a variable has a zero or nonzero value. The program first reads a number and places it in the **num** variable using the **scanf** function. Next, it prints the value of **num** if it is nonzero. Otherwise, it prints the message "Number is zero."

```
/*********************************************
This program illustrates the use of if statement
**********************************************/

#include <stdio.h>

main()
{
   int num = 0;

   scanf( " %d \n", &num );

   if ( num )

     printf( "Number is %d \n", num );

   else

     printf( "Number is zero \n" );
}
```

If replaced **num** with a relational expression **num != 0**, the result would be the same. For example,

```
if ( num != 0 )

   printf( "Number is %d \n", num );
```

In the next program, the conditional *expression* of the **if** statement consists of both relational and logical operators. A keyboard character is read by a **getchar** function and placed in the **chr** variable. The *expression* of the **if** statement is to test whether a character is numeric. According to the ASCII (American Standard Code for Information Interchange) table, all numeric characters are between '0' and '9'. When the *expression*

```
        ( chr > '0' && chr <= '9' )
```

is evaluated to be FALSE (0), the message "Character is not numeric" is printed to the standard output stream. Otherwise, the numeric character is printed.

```c
/***********************************************
This program illustrates the use of if statement.
***********************************************/

#include <stdio.h>

main()
{
    char chr;

    chr = getchar();

    if ( chr > '0' && chr <= '9')

        printf( "Numeric character is %c \n", chr );

    else

        printf( "Character is not numeric \n" );
}
```

◨ if-else-if statement

- General form

```
if( expression )
    statement;
else if ( expression )
    statement;
    .
    .
    .
else
    statement;
```

- Description

An **if-else-if** statement is an extension of the **if** statement. The evaluation of *expression* starts from the top. As soon as an expression is found to be TRUE (nonzero), the associated statement is executed and the rest of the ladder is skipped. If none of the expression is evaluated to be TRUE, the *statement* linked to the last *else* is executed.

In the following example a message is printed when the input character is one of the following:

1. Numeric character
2. Space character
3. Plus sign
4. None of the above; default

```c
/*****************************************************
This program illustrates the use of if-else-if ladder.
*****************************************************/

#include <stdio.h>

main()
{
   char chr, *strp = " ";

   int y;

   if ( scanf( "%c", chr ) != EOF )
   {

     if ( chr >= '0' && chr <= '9' )
     {
       *strp = chr;

       y = atoi( strp );

       printf( "Number is %d \n", y );
     }

     else if ( chr == ' ' )

       printf( "Space character \n" );

     else if ( chr == '+' )

       printf( "Plus sign \n" );

     else

         printf("Not numeric character, space or + \n");
   }
   else

     printf( "Input Error " );
}
```

◻ Switch statement

● General form

```
switch( expression )
{
   case constant1:
       statement;
       break;
   case constant2:
       statement;           switch body
       break;
        .
        .
        .
   default:
     statement;
}
```

● Description

The **switch** statement is a multiple-branch decision statement. This statement not only replaces some forms of **if-else-if** ladder construction discussed earlier but also infuses clarity and elegance to a program. The switch body, enclosed in braces, has *case* labels, empty statements, and *default* labels.

expression must evaluate to an integral type. Starting from the top, the *expression* is checked against the constants successively. If a match is found, control is transferred to the statement associated with that constant. Execution will continue until a **break** statement is encountered or the end of the switch body is reached. If there is no match, the computer executes the optional **default** statement. If a **default** label is not present, no action is taken if no match occurs.

The **break** statement is not part of the **switch** statement but is used to stop execution of the statement sequence of the **case** clause. As shown in an example later, you might want to omit a **break** statement in certain instances. This is when a common processing is suitable for many situations.

There are a few things to keep in mind when using a **switch** statement:

● The expression and constants must be of integral type, and each constant must be different.
● There must be only one **default** label.

- A switch body can have definitions and declarations.
- A **case** clause can have a **switch** statement; therefore, nested **switch** is allowed.
- A **case** clause can be empty.

- Example

One way of using a **switch** statement is to process a menu selection. In the next program, a menu of three items is printed. Then, it reads a selection character from the user.

```c
/*****************************************************
This program illustrates the use of switch statement.
*****************************************************/
#include <stdio.h>
main()
{
   char key;

   printf( "1. Add Customer Record \n");
   printf( "2. Change Customer Record \n");
   printf( "3. Delete Customer Record \n" );
   printf( "   Enter a selection (1, 2 or 3 ) \n");
   printf( "   Press any other key to skip \n" );

   key = getchar() ; /* read the selection from the
        standard input stream */

   switch( key )
   {
     case '1':
        CustAdd();
        break;
     case '2':
        CustChg();
        break;
     case '3':
        CustDel();
        break;
     default:
        printf("No selection made \n" );
   }
   return;
}
```

The **key** variable is compared to each character constant: '1', '2', and '3'. If there is a match, the corresponding function is called. If it is '1', then the **CustAdd** function is called. On return from **CustAdd**, the **switch** statement is terminated because of **break** and control is transferred to the next statement, which is **return**. Similarly, **CustAdd** and **CustDel** functions are called if key is '2' or '3', respectively.

In case of no match—the key is not '1', '2', or '3'—the message "No selection made" is printed to the standard output stream. This is a result of executing the statement part of the **default** label.

The following program illustrates an empty **case** statement and a **case** statement having one or more statements. Note that the constants are both integer and character constants. For example, '1', '2', and '3' are character constants and decimal 52 (ASCII code for '4') and SPACE defined as hex 20, are integer constants.

```
/**********************************************
This program illustrates the use switch statement.
**********************************************/

#include <stdio.h>
#define SPACE  0x20     /* ASCII code for space character*/

main()
{
    int y;
    char key, *strp = " ";

    key = getchar();

    switch( key )
    {
      case '1':
      case '2':
      case '3':
         printf("Key is %c", key );
         break;

      case 52: /* EBCDIC code for '4' */
         *strp = key;
         y = atoi( strp );
         printf( "Number is %d ", y );
         break;

      case SPACE:
         printf( " Key is space bar " );
         break;
    }
}
```

The **case** clauses with constant '1' and '2' have no statements; therefore, they use the same code as the **case** clause with constant '3'. This shows that different conditions can use the same portion of a program. In the fourth **case** clause, the constant is an integer constant 244 which is equivalent to the EBCDIC character '4'. This **case** clause has three statements. The first is

```
*strp = key;
```

to move the character into a string. The second is a call to **atio(strp)** function to convert the key stroke from a character to integer value, which is placed in **y**. Next, the converted integer **y** is printed. The fifth **case** label has an integer constant representing a space character. Note that this **switch** statement does not have a **default** label. This means that the **switch** statement does not execute anything if none of the five conditions is met.

◘ For statement

● General form

```
for ( expression1; expression2; expression3 )
        statement ;
```

● Description

The **for** statement can have an empty statement, single statement or a block of statements. More than one statement must be enclosed in a pair of braces. The statement forms the body of the **for** loop.

Expression1 is an expression evaluated only once before the loop starts. It can be used to initialize a variable to control the loop.

Expression2 is an expression evaluated every time the body is executed. The result of *expression2* determines when to exit the loop. If it yields a zero value (0), the **statement** of the **for** loop is not executed and control goes to the next statement of the program. Otherwise, the statement is executed.

expression3 is an expression evaluated every time but only after the statement of the loop is executed. It can be used to increment, decrement, or initialize variables that determine whether to exit or continue the loop.

Any or all of these expressions can be omitted, but in each case it affects how the loop is executed. Later we will discuss some of the variations of the **for** loop. First, we want to show you a simple example of the **for** loop.

● Example

In the following program, the **for** loop is used to print numbers 1 through 5 to the standard output stream. First, the **i** variable is set to value 1. Next, the expression **i <= 5** is evaluated. If it is TRUE (1), then the value is printed; otherwise, the loop terminates. Every time **i** is printed with the **printf** function, it is incremented by 1. The loop stops when **i** reaches the value 5.

```
/**********************************************
This program illustrates the use of the for loop.
**********************************************/

#include <stdio.h>

main()
{
   int i;

   for( i = 1; i <= 5; i++ )

     printf( "%d ", i );

}
```

In a **for** loop, C does not restrict you in the composition of expressions as long as they are valid. In the following example, *expression1* sets **i** to 5, *expression2* tests whether **i**, greater than 0, and *expression3* decrements **i** by 1. In this case, the statement prints numbers in descending order from 5 through 1.

```
for ( i = 5; i > 0 ; x-- )
   printf( "%d ", i );
```

C allows many variables of the **for** loop, which can add power and flexibility to your programs. You can omit the *expression1*, but you have to ensure that the variable controlling the loop is properly initialized before the execution of the **for** loop. If it is not set properly, an undesired result may occur.

In the following situation **i** is set to 5 before the loop starts.

```
i = 5;

for ( ; i > 0 ; x-- )
   printf( "%d ", i );
```

In the next example, the *expression2* is missing. When this expression is omitted, the compiler replaces the expression with a nonzero contant. Therefore, the loop will be executed infinitely. To break out of the loop, you use the **break** as shown here.

```
for ( i = 0 ; ; i++ )
{
   if ( i > 5 )
     break;
   printf( "%d ", i );
}
return;
```

This will end the loop when **i** is greater than 5 and give control to the next statement in the function:

```
   return;
```

Note that there is more than one statement associated with this **for** loop; therefore, the loop is enclosed in braces. Other ways to end a **for** loop are by using **return** and **goto** statements. The **return** statement will terminate the function, while **goto** will transfer control to a portion of the function identified by a label. The **break** and **goto** statements are dicussed later.

You can include a **for** statement within another one, thus forming many levels of nested **for** loops. The next example uses two levels of **for** loops to initialize a two-dimensional array called **table**. The outer **for** loop increments i by 1 from 0 to 10. The inner **for** loop is included in the body of the outer loop. Before every increment of **i**, the inner loop increments **j** from 0 to 20. The body of the inner loop first calculates the sum if **i** and **j** and places it in the **i**th and **j**th elements of the **table** array.

```
/**********************************************
This program illustrates two levels of for loop.
**********************************************/
#include <stdio.h>

main()
{
   int table[10][20] ;
   int sum, i,j;

   for ( i = 0 ; i >= 10 ; i++ ) /* outer loop */
     for ( j = 0 ; j >= 20 ; j++ ) /* inner loop */
     {
        sum = i + j ;
        table[i][j] = sum ;
     }
}
```

So far we have seen *expression1* and *expression3* having only one part; however, they can have more than one part. In the following example, the initialization expression sets **x** to 0 and **y** to 1. And the *expression3* first increments **y** by 1 and **x** becomes the sum of **y** and 5.

```
for ( x = 0 , y = 1; y <= 5 ; y++, x = y + 5 )
   printf( "y = %d, x = %d \n", y, x );
```

An empty **for** loop does not have any statement. For example,

```
if ( i = 0 ; i > 1000    ; i ++ );
```

◻ While statement

● General form

```
while( expression )
   statement ;
```

● Description

The **while** statement allows you to repeatedly do a task within a program until a specific condition is met. You can break out of the **while** loop by using a **break, return,** or **goto** statement.

expression determines the duration of the loop. Before every iteration, the expression is evaluated. If it yields a FALSE value (0), the loop is terminated. Otherwise, the statements of the body are executed.

statement consists of either an empty statement, a single statement, or a block of statements, forming the body of the **while** loop.

● Example

The following example is a simple program to determine the length of a string and the number of spaces. Using the **while** loop, the program scans the **string** buffer until a NULL character is found. The expression of the **while** loop checks whether the ith element is '\0'. If it is TRUE, then the body is executed. In the body a space counter is incremented by 1 in case a space character is encountered. Next, the **i** index is incremented by 1 when the **ith** element of **string** is '\0', then the loop is terminated. The variable **i** has the length of the string, and **spaces** has the number of spaces in the string. Both counts are printed before the program ends.

```
/***********************************************
This program illustrates the use of the while loop.
***********************************************/

#include <stdio.h>
```

```c
#define SPACE ' '
main()
{
   char string[] = "This is a complex world";
   int i, spaces ;

   i = 0;
   space = 0;

   while( string[i] != '\0' )
   {
     if ( string[i] == SPACE )
        spaces++;
     i++;
   }

   printf("length of string is %d \n", i );
   printf("number of spaces are %d \n", spaces );
}
```

◘ Do/while loop

● General form

```c
do
{
    statement;
} while( expression );
```

● Description

The **do/while** statement executes the body of the loop and then evaluates
the *expression*. The body is made up of either an empty statement, a
single statement, or a block of statements. If the *expression* of the **while**
clause evaluates to nonzero, the loop is executed again; otherwise, the
loop ends.

Unlike **for** and **while** loops, the **do/while** loop executes the body at least
once, regardless of the form of the expression. The loop can also be
ended with a **break, return**, or **goto** statement within the body of the
do/while loop.

● Example

One possible use of the **do/while** loop is to process a menu selection.
The following program first prints all the items of a menu and then
enters the body of the **do** loop. Within the body, the program accepts a
key, which is executed at least once. The **switch** statement is used to
process the selection. For example, if the key is '1', **CustAdd** function

is called and **CustChg** and **CustDel** functions are called if the key is '2' and '3', respectively. The expression of the **while** clause checks whether the key is '4'; if it is, the loop is terminated. Otherwise, it reads another key from the keyword and does another iteration.

```c
/*************************************************
This program illustrates the use of the do/while loop.
*************************************************/
#include <stdio.h>

main()
{
   char key ;

   printf("1. Add Customer Record \n");
   printf("2. Change Customer Record \n");
   printf("3. Delete Customer Record \n");
   printf("4. Exit \n" );
   printf("   Enter selection (1,2,3 or 4) \n");

   do
   {
     key = getchar(); /* read the selection */
     switch( key )
     {
       case '1':
           CustAdd();
           break;
       case '2':
           CustChg();
           break;
       case '3':
           CustDel();
           break;
       }
   } while ( key != '4' );
}
```

◖ Break statement

- General form

```c
break;
```

- Description

The **break** statement has been used earlier in this chapter to terminate loops and **switch** statements. The **break** statement can be placed within the body of **do, for, while,** and **switch** statements. Any loop or **switch** statement is immediately terminated without testing the conditional expression when a **break** statement is encountered.

When a loop or **switch** statement is ended with a **break**, the control moves to the next statement outside the loop or **switch** body. Within nested statements, **break** terminates only the lower level of the loop or **switch** statement. A **break** statement cannot be used outside a loop or **switch** body.

● Example

The following program illustrates how to use a **break** within a **while** loop by stopping a search when the first space character within a string is found. The **while** loop scans a character array called **string**. It starts from the first element and continues as long as the **i**th element is not NULL character ('\0'). Within the loop body, when the first space character is encountered, the loop is ended after printing the position of the space in the string. The loop exits regardless of the conditional expression of the **while** statement. If the **i**th element is not a NULL or space character, the **i** variable is incremented by one.

```
/*********************************************************
This program illustrates the use of the break statement.
*********************************************************/
#include <stdio.h>
#define SPACE ' '

main()
{

    int rc;
    char string[] = "It is a wonderful world";

    i = 0 ;

    while ( string[i] != '\0' )
    {
     if ( string[i] == SPACE )
     {
          printf( "Space character is at position %d \n",
                     i );
         break;
     }
     i++;
    }
}
```

The preceding program with a **break** statement can be coded using a **do/while** loop. For example,

```
do
{
   if ( string[i] == SPACE )
   {
    printf( "Space character is at position %d \n",
                 i );
```

```
      break;
   }
   i++;
} while ( string[i] != '\0' );
```

◘ Continue statement

● General form

```
continue;
```

● Description

The **continue** statement forces the next iteration of a loop to occur. Within the body of the **do, for,** or **while** loop, the current iteration stops when **continue** is executed, and control is passed to the expression of the loop. If it is a **for** statement, the third expression is executed, followed by the second expression.

● Example

The following program illustrates how to use the **continue** statement to count nonblank characters in a string array. This **for** loop scans the string array starting from the first element until a NULL character is found. Every time the body of the loop is executed, the **i**th element is tested. If it is a blank character, the rest of the loop is skipped by using the **continue** statement. The next iteration starts after incrementing the **i** index and testing if the **i**th element is not NULL. If it is a nonblank character, a counter is incremented by 1.

Within nested statements, the **continue** statement ends the current iteration of the loop where it is found. The **continue** statement can be used only within a loop body.

The following program counts all nonblank characters of the variable **string**.

```
/***************************************************************
This program illustrates the use of the continue statement.
***************************************************************/

#include <stdio.h>

main()
{
    int count, i ;
```

```c
char string[] = "This is a very vast universe" ;
count = 0;

for ( i = 0 ; string[i] = '\0' ; i ++ )
{
  if ( string[i] == ' ' )
     continue;
  count++;
}
printf( "Number of nonblank characters is %d \n",
                  count );
}
```

◘ Goto statement

● General form

```c
goto label;
```

● Description

Because of the emphasis on structured programming techniques, the **goto** statement has fallen out of favor among programmers. Although it is possible to avoid **goto** entirely in many programming situations, there are times when the use of **goto** statement simplifies and clarifies a program. However, with the rich control verbs of C, there may never be a need to use the **goto** statement.

The **goto** transfers control unconditionally to a statement associated with a label.

● Example

This program scans the character **string** array for the first space character. When it is found, the control is transferred to the label **found**, where the position of the space character is printed.

```c
/************************************************************
This program illustrates the use of the goto statement.
************************************************************/

#include <stdio.h>

#define SPACE ' '

main()
{
   int i;
   char string[] = "Humanity will live in harmony" ;
```

```
i = 0;

while ( string[i] != '\0' )
{
  if ( string[i] == SPACE )
    goto found ;
  i++;
}
not_found: printf( "Space character not found \n" );

return
found: printf( "Space character is at position %d \n",
                  i );
}
```

◘ Empty statement

- General form

```
;
```

- Description

An **empty** or **NULL** statement performs no operation. It is simply a
semicolon (;). For example, as discussed earlier, a **for** loop consists of
expressions within parentheses, followed by one of more statements.
However, there are situations when the statement—any one discussed in
the preceding paragraphs—is not needed. In such a case, the **for** loop as
to be completed with an empty statement. Sometimes, it is easy to place
a semicolon inadvertently in a wrong spot; consequently, your program
may not work as expected. In case of logical errors in your code, check
closely whether all semicolons are placed correctly.

```
for( i = 0; i < 100 ; i++ );
```

C++ Language

In the previous Chapter we discussed some of the basic features of C, such as statements, data types and operators. Because C is a subset of C++, all the features described in Chap. 1 apply to C++. This section provides an overview of the main concepts found in C++ which do *not* apply to C. These aspects of C++ support the principle of object-oriented programming (OOP). The main reason for this OPP extension of C is to create and maintain software for an ever increasing complexity of information systems of today and tomorrow.

In the last few decades, as programmers, we have practiced what is known as the *structured programming*. The limitations of this methodology are causing a crisis in the present software industry. Simply put, intricate software systems are not easy to design, program, and maintain using the old methods. The state of the art is crying for a change, as part of an evolution in the history of software development. This has given way to the development of object-oriented concepts and programming.

The object-oriented paradigm is based on three general principles, which we'll discuss closely in a moment:

- Encapsulation
- Inheritance
- Polymorphism

This chapter shows how these concepts are translated into a programming language. One chapter is not sufficient to describe comprehensively all aspects of OOP. Many books and manuals on object-oriented concepts are available in the literature and if you need more information on OOP or related subjects, you can refer to any of these works. Here, we'll briefly review them, to refresh your memory.

Encapsulation: In the object-oriented concept, data and functions are combined. This fusion is called *encapsulation*. In programming terms, the data is called the *object* and the function is referred to as the *method*. The method is composed of a finite set of actions on the object; the collective term for the object and the method is the *class type*.

Inheritance: The principle of *inheritance* dictates that a new class can acquire the object and methods of an existing class. This is similar to the biological inheritance of genetic characteristics such as hair, skin and eye (iris portion) pigment from one's parents.

The inheritance concept does not exist in our traditional structured programming. Inheritance, when applied to software development, enables the programmer to reuse code. It is true that programmers write functions and place them in a library for others to use after the functions attain a certain maturity. Such functions are called in different applications. For instance, a string manipulation function can be called from a database application or an inventory program. Unfortunately, the reuse of code is not widwspread, except for a few commonly used functions. For example, if you have a class called **quadrupled**, you can define a subclass called "horse." The new class will inherit all the properties of the **quadrupled** class and will have creatain additional characteristics, such as the ability to eat grass and participate in polo games.

Polymorphism. *Polymorphism* means having many forms. In programming terms this means that one interface can be used to call one generic function. Depending on the characteristic of this interface, different functions are performed. The specific action is determined by the type of data passed to the function. The programmer need not worry about how this is done; an object-oriented language accomplishes the mechanics of determining when and how to process a particular aspect of a function. Essentially, polymorphism allows a program to use many, but related functions through one interface.

In the rest of this chapter, we'll discuss the following:

- Elements of C++
- Class and object
- Constructors and destructor functions
- Function and operator overloading

2.1 Elements of C++

Because C is a subset of C++, you can write a C++ program in the same way as you would write a C program. There is no rule to prevent you from doing this, but you might not be taking advantage of the extra features related to OOP. This is like watching your favorite show in black and white on a color TV.

Next is a short C++ program. At first glance it is similar to a C program starting with an **#include** directive, followed by a **main** function. It also has curly brackets (braces), a **return** statement, and a variable definition familiar to the C programmer. At close look, this C++ program is different; a C compiler cannot successfully compile this program.

Three features are peculiar to C++ programming and style:

- Comment lines
- I/O (input/output) operators
- I/O operations

■ General form of a C++ program

Each programmer has an individual style of writing C++ code, but most programs will have the following general form:

#includes
base-class declarations
derives class declarations
nonmember function prototypes

main()
{

.

.

.

}

nonmember function definitions

This format applies to small programs. For large projects, the class definitions, like macros, will likely be found in header files included with each module.

The following is an example of a short C++ program. It includes the **my_class** class. This class has two data variables: **x** and **y** **and** two function members called **sum** and **set_xy**, where **sum** adds two number and **set_xy** sets the values of **x** and **y**. In the main function, the **x** object is created and the values of **x** and **y** are set to 7 and 8, respectively. Also, the sum of **x** and **y** is shown by calling **z.sum(z)** using the **cout** function.

```
#include "iostream.h"

class my_class
{
  int x, y;
public:
  int sum(my_class m) ;
  void set_xy(int p, int q)
    {x=p; y=q;}

};

// sum() is not a member of my_class
// As a member of my_class it can access
// x and y private variables

my_class::sum(my_class m)
{
  return m.x + m.y;
}
```

```
main()
{
  my_class z;

  z.set_xy(7,8);
  cout << z.sum(z); // prints 15

  return 0;
}
```

◻ Comment lines

In C++ there are two ways of marking a line in a program as a
comment. First is the C style, where a comment line starts with /* and
ends with */. Also, you can designate a line as a comment when it starts
with two slashes (//). The slashes can appear anywhere in a line, and
anything following them is considered a comment. The following lines,
taken from the previous program, are examples of these two types of
comment lines.

```
// This is my first C++ program
cin >> string;   /* C style comment line */
```

◻ I/O operators

You may have noticed characters such as << and >> in the previous
program. They resemble left and right shift operators. In the following
examples,

```
cout << "Enter integer: ";
cin >> integer;
```

where **<<** is an output operator and **>>** is an input operator. This takes
us to the C++ I/O operations. Note that to use these operators, you must
include the **iostream.h** header file.

◻ I/O operations

In the line

```
cout << "Enter integer: ";
```

we have **cout**, which performs the same operation as the **printf** function.
It writes **Enter integer:** to the screen. In C++, the term **cout** refers to

the screen. With the output operator <<, it sends any built-in data type and character string to the screen.

In contrast, **cin** refers to the keyboard; for example in

```
cin >> integer;
```

is like the input data is placed in the variable **integer** and a replacement for the **scanf** function. The main reason for using **cout** and **cin** rather than **printf** and **scanf** is that they are more versatile, especially for applications of the object-oriented concepts. In the C++ program, **cin** writes to variables of three different types of data (**float**, **char** and **int**); you cannot do this with **scanf**.

A more interesting line of the program is:

```
cout << floating_point << " " << string << " " << integer;
```

which writes to the screen the content of **floating_point**, followed by one blank, the contents of **string**, one blanks and the contents of **integer**.

◻ C++ keywords

Earlier in this chapter we discussed some of the keywords for the C language. Additional C++ keywords are listed in Fig. 2.1.

asm	private
catch	protected
class	public
delete	template
friend	this
inline	throw
new	try
operator	virtual
overload	

Figure 2.1 C++ keywords.

◘ C++'s predefined streams

When a C++ program is executed, four streams are automatically opened:

Stream	Description	Default Device
cin	Standard input	Keyboard
cout	Standard output	Screen
cerr	Standard error output	Screen
clog	Bufferred version of cerr	Screen

The first three streams correspond to C's **stdin**, **stdout**, and **stderr**.

2.2 Class and Object

The basic elements of C++ are *class* and *object* which constitute the foundation for object-oriented concepts. As we will see shortly, class and object are closely related, and acquiring a sound understanding of these two building blocks is crucial to object-oriented programming (OOP).

This section first gives the general format of class and object, followed by examples. It also discusses a few topics related specifically to class, such as

- Structure and class
- Union and class
- Friend function
- Inline function
- Static data member
- Static function member
- Local class
- Passing objects to function
- Returning objects
- Object assignment

Class: By definition, a class links code and data together. In some ways class is like structure, but without the functions. It is possible to define one class within another; this is called a *nested class*.

Object: Once a class is defined, it can be used to create an object of that class. Again, this can be compared to the declaration of a structure variable (or an object) after the particular structure is defined.

● General format

The general form of a class definition is

    class *class-name*
    {
        private *data* and *function*
        access-specifier: *data* and *function*
           .
           .
           .
        access-specifier: *data* and *function*

    } [*object-list*];

class-name object-list;

    class-name::*function*([*parameter-list*])
    {
        // body
    }

class is the keyword defining a class.

class-name is used to specify the name of the class that is being defined.

access-specifier is one of the following three keywords: **private, public,** or **protected**. This specifies whether a class member—data or function—is accessible to the world outside the class. The default access specifier is **private**.

private is a specifier meaning that the data or function declared within a class is accessible only to other members of the class. In other words, the members with private access are not known outside the scope of the class.

public is a specifier indicating that data or functions can be accessed by other parts of a program as well as by other members of a class.

protected is a specifier similar to private access, except that a derived class has access to the data or functions of the base class. For more information, see the section on inheritance.

data is the name of a variable declared within a class. It is referred to as a *member variable* or a *data member*. This declaration must conform to the same rules as those used in declaring a variable anywhere else in a program. In general, all data elements are private to the class. However, in some situations you may want to make a few data members public.

function is a function within a class. A member function can access any element—data or function—of the class to which it belongs. All functions must be prototyped; prototypes are not optional.

object-list is optional and, if present, declares one or more objects of a class. This is another way of declaring an object to a preceding object name with the class name and ending the statement with a semicolon (;).

The scope resolution (::) is used to link a class name to its members, especially during definition of a function.

parameter-list is one or more parameter(s), if any, passed to the function being defined.

● Example

The following program illustrates the definition and use of a class called **my_swap**. In the main function, first **s** is created as an object of **my_swap** class. Next, u is assigned a value of 599123, followed by swapping the characters in array **c** and showing the result.

```
#include "iostream.h"

class my_swap
{
  void swap();
  void set_data(unsigned i);
  void show();

  unsigned u;
  unsigned char c[2];

};
```

```cpp
void my_swap::swap()
{
  unsigned char x;

  x = c[0];
  c[0] = c[1];
  c[1] = x;
}

void my_swap::show()
{
  cout << u ;
}

void my_swap::set_data(unsigned i)
{
  u = i;
}

main()
{
  my_swap s;  // create an object

  s.set_data(59123);  // set initial values
  s.swap();  // switch characters
  s.show();  // show the result 62438
  return 0;
}
```

◘ Structure and class

In C, a structure is used to group data together. In C++, we define a structure, and syntactically it looks like C, except that in C++ its role has been expanded. In fact, you can use the **struct** keyword to define a class, as we saw in the previous example. In all respects, a class defined by **class** or **struct** is the same, except that by default all members in **struct** are public and in **class** they are private.

This begs the question as to why **struct** and **class** keywords do virtually the same task. The main reason is that classes and structures are related, and this expansion makes it easier to port C programs to C++. Also, it leaves room for classes to expand while leaving structures at their present levels. Generally, it is advisable not to use **struct** for **class**.

Union and class

The **union** keyword can be used to define a class. This definition is similar to a **union** definition in C, except in C++, the members are both variables and functions. Like the structure, the default access of the union members is public. You must also remember that all data elements share the same memory location.

When using the C++ **union**, you must keep in mind a few restrictions:

- A **union** cannot inherit another class of any type.
- A **union** cannot be a base class.
- A virtual function cannot be a member.
- A member of any object cannot overload the = operator.
- A **union** cannot have destructor or constructor function.
- If an object has a constructor or destructor function, it cannot be a member of a member.

With all these restrictions, the only compelling reason to use **union** over **class** is when memory is shared by all the variables.

- Example

The following program illustrates the use of **union**.

```
#include "iostream.h"

union my_swap
{
  void swap();
  void set_data(unsigned i);
  void show();

  unsigned u;
  unsigned char c[2];

};

void my_swap::swap()
{
  unsigned char x;

  x = c[0];
  c[0] = c[1];
  c[1] = x;

}
```

```cpp
void my_swap::show()
{

  cout << u ;

}

void my_swap::set_data(unsigned i)
{

  u = i;

}

main()
{

  my_swap s; // create the object

  s.set_data(59123); // set the initial value
  s.swap(); // swap the characters
  s.show(); // prints 62438
  return 0;

}
```

◘ Friend function

It is possible to grant a nonmember function to access private or protected members of a class. Such a member is called a **friend** function; and it is defined with the **friend** keyword placed in front of the function declaration in the **class** definition.

● Example

The following example illustrates the usage of a **friend** function.

```cpp
#include "iostream.h"

class my_class
{

  int x,y;
public:
  friend int sum(my_class m) ; // friend member

  void set_xy(int p, int q)

  { x=p; y=q;}

};

// sum() is not a member of my_class
// As a friend member of my_class it can access
// x and y private variables
```

```
int sum(my_class m)
{
  return m.x + m.y;
}

main()
{

  my_class z; // create an object

  z.set_xy(7,8); // set values

  cout << sum(z); // prints 15

  return 0;

}
```

◘ Inline function

In C++, there is the **inline** function; it is similar to a C-like macro. An inline function is not called; rather, its code is expanded by the compiler at the point where it is encountered. To declare such a function, you would place the **infile** keyword in front of the declaration.

● Example

In the following example, **max** is an **infile** function. In **main** it is invoked, and this example shows the point of invocation and the expanded version.

```
#include "iostream.h"

inline int max(int x, int y)
{

  return x > b ? x : y;

}

main ()
{

  count << max(5,10); // prints 10
  return 0;

}
```

The expanded version of the **inline** function in **main** looks like this:

```
main ()
{
  count << 5 > 10 ? 5 : 10;
  return 0;
}
```

◘ Static data member

When you place the **static** keyword in front of a variable declaration in a **class**, you are telling the computer to treat this variable in a special way. If you declare more than one object for a **class** and if there is a **static** variable within the **class**, the compiler keeps *only* one copy of such a variable. In other words, the same copy of the variable is showed among all the objects.

There are many cases where a **static** variable can be useful. One example is when two or more objects want to check a **static** variable, which holds the status of a file before performing any operation. If you use **static** variables, you will virtually eliminate the need to use global variables.

● Example

The following illustrates how a static variable works. In the declaration of **share_x class**, **x** is **static** and **y** is nonstatic. In the **main** function, the **a** and **b** objects are first declared, and subsequently the **set_xy** and **show_xx** functions are called to show how **x** is shared between **a** and **b** objects.

```
#include "iostream.h"

class share_x
{

  static int x;
  int y;
public:
  void set_xy(int i, int j)
    {x=i;y=i;}
  void show_xy();

};
```

```cpp
void share_x::show_xy()
{
  cout << "Value of static x: " << x << "\n";
  cout << "Value of nonstatic y: " << y << "\n";
  cout << "\n";
}

main()
{

  share_x a , b;

  a.set_xy( 1, 1 ); // set x and y to 1
  b.show_xy();      // show the values of x and y
  b.set_xy( 2, 2); // set x and y to 2
  b.show_xy(); // show the values of x and y
  a.show(); //show the values of x and y

  return 0;

}
```

◘ Static function member

Similar to a member variable, a function may also be declared as **static**.
When using **static** functions, there are two points to remember:

- A static function may access only other static members of the class
  except for global data and functions.

- A **static** function does not have a **this** pointer.

- Example

The next program illustrates the use of **static** functions. In the definition
of **my_x class**, the **static** variable, called **x**, represents the availability of
a resource. The **static** function called **allocate_x** sets the value of **x** to
1, indicating that it is in use. And a nonstatic function called **free_x** sets
x to 0.

```cpp
#include "iostream.h"

class my_x
{
  static int x;
public:
  static int allocate_x();
  void free_x()
     {x=0;}
};
```

```
    int my_x::allocate_x()
    {
      if (x) return 0; // already allocated

      else
      {
        x = 1;
        return 0;
      }
    }

    main()
    {

      my_x a, b;

    // the static function can be called directly,
    // independent of any object

      if (my_x.allocate_x())
         cout << "a has resource  \n";

      if (!my_x.allocate_x())
         cout << "b denied resource \n";

      a.free_x();

    // now use b object to access allocate_x()

      if (b.allocate_x())
         cout << "b can used the resource";

      return 0;
    }
```

◘ Local class

A class may be defined with a function. Such a class is known to the function only where it is defined and unknown outside the function. When using local class, there are a few restrictions to keep in mind:

- All member functions must be defined inline.

- Static variables cannot be part of a local class.

Generally, local classes are not common in C++ programming because of these restrictions.

● Example

In the next example, the local class calling **my_local_class** is defined in **my_func** function.

```
#include "iostream.h"

void my_func();

main()
{

  my_func();

  // my_local_class is not known to main()

}


void my_func()
{

  class my_local_class
  {
     int i;

  public:
     void set_i (int n)
         {i = n;}

     int  get_i ()
         {return i;}

  } object1;

  object1.set_i( 20 );

  cout << object1.get_i(); // prints 20

}
```

Passing objects to functions

Like any other variables, you may pass an object to a function. C++ uses the standard call-by-value mechanism to pass objects to functions. A copy of the object being passed to the function is created. This raises two issues: whether the constructor is executed at the time the copy of the object is created and whether the destructor is executed when the copy of the object is destroyed. (Constructors and destructors are dealt with in detail later in this chapter.) The solutions to both these issues are found in the next section.

● Example

The next example demonstrates passing an object to a function.

```cpp
#include "iostream.h"

class my_class
{
  int x;

public:
  void set_x (int n)
    {x=n;}

  int get_x()
    {return x;}
};

void func(my_class obj1);

main()
{
  my_class obj2;

  obj2.set_x(1);

  func(obj2);

  cout << "This copy is in main  ";
  cout << obj2.get_x() << "\n";

  return 0;
}

void func( my_class obj1)
{

  obj1.set_x(2);

  cout << "This copy is passed to function " ;
  cout << obj1.get_x() << "\n";

}
```

After execution of the program, the following lines are printed:

```
This copy is passed to function 2
This copy is in main  1
```

◪ Returning objects

As you can pass an object to a function, you can also return an object from a function.

- Example

The following example shows how the **func** function returns an object of **my_class** class.

```cpp
#include "iostream.h"

class my_class
{
  int x;

public:
  void set_x (int n)
    {x=n;}

  int get_x()
    {return x;}
};

my_class func() ; // returning my_class object

main()
{
  my_class ob1;

  ob1 = func();

  cout << ob1.get_x() << "\n"; // prints 1

  return 0;
}

my_class func()
{
  my_class y;

  y.set_x(1);

  return y;  //returning an object
}
```

◻ Object assignment

If two objects are of the same type, one object may be assigned to another using the assignment operator (=). The data of the object on the right side of the operator is copied to the left side of the operator.

- Example

The following program illustrates object assignment. In the **main** function, there are **ob1** and **ob2** objects of **my_class** class. First, set the variable to 11, then assign **ob1** to **ob2**, and check the value of **ob2**.

```
#include "iostream.h"

class my_class
{
  int x;

public:
  void set_x (int n)
    {x=n;}

  int get_x ()
    {return x;}
};

main()
{
  my_class ob1, ob2; // create objects

  ob1.set_x(11); // set the variable to 11

  ob2 = ob1 ; // assign ob1 to ob2

  cout << "The value of ob2's x is: "" \
        << ob2.get_x() << "\n";
}
```

After execution of the program, the following line is printed:

```
The value of ob2's x is: 11
```

2.3 Constructor and Destructor Functions

As you may be aware, sometimes you have to set a variable to an initial value or open a file before processing a task. Similarly, an object may require initialization before it is used; you can define an initialization function, called a *constructor*, within a class that has the task of setting initial values.

Also, when the task ends, you may want to perform a few subtasks such as setting variables to certain values, closing a file, deallocating memory, or destroying windows. In an object, such a termination function, called a *destructor*, is the complement of a constructor.

This section discusses various aspects of constructor and destructor functions in more detail. These are

- Constructor function
- Destructor function
- Passing arguments to constructors
- Execution of constructors and destructors

◻ Constructor function

A *constructor* is part of a class definition, and its main purpose is to
take action before an object is used. The name of the constructor
function is the same as the name of the class; therefore, when the
compiler encounters a function with such a name, it is considered a
constructor function. Such a function is similar to any other function,
except that it is executed automatically at the time an object is created.
It is important to know when this execution takes place, and we'll deal
with it shortly.

A local object is created when the block where it is found is entered. A
global object is created when the program is entered.

● Example

The following example shows how to define a constructor function for
the **my_class** class.

```
#include "iostream.h"

class my_class
{
  int x;
public:
  my_class(); // constructor
  void set_x(int n)
    {x=n;}
  int get_x()
    {return x;}
};

// my_class constructor function
my_class::my_class()
{
  x = 1;
  cout << "x is initialized " << "\n";
}

main()
{
  my_class ob;

  cout << "The value of x is " << ob.get_x << "\n";
}
```

After execution of the program, the following lines are printed:

```
x is initialized
The value of x is 1
```

◘ Destructor function

A *desctructor* function is part of a class definition, and its main purpose is to take action before an object goes out of scope. You supply the function, but the compiler adds code to ensure that it is automatically executed.

A local object vanishes when a block where it is found is ended. A global object is destroyed when the program ends.

The name of the destructor function is the same as the class name or the constructor name, except that it is preceded by a tilde ($\sim$).

● Example

The following program illustrates the definition and usage of both constructor and destructor functions.

```cpp
#include "iostream.h"

class my_class
{
  int x;

public:
  my_class(); // constructor

  ~my_class(); // destructor

  void set_x(int n)
    {x=n;}
  int get_x()
    {return x;}
};

// my_class constructor function
my_class::my_class()
{
  x = 1;
  cout << "x is initialized " << "\n";
}

my_class::~my_class()
{
  x = 0 ; // set x to 0
  cout << "x is set to 0 at termination" << "\n";
}

main()
{
  my_class a, b; //create two objects

  a.set_x(2);
  b.set_x(3);
```

```
cout << "Value of a.x is " << a.get_x() << "\n";
cout << "Value of b.x is " << b.get_x() << "\n";

return 0;
}
```

After execution of the program, the following lines are printed:

```
x is initialized
x is initialized
Value of a.x is 2
Value of b.x is 3
x is set to 0 at termination
x is set to 0 at termination
```

◘ Passing arguments to constructors

Earlier, we saw how to define a constructor. Now, let's see how arguments are passed to constructor functions. These arguments are passed when declaring objects, and these values passes are typically used to initialized the object. You would pass these arguments the same way as in any other function, simply by adding parameters to the function.

- Example

This example shows how to pass an argument to a constructor function of **my_class**. Note that the **my_class** function—the constructor—has one parameter and the argument is passed when the **ob** object is created.

```
#include "iostream.h"

class my_class
{
  int x;

public:
  my_class (int y );

  ~my_class();

  int get_x()
     {return x ;}
}

// my_class contructor function with one parameter

my_class::my_class(int y)
{
  x = y;
  cout << "x is initialized " << "\n";
}
```

```
my_class::~my_class()
{
  x = 0 ; // set x to 0
  cout << "x is set 0 at termination" << "\n";
}

main()
{
  my_class ob(1);

  cout << "Value of a.x is " << ob.show() << "\n";

  return 0;
}
```

After execution of the program, the following lines are printed:

```
x is initialized
Value of a.x is 1
x is set to 0 at termination
```

◘ Execution of constructors and destructors

Earlier, we mentioned you would define the constructor and destructor functions; however, they are not explicitly called as part of the logic of your program. They are automatically invoked by special code generated by the compiler. Because they are written to accomplish initialization and termination tasks of your program, it is important to know when the computer executes these functions.

A constructor function is executed when the object is created, and this depends whether is a local or global object. The constructor of a local object is invoked when the compiler encounters the statement where the object declaration is found. One should also remember the order in which these functions are executed. In a statement with several object declarations, they are executed from left to right and within a file are from top to bottom.

The constructors of a global object are invoked before the **main** function is executed. And, as in a local object, the order of execution is from left to right within a statement and from top to bottom within a file.

The destructors are executed when an object is ended. A local object vanishes when a block end, and destructors of global objects are executed after the **main** function is completed.

When an object is passed as an argument, there are a few points to remember as to when constructor and destructor functions are executed. When an object is passed to a function, a copy of the object is made before the function call. Remember that at this point the constructor function is not called because you want to preserve the state of the object. However, when the *copy* of the object is destroyed, the destructor is executed.

● Example

The following example illustrates the time at which the constructors and destructors are executed.

```cpp
#include "iostream.h"

class my_class
{
  int i;
public:
  my_class(int x);
  ~my_class();
  show()
    {cout << i;}
};

my_class::my_class(int x)
{
  i = x;

  cout << "Executing constructors " << i << "\n";
}

my_class::~my_class()
{
  i = 0;
  cout << "Executing desctructor \n";
}

// declaring global objects

my_class go1(1), go2(2);
my_class go3(3);

int func();

main()
{
  my_class main_ob1(4);
  my_class main_ob2(5);

  func( main_ob1 );

  return 0 ;
}
```

```
    int func(my_class f_obx)
    {
      my_class f_o1(6);

      f_o1 = f_obx;

      cout << "In func, value of i is ";

      f_o1.show();

      cout << "\n";

      return 0;
    }
```

After execution of the program, the following lines are printed:

```
Executing constructors 1
Executing constructors 2
Executing constructors 3
Executing constructors 4
Executing constructors 5
Executing constructors 6
In func, value of i is 4
Executing desctructor
Executing desctructor
Executing desctructor
Executing desctructor
Executing desctructor
Executing desctructor
```

2.4 Function and Operator Overloading

Earlier, we considered the principle of polymorphism of the object-oriented concept. This means that one object can do many things or have many forms. In programming terms, polymorphism is accomplished with function and operator overloading.

This section describes various aspects of overloading, such as

- Function overloading
- Function overloading and ambiguity
- Overloading constructor functions
- Address of an overloaded function
- Operator overloading
- Operator overloading and **friend** function
- Overloading **new** and **delete**
- Overloading [] operator
- Overloading () operator
- Overloading -> operator

◘ Function overloading

Function overloading simply means that the same function name is used for two or more operations. This allows for many definitions of a function and stipulates that with each redefinition the function must use either different types of parameters or a different number of parameters. Because of these definitions, the function name is used in any situation. However, the type of return value does not make any difference; these values may be different or the same.

● Example

The next example illustrates function overloading by definition of three functions called **func**. One has one parameter of **int** type; the second has one parameter of **double** type; the third has two **int** paramters.

```
#include "iostream.h"

//one function name but the functions are different

int func(int x);

int func(int x, int y);

double func(double x);

main()
{
  cout << func(20) << "\n";
  cout << func(20, 10) << "\n";
  cout << func(20, 10) << "\n";

}

// This function has one parameter of int type

int func(int x)
{
  return x;
}

//This function has two parameters of int type

int func(int x, int y)
{
  return x*y;
}

// This function has one parameter of double type

double func( double x )
{
  return x;
}
```

▣ Function overloading and ambiguity

Earlier, we saw function overloading where two or more functions are defined with the same name but different types or numbers of parameters.

It is possible to create a situation where the compiler cannot decide which function to choose. In an ambiguous situation the compiler simply flags the statement as an error; in such cases the compilation will not be successful.

C++ automatically converts data from one type to another and this also applies to arguments passed to a function. Let's say a function receives a **double** value:

```
int func( double x );
```

When it is invoked, you may pass a character, for example,

```
cout << func('c')); // not an error
```

The statement where **func** is invoked is not erroneous because the compiler applies a data conversion.

● Example

The following example illustrates a case of ambiguous and unambiguous calls.

```
#include "iostream.h"
float func(float x);
double func(double x);
main()
{
  cout << func(20.2) << "\n"; // unambiguous call
  cout << func(20) << "\n"; //ambiguous call
}
float func(float x)
{
  return x;
}
```

```
double func(double x)
{
  return x;
}
```

◘ Overloading constructor functions

Earlier, we discussed constructor functions and their main purpose, to perform initialization tasks. These functions are no different from other functions, except they are automatically called when an object is created. Therefore, it is valid to overload a constructor function.

● Example

The following example illustrates overloading constructor functions. In the definition of **my_class class**, there are two constructors; the first with one integer parameter; and the second, with two integer parameters. Note that when **ob1** and **ob2** objects are created, the arguments are different for each, and the compiler decides which constructor function to call.

```
#include "iostream.h"

class my_class
{
  int i,j;
public:
  my_class (int x);
  my_class (int x, int y);
  show();
};

// Constructor with one parameter

my_class::my_class(int x)
{
  i = x;
  cout << "Constructor with one parameter \n";
}

// constructor with two parameters
my_class::my_class(int x, int y)
{
  i = x;
  j = y;
  cout << "Constructor with two parameters \n";
}

my_class::show()
{
  cout << "Value of i: " << i <<   "\n";
  cout << "Value of j: " << j <<   "\n";
}
```

```
main()
{
  my_class ob1(2);
  ob1.show();

  my_class ob2(3, 4);
  ob2.show();

}
```

After execution of the program, the following lines are printed:

```
Constructor with one parameter
Value of i: 2
Value of j: 0
Constructor with two parameters
Value of i: 3
Value of j: 4
```

◻ Address of an overloaded function

In C, as you probably know, assigning the address of a function to a pointer is straightforward; for example,

```
pfunc = func;
```

This statement stores the address of **func** function into the **pfunc** function pointer. In a C program, there can be one and only one function called **func**. Of course, this also applies to a C++ program if **func** is unique.

Now, with function overloading, it is possible to have two or more functions by the same name. The question is, if you assign the address of a function, as we just did, and there are many functions by **func**, which address will the compiler be assigned?

To find the correct address of an overloaded function, you have a corresponding pointer whose return type and type and number of parameters match the overloaded function.

● Example

The following example shows how to assign the address of an overloaded function **func** with one parameter to a pointer. Also, it illustrates how to call this function using the pointer **pfunc**.

```cpp
#include "iostream.h"

int func(int x);
int func(int x, int y);

main()
{

   // declare a pointer for a function that returns
   // int and its one parameter is also int.

   int (*pfunc) (int x);

   // point to func(int x)
   pfunc = &func();
   cout << pfunc(10);
   return 0;

}

int func(int x)
{
  return x;
}

int func(int x, int y)
{
  return x*y;
}
```

◘ Operator overloading

Previously, we discussed function overloading, which leads us to operator overloading. Both are closely related. In C++, overloading of a function simply means that the function performs a special operator in relation to a class. To do this special task, you create an operator function. The operator function defines the specific operations that the overloaded operator accomplishes in relation to a class. An operator function can be a member or nonmember of a class. If it is not a member, then it must be a **friend** function (discussed earlier in this chapter).

The general format of a member operator function is

```
type class-name::operator#(argument-list)
{
   //body to define the operations
}
```

type is the return data type of the operator function, and it can be any valid return type. Often, the operator function returns an object of the class of which it is a member.

class-name is the name of the class that the operator function operates on.

operator is a keyword defining an operator function.

is a placeholder which is substituted with an operator for which an operator function is created.

argument-list is one argument when you overload a binary operator. For a unary operator, the argument list of the function is empty.

● Example

The following is a simple example of overloading the + operator. First we define a class, called **xy**, which stores values in **x** and **y** variables. In addition, it overloads the + operator relative to the **xy** class.

```
#include "iostream.h"

class xy
{
  int x,y;

public:
  xy()
  {
    x=0, y=0;
  }

  xy(int a, int b)
  {
    x=a; y=b;
  }

  void show()
  {
    cout << "x is " << x << "\n";
    cout << "y is " << y << "\n";
  }

  xy operator+(xy op2)
  {
    xy temp;
    temp.x = op2.x + x;
    temp.y = op2.y + y;
    return temp;
  }
};

main()
{
  xy ob1(100, 200), ob2(50, 300);

  ob1.show(); // prints 100 and 200
```

```cpp
  ob2.show(); // prints 50 and 300

  ob1 = ob1 + ob2;

  ob1.show(); // prints 150 amd 500

  (ob1 + ob2).show(); // prints 200 and 800
}
```

The following example overloads the +, -, =, and ++ operators.

```cpp
#include "iostream.h"

class xy
{
  int x, y;

public:
  xy()
  {
    x=0, y=0;
  }

  xy(int a, int b)
  {
    x=a; y=b;
  }

  void show()
  {
    cout << "x is " << x << "\n";
    cout << "y is " << y << "\n";
  }

  xy operator+(xy op2);
  xy operator-(xy op2);
  xy operator=(xy op2);
  xy operator++();

};

xy xy:: operator+(xy op2)
{

  xy temp;
  temp.x = op2.x + x;
  temp.y = op2.y + y;
  return temp;

}

xy xy:: operator-(xy op2)
{
  xy temp;
  temp.x = x - op2.x ;
  temp.y = y - op2.y ;
  return temp;
}
```

```
xy xy:: operator=(xy op2)
{
  xy temp;
  x  = op2.x ;
  y  = op2.y ;
  return *this;
}

xy xy:: operator++()
{
  xy temp;
  x++;
  y++;
  return *this;
}

main ()
{
  xy ob1(100,200), ob2(50,300), ob3(900,900);

  ob1.show();
  ob2.show();

  ob1++;
  ob1.show(); // prints 100 and 201

  ob2 = ob1++;
  ob1.show(); // prints 102 and 202

  ob1 = ob2 = ob3;
  ob1.show(); // prints 900 and 900
  ob2.show(); // prints 900 and 900
}
```

◘ Operator overloading and friend function

It is possible to overload an operator in relation to a **class** by using a **friend** function. When doing so, there are a few points to remember:

- A friend can never be a member of a class, and it does not have a **this** pointer.
- A **friend** function that overloads a binary operator has two paramters.
- A **friend** function that overloads a unary operator has one parameter.

● Example

In this program, the operator +( ) function is defined as a **friend**. This example is similar to the previous one, where +, =, -, and ++ operators were overloaded, except that the + operator is overloaded relative to the **xy** class using the **friend** function.

```cpp
#include "iostream.h"

class xy
{
  int x, y;
public:
  xy()
  {
    x=0, y=0;
  }

  xy(int a, int b)
  {
    x=a; y=b;
  }

  void show()
  {
    cout << "x is " << x << "\n";
    cout << "y is " << y << "\n";
  }

  friend xy operator+(xy op2);
  xy operator-(xy op2);
  xy operator=(xy op2);
  xy operator++();

};

xy xy:: operator+(xy op1, xy op2)
{
  xy temp;
  temp.x = op2.x + op1.x;
  temp.y = op2.y + op2.y;
  return temp;
}

xy xy:: operator-(xy op2)
{
  xy temp;
  temp.x = x - op2.x ;
  temp.y = y - op2.y ;
  return temp;
}

xy xy:: operator=(xy op2)
{
  xy temp;
  x  = op2.x ;
  y  = op2.y ;
  return *this;
}

xy xy:: operator++()
{
  xy temp;
  x++;
  y++;
  return *this;
}
```

```
main ()
{
    xy ob1(100,200), ob2(50,300);

    ob1 = ob1 + ob2;

    ob1.show();

    return 0;

}
```

▣ Overloading new and delete

Now, let's see how to overload **new** and **delete**. The main reason for overloading **new** and **delete** is when you are using some special allocation method.

The general format of functions that overload **new** and **delete** is:

```
void *operator new(size_t size)
{

  // perform allocation
     .
     .
     .
  return p_to_memory; //pointer to memory

}
void operator delete (void *p)
{

  // free memory pointed by p

}
```

size_t is an unsigned integer type.

size is the number of bytes required to hold the object.

p_to_memory is a pointer to the memory allocated by the overloaded function. It can be a NULL pointer, if no allocation occurs as a result of error.

p is the pointer to the memory that is to be freed.

● Example

This program shows how to overload the **new** and **delete** operators relative to the **xy** class.

```cpp
#include "iostream.h"
#include "stdio.h"

class xy
{
  int x, y;

public:
  xy() {};
  xy(int a, int b) {x=a; y=b;}

  void show()
  {
    cout << "x is " << x << "\n";
    cout << "y is " << y << "\n";
  }
  void *operator new(size_t size);
  void operator delete(void *p);
};

// new overloaded relative to xy

void *xy::operator new (size_t size)
{
  cout << "In function for overloaded new operator \n";
  return malloc(size);
}

// delete overloaded relation to xy

void xy::operator delete (void *p)
{
  cout << "In function for overloaded delete operator \n";
  free (p);
}

main()
{
  xy *p1;

  p1 = new xy(100, 200);

  if (!p1)
  {
    cout << "Could not allocate \n";
    return 1;
  }

  p1->show();

  delete p1;

  return 0;
}
```

After execution of the program, the following lines are printed:

```
In function for overloaded new operator
x is 100
y is 200
In function for overloaded delete operatos
```

◘ Overloading [ ] operator

When the [ ] operator is overloaded, it is considered a binary operator. Typically, the operator [ ]( ) function is used to provide array subscripting. The general format of the operator [ ]( ) function as a member of a **class** is

```
type class-name::operator[](int i)
{

    // body
}
```

● Example

The following is an example of overloading the [ ] operator.

```
#include "iostream.h"

class x_array
{
  int x[3];

public:
  x_array(int a, int b, int c)
    {
      x[0] = a;
      x[1] = b;
      x[2] = c;
    }

  int operator[](int y)

  { return x(y);}
};

main()
{

  x_type ob(1, 2, 3);

  cout << ob[2]; //prints 3

  return 0;
}
```

◘ Overloading ( ) operator

When overloading the ( ) function call operator, you create an operator
function to which you can pass an arbitrary number of parameters.

● Example

This example illustrates overloading ( ) relative to the **xy class**. In this
case, the values of the two arguments are assigned to **x** and **y** of the
object to which they are applied.

```
#include "iostream.h"

class xy
{
  int x, y;
public:
  xy() {};
  xy(int a, int b)
  {
    x = a;
    y = b;
  }
  void show()
  {
    cout << "x is " << x << "\n";
    cout << "y is " << y << "\n";
  }
  xy operator+(xy op2);
  xy operator ()(int s, int r);
};

xy xy::operator+(xy op2)
{
  xy temp;

  temp.x = op2.x + x;
  temp.y = op2.y + y;
  return temp;
}

xy xy::operator()(int s, int r)
{
  x = s;
  y = r;
  return *this;
}

main()
{
  xy ob1(100, 200), ob2(10, 10);

  ob1.show();
  ob1(70, 80);
  ob1.show();
  ob1 = ob2 + ob1(100, 100);
```

```
    ob1.show();
    return 0;
}
```

After execution of the program, the following lines are printed:

```
x is 100
y is 200
x is 70
y is 80
x is 110
y is 110
```

◘ Overloading -> operator

When the -> operator is overloaded, it is cosidered to be a unary operator. The operator ->() function must return a pointer to an object that the -> operator acts on. The general usage is

```
object->element;
```

object is the object that imitates the call.

element is an element that is accessible within the object pointed to.

● Example

The following program illustrates the use of the -> pointer operator. It shows that **ob->a** is the same as **ob.a**.

```
#include "iostream.h"

class my_class
{

public:

  int a;

  my_class *operator->(){ return this;}
};

main()
{
  my_class ob;

  ob->a = 100;
  cout << ob.a << " " << ob->a;
  return 0;
}
```

2.5 Inheritance

Earlier, we saw how to create a class. In this section, we'll study how to derive a class from another. This is called *inheritance*, one of the fundamental principles of object-oriented programming. Now, the derived class inherits the characteristics of the *base* class. In turn, a derived class can become a base class from which other classes are derived. This is the basic concept of inheritance.

In general, a base class is defined to have characteristics that are common to a set of items. Therefore, inheritance allows you to build many classes in a hierarchical structure where the classes of the lower level are derived from the higher levels. From top to bottom, classes range from generic to specific. In this section, we'll look at the following areas:

- Base class access control
- Inheritance and protected members
- Inheriting multiple classes
- When constructors and destructors are executed
- Passing parameters to base-class constructors
- Granting access
- Virtual base classes

◼ Base class access control

The general form used to define a derived class is

```
class derived-class:access-specifier  base-class
{
    // body of the derived class
}
```

class is the keyword required to define a derived class from the base class.

derived-class is the name of the class that inherits the characteristics of a base class. After the definition, this name is used to create an object.

access-specifier is either **public** or **private** and determines how base-class members are accessed inside the derived class. In case the access specifier is omitted, the default is **private**, if the derived class is a **class**. If the derived class is defined with **struct**, the default access is **public** in case the access specifier is omitted.

public means that all public members of the base class become **public** in the derived class, and all protected members of the base class become **protected** in the derived class.

private means that the private elements of the base class are not accessible in the derived class.

base-class is the name of the class whose characteristics are inherited by the derived class.

● Example

The following program illustrates inheritance of a class. In this case, **xy_base** is the base class and its characteristics are inherited by the **z_derived** class. Note that the access specifier is public; therefore, all public elements of xy_base are accessible to **z_derived**.

```
#include "iostream.h"

class xy_base
{
  int x,y;

public:

  void set_xy(int a, int b)
    {x=a; y=b;}

  void show_xy()
    {cout << x << " " << y << "\n";}
};

class z_derived:public xy_base
{
  int z;

public:

  z_derived (int d)
    {z=d;}

  void show_z()
    {cout << z << "\n";}
};

main()
{
  z_derived ob(300);

// x and y are accessed from ob of z_derived class

  ob.set_xy(100, 200);
```

```
    ob.show_xy(); // prints 100 and 200

    ob.show_z(); // access member of derived class
              // prints 300
    return 0;
}
```

Now, let's define **z_derived** with the **private** access specifier.

```
#include "iostream.h"

class xy_base
{
  int x,y;

public:

  void set_xy(int a, int b)
    {x=a; y=b;}

  void show_xy()
    {cout << x << " " << y << "\n";}
};

class z_derived:private xy_base
{
  int z;

public:
  z_derived (int d)
    {z=d;}

  void show_z()
    {cout << z << "\n";}
};

main()
{

  z_derived ob(300);

// it will produce an error:
// set_xy() and show_xy are not accessible from ob
// This program will not compile successfully.

  ob.set_xy(100, 200);

  ob.show_xy();

  ob.show_z(); // access member of derived class

  return 0;

}
```

◘ Inheritance and protected members

Earlier in this chapter, we briefly looked at **protected** members of a class. The **protected** member is of great interest to us particularly in relation to derived classes as it adds more flexibility to the mechanism of inheritance. When a member is protected, it is similar to a **private** one; both are accessible to members of the class but not to nonmembers. However, both differ significantly when class members are inherited.

A member that is declared as **private** in the base class, is not accessible in any derived class. Now, if a member is **public** and a base class is inherited as **public**, all the **protected** members of the base class become **protected** members of the derived class; therefore, such members are accessible in the derived class. In conclusion, by using the **protected** keyword, members can be **private** to the base class, yet accessible by the derived class.

A derived class can be a base class for another derived class. As we saw previously, the **protected** members of the original base class become **protected** in both the first and second derived classes. In this situation, the first derived class is the base class of the second.

● Example

In the next example, **my_class** is the base class which is used to derive **derived_class**. Note that the elements of **my_class** are accessible in **derived_class** by using the **protected** keyword in the base class and declaring the derived class as **public**.

```
#include "iostream.h"

class my_class
{

protected:

  int x,y; //private to base,
           //yet accessible in derived class
public:

  void set_xy(int a, int b)
    {x=a;y=b;}

  void show_xy()
    {cout << x << " " << y << "\n";}
};
```

```
class derived_class:public my_class
{
  int z;

public:

  // derived class can access base members
  void set_z ()
     {z=x+y;}
  void show_z()
     {cout << z << " \n";}
};

main()
{
  derived_class ob;

  ob.set_xy(2, 3); // x and y are known
             // to derived_class

  ob.show_xy(); // x and y known to derived_class
             // prints 2 and 3

  ob.set_z();
  ob.show_z(); // prints 5
  return 0;
}
```

The next example shows how a derived class can be a base class for a
second derived class. The protected members **x** and **y** of **my_class** are
accessible by **derived_class2**.

```
#include "iostream.h"

class my_class
{
protected:
  int x,y; //private to base,
                  //yet accessible in derived class
public:
  void set_xy(int a, int b)
     {x=a;y=b;}
  void show_xy()
     {cout << x << " " << y << "\n";}
};


// x and y are accessible
class derived_class1: public my_class
{
  int z;
public:
  void set_z()
     {z=x+y;}
  void show_z()
     {cout << z << "\n";}
};
```

```cpp
        // x and y are accessible

        class derived_class2: public derived_class1
        {
          int n;
        public:
          void set_n()
             {n=x-y;}
          void show_n()
             {cout << n << "\n";}
        };

        main()
        {

          derived_class1 ob1;
          derived_class2 ob2;

          ob1.set_xy(20, 30);

          ob1.show_xy(); // prints 20 and 30

          ob1.set_z();

          ob1.show_z(); // prints 50

          ob2.set_xy(30, 40);

          ob2.show_xy();     // prints 30 and 40

          ob2.set_z();

          ob2.set_n();

          ob2.show_z(); // prints 70

          ob2.show_n(); // prints -10

          return 0;
        }
```

◘ Inheriting multiple classes

It is possible for a class to be derived from two or more base classes.

● Example

The following example illustrates how a derived class, called
derived_xy, inherits two base classes **my_x** and **my_y**.

```cpp
        #include "iostream.h"

        class my_x
        {
        protected:
```

```
   int x;
public:
  show_x()
    {cout << x << "\n";}
};

class my_y
{
protected:
  int y;
public:
  show_y()
    {cout << y << "\n";}
};

//derived_xy inherits 2 base classes
class derived_xy: public my_x, public my_y
{
public:
  void set_xy(int a, int b)
    {x=a; y=b;}
};

main()
{
  derived_xy ob;

  ob.set_xy(100, 200); // set_xy found
                       // in derived class
  ob.show_x(); // show_x found in base class
                       // prints 100
  ob.show_y(); // show_y found in base class
                       // prints 200
  return 0;
}
```

◻ When constructors and destructors are executed

It is possible to have constructors and destructors in both base and derived classes. It begs the question of when constructors and destructors are executed.

At the moment an object of a derived class is created, if the base class consists of a constructor, it will be executed first, followed by a constructor of a derived class. Conversely, when a derived class is destroyed, its constructor function is called first, followed by the execution of any destructor function of the base class.

If a derived class becomes the base class of another derived class, the same general rule applies. Constructor functions are executed from the higher to lower derivations, and the destructor functions are called in reverse order.

● Example

The following example shows the order in which constructors and destructor functions are called in both base and derived classes.

```
#include "iostream.h"

class my_base
{
public:

  my_base()
    {cout << "Constructor function of my_base \n";}

  ~my_base()
    {cout << "Destructor function of my_base \n";}
};

class my_derived: public my_base
{
public:

  my_derived()
  { cout << "Constructor function of my_derived \n";}

  ~my_derived()
  { cout << "Destructor function of my_derived \n";}
};

main()
{
  my_derived ob;

  return 0;

}
```

After execution of the program, the following lines are printed:

```
Constructor function of my_base
Constructor function of my_derived
Destructor function of my_derived
Destructor function of my_base
```

◻ Passing parameters to base class constructors

You can pass parameters to base constructor functions when you create an object of a derived class. This is done by declaring the derived constructor with an expanded form of the constructor function of the derived class. This allows you to pass parameters to one or more base constructors. The general form of this expansion version is

```
derived_constructor (arg_list): base1(arg_list),
                      base2(arg_list),
                          .
                          .
                          .
                  baseN(arg_list)
{
  // body of the derived constructor
}
```

derived_constructor is the name of the constructor function of the derived class.

base1 through *baseN* are names of the base classes used to derive the new class.

arg_list is the list of arguments that are passed to the base or derived functions.

● Example

In the next program, the constructor function called **my_derived** is declared using an extended form where **a** and **b** are arguments. Note that **a** belongs to **my_derived** and **b** to **my_base**.

```
#include "iostream.h"
class my_base
{
protected:
  int x;
public:
  my_base (int a)
  {
    x = a;
      cout << "In Constructor function of my_base \n";
  }
  my_base()
  {
    cout << "In Destructor function of my_base \n";
  }
};

class my_derived: public my_base
{
  int y;
public:

  // my_derived uses a ; my_base uses b
  void my_derived(int a, int b) : my_base(b))
  {
    y = a;
    cout << "In constructor of my_derived \n";
  }
```

```
    void ~my_derived()
    {
      cout << "In destructor of my_derived \n";
    }

    void show_xy()
    {
     cout << x << "   " << y << " \n";
    }
};

main()
{
    // 30 is passed to my_derived and 40 to my_base
    my_derived ob(30, 40);

    ob.show_xy(); // prints 30 and 40

    return 0;

}
```

◘ Granting access

In some situations you may want to grant access to a member of a derived class by a nonmember. One such case is when a base class is inherited as **private**, and all the members of the derived class—public, protected, or private—automatically become private. You can grant access to any one of these inherited members by using an access declaration in the definition of the derived class.

The general form is

```
base_class::member;
```

This declaration is placed in the appropriate access category (**public, private**, or **protected**) of the derived class.

● Example

In the following program fragment, **my_base** class is inherited as private by **my_derived** class. And **x** is granted **public** access in the definition of **my_derived**.

```
class my_base
{

public:

  int x; // public in my_base
};
```

```
// my_class is inherited as private

class my_derived: private my_base
{

  // x is granted public access

  my_base::x;

};
```

⬤ Virtual base classes

When a class is derived from one or more base classes, there is a chance of introducing ambiguity; such a program will not compile successfully. When two or more objects are derived from the same base class, multiple copies of the base class are present in the derived object. There are two ways of resolving ambiguity: by using a resolution operator or a virtual base. The scope resolution operator (::) is used to explicitly refer to a member of a base class. The following example shows the ambiguity and how it is remedied using the scope resolution operator. The other way is to prevent multiple copies of the base class from being present in a derived class when the base class is declared as **virtual**. To do so, you simply place the **virtual** keyword in front of the base-class name when it is inherited.

● Example

The following example shows how ambiguity occurs and how it is resolved with a scope resolution operator. Because of errors, this program will not compile successfully.

```
#include "iostream.h"

class my_base
{
public:
  int x;
};

// derived_class_1 inherits my_base

class derived_class_1: public my_base
{

public:

  int y;
};
```

```cpp
// derived_class_2 also inherits my_base

class derived_class_2 : public my_base
{
public:
  int z;
};

// derived_class_3 inherits derived_class_1 and
// derived_class_2. Therefore there are two copies
// of my_base in derived_class_3.

class derived_class_3 : public derived_class_1,
                public derived_class_2
{
public:
  int a;
};

main()
{
  derived_class_3 ob;

  ob.x = 10 ; // This is ambiguous

  // This not ambiguous

  ob.derived_class_2::x = 10 ;

  ob.y = 20;
  ob.z = 20 ;

  // ambiguous, which x ?

  ob.a = ob.x + ob.y + ob.z;

  // resolved with the scope operator

  ob.a = ob.derived_class_1::x + ob.y + ob.z;

  cout << "Sum is " << ob.a << "\n";

  return 0;
}
```

The next program is similar to the previous one, except that only one copy of **my_base** is created in the **ob** object. This is achieved by using **virtual** base classes.

```cpp
#include "iostream.h"

class my_base
{
public:
  int x;
};
```

```cpp
// derived_class_1 inherits my_base

class derived_class_1: virtual public my_base
{
public:
  int y;
};

// derived_class_2 also inherits my_base

class derived_class_2 : virtual public my_base
{
public:
  int z;
};

// only one copy of my_base is created

class derived_class_3 : public derived_class_1,
                public derived_class_2
{
public:
  int a;
};

main()
{
  derived_class_3 ob;

  ob.x = 10 ; // not ambiguous,
          // only one copy of x is created

  ob.y = 20;
  ob.z = 30;

  ob.a = ob.x + ob.y + ob.z ;

  cout << "Sum is " << ob.a << "\n";
              // prints "Sum is 60"
  return 0;
}
```

2.6 Virtual Functions

A **virtual** function is declared in a base class with the virtual keyword and
then it is redefined.

Before we go any further, let's consider at why you would want to use
a **virtual** function. Earlier in this chapter, we discussed polymorphism in
relation to functions. In other words, you can have one interface but
multiple functions by overloading. This is called *compile-time
polymorphism.* At this time, the compiler decides which one of the many
functions to call. However, in C++ there is a run-time polymorphism. This
is accomplished by both inheritance and polymorphism, which is the topic
of discussion in this section.

To understand the run-time polymorphism, let's look at a pointer of a base class. Such a pointer can be used to access any derived-class function. The value of such a pointer is not known until the program is executed. Let's say there is a function called **func** defined in the base class which is inherited in two derived classes, **derived1** and **derived2**. Also, there are two objects of the derived classes called **ob1** and **ob2**. The ambiguity occurs when the base pointer is to call a base function from an object of the derived class. In the case we described above there are two versions of **func** in the two objects of the derived class. Now, the question is which function the pointer will point to.

The following example shows a **virtual** function. **virtual_func** is declared in the **my_base** base class. Subsequently, **derived_1** and **derived_2** are derived classes of **my_base**. In both cases, **virtual_func** is redefined.

In the **main** function, we see how three functions called by one name (**virtual_function**) is called using a pointer of the base class. In this example, the **virtual** functions in base and derived classes are executed. Note that the **virtual** keyword is used in the base class and *not* in the derived classes.

```cpp
#include "iostream.h"

class my_base
{
public:

  virtual void virtual_func()
  {
    cout << "Executing virtual_func of my_base \n";
  }

};

class derived_1: public my_base
{

public:

  void virtual_func()
  {
    cout << "Executing virtual_func of derived_1 \n";
  }
};

class derived_2: public my_base
{
public:

  void virtual_func()
  {
    cout << "Executing virtual_func of derived_2 \n";
  }
};
```

```cpp
main()
{
    my_base *pfunc, ob1;

    derived_1 ob2;
    derived_2 ob3;

    // point to the my_base

    pfunc = &ob1;

    // access virtual_func of my_base

    pfunc->virtual_func();

    // point to derived_1

    pfunc = &ob2;

    // access virtual_func of derived_1

    pfunc->virtual_func();

    // point to derived_2

    pfunc = &ob3;

    // access virtual_func of derived_2

    pfunc->virtual_func();

    return 0;
}
```

After execution of the program, the following lines are printed:

```
Executing virtual_func of my_base
Executing virtual_func of derived_1
Executing virtual_func of derived_2
```

3

Compiling and Linking C and C++ Programs

This chapter is designed as a reference guide for programmers. It discusses the processes of compiling and linking programs using C Set++. It covers various topics to give developers helpful information such as

- Software requirements
- Compiler files
- Invoking the compiler
- Compiler options
- Compiler return codes
- Invoking the linker
- Linker environment variables
- Linker error messages
- Correct compiler options
- Correct run-time libraries
- Static and dynamic linkage
- Multithreading

3.1 Software Requirements

Before using the C Set++ compiler, you must install several pieces of software as well as set up the environment.

◻ Compiler

The compiler is automatically installed when you install the C Set++ product. The *compiler* is a program that translates a C or C++ source program into object code. The rest of this chapter describes the input files, output files, format, options, and how to invoke the compiler.

◻ Linker

The linker is called LINK386. It is distributed with the OS/2 Toolkit. This program combines object files, produced by the compiler, and converts them into an executable module. In other words, you can run the program. The linker is discussed in more detail later.

◻ Run-time libraries

The C Set++ compiler is supplied with object code that is used by your program while it is running. The linkage to this library code is resolved by the linker; you need not be concerned with how it is done. However, these run-time libraries must be installed in the directories known to OS/2.

◻ Debugger

The debugger comes with the C Set++ and is a software product to help you locate logical errors in your program.

◻ Editor

An editor is required to create and change your C source program. OS/2 comes with two editors. One editor performs basic editing functions and is invoked by typing the E command. The other is Enhanced Editor, invoked by typing the **EPM** command. In addition to basic functions, it has many features specially geared toward software development.

◻ Class browser

The C++ class browser allows the user to understand the complex relationships between C++ objects. It comes with the C Set++ product.

◻ Environment setup

The compiler uses many OS/2 environment variables when compiling a program. For the compiler to work properly, these variables must be initialized with the appropriate values. After the installation of any of the software mentioned earlier, the **CONFIG.SYS** file is changed such that the values are initialized during the OS/2 startup time. In case you notice that the compile and link processes are not going well and you suspect that the variables are not set up properly, then run a command file called **CSETENV.CMD**. This command file is supplied with the C Set++.

You should keep in mind that the value lasts as long as the current OS/2 session. In other words, when you boot OS/2, subsequently you will have to set up the variable values again during startup time or at the command line. The variables are **PATH, DPATH, INCLUDE, LIB, TMP,** and **ICC**.

◻ PATH

The **PATH** variable contains directories that are used by the OS/2 system to locate executable files. In this case, you specify directories, separated by a semicolon (;), of the compiler and linker programs. Remember that OS/2 uses the **PATH** variable to search for many other executable modules; therefore, their directory entry must not be changed.

● Example

In the following example, the paths **C:\CSET2\BIN** and **C:\LINK** are added to the environment variable. The parameter **%PATH%** means to append the new values to the original one.

```
SET PATH=C:\CSET2\BIN;C:\LINK;%PATH%
```

◘ DPATH

The **DPATH** variable is used to specify directories which are to be searched by the compiler for help and message files.

● Example

In the following example, two paths, **C:\CSET2\MESS** and **C:\CSET2\HELP**, are added to the original value of **DPATH**.

```
SET DPATH=C:\CSET2\MESS;C:\CSET2\HELP;%DPATH%
```

◘ INCLUDE

The **INCLUDE** variable is used to specify directories which are searched by the compiler for header (include) files.

● Example

In this example, the path **C:\CSET2\INCLUDE** is added to the original value of **INCLUDE**.

```
SET INCLUDE=C:\CSET2\INCLUDE;%INCLUDE%
```

◘ LIB

The **LIB** variable is used to specify C Set++ libraries, used by the linker.

● Example

In the following example, the path **C:\CSET2\LIB** is added to the original value of **LIB**.

```
SET LIB=C:\CSET2\LIB;%LIB%
```

◘ TMP

The compiler uses a directory listed in the **TMP** variable to create working files. After compilation is terminated, all these temporary files are erased.

● Example

In the following example, the variable **TMP** is initialized to the path **C:\CSET2\TMP**. Make sure that the specified path exists before using it with the SET command.

```
SET TMP=C:\CSET2\TMP
```

◻ ICC

The ICC variable is used to list all the default compiler options. With this variable you can also include any filenames. You would use this facility to list options that are used frequently. These options are overridden by options on the command line when invoking the compiler. All the compiler options are listed later in this chapter.

● Example

In the following example, the **ICC** variable is set to compile source files **help.c** and **action.c** and include /C option. You can override any option at the time the compiler is invoked.

```
SET ICC= help.c action.c /C
```

3.2 Compiler Files

The compiler uses many different types of files. These files can be grouped into three categories: input files, output files, and work files. Each file has a specific extension to distinguish it from other files. The following is a list of default files with an indication of the type and a brief description of the content.

Extension	Type	Description
.asm	Output	This file contains assembly listings for each C source program produced by the compiler.
.brs	Output	This file, generated by the compiler, contains information for browsing program source code.
.c	Input	This file contains the C source program for which the compiler produces the object file.

Extension	Type	Description
.cpp	Input	This file contains the C++ source program for which the compiler produces the object file.
.cxx	Input	This file contains the C++ source program for which the compiler produces the object file.
.ctn	Work	Temporary file.
.def	Input	Definition file.
.dll	Output	This file contains dynamic-link libraries produced by the linker from one or more object modules.
.exe	Output	This module contains executable code produced by the linker from one or more object modules.
.h	Input	This is a header or include file that contains portions of C programs (macros, data definitions, statements, etc.) to be incorporated during compilation. The **#INCLUDE** directive is used to merge the include file with the source.
.hpp	Input	This is a header or include file that contains portions of C++ programs that are merged with the main source program during compilation. The **#INCLUDE** directive is used to specify an include file in the source program.
.i	Output	This file is produced by the preprocessor for each source program. It contains information that can be used for debugging your program.
.l	Work	Temporary file.
.lst	Output	This file is produced by the compiler; it contains information such as the source program, any error message, date and time of compilation, and compiler options.

Extension	Type	Description
.lib	Input	This file is an object library that contains one or more object modules. It is used by the linker when generating an executable file.
.m	Input or Output	Temporary file.
.map	Output	This file contains a memory map produced by the linker. This file is useful for program debugging.
.obj	Output or input	This file contains object code for each source program produced by the compiler. Subsequently, this file is used by the linker to produce an executable file.
.w	Work	Intermediate file.
.wh	Work	Intermediate file.
.wl	Work	Intermediate file.
.wli	Input or output	Temporary file.

3.3 Invoking the Compiler

● General format

```
ICC [/option..] [source-name or
        object-name or
        library-name or
        def-file-name] ...]
```

● Description

The C Set++ compiler is invoked in three ways: OS/2 command line, WorkFrame/2, or command file (**.CMD**). In all cases the syntax is the same. If the compilation of a source program is successful, **ICC** automatically calls the linker (**LINK386**). However, if you do not want the linker to be invoked, use /C+ options with the **ICC** command. **ICC** is the compiler program.

option specifies a task that the compiler must or must not perform. There are two types of options. One type applies to a file such as a source program, object file, library, or definition file. Other options apply globally to all the files in the **ICC** command. The options are discussed in more detail in the next section.

source-name is the name of a source program.

object-name is the name of an object module.

library-name is the name of a C library.

def-file-name is the name of a definition file.

● Example

To compile and link a program **myprog.cpp**, enter

```
ICC myprog.cpp
```

The compiler will create an object file **MYPROG.OBJ** in the current directory (e.g., **\MYWORK**) and an executable file **MYPROG.EXE**. To run this program, at the command line, simply enter

```
myprog <Enter>
```

Now, if you want to compile only, enter

```
ICC /C+  myprog.cpp
```

In the example,

```
ICC myprog.cpp routine1.c routine2.c
```

the compiler will compile three programs (**myprog.cpp**, **routine1.c**, and **routine2.c**) and produce three object files (**myprog.obj**, **routine1.obj**, and **routine2.obj**). Next, the linker uses these object files to produce one executable file **MYPROG.EXE** in the current directory (e.g. **\MYWORK**). If an executable file is not explicitly specified, when you call the compiler, it will assign to the executable file the same name as the first source name of the command.

In these previous examples only a few programs are involved. In a large scale program, you could conceivably have hundreds of files. For a larger number of files, it is impractical to issue compiler commands as we have just seen. Another way to handle source files, where they are compiled and linked automatically is to use the **NMAKE** utility. This utility is discuused in detail later in this book.

3.4 Compiler Options

As mentioned earlier, options are used to instruct the compiler to do special processing. This section lists all the options available with C Set++. This list is extensive and often cryptic. It is very unlikely that you will use all of them during your programming career.

Earlier in this chapter, we discussed the general format of invoking the compiler, namely, the **ICC** (compiler name) followed by option and filenames. Before using the option it is important to understand the format, primary option, suboption, and parameters.

- General option format

  `< / or - > options [suboption][parameter]`

- Description of format

  The options are not case-sensitive; therefore you can use lowercase, -uppercase, and mixed-case characters. For example, /Ls is the same as /ls. Depending on the needs, you can specify no option or many options, but always bear in mind that the compiler uses the default values for the options not listed.

  / or -, as mentioned before, is the start of an option.

  suboption specifies different operations with an option. In this book it will be in lowercase characters.

  parameter is optional and can be a string, filename, switch, or number.

  String: A string, if required by an option, must be placed immediately after the option. If a blank is part of the string, it should be enclosed in double quotes, for example, /V"Version 2.1".

Filename: With a filename you can specify a full path, such as **/Fe C:\bin\prop.exe**. If you omit the extension, the compiler will use the default values (see section on compiler files).

Switch: Some options require a switch which is a plus (+) or minus (-). A switch indicates to the compiler whether to perform a task. For example, **/Gf+** means to generate code for fast floating-point execution, and **/Gf-**, not to generate such a code. If you omit the switch, then the compiler assumes a plus, for example, **/Gf** is the same as **/Gf+**. Some examples of switches are

```
ICC /La /C- /O+ main.cpp
```

Numbers: A number, if required by an option, must be placed immediately after the option, following a space. If more than one member is specified, they should be separated by commas; for example,

```
/Sg 10,32
```

option is a character symbol denoting the facility and will appear in uppercase characters throughout this book.

The options are divided into the following categories:

- Output management
- **#include** file search
- Program listing file
- Debugging and diagnostic Information
- Source code
- Preprocessor
- Code generation

The following is a description of all the compiler options.

◘ /B—pass parameter to the linker

/B"*parameter*" is used to pass options to the linker, when the compiler is invoked.

parameter is a string, enclosed in double quotes, that is sent to the linker. The default is that the compiler does not send any parameter to the linker.

● Example

Pass /NOI parameter to the linker:

```
ICC /B"/NOI" myprog.c
```

◘ /C—invoke the linker

/C+ Produce object module only (compile only, not link).
/C- Produce executable file (compile and link a program). This is the default.

● Example

Compile program only:

```
ICC /C+ myprog.c
```

◘ /D—define preprocessor macro

/D *name*[::*n*] or /D*name*[=*n*]
  Define a preprocessor macro, where *name* is the name of the macro and *n* is the value assigned to it.

● Example

Define **DEBUG** macro:

```
ICC /D DEBUG=1  myprog.c
```

◼ /F—output file management

/Fa-	Do not produce an assembler listing file. This is the default.
/Fa+	Produce an assembly listing file; the filename is the same as the source file, but with extension .ASM.
/Fa *name*	Produce an assembler listing file and call it *name*.ASM.
/Fb-	Do not produce a browser file. This is the default.
/Fb+	Produce a browser file with extension .BRS.
/Fc-	Compile and produce output files depending on other options. This is the default.
/Fc+	Check the syntax of the program only. With this option an object file is not produced, but you can request a program listing with this option.
/Fd-	Produce internal work files in memory. This is the default for C code, and this option cannot be specified for C++ code.
/Fd+	Produce work files on disk in the directory specified in the **TMP** variable.
/Fe *name*	Specify the name of an executable file or DLL. The default is to assign the executable file the same name as the first source file, but with extension .EXE or .DLL.
/Fi-	Do not produce a precompiled include file. This is the default.
/Fi+	Produce a precompiled include file.
/Fl-	Produce a listing file and give it the same name as the source file. This is the default.
/Fl *name*	Specify the name of the listing file, where name is the filename.
/Fm-	Do not produce a map file. This is the default.

/Fm+   Produce a map file and give it the same name as the source file with extension .MAP.

/Fm *name* Produce a map file, where *name* is the filename.

/Fo+   Produce an object file and give it the same name as the source file with extension .OBJ. This is the default.

/Fo-   Specify not to produce an object file.

/Fo *name* Specify a name of the object file, where *name* is a filename with extension .OBJ.

/Ft+   Produce files for template resolution in the TEMPINC subdirectory. This is the default.

/Ft-   Do not produce files for template resolution.

/F *dir*   Produce files for template resolution in a specified directory.

/Fw-   Do the compilation and do not save the intermediate files. This is the default.

/Fw+   Do the intermediate compilation only; it does not complete the compilation.

/Fw *name* Do the intermediate compilation and save the output in file *name*.W, *name*.WH, and *name*.WI.

● Example

Produce an assembly listing file:

```
ICC /Fa+ myprog.c
```

Check the systax of the program:

```
ICC /Fc+ myprog.c
```

Produce a listing file:

```
ICC /Fl prog.lst myprog.c
```

◘ /G—code generation

/Gd-	Statically link the run-time libraries. This is the default.
/Gd+	Dynamically link the run-time libraries.
/Ge+	Build an .EXE file. This is the default.
/Ge-	Build a .DLL file.
/Gf-	Disable the compiler to use the fast floating-point execution. This is the default.
/Gf+	Enable the compiler to use the fast floating-point execution.
/Gh-	Disable code for EXTRA. This is the default.
/Gh+	Enable code for EXTRA. (You must also specify /Ti with this option.)
/Gi-	Disable use of fast integer execution. This is the default.
/Gi+	Enable use of fast integer execution.
/Gm-	Link with the single-thread version of the library. This is the default.
/Gm+	Link with the multithread version of the library.
/Gn-	Search the default libraries, according to the /G option. This is the default.
/Gn+	Do not search the default libraries; all libraries must be explicitly specified.
/Gr-	Disable object code to run at ring 0. This is the default.
/Gr+	Enable object code to run at ring 0.
/Gs-	Do not remove stack probes. This is the default.
/Gs+	Remove the stack probes.

/Gt-   Do not allow variables to be passed to 16-bit functions. This is the default.

/Gt+   Allows all variables to be passed to 16-bit functions.

/Gu-   Allow external functions be use data defined in intermediary files. This is the default.

/Gu+   Let the data be used only within the intermediate files being linked.

/Gv-   Do not handle DS and ES registers in any special way. This is the default.

/Gv+   Save the content of DS and ES registers on entry to an external function, set them to the selector for **DGROUP**, and restore them when returning from the function.

/Gw-   Do not execute **FWAIT** instruction after each floating-point load instruction. This is the default.

/Gw+   Execute an **FWAIT** instruction after each floating-point load instruction.

/Gx-   Do not remove C++ exception handling data. This is the default.

/Gx+   Remove C++ exception handling data.

/G3   Optimize the code for 80386 processor. This is the default.

/G4   Optimize the code for 80486 processor.

● Example

Optimize the code for 80486:

```
ICC /G4 myprog.c
```

Disable the use of fast integer execution:

```
ICC /Gi- myprog.c
```

◘ /H—set significant length of external names

/H255　　　Set the first 255 characters of external names to be significant. This is the default.

/H *num*　　Specify the first number of characters of the external names to be significant, where *num* ranges between 6 and 255.

● Example

Specify the 40 first characters of external names to be significant:

```
ICC /H 40 myprog.c
```

◘ /I—specify include file

/I *path*[;*path*]　　tells the compiler which directories to search for files specified in the **#include** directive. The default is to look for include files in the directory where source files are found, and then look at the directories listed in the **INCLUDE** environment variable.

● Example

Specify the path for the include file:

```
ICC /I C:\MYWORK\INCLUDE myprog.c
```

◘ /J—set default char type

/J+　　Set unspecified variables of **char** type to **unsigned char**. This is the default.

/J-　　Set unspecified variables of **char** type to **signed char**.

● Example

Set unpsecified **char** variables to **signed char**:

```
ICC /J- myprog.c
```

◼ /K—diagnostic and debugging information

/Ka-   Suppress messages about assignment operations that may diminish precision. This is the default.

/Ka+   Produce messages if assignment operations are inappropriate for long values.

/Kb-   Suppress all basic diagnostic messages. This is the default.

/Kb+   Generate all basic diagnostic messages.

/Kc-   Suppress warning messages produced by the preprocessor. This is the default.

/Kc+   List warning messages produced by the preprocessor.

/Ke-   Suppress all messages that are caused by usage of **enum**. This is the default.

/Ke+   Produce messages that are caused by the usage of **enum**.

/Kf-   Set all diagnostic messages off. This is the default.

/Kf+   Set all diagnostic messages on.

/Kg-   Suppress messages caused by the usage of the **goto** statement. This is the default.

/Kg+   List all messages caused by the usage of the **goto** statement.

/Ki-   Suppress messages caused when variables are not initialized. This is the default.

/Ki+   List all messages caused when variables are not initialized.

/Ko-   Suppress all messages caused by portability. This is the default.

/Ko+   List all messages caused by portability.

/Kp-   Suppress messages caused when unused function parameters are encountered. This is the default.

/Kp+   List all the messages caused when unused function parameters are encountered.

/Kr-   Suppress messages about name mapping. This is the default.

/Kr+   List messages caused by name mapping.

/Kt-   Suppress messages caused by the preprocessor trace. This is the default.

/Kt+   List all the messages caused by the preprocessor trace.

/Kx-   Suppress messages when unreferenced external variables are found. This is the default.

/Kx+   List messages when unreferenced external variables are found.

● Example

List all the messages caused by the preprocessor trace:

```
ICC /K+ myprog.c
```

■ /L—listing file

/L-   Do not produce a listing file. This is the default.

/L+	Produce a listing file with heading, source program, and error messages.
/La-	Do not include a layout. This is the default.
/La+	Include a layout.
/Lb-	Do not include a layout. This is the default.
/Lb+	Include a layout.
/Le-	Do not expand macros. This is the default.
/Le+	Expand all macros.
/Lf-	Turn off all listing options. This is the default.
/Lf+	Turn on all listing options.
/Li-	Do not expand user **#include** files. This is the default.
/Li+	Expand user **#include** files.
/Lj-	Do not expand any **#include** files (system or user). This is the default.
/Lj+	Expand all **#include** files (system and user).
/Lp66	Set the page length limit to 66 lines. This is the default.
/Lp *num*	Set the page length limit as specified by *num*.
/Ls-	Exclude the source code. This is the default.
/Ls+	Include the source code.
/Lt ""	Specify a null string as the title. This is the default.
/Lt "*string*"	Specify a title, where *string* is the title.
/Lu""	Specify a null string as the title. This is the default.
/Lu "*string*"	Specify a subtitle, where *string* is the subtitle.

/Lx-	Do not generate a cross-reference table. This is the default.
/Lx+	Generate a cross-reference table.
/Ly-	Do not generate a cross-reference table. This is the default.
/Ly+	Generate a cross-reference table.

● Example

Produce a listing file with heading, source program, and error messages:

```
ICC /L+ myprog.c
```

◘ /M—set calling convention

/Mp   Use **_optlink** linkage for functions. This is the default.

/Ms   Use **_system** linkage for functions.

● Example

Use **_system** linkage for functions:

```
ICC /Ms myprog.c
```

◘ /N—set error limits before aborting compilation

/N*n*   Set the number errors before compilation is terminated, where n is the count limit. The default is not to set any limit on the number of errors generated before the compilation aborts.

● Example

Set maximum number of errors to 20:

```
ICC /N20 myprog.c
```

◾ /O—optimization switch and code generation

/O-   Turn the optimization of the code off. This is the default.

/O+   Turn the optimization of the code on.

/Oi-   Do not inline any user code. The option is the default, except when /Oi+ is used.

/Oi+   Inline all user functions with the **_Inline** or **inline** keyword.

/Oi *value*   Inline all user functions qualified with *value*.

/Ol-   Do not process the code at the intermediate level of the linker. This is the default.

/Ol+   Process the code at the intermediate level of the linker before the object file is generated.

/Om-   Do not limit the working set size. This is the default.

/Om+   Limit the working set size to 35 Mbytes.

/Op+   Opitimize the code when the stack pointer is used. This is the default.

/Op-   Do not optimize the code when the stack pointer is used.

● Example

Do not optimize the code when the stack pointer is used:

```
ICC /Op- myprog.c
```

◘ /P—preprocessor options

/P-   Run the preprocessor and the compiler. It does not produce preprocessor output. This is the default.

/P+   Run the preprocessor only and produce a file, with extension **.I**, containing the preprocessor output.

/Pc- Run the preprcessor only and produce an output file without comments. The output file has the same name as the source with extension **.I**. This is the default.

/Pc+ Run the preprocessor only and produce an output file containing the comments from the source code. The output file has the same name as the source with extension **.I**.

/Pd- Run the preprcessor only and produce an output file without comments. The output file has the same name as the source with extension **.I**. This is the default.

/Pd+ Run the preprocessor only and redirect the output to **stdout**.

● Example

Run the preprocessor only and redirect the output to **stdout**:

```
ICC /Pd+ myprog.c
```

◘ /Q—compiler logo display

/Q- Show the logo on the **stderr**. This is the default.

/Q+ Do not display the logo.

● Example

Do not display logo:

```
ICC /Q+ myprog.c
```

◙ /R—control executable run-time environment

/Re   Produce an executable output that runs in the C/C++ Tools run-time environment. This is the default.

/Rn   Produce an executable output that will run as a subsystem. This code does not need a run-time environment.

● Example

Produce an executable file to run as a subsystem:

```
ICC /Rn myprog.c
```

◙ /S—source code options

/Se   Incorporate all C/C++ Tools language extensions. This is the default.

/Sa   Conform to ANSI standards.

/Sc   Conform to older versions of C++ language.

/S2   Conform to SAA (IBM Systems Application Architecture) Level 2 standards (only for C programs).

/Sd-   Set the default file extension to .OBJ. This is the default.

/Sd+   Set the default file extension to .C.

/Sg-   Do not set any margin; the entire file is used an input. This is the default.

/Sg[l][,r or *]   Set margins, where l is the left margin, r is the right margin, and * means no margin.

/Sh-   Do not allow data definition names (**DDNAME**). This is the default.

/Sh+	Allow data definition names (DDNAME).
/Si-	Do not use precompiled include files. This is the default.
/Si+	Use precompiled include files, only if they are in current state.
/Sm-	Process unsupported 16-bit keywords in the same way as any other identifier. This is the default.
/Sm+	Do not process unsupported 16-bit keywords.
/Sn-	Disable double-byte character set (DBCS). This is the default.
/Sn+	Process DBCS.
/Sp4	Align structures and unions along 4-byte boundaries. This is the default.
/Sp[1 or 2]	Align structures and unions along 1-byte or 2-byte boundary.
/Sq-	Do not use sequence numbers. This is the default.
/Sq[l][,r]	Use sequence numbers specified between l and r, where l and r are columns of each line.
/Sr-	Use new-style rules when processing type conversion. This style is more accurate. This is the default.
/Sr+	Use old-type rules when processing type conversion.
/Ss-	Allow only one slash (/) for comments. This is the default.
/Ss+	Allow two slashes (//) for comments.
/Su-	Make all **enum** variables the same size as small **int.** This is the default.

/Su+	Specify all **enum** variables to occupy 4 bytes.
/Su1	Specify all **enum** variables to occupy 1 byte.
/Su2	Specify all **enum** variables to occupy 2 bytes.
/Su4	Specify all **enum** variables to occupy 4 bytes.
/Sv-	Do not make use of memory files. This is the default.
/Sv+	Use memory files.

● Example

Conform to ANSI standards:

```
ICC /Sa myprog.c
```

◘ /T—specify C and C++ source file

/Tc	Compile the following files as C files. The default is to compile files with extension .CPP and .CXX as C++ files and with any other extension as C files.
/Td	Compile files with extension .CPP and .CXX as C++ files and files with any other extensions as C files. This is the default.
/Tdc	Compile the following files as C files.
/Tdp	Compile the following files as C++ files.
/Tp	Compile files with extension .CPP and .CXX as C++ files, and files with .C or any other extension as C files.

● Example

Compile source file as a C file:

```
ICC /Tc myprog.c
```

◼ /U—undefine macros

/U*   Undefine all macros. The default is to retain all macros.

/U *name*   Undefine a macro, where *name* is the name of a macro.

● Example

Undefine DEBUG macro:

```
ICC /U DEBUG myprog.c
```

◼ /V—version string

/V""   Set a null string as version. This is the default.

/V"*string*"   Set *string* as version.

● Example

Set version:

```
ICC /V"Version 1.2" myprog.c
```

◼ /W—message control

/Wall- Do not produce diagnostic messages. This is the default.

/W *grp* Produce messages as specified by *grp*.

/W3   Produce messages of all types.

/W0   Produce messages for severe types only.

/W1   Produce messages for all errors.

/W2   Produce messages for all errors and warnings.

● Example

Produce messages of all types:

```
ICC /W3 myprog.c
```

◻ /X—search control

/Xc-   Search paths listed in the /I option. This is the default.

/Xc+   Do not to search paths listed in the /I option.

/Xi-   Search path listed in the **INCLUDE** environment variable. This is the default.

/Xi+   Do not to search paths listed in the **INCLUDE** environment variable.

● Example

Do not search paths listed in the **INCLUDE** environment variable:

```
ICC /Xi myprog.c
```

3.5 Compiler Return Codes

The compiler of C Set++ returns a return code after compiling every source file. The return code indicates the status of the compilation process—whether the source program is error free and linking task can proceed. The compiler returns one of the following codes:

Return code	Description
0	Successful completion of the compilation.
12	Compilation was completed, but errors were encountered during the compilation.

16   Compilation was aborted abnormally and severe error was encountered during the compilation.

20   Compilation was aborted abnormally and fatal error was found during the compilation.

Along with the return code, the compiler also produces messages showing which line of the program caused an error or warning.

The message format is

   filename.ext(*line:col*):SS EDC*nnnn:text*

where

filename.ext is the name of the source program where the error or warning occurred

line is the line number of the program where the error or warning occurred

col is the column within a line where the error or warning occurred

SS is a two digit number which is one of the following:

   00   Informational
   10   Warning
   30   Error
   40   Severe error
   50   Fatal error

nnnn is an error message number
text is description of the error or warning

3.6 Invoking the Linker

• General format

```
LINK386 objfile...
[+ or BLANK][,exefile,mapfile,libraries,deffile]
```

```
[option...][;]
```

or

```
LINK386
```

or

```
LINK386 @response-file
```

● Description

Earlier we saw the compiler invoking the linker. While developing programs, you may encounter situations where it seems more advantageous to link programs separately from the compile step. This section describes how to invoke the linker. The following sections deal with other related aspects of the linker, such as environment variables and error messages.

There are three ways to run the linker at the command line

- Type LINK386, followed by all the input files and options and press ENTER.

- Type LINK386 and press ENTER. The linker will prompt you for all the necessary information, such as the object file, library file, and types of output.

- Type LINK386 followed by character @ and a name of a response file. The content of the response file is dicussed later.

When the linker is processing, it can be stopped at any time by pressing CTRL+C, and control will be returned to OS/2.

objfile is the name of the object file, previously produced by the compiler. If you list more than one object file, separate them with a plus (+) or blank. This parameter is required.

exefile is the name of the output file. It can be one of the following types: executable file, dynamic-link library or device driver. If you omit this parameter, the linker uses the name of the first object file as the output filename and adds .EXE, DDL, or SYS as the extension.

mapfile is the name of the map file. If you do not require the map file enter NUL.MAP. For more information about this file, see the /M option. The default map filename is the same as the executable output file with extension .MAP.

libraries is the name of one or more libraries needed to resolve some of the external references that are not resolved by other object files. Multiple library names must be separated by a plus (+) or a blank. The library files are searched for in the current directory or default directories defined in the environment variable **LIB**. Also you can enter a specific path for the directory.

deffile is the name of a module definition file. A definition file contains module statements that define names, attributes, export functions, import functions, and other characteristics of an OS/2 application. If you are creating a dynamic link library or device drivers, a definition file is absolutely required. When creating or updating a module definition file, there are a few rules to follow:

- **A NAME, VIRTUAL DEVICE,** or **PHYSICAL DEVICE** statement must precede all other statements.

- A comment must start with a semicolon (;) and is ignored by the linker.

- All module definition keywords, such as **NAME, LIBRARY,** and **OLD,** must be in all-uppercase characters.

The following is a list of module statements with a brief description.

Statement	Description
BASE	Base
CODE	Gives default attributes for code segments
DATA	Gives default attributes for data segments
DESCRIPTION	Describes the mode
EXETYPE	Identifies the operating system

Statement	Description
EXPORTS	Defines export functions
IMPORTS	Defines import functions
HEAPSIZE	Names a dynamic-link library
NAME	Names an application
OLD	Preserves import information
PHYSICAL DEVICE	Names a physical device
PROTMODE	Specifies that the module runs in protected mode
SEGMENTS	Defines the attributes of one or more segments in the application or library on a segment-by-segment basis
STACKSIZE	Controls the stack size of a program, same as the linker /ST option
STUB	Adds a DOS (disk operating system) executable file to the beginning of the application or library
VIRTUAL DEVICE	Names a virtual device

option is a parameter used to change the processing of the linker. Each option starts with a slash (/), and you can list one or many options when running the linker. The following is a list of all the linker options.

Option	Description
/?	Show the linker command line syntax
/A[LIGNMENT]	Align
/BASE[E]	Base

Option	Description
/BAT[CH]	Run in batch mode
/C[ODEVIEW]	Prepare output for debugger **CODEVIEW**
/DE[BUG]	Prepare output for debugger **DEBUG**
/DO[SSEG]	Prepare output for debuuger
/E[XEPACK]	Exepack
/F[ARCALLTRANSLATION]	Optimize **far** calls
/H[ELP]	Display help information
/I[INFORMATION]	Display process information
/L[INENUMBERS]	Include line numbers
/M[AP]	List public symbols
/NOD[EFAULTLIBRARYSEARCH]	Ignore default libraries
/NOE[XTDICTIONARY]	Ignore extended dictionary
/NOF[ARCALLTRANSLATION]	Disable far optimizations
/NOI[GNORECASE]	Preserve case sensitivity
/NOL[OGO]	Disable sign-on logo
/NON[ULLSDOSSEG]	Order segments without NULLS
/NOP[ACKCODE]	Do not pack contiguous code
/PACKD[ATA]	Pack contiguous code
/PAU[SE]	Pause during link processing

Option	Description
/PM[TYPE]	Name application type
/SE[GMENTS]	Set maximum number of segments
/ST[ACK]	Control stack size
/W[ARMFIXUP]	Warm fixup

response-file contains the entries to the prompts of LINK386 that can be passed to the linker in a response file. In other words, the input to the linker is supplied through this file. The 'at' (@) symbol tells the linker to use the filename as a response file, containing parameters. For further clarification, see examples given later in this chapter.

● Example

In this example,

```
LINK386 main;
```

the linker links the object file **main.obj**, resolves any external references using the default libraries, and produces an executable file **main.exe**. It does not create a map file.

In the next command, there are more parameters, including files and options.

```
LINK386 label+readfile+print,,,mylib.lib /DE;
```

To understand this example, you have to recall the general format, discussed earlier, especially the position of each parameter. The first three parameters **label**, **readfile**, and **print**, are object files. The following three commands mean to produce an executable file **label.exe** and a map file **label.map**. The linker searches the library file **mylib.lib**, and default files to resolve external references. The /D option tells the linker to prepare the output for debugging, and the semicolon (;) means to ignore the module definition file.

The next example is similar to the previous one except that it uses a module definition file **label.def**.

```
LINK386 label+readfile+
        print,,,mylib.lib,label.def /De
```

Note that the semicolon at the end is omitted because all the input files are implicitly or explicitly specified.

3.7 Linker Environment Variable

When LINK386 is doing a link process, it uses vital information from the **LINK** environment variable. If this variable is initialized with one or more options, the linker uses them. This variable is set to a value with the **SET** command in the **CONFIG.SYS** or at the command line, for example,

```
SET LINK=/NOI /SE:256 /CO
```

If LINK386 is invoked subsequently, it will use the /NOI, /SE:256, and /CO. In the example

```
LINK386 MYPROG;
```

the file **MYPROG.OBJ** is linked with the options /NOI, /SE:256, and /CO.

LINK386 expects to find options listed in the variable exactly as you would type them on the command line. And you should not add any thing else, for example filenames in the environment variable cause the following error message:

```
unrecognized option
```

Using the **LINK** environment variable is a practical way of using options that are frequently used. Each time you run the linker, you can specify other options in addition to the ones specified in the LINK386 environment variable. If you give an option at the command line which is the same as in the environment variable, the effect is the same as if the option were given once. But if an option given at the command line is in conflict with the one listed in the environment variable, the command line option overrides the effect of the environment-variable option. If you want to change the environment-variable option, you reissue the **SET LINK** command with new options.

3.8 Linker Error Messages

LINK386 produces three kinds of messages: fatal, nonfatal, and warning. The following briefly describes each type and gives a message format.

Fatal errors: These messages are caused when the linker encounters very serious problems with the linkage and processing steps. The format is

```
filename:fatal error L1xxx:text
```

Nonfatal errors: These messages are caused when problems are encountered in the executable output file. Although the linker creates an excutable file, it cannot be run from OS/2. The format is

```
filename: error L2xxx:text
```

Warnings: These messages are caused when potential problems are encountered in the executable output file. The executable file is created and you can run it, unlike nonfatal errors. The format is

```
filename:Warning L4xxx:text
```

filename is the name of the file where the error occurred. It can be an object file, library file, module definition file, or the linker. In case it is a definition file, the messages include the line number associated with the error; for example,

```
label.def(3):fatal error L1030:missing internal name
```

If *filename* is an object or library file, then the source name, if it exists, is shown in parentheses; for example,

```
mylib.lib(_export)
print.obj(print.c)
label.obj
```

If the error encountered is with LINK386 itself, then *filename* is omitted.

xxx is a number associated with the message.

text is the description of the message.

3.9 Correct Compiler Options

Developing software in the OS/2 environment can be quite complicated; there are many aspects to consider. To get the right result from the compiler it is important to choose the correct compiler option for the right type of application. The options vary depending on many aspects, such as

- Linkage: static or dynamic
- Type of threading: single or multithread
- Library: standard, migration, or subsystem
- Output: executable or ddl

Figure 3.1 lists the correct options needed for the compiler with the right combination of linkage, type of threading, library, module, and options.

Linkage	Type of Threading	Library	Module	Options Required
Static	Single	Standard	EXE	None
Static	Single	Standard	DLL	/Ge-
Static	Single	Migration	EXE	/Sm
Static	Single	Migration	DLL	/Sm /Ge-
Static	Multiple	Standard	EXE	/Gm+
Static	Multiple	Standard	DLL	/Gm+ /Ge-
Static	Multiple	Migration	EXE	/Gm+ /Sm
Static	Multiple	Migration	DLL	/Gm+ /Sm /Ge-
Static	N/A	Subsystem	EXE	/Rn
Static	N/A	Subsystem	DLL	/Rn /Ge-
Dynamic	Single	Standard	EXE	/Gd+
Dynamic	Single	Standard	DLL	/Gd+ /Ge-
Dynamic	Single	Migration	EXE	/Gd+ /Sm
Dynamic	Single	Migration	DLL	/Gd+ /Sm- /Ge-
Dynamic	Multiple	Standard	EXE	/Gd+ /Gm+
Dynamic	Multiple	Standard	DLL	/Gd+ /Gm+ /Ge-
Dynamic	Multiple	Migration	EXE	/Gd+ /Gm+ /Sm
Dynamic	Multiple	Migration	DLL	/Gd+ /Gm+ /Sm /Ge-
Dynamic	N/A	Subsystem	EXE	/Gd+ /Rn
Dynamic	N/A	Subsystem	DLL	/Gd+ /Rn /Ge-

Figure 3.1 Combination of compiler options and specific libraries.

3.10 Correct Run-Time Library

It is important to specify the right run-time library for the different types of application programs. To identify the right linker filename, with the correct combination, the naming convention listed in Figure 3.2 is convenient to use. The first four characters of the library name are constant, but the last four position vary according to the different types and significance of the libraries. Both Figures 3.1 and 3.2 cover all the combinations that you would need for any kind of development.

Character position Description	
12345678	
DDE4	
S	Single-thread library
M	Multithread library
N	Subsystem
B	EXE or DLL
S	Standard library
M	Migration library
I	Import library
O	Object library

Figure 3.2 Naming convention for libraries.

● Example

For example, the library name DDE4SBSI is used for single-thread programs, executable or DLL outputs, and standard and import libraries.

3.11 Linkage: Static or Dynamic

There are two types of linkages: static and dynamic; this should not be confused with dynamic-link libraries.

Static linkage: This means that all the run-time functions are included in the final copy of the program, whether it is executable or DLL. Obviously, this makes the output files larger because they contain all the C or C++

functions. Although this method requires more storage, on disk or memory, for programs, it is easier to distribute and may even run faster than its counterpart dynamic linkage.

Dynamic linkage: Unlike the static linkage, in this method the target rules do not include run-time library functions. At runtime all the external references are resolved, thus making the output files smaller than the static linkage method. The down side of this method is that it may decrease execution performance.

3.12 Multithread Programming

Multithread is a method of dividing a program or process into many threads. A *thread* is a small unit of execution within a process. Execution of many threads occurs concurrently, while in a single-thread program, each function—a process— starts and ends after another one is completed.

Because of the nature of multithreading, programming of this method is complex. This section is not about concepts and theoretical aspects of multithreads. It describe a few programming steps that you might find useful if you are already familiar with this technique. For more in-depth discussion of multithread and multitasking, refer to *IBM Programming Guide*.

This section will first make you aware of some of the variables and functions related to multithread programming. Then, we will look at an example of multithread programming, using some of these functions and variables. Finally, we will see how to compile, link, and execute the sample program.

3.12.1 Functions

This section gives specific information about some functions found in C or C++ libraries or OS/2. You will find this information useful when writing multithread programs. This section discusses some of the restrictions and nature of the **_beginthread** function. This function produces a new thread. Under OS/2 you can produce up to **x** threads. You must use this function if your program is calling any of the language library functions. This allows the the C and C++ intialization routines to handle resources and data between threads. There is an OS/2 function to produce threads called **DosCreatThread**. You must remember that this function does not have access to the resource management facilities. **DosCreatThread** is used with the subsystem libraries.

_endthread: This function is used to end a thread.

abort: This function ends all threads within a process.

exit: This function ends all threads within a process.

signal: This function registers signal handlers independently for each thread.

_putenv: A thread can call this function to set the environment variables. You can access the latest data from the environment variables with the **_getenv** function.

DosCreateThread: This function produces an asynchronous thread within a process.

DosEnterCritSec: This function is used to disable thread switching for the current process.

DosExit: This function ends a thread within a process.

DosExitCritSec: This function enables the thread switching for the current process.

DosGetInfoBlocks: This function gets the address of the thread information block (TIB) and process information block (PIB).

DosKillThread: This function ends a thread in the current process.

DosResumeThread: This function restarts a previously suspended thread.

DosSetPriority: This function is used to change the priority of a process or thread.

DosSuspendThread: This function is used to suspend execution of a thread within a process.

DosWaitThread: This function is used to wait for another thread to end.

3.12.2 Variables and data structures

There are a few variables to consider when you write multithread programs. This section briefly describes these variables.

Name	Description
_thread	A global variable that contains the current thread
errno	A variable containing the current error number for each thread, implemented as a per-thread global variable
_environ	An environment variable implemented as a per-thread global variable and is shared by multithread and single thread programs
_doserrno	A variable that contains the current error for each thread; implemented as a per-thread global variable.

3.12.3 Examples

The next program illustrates in a simple way the concept of multithread programming. Let's call it **mthread.c**. It contains two threads, **thread1** and **thread2**.

```c
/*-------------------------------------------------
/* Program: MTHREAD.C
/* This program illustrates multithread programming.
/*-------------------------------------------------

#include <stdio.h>

int done_1 = 0;

int done_2 = 0;

void thread1( void )
{
   fprintf(stderr,"This is thread 1 \n");

   fprintf(stderr,"More from 1 \n");

   done_1 = 1;
}

void thread2( void )
{
   fprintf(stderr,"This is thread 2 \n");

   fprintf(stderr,"More from 2 \n");

   done_2 = 1;
}

int main( void )
{
   _beginthread(thread1, NULL, 4096, NULL);

   _beginthread(thread2, NULL, 4096, NULL);

   while(1)
   {
     if (done_1 && done_2)

        break;
   }

   return 0;

}
```

Each function prints two lines of data to the error standard stream **strerr**. In the **main** function both of these threads, which are also functions, are created using the **_beginthread** function. When both threads are executed, the program terminates.

3.12.4 Compile, link, and run multithread program

In this section we will go through the steps of compiling, linking, and running the program **mthread.c**.

Compiling and linking: In this process, you have to make sure that the correct compiler option is specified to use the multithread libraries. In a multithread environment such as OS/2, the library routines are designed to share data without running into each other. To use the multithread library, use the compiler option /Gm+ when compiling and linking the program **mthread.c**, for example,

```
ICC /Gm+ mthread.c
```

This command will create an executable file **mthread.exe.**

Link: If you want to compile and link separately, then use the /C+ option when invoking the compiler; for example,

```
ICC /Gm+ /C+ mthread.c
```

This will generate an object file **mthread.obj**. To genrate an executable file **mthread.exe** type the command

```
LINK386 mthread
```

Run: To run the this program, change to the directory where **mthread.exe** is found and type

```
mthread
```

at the command line. Possible result will be

```
This is thread 1
This is thread 2
More from 1
More from 2
```

or

```
This is thread 1
More from 1
This is thread 2
More from 2
```

or

```
This is thread 1
This is thread 2
More from 2
More from 1
```

COBOL

This chapter is a reference guide for programmers using the COBOL language. It provides the syntax and descriptions of the divisions, sections, paragraphs, clauses, and statements of the language. This chapter covers several aspects of COBOL:

- General program format
- Language element
- IDENTIFICATION DIVISION
- ENVIRONMENT DIVISION
- DATA DIVISION
- PROCEDURE DIVISION

For OS/2 there many compilers; each conforms primarily to ANSI COBOL with special additions. As it is impossible to cover all the differences of OS/2 COBOL compilers in this chapter, the discussion in this chapter is limited to the ANSI standard.

General format: The general format of a COBOL source program is

```
<IDENTIFICATION DIVISION. or ID DIVISION.>
PROGRAM-ID. program-name.
   [identification-division-content]
[ENVIRONMENT DIVISION.]
   [environment-division-content]
[DATA DIVISION.]
   [data-division-content]
[PROCEDURE DIVISION.]
   [procedure-division-content]
[END PROGRAM program-name.]
```

A COBOL program generally has four divisions:

IDENTIFICATION DIVISION—identifies the program

ENVIRONMENT DIVISION—describes the hardware being being used
to compile and run the program

DATA DIVISION—defines the data being processed in the program

PROCEDURE DIVISION—consists of procedures to process the data

These divisions are further divided into sections, paragraphs, and
sentences. They also consist of statements and clauses. All these different
parts of a program are discussed later in this chapter. Next is a short
program, called **sample.cbl**, as an example of all these four divisions.

```
*-----------------------------------------------------------
*
* -- File name
*       sample.cbl
*
* -- Dependencies / External references
*
*
* -- Purpose
*    This module is an example of a COBOL program.
*    It accepts a system date, then prints it in a
*    formatted way.
*
*-----------------------------------------------------------
*
* -- Revision History
*
* Author          Date       Summary
* ---------       ---------   ----------------------------
* M. Gopaul       94/02/17   Original development.
*
*
```

```cobol
*
*/


      IDENTIFICATION DIVISION.
      PROGRAM-ID.                  sample.
      DATE-WRITTEN.                February 17, 1994.
      DATE-COMPILED.


      ENVIRONMENT DIVISION.
      CONFIGURATION SECTION.
          SOURCE-COMPUTER.    ibm-pc.
          OBJECT-COMPUTER.    ibm-pc.

      DATA DIVISION.

      WORKING-STORAGE SECTION.

      01   WS-CURRENT-DATE      PIC S9(08).
      01   WS-DATE.
           10 WS-YEAR           PIC X(04) VALUES SPACES.
           10 WS-MONTH          PIC X(02) VALUES SPACES.
           10 WS-DAY            PIC X(02) VALUES SPACES.
      01   WS-FORMATTED-DATE.
           05 YEAR-OF-DATE      PIC X(04) VALUES SPACES.
           05 FILLER            PIC X(01) VALUES "/".
           05 MONTH-OF-DATE     PIC X(02) VALUES SPACES.
           05 FILLER            PIC X(01) VALUES "/".
           05 DAY-OF-DATE       PIC X(02) VALUES SPACES.


      ****************************************************************
      * Mainline                                                    *
      ****************************************************************
      PROCEDURE DIVISION.


      MAINLINE.

          ACCEPT WS-CURRENT-DATE FROM DATE.
          ADD 19000000                      TO WS-CURRENT-DATE
          MOVE WS-CURRENT-DATE               TO WS-DATE
          MOVE WS-YEAR                       OF WS-DATE
            TO YEAR-OF-DATE                  OF WS-FORMATTED-DATE
          MOVE WS-MONTH                      OF WS-DATE
            TO MONTH-OF-DATE                 OF WS-FORMATTED-DATE
          MOVE WS-DAY                        OF WS-DATE
            TO DAY-OF-DATE                   OF WS-FORMATTED-DATE

          DISPLAY " DATE IS "
          DISPLAY WS-FORMATTED-DATE


          EXIT PROGRAM
            .
      END PROGRAM sample.
```

4.1 Source Format

Each line of a COBOL program is limited to 72 columns. These columns
are divided into four areas

Sequence number   Columns 1-6
Indicator area   Column 7
Area A   Columns 8-11
Area B   Columns 12-72

Sequence number: A *sequence number* is made up of six digits and is
used to number each line of a source program. In this area, you can also
place characters that are treated in a special way by the compiler. If
column 1 has an asterisk (*), or if columns 1 and 2 contain a formfeed
character and an asterisk, then the entire line is ignored by the compiler
and these special characters do not appear in the list file. This allows you
to use a list file as a source file.

Indicator area: This column is used for special indicators:

*   Indicates a comment line
/   Causes a formfeed
D   Indicates a debugging line (any COBOL sentence can follow this
    indicator)
-   Indicates continuation of the previous line

Areas A and B: In these areas you start section names and paragraph
names. Level indicators such as FD, SD, and FD are placed in area A
followed by the appropriate file. Also level numbers such as 01, 66, 77,
78, and 88 begin in area B followed by the record description.

4.2 Language Elements

■ Character set

The basic unit of a COBOL program is the *character*. The following is a list of valid characters that can be used to form divisions, sections, strings and other elements of a program.

Character	Meaning
0-9	Digits
A-Z	Uppercase letters
a-z	Lowercase letters
Space	
+	Plus sign
-	Hyphen or minus sign
*	Asterisk
/	Forward slash
=	Equal sign
$	Dollar sign
.	Decimal point or period
,	Decimal point or comma
;	Semicolon
"	Quotes
'	Apostrophe
(	Left parenthesis
)	Right parenthesis
>	Greater-than symbol
<	Less-than symbol
:	Colon
&	Ampersand

■ Data types

As mentioned before, the DATA DIVISION defines the storage which the program processes. The data has many types:

DISPLAY, INDEX, POINTER, BINARY, PACKED-DECIMAL, COMPUTATIONAL, COMPUTATIONAL-1, COMPUTATIONAL-2, COMPUTATIONAL-3, and **COMPUTATIONAL-4.**

DISPLAY specifies storing 1 character of data in 1 byte, corresponding to print format. This phrase can be used with the following types of data:

- Alphanumeric
- Alphabetic
- Alphanumeric—edited
- Numeric—edited
- External decimal (numeric)
- External floating-point

INDEX specifies that the data area is an index; therefore, it is used to store index name values. An elementary data area is 4 bytes long.

POINTER specifies that the data area is a pointer; therefore, it is used to store limited base addresses. An elementary data area is 4 bytes long.

BINARY specifies that the data area is for binary values and its size depends on the number of digits.

Digits	Size in bytes
1—4	2 (halfword)
5—9	4 (fullword)
10—18	8 (doubleword)

PACKED-DECIMAL specifies internal decimal items. Each item contains up to 18 decimal digits stored, and two items are stored in 1 byte.

COMPUTATIONAL or **COMP** specifies a binary data item.

COMPUTATIONAL-1 or **COMP-1** specifies a single-precision internal floating-point data item.

COMPUTATIONAL-2 or **COMP-2** specifies a double-precision internal floating-point data item.

COMPUTATIONAL-3 or **COMP-3** specifies a packed-decimal data item.

COMPUTATIONAL-4 or **COMP-4** specifies a binary data item.

◻ Arithmetic operators

There are two kinds of arithmetic operators: binary and unary. The
following is a list of the operators and their operations.

Operator   Operation

BINARY
+   Addition
-        Subtraction
*   Multiplication
/   Division
**   Exponential

UNARY
+   Multiplication by +1
-        Multiplication by -1

◻ Conditional expressions

A *conditional expression* is evaluated, and its result is either true or
false. Usually the result of a conditional expression is used to choose
logical paths in a program. Condition expressions are specified in
EVALUATE, IF, PERFORM, and **SEARCH** statements. There are two
types of conditional expression: simple conditions and complex
conditions. There are five simple conditions:

- Class condition
- Condition-name condition
- Relation condition
- Sign condition
- Switch-status condition

There are two complex conditions:

Negated simple condition
Combined condition

4.3 IDENTIFICATION DIVISION

In a COBOL source program, the IDENTIFICATION DIVISION must always be the first division. This division has several paragraphs, each specifying pieces of information to document a program. The general format of this division is

```
IDENTIFICATION DIVISION or ID DIVISION.
PROGRAM-ID. program-name.
[AUTHOR. comment-entry]
[INSTALLATION. comment-entry]
[DATE-WRITTEN. comment-entry]
[DATE-COMPILED. comment-entry]
[SECURITY. comment-entry]
[REMARKS. comment-entry]
```

The **PROGRAM-ID** paragraph is for the program name and it is mandatory. The other paragraphs—**AUTHOR, INSTALLATION, DATA-WRITTEN, DATE-COMPILED, SECURITY**, and **REMARKS**—are optional, but when used they must appear in the order shown in the general format.

All these elements of this division are discussed below.

The following is an example of the IDENTIFICATION DIVISION, where the PROGRAM-ID, DATA-WRITTEN, and DATE-COMPILED paragraphs are used.

```
IDENTIFICATION DIVISION.
PROGRAM-ID.            sample.
DATE-WRITTEN.          February 17, 1994.
DATE-COMPILED.
```

◘ PROGRAM-ID paragraph

● General format

```
PROGRAM-ID. program-name.
```

● Description

The PROGRAM-ID paragraph specifies the name of the program; it must be the first paragraph in the IDENTIFICATION DIVISION.

program-name is a user-defined name of a program. The first eight characters of the name must be unique within the system. The first character must be alphabetic; if it is not, a translation will take place. A hyphen in positions 2 through 8 of the name is converted to a zero.

◘ AUTHOR paragraph

- General format

```
AUTHOR. comment-entry
```

- Description

The AUTHOR paragraph specifies the name of the person who wrote the program.

◘ INSTALLATION paragraph

- General format

```
INSTALLATION. comment-entry
```

- Description

The INSTALLATION paragraph is used to enter the name of the location where the program is written.

◘ DATE-WRITTEN paragraph

- General format

```
DATE-WRITTEN. comment-entry
```

- Description

The DATE-WRITTEN paragraph is used to specify the date when the program was written.

◘ DATE-COMPILED paragraph

- General format

```
DATE-COMPILED. comment-entry
```

- Description

The DATE-COMPILED paragraph is used to specify the date when the program was compiled.

◘ SECURITY paragraph

- General format

```
SECURITY. comment-entry
```

- Description

The SECURITY paragraph is used to specify the level of security of a program.

◘ REMARKS paragraph

- General format

```
REMARKS. comment-entry
```

- Description

The REMARKS paragraph is used to write a brief remark about the program.

4.4 ENVIRONMENT DIVISION

The ENVIRONMENT DIVISION of a program is optional and consists of two sections:

- CONFIGURATION SECTION
- INPUT-OUTPUT SECTION

The general format of this division is

```
ENVIRONMENT DIVISION.
[CONFIGURATION SECTION.]
    [configuration-section-entry]
[INPUT-OUTPUT SECTION.]
    [input-output-section-entry]
```

The following is an example of an ENVIRONMENT DIVISION, which consists of a CONFIGURATION SECTION and an INPUT-OUTPUT SECTION. Both sections contains several paragraphs.

```
ENVIRONMENT DIVISION.

CONFIGURATION SECTION.
    SOURCE-COMPUTER. ibm-pc.
    OBJECT-COMPUTER. ibm-pc.

SPECIAL-NAMES.
    CONSOLE IS CRT.

INPUT-OUTPUT SECTION.
FILE-CONTROL.

SELECT INPUT-TEST
    ASSIGN TO "tip.input.test"
    ORGANIZATION IS LINE SEQUENTIAL
    ACCESS MODE IS SEQUENTIAL
    FILE STATUS IS WS-FILE-STATUS.

SELECT OUTPUT-TEST
    ASSIGN TO "tip.output.test"
    ORGANIZATION IS LINE SEQUENTIAL
    ACCESS MODE IS SEQUENTIAL
    FILE STATUS IS WS-FILE-STATUS.
```

In the rest of this section, we discuss in detail all the sections, paragraphs, and clauses, listed in alphbetical order, associated with the ENVIRONMENT DIVISION.

◘ CONFIGURATION SECTION

● General format

```
CONFIGURATION SECTION.
    [SOURCE-COMPUTER. source-computer-entry]
    [OBJECT-COMPUTER. object-computer-entry]
    [SPECIAL-NAMES. special-names-entry]
```

● Description

The CONFIGURATION SECTION, an optional entry within the ENVIRONMENT DIVISION, specifies

- The computer where the program is compiled

- The computer where the program is run

- The configurations

The SOURCE-COMPUTER, OBJECT-COMPUTER, and SPECIAL-NAMES paragraphs are discussed next.

● Example

```
CONFIGURATION SECTION.
    SOURCE-COMPUTER. ibm-pc.
    OBJECT-COMPUTER. ibm-pc.
    SPECIAL-NAMES. CONSOLE IS CRT.
```

◘ SOURCE-COMPUTER paragraph

● General format

```
SOURCE-COMPUTER. computer-name [WITH] DEBUGGING MODE.
```

● Description

The SOURCE-COMPUTER paragraph, an optional entry in the CONFIGURATION SECTION of the ENVIRONMENT DIVISION, specifies the computer environment in which the source program is to be compiled.

computer-name is the computer system name.

DEBUGGING MODE specifies that a switch is to be turned on during compilation to write debugging lines in the source program.

● Example

```
CONFIGURATION SECTION.
    SOURCE-COMPUTER. ibm-pc.
```

◘ OBJECT-COMPUTER paragraph

• General format

```
OBJECT-COMPUTER. computer-name
     MEMORY SIZE integer
          <WORDS or CHARACTERS or MODULES>
     PROGRAM COLLATING SEQUENCE [IS] alphabet-name
     SEGMENT-LIMIT IS priority-number
```

• Description

The OBJECT-COMPUTER paragraph, an optional entry in the CONFIGURATION SECTION of the ENVIRONMENT DIVISION, specifies the computer environment where the object program runs.

computer-name is the computer system name.

MEMORY SIZE is obsolete; its systax is checked, but it is otherwise ignored.

PROGRAM COLLATING SEQUENCE IS specifies the collating sequence used for this program.

alphabet-name is the alphabet name which is used for the collating sequence.

SEGMENT-LIMIT IS is obsolete.

• Example

```
     CONFIGURATION SECTION.

          SOURCE-COMPUTER. ibm-pc.

          OBJECT-COMPUTER. ibm-pc.
```

◘ SPECIAL-NAMES paragraph

• General format

```
SPECIAL-NAMES. [[environment-name-1 or environment-name-2]
      [[IS] mnemonic-name-2 [phase-1 or phase-2]
          or
            phase-1
          or
            phase-2]]...
```

```
[ALPHABET. alphabet-entry]
[SYMBOLIC. symbolic-entry]
[CLASS. class-entry]
[CURRENCY. currency-entry]
```

where

phase-1 is ON [STATUS IS] *condition-1*

phase-2 is OFF [STATUS IS] *condition-2*

● Description

The SPECIAL-NAMES paragraph, an entry in the CONFIGURATION SECTION of the ENVIRONMENT DIVISION, specifies configuration options.

environment-name-1	Meaning	Statement
SYSIN SYSIPT	System logical Input unit	**ACCEPT**
SYSOUT SYSLST	System logical Ouput unit	**DISPLAY**
SYSPUNCH SYSPCH	System unit Device	**DISPLAY**
CONSOLE	Console typewriter	**ACCEPT** or **DISPLAY**
C01—C12	Skip to channel 1—12	**WRITE ADVANCING**
CSP	Suppress spacing	**WRITE ADVANCING**
S01—S05	Pocket select 1 or 2 on punch devices	**WRITE ADVANCING**

environment-name2 is an UPSI switch of 1 byte long. It can be UPSI0 through UPSI7.

mnemonic-name is a user-defined name used in the **ACCEPT, SET, DISPLAY,** and **WRITE** statements.

mnemonic-name-2 is an user-defined name used in the **SET** statement.

condition-1 and *condition-2* are conditions that follow the rules for user-defined names.

◨ ALPHABET clause

- General format

```
ALPHABET alphabet-name [IS]
         < STANDARD-1 or
           STANDARD-2 or
           NATIVE      or
           ASCII       or
           <literal-1 <THROUGH or THRU>
            literal-2 ALSO literal-3>
           >
```

- Description

The ALPHABET clause specifies a relation between an alphabet and a character code or collating sequence. This clause is an optional entry in the SPECIAL-NAMES paragraph of the CONFIGURATION SECTION.

alphabet-name is the name of the character. A collating sequence is specified when *alphabet-name* is used in either the PROGRAM COLLATING SEQUENCE clause of the OBJECT-COMPUTER paragraph or the COLLATING SEQUENCE phrase of the **SORT** or **MERGE** statment.

A character code set is specified when *alphabet-name* is specified in either the FD entry CODE-SET clause (discussed later in the DATA DIVISION section) or the SYMBOLIC CHARACTERS clause.

STANDARD-1 specifies the ASCII character set.

STANDARD-2 specifies the International Reference Version of the ISO (International Standards Organization) 7-bit code.

NATIVE specifies the native character code set.

ASCII specifies the ASCII character set.

literal-1, *literal-2*, and *literal-3* specify that the collating sequence is to be determined by the program.

◘ CLASS clause

● General format

```
CLASS class-name [IS]   literal-1
     [<THROUGH or THRU> literal-2]
```

● Description

The CLASS clause, an entry in the SPECIAL-NAMES paragraph of the CONFIGURATION SECTION, associates a name with a set of characters.

class-name may be a DBCS (double-byte character set) user-defined word.

literal-1 and *literal-2* define a set of characters to be associated with *class-name*.

◘ CURRENCY SIGN clause

● General format

```
CURRENCY [SIGN IS] literal [DECIMAL-POINT IS COMMA].
```

● Description

The CURRENCY sign clause, an optional entry in the SPECIAL-NAMES paragraph of the CONFIGURATION SECTION, specifies a currency symbol.

literal is the current symbol used in the PICTURE clause (discussed later in the DATA DIVISION section). It must be a single character and nonnumeric. It cannot be any of the following characters:

Digits 0 to 9
Uppercase characters A B C D P R S V X Z
Lowercase characters a to z (except d, f, g, h, i, j, k, m, n, o, q, t, u, w, y)
Space character
Characters * + - / ' . ; ( ) = "

The default is the dollar sign character ($).

◘ SYMBOLIC CHARACTERS clause

● General format

```
SYMBOLIC [CHARACTERS] symbolic-character <ARE or IS>
               integer IN alphabet-name
```

● Description

The SYMBOLIC CHARACTERS clause, an optional entry in the SPECIAL-NAMES paragraph of the CONFIGURATION SECTION, specifies one or more symbolic characters.

symbolic-character is a user-defined word (DBCS word) or a series of user-defined words.

integer is a single number or a series of corresponding numbers.

◘ INPUT-OUTPUT SECTION

● General format

```
INPUT-OUTPUT SECTION.
   FILE-CONTROL. file-control-entry...
   [I-O-CONTROL.] [input-output-entry]
```

● Description

The INPUT-OUTPUT SECTION, an optional entry in the ENVIRONMENT DIVISION, describes the external files that a program processes. It contains two paragraphs:

● FILE-CONTROL paragraph
● I-O-CONTROL paragraph

● Example

```
INPUT-OUTPUT SECTION.
FILE-CONTROL.

SELECT INPUT-TEST
    ASSIGN TO "tip.input.test"
    ORGANIZATION IS LINE SEQUENTIAL
    ACCESS MODE IS SEQUENTIAL
    FILE STATUS IS WS-FILE-STATUS.
```

```
SELECT OUTPUT-TEST
      ASSIGN TO "tip.output.test"
      ORGANIZATION IS LINE SEQUENTIAL
      ACCESS MODE IS SEQUENTIAL
      FILE STATUS IS WS-FILE-STATUS.
```

◘ I-O-CONTROL paragraph

● General format

```
Sequential files:

  I-O-CONTROL. RERUN clause]...
     [SAME RECORD AREA clause]...
     [MULTIPLE FILE TAPE clause]...
     [APPLY WRITE-ONLY clause]...


Relative and indexed files:

  I-O-CONTROL. [RERUN clause]...
     [SAME RECORD AREA]...
     [APPLY WRITE-ONLY]...
```

● Description

The I-O-CONTROL paragraph, an optional entry in the INPUT-OUTPUT SECTION of the ENVIRONMENT DIVISION, specifies storage areas that are to be shared among different files. It also specifies when checkpoints are to take place. There are three formats for the I-O-CONTROL paragraph, those for sequential files, relative files, and indexed files.

◘ FILE-CONTROL paragraph

● General format

```
Sequential file entry:

  FILE-CONTROL. SELECT clause
       ASSIGN clause
        [RESERVE clause]
        [ORGANIZATION clause]
        [PADDING CHARACTER clause]
        [RECORD DELIMITER clause]
        [ACCESS MODE clause]
```

```
        [PASSWORD clause]
        [FILE STATUS clause]


Indexed file entry:

  FILE-CONTROL. SELECT clause
        ASSIGN clause
        [RESERVE clause]
        INDEXED
        [ACCESS MODE clause]
        RECORD KEY clause
        [ALTERNATE RECORD KEY clause]
        [PASSWORD clause]
        [FILE STATUS clause]


Relative file entry:

  FILE-CONTROL. SELECT clause
        ASSIGN clause
        [RESERVE clause]
        [ORGANIZATION clause]
        RELATIVE
        [ACCESS MODE clause]
        [PASSWORD clause]
        [FILE STATUS clause]
```

● Description

The FILE-CONTROL paragraph, an entry in the INPUT-OUTPUT
SECTION of the ENVIRONMENT DIVISION, associates each file that
is being accessed in a program with its external file. It also describes the
file organization, access mode, and other information useful in file
processing.

Each file described in this paragraph must have an FD or SD entry in
the DATA DIVISION.

● Example

```
        FILE-CONTROL.

        SELECT INPUT-TEST
            ASSIGN TO "tip.input.test"
            ORGANIZATION IS LINE SEQUENTIAL
            ACCESS MODE IS SEQUENTIAL
            FILE STATUS IS WS-FILE-STATUS.

        SELECT OUTPUT-TEST
            ASSIGN TO "tip.output.test"
            ORGANIZATION IS LINE SEQUENTIAL
```

```
ACCESS MODE IS SEQUENTIAL
FILE STATUS IS WS-FILE-STATUS.
```

◘ ACCESS MODE clause

- General format

```
Sequential file entries:

  ACCESS [MODE IS] SEQUENTIAL


Indexed file entries:

  ACCESS [MODE IS] <SEQUENTIAL or RANDOM or DYNAMIC>


Relative file entries:

  ACCESS [MODE IS] <SEQUENTIAL or RANDOM or DYNAMIC>
```

- Description

The ACCESS MODE clause specifies how a file is to be accessed. This clause is an optional entry in the FILE-CONTROL paragraph of the INPUT-OUTPUT SECTION. Files are accessed in three different modes: sequential, random, and dynamic. If this clause is omitted, the default is sequential mode.

SEQUENTIAL is used to process records sequentially for three types of files:

- Sequential files
- Indexed files
- Relative files

RANDOM is used to process records randomly for two types of files:

- Indexed files
- Relative files

DYNAMIC is used to process records sequentially and randomly for two types of files:

- Indexed files
- Relative files

● Example

```
SELECT INPUT-TEST
      ASSIGN TO "tip.input.test"
      ORGANIZATION IS LINE SEQUENTIAL
      ACCESS MODE IS SEQUENTIAL
      FILE STATUS IS WS-FILE-STATUS.
```

◘ ALTERNATE RECORD KEY clause

● General format

```
ALTERNATE [RECORD KEY IS] data-name [WITH] [DUPLICATES]
```

● Description

The ALTERNATE RECORD KEY clause, an optional entry in the FILE-CONTROL paragraph of the INPUT-OUTPUT SECTION, specifies an alternative path to the data of an indexed file.

data-name contains the alternative key. Also, it must be an alphanumeric item within only one of the record description entries of a file.

◘ APPLY WRITE-ONLY clause

● General format

```
APPLY WRITE-ONLY [ON] filename
```

● Description

The APPLY WRITE-ONLY clause, an optional entry in the I-O-CONTROL paragraph of the INPUT-OUTPUT SECTION, optimizes buffer and device space allocation for sequential files with blocked variable-length records.

filename is the name of the file, entered in the FILE-CONTROL paragraph, to which the WRITE-ONLY applies. You can enter one or more file names with this parameter.

◻ ASSIGN clause

- General format

```
ASSIGN [TO] assignment-name...
```

- Description

The ASSIGN clause, an entry in the FILE-CONTROL paragraph of the INPUT-OUTPUT SECTION, associates a file used in a program with the external name of a file or device. This clause is used along with the SELECT clause, which specifies the file.

assignment-name is either a user-defined word or a nonnumeric literal.

- Example

```
SELECT INPUT-TEST

    ASSIGN TO "tip.input.test"

    ORGANIZATION IS LINE SEQUENTIAL

    ACCESS MODE IS SEQUENTIAL

    FILE STATUS IS WS-FILE-STATUS.
```

◻ FILE STATUS clause

- General format

```
FILE STATUS [IS] data-name1  data-name2
```

- Description

The FILE STATUS clause, an optional entry in the FILE-CONTROL paragraph of the INPUT-OUTPUT SECTION, associates a file with a file status key.

data-name1 is an alphanumeric data area 2 bytes long in DATA DIVISION. It must not be defined in the FILE SECTION.

data-name2 must be defined as a group item of 6 bytes in the WORKING-STORAGE SECTION or LINKAGE SECTION.

● Example

```
SELECT INPUT-TEST

    ASSIGN TO "tip.input.test"

    ORGANIZATION IS LINE SEQUENTIAL

    ACCESS MODE IS SEQUENTIAL

    FILE STATUS IS WS-FILE-STATUS.
```

◼ MULTIPLE FILE TAPE clause

● General format

```
MULTIPLE FILE [TAPE CONTAINS] <filename
        [POSITION integer]>...
```

● Description

The MULTIPLE FILE TAPE clause is an entry in the I-O-CONTROL paragraph of the INPUT-OUTPUT SECTION. It specifies that two or more files are found in the same reel of tape.

filename is the name of the file found on tape.

POSITION specifies an integer value at which the file starts.

◼ ORGANIZATION clause

● General format

Sequential file entries:

```
ORGANIZATION [IS] SEQUENTIAL
```

Indexed file entries:

```
ORGANIZATION [IS] INDEXED
```

Relative file entries:

```
ORGANIZATION [IS] RELATIVE
```

● Description

The ORGANIZATION clause, an entry in the FILE-CONTROL

paragraph of the INPUT-OUTPUT SECTION, specifies the logical structure of a file processed in a program. There are three types: sequential, indexed, and relative. The default is sequential.

SEQUENTIAL specifies that the records in a file are accessed in the same order in which they were written. A record is added at the end of the file.

INDEXED specifies that the position of each logical record is determined by an index.

RELATIVE specifies that the position of each logical record is determined by its relative record number.

- Example

```
SELECT INPUT-TEST

    ASSIGN TO "tip.input.test"

    ORGANIZATION IS LINE SEQUENTIAL

    ACCESS MODE IS SEQUENTIAL

    FILE STATUS IS WS-FILE-STATUS.
```

◻ PADDING CHARACTER clause

- General format

PADDING [CHARACTER IS] *data-name* or *literal*

- Description

The PADDING CHARACTER clause, an optional entry in the FILE-CONTROL paragraph of the INPUT-OUTPUT SECTION, specifies the character to be used for block padding on sequential files.

data-name is an alphanumeric data area defined in the DATA DIVISION as 1 byte long.

literal is a 1-byte nonnumeric literal.

◻ PASSWORD clause

● General format

```
PASSWORD [IS] data-name
```

● Description

The PASSWORD clause, an entry in the FILE-CONTROL paragraph of the INPUT-OUTPUT SECTION, specifies a password for files.

data-name is a data area, defined as an alphanumeric item in the WORKING-STORAGE SECTION of the DATA DIVISION, that contains a password associated with a file.

◻ RECORD KEY clause

● General format

```
RECORD [KEY IS] data-name
```

● Description

The RECORD KEY clause, an entry in the FILE-CONTROL paragraph of the INPUT-OUTPUT SECTION, defines the data within a record as the prime key. This clause is mandatory for indexed files.

data-name is the prime key and must be an alphanumeric item within one of the record description entries associated with the file.

◻ RECORD DELIMITER clause

● General format

```
RECORD DELIMITER [IS]
     <STANDARD-1 or character-string>
```

● Description

The RECORD DELIMITER clause, an entry in the FILE-CONTROL paragraph of the INPUT-OUTPUT SECTION, specifies the method for determining the size of variable-length records.

STANDARD-1 specifies that the external medium of the file is magnetic tape.

character-string is a user name or a literal, but it cannot be a COBOL keyword.

(**Note**: This clause has no effect during run time; however, its syntax is checked during compilation.)

◻ RELATIVE KEY clause

● General format

```
RELATIVE [KEY IS] data-name
```

● Description

The RELATIVE KEY clause, an entry in the FILE-CONTROL paragraph of the INPUT-OUTPUT SECTION, specifies the data area that contains the relative record number of the next record in a relative file.

data-name is a data area that contains the relative record number used for each input or output operation. It is defined as an unsigned integer.

This clause is required for random and dynamic access of files. For sequential files, it is required only if the file is referenced by a START statement.

◻ RERUN clause

● General format

```
Sequential files:

  RERUN [ON assignment-name] [EVERY]
    < integer RECORDS or END [OF] <REEL or UNIT>>
      [OF] filename

Relative or indexed files:

  RERUN ON assignment-name [EVERY] integer RECORDS
            [OF] filename
```

- Description

The RERUN clause, an optional entry in the I-O-CONTROL paragraph of the INPUT-OUTPUT SECTION, specifies that checkpoints are to take place.

assignment-name is a sequential external file, a user name or a literal, but it cannot be a keyword.

integer is a number; for every occurrence of this number of records in *filename*, a checkpoint record is written.

filename is a sequential file.

RESERVE clause

- General format

```
RESERVE integer <AREA or AREAS>
```

- Description

The RESERVE clause, an entry in the FILE-CONTROL paragraph of the INPUT-OUTPUT SECTION, specifies the number of buffers to be allocated for I/O operation.

integer is the number of buffers; it must not exceed 255.

SAME SORT AREA clause

- General format

```
SAME <RECORD or SORT or SORT-MERGE>
     filename-1...
```

- Description

The SAME SORT AREA clause, an optional entry in the I-O-CONTROL paragraph of the INPUT-OUTPUT SECTION, optimizes storage area if the **SORT** statement is used.

filename-1 is a file that must be defined in the FILE-CONTROL paragraph of the same program in which the SAME SORT AREA clause is used.

▣ SAME RECORD AREA clause

● General format

```
Sequential files:

  SAME [RECORD] [AREA FOR] filename-1 filename-2...

Relative and indexed files:

  SAME [RECORD] [AREA FOR] filename-1...
```

● Description

The SAME RECORD AREA clause, an optional entry in the I-O-CONTROL paragraph of the INPUT-OUTPUT SECTION, specifies that two or more files can use the storage area while processing the current logical record.

filename-1 and *filename-2* are the names of files that share the storage area. Both must be defined in the FILE-CONTROL paragraph of the same program in which the SAME RECORD AREA clause is used.

▣ SELECT clause

● General format

```
SELECT [OPTIONAL] filename
```

● Description

The SELECT clause, the first entry in the FILE-CONTROL paragraph of the INPUT-OUTPUT SECTION, specifies a filename in a COBOL program that is associated with an external file. The ASSIGN clause describes the external file; it must follow the SELECT clause.

filename is a user-defined name that is unique to a program. Also, there must be a corresponding FD or SD entry in the DATA DIVISION.

OPTIONAL specifies that the file(s) are not necessarily present each time the program is run.

● Example

```
SELECT INPUT-TEST
    ASSIGN TO "tip.input.test"
    ORGANIZATION IS LINE SEQUENTIAL
    ACCESS MODE IS SEQUENTIAL
    FILE STATUS IS WS-FILE-STATUS.
```

4.5 DATA DIVISION

The DATA DIVISION is an optional entry which defines the data area to be used by a program during processing. It consists of three sections:

- FILE SECTION
- WORKING-STORAGE SECTION
- LINKAGE SECTION

The general format of the DATA DIVISION is

```
DATA DIVISION.
[FILE SECTION.]
    [file-description-entry record-description-entry...]

[WORKING-STORAGE SECTION.]
    [record-description data-item-description]...

[LINKAGE SECTION.]
    [record-description data-item-description]...
```

All these sections of the division and related clauses are discussed in detail below.

● Example

```
DATA DIVISION.
FILE SECTION.

FD   INPUT-TEST.
01   INPUT-LINE                        PICTURE X(512).

FD   OUTPUT-TEST.
01   OUTPUT-LINE                       PICTURE X(332).


WORKING-STORAGE SECTION.

01   WS-FILE-STATUS                    PIC X(02) VALUE "00".
```

```cobol
          88   IO-OK                             VALUE "00".
          88   END-OF-FILE                       VALUE "10".
          88   NOT-FOUND                         VALUE "23".
          88   SEVERE-ERROR                VALUE "01" THRU "09"
                                                "11" THRU "22"
                                                "24" THRU "99".


      01   WS-INPUT-TEST-STATUS             PIC X(02) VALUE "00".
          88   IO-OK                             VALUE "00".
          88   END-OF-FILE                       VALUE "10".
          88   NOT-FOUND                         VALUE "23".
          88   SEVERE-ERROR                VALUE "01" THRU "09"
                                                "11" THRU "22"
                                                "24" THRU "99".


  01   WS-POST-DATE.
          10 WS-POST-YYYY.
             12 WS-POST-CN                  PIC X(02).
             12 WS-POST-YY                  PIC X(02).
          10 FILLER                         PIC X VALUE '-'.
          10 WS-POST-MM                      PIC X(02).
          10 FILLER                         PIC X VALUE '-'.

      01   WS-POSTED-DATE REDEFINES WS-POST-DATE PIC X(10).

      01   WS-DATE-TABLE                    PIC 9(8)
              OCCURS 10 TIMES.

      01   WS-TOTAL-LTD-NET-REV  PIC S9(7) COMP-3 VALUE +0.

      01   WS-OUTPUT-TEST-STATUS            PIC X(02) VALUE "00".
          88   IO-OK                             VALUE "00".
          88   END-OF-FILE                       VALUE "10".
          88   NOT-FOUND                         VALUE "23".
          88   SEVERE-ERROR                VALUE "01" THRU "09"
                                                "11" THRU "22"
                                                "24" THRU "99".

      01   WS-SEVERE-ERROR-STATUS           PIC X(01).
          88   NOT-SEVERE-ERROR                      VALUE " ".
          88   SEVERE-ERROR                          VALUE "T".


  LINKAGE SECTION.

      01   WS-FILE-ERROR-LINE.
          05   FILLER                       PIC X(11)
               VALUE "FILE ERROR ".
          05   FILLER                       PIC X(08)
               VALUE "FILE =  ".
          05   WS-FILE-ERROR-FILE           PIC X(16).
          05   FILLER                       PIC X(14)
               VALUE "FILE STATUS = ".
          05   WS-FILE-ERROR-STATUS         PIC X(02).
```

◻ FILE SECTION

● General format

```
FILE SECTION
file-description-entry record-description-entry
```

Format for sequential file:

```
FD filename

    [EXTERNAL clause]
    [GLOBAL clause]
    [BLOCK CONTAIN clause]
    [RECORD clause]
    [LABEL RECORDS clause]
    [VALUE OF clause]
    [DATA RECORDS clause]
    [LINAGE clause]
    [RECORDING MODE clause]
    [CODE-SET clause]
```

Format for relative or indexed file:

```
FD filename

    [EXTERNAL clause]
    [GLOBAL clause]
    [BLOCK CONTAIN clause]
    [RECORD clause]
    [LABEL RECORDS clause]
    [VALUE OF clause]
    [RECORDING MODE clause]
    [DATA RECORDS clause]
```

Format for sort or merge file:

```
SD filename

    RECORD clause
    DATA RECORDS clause
```

● Description

The FILE SECTION, the first, and optional, entry in the DATA DIVISION, defines the filenames to be used within a program and associates each of them with its attributes. In this section, there are two types of entries: file description and record description. There must be only one file description entry for each file followed by one or many record description entries.

You can specify three kinds of files: sequential files, indexed or relative files, and sort or merge files. The preceding formats for each type of file show all the different entries for record descriptions.

filename is the filename used in the program. It must also be specified in the SELECT clause of the IDENTIFICATION DIVISION. Following the filename, you can enter one or many record descriptions.

FD specifies a sequential, indexed, or relative file. Following this is a series of clauses describing the file.

SD specifies a sort or merge file. Following this is a series of clauses describing the file.

◘ WORKING-STORAGE SECTION

● General format

```
level-number <data-name or FILLER>

[REDEFINES clause]
[BLANK WHEN ZERO clause]
[EXTERNAL clause]
[GLOBAL clause]
[JUSTIFIED clause]
[OCCURS clause]
[PICTURE clause]
[SIGN clause]
[SYNCHRONIZED clause]
[USAGE clause]
[VALUE clause]
[RENAMES clause]
```

● Description

The WORKING-STORAGE SECTION, an optional entry in the DATA DIVISION, defines data structures that use a program. These working data areas include counters, variables, flags, and accumulators required to accomplish programming tasks. This section consists of one or many data description entries. Each entry is made up of a level number, a data name, and optional clauses.

level-number is a number representing a hierarchy within a group of related data. The level number is a value between 01 and 49, 66, 77, or 88.

01 to 49 may begin in area A or B and be followed by a period or space.

66 and 88 may begin in area A or B and are followed by a space.

data-name is the name of the data area. In the program the data item is referenced by this name. This name follows a level number.

FILLER is a data area that does not have a specific name and is not referenced in a program.

◘ LINKAGE SECTION

● General format

```
LINKAGE SECTION.

    record-description data-item-description
```

● Description

The LINKAGE SECTION, the third—and optional—entry in the DATA DIVISION, defines the data area that is made available to a calling program. The data is actually stored in the program storage area and passed to another program. There are two entries: record and data descriptions.

record-description defines a record, which is made up of a group of related data items. There must be one record entry for each record.

data-item-description defines each data area, which can be an independent item or one of the elements of a record.

◘ BLANK WHEN ZERO clause

● General format

```
BLANK [WHEN] ZERO
```

● Description

The BLANK WHEN ZERO clause, an optional entry in the WORKING-

STORAGE SECTION of the DATA DIVISION, specifies that whenever a zero value occurs in a data area it is to be replaced with spaces.

◻ BLOCK CONTAINS clause

● General format

```
BLOCK [CONTAINS] [integer1 TO] integer2
        <CHARACTERS or RECORDS>
```

● Description

The BLOCK CONTAINS clause, an optional entry in the FILE SECTION of the DATA DIVISION, specifies the number of physical records in a blocked sequential file.

integer1 is an unsigned nonzero number that specifies the minimum number of characters or logical records.

integer2 is an unsigned nonzero number that specifies the maximum number of characters or logical records.

CHARACTERS specifies the size of the record in characters.

RECORDS specifies the number of logical records in a physical record.

◻ CODE-SET clause

● General format

```
CODE-SET [IS] alphabet-name
```

● Description

The CODE-SET clause, an optional entry in the FILE SECTION of the DATA DIVISION, specifies the character set used to represent data in a file.

alphabet-name is a name defined in the SPECIAL-NAMES paragraph of the ENVIRONMENT DIVISION. It can be **STANDARD-1**, **STANDARD-2**, or **ASCII**. The default is **ASCII**.

◘ DATA RECORDS clause

● General format

```
DATA <RECORD IS or RECORDS ARE> data-name...
```

● Description

The DATA RECORDS clause, an optional entry in the FILE SECTION of the DATA DIVISION, specifies a name for the data records of a file.

data-name is a data area that contains the name of the data records associated with a file.

(**Note**: The DATA RECORDS clause is used for documentation purposes only.)

◘ EXTERNAL clause

● General format

```
FD filename [IS] EXTERNAL

level-number data-name EXTERNAL
```

● Description

The EXTERNAL clause, an optional entry in the FILE SECTION or the WORKING-STORAGE SECTION of the DATA DIVISION, allows the same file or data area to be shared by several programs running concurrently.

filename is the name of the file to be shared.

data-name is the name of the data area to be shared. The data area must defined at *level-number* 01.

◘ GLOBAL clause

- General format

```
FD filename [IS] [GLOBAL]
level-number <data-name> [GLOBAL]
```

- Description

The GLOBAL clause, an optional entry in the FILE SECTION or the WORKING-STORAGE SECTION of the DATA DIVISION, allows the same file or data area to be shared by subprograms of a program.

filename is the name of the file to be shared.

data-name is the name of the data area to be shared. The data area must be defined at *level-number* 01.

◘ JUSTIFIED clause

- General format

```
<JUSTIFIED or JUST> [RIGHT]
```

- Description

The JUSTIFIED clause, an optional entry in the WORKING-STORAGE SECTION of the DATA DIVISION, specifies that the data moved into a data area be right-justified, instead of following the default justification rules.

◘ LABEL RECORDS clause

- General format

```
LABEL <RECORD IS or RECORDS ARE>
    < STANDARD or OMITTED or data-name>
```

● Description

The LABEL RECORDS clause, an optional entry in the FILE SECTION of the DATA DIVISION, specifies whether a file has a label.

STANDARD specifies that the label in the file conforms to system standard.

OMITTED specifies that the file does not have a label.

data-name specifies that user labels are present in addition to standard labels.

◘ LINAGE clause

● General format

```
LINAGE [IS] <data-name-1 or integer-1> [LINES]
       [WITH] FOOTING [AT] <data-name-2 or integer-2>
       [LINES AT] TOP <data-name-3 or integer-3>
       [LINES AT] BOTTOM <data-name-4 or integer-4>
```

● Description

The LINAGE clause, an optional entry in the FILE SECTION of the DATA DIVISION, specifies the number of lines per page, and the top margin, bottom margin, and footing for a report.

data-name-1 is the data area that contains the number of lines for each page.

integer-1 is the number of lines on each page.

data-name-2 is the data area that contains the last printed line of each page.

integer-2 is the last printed line of each page.

data-name-3 is the data area that contains the number of blank lines at the top of each page.

integer-3 is the number of blank lines at the top of each page.

data-name-4 is the data area that contains the number of lines at the bottom of each page.

integer-4 is the number of lines at the bottom of each page.

◻ OCCURS clause

● General format

```
Fixed-length tables:

    OCCURS integer1 [TIMES]
    <ASCENDING or DESCENDING> [KEY IS] data-name2...
    INDEXED [BY] index-name1...


Variable-length tables:

    OCCURS integer1 TO integer2 [TIMES]
    DEPENDING [ON] data-name1
    <ASCENDING or DESCENDING> [KEY IS] data-name2...
    INDEXED [BY] index-name1...
```

● Description

The OCCURS clause, an optional entry in the WORKING-STORAGE SECTION of the DATA DIVISION, specifies that the data area must be arranged as a table or array. Each element of the table is referenced with an index or subscript. There are two formats for the OCCURS clause: fixed-length table and variable-length table.

integer1 is the exact number of elements in a fixed-length table and the minimum number of elements in a variable-length table.

integer2 is the maximum number of elements in a variable-length table.

data-name1 is a data area containing a value which is the current number of elements in a variable-length table.

data-name2 is a data area containing a value by which the data is arranged in either ascending or descending order.

index-name1 is a data area used in a program to access a particular element of a table.

◘ PICTURE clause

- General format

```
<PICTURE or PIC> [IS] character-string
```

- Description

The PICTURE clause, an optional entry in the WORKING-STORAGE SECTION of the DATA DIVISION, defines the type and size of an elementary data area. It also specifies the editing requirements of the data.

character-string is a combination of symbols that defines the characteristics of the data. The following is a list of all the symbols and their descriptions.

SYMBOL	Description
A	Alphabetic character or space
B	Space
E	Exponential
G	Double-byte character
P	Decimal position
S	Operational sign
V	Decimal sign
X	Alphanumeric character
Z	Leading zeros replaced by spaces
9	Numeric character
/	Insert a slash
,	Insert a comma
.	Insert a period
+	Editing control character
-	Editing control character
CR	Editing control character
DB	Editing control character
*	Replace leading zeros with asterisk
$	Currency symbol

◘ RECORD clause

● General format

```
Fixed-length records:

  RECORD [CONTAINS] integer-1 [CHARACTERS]

Fixed- or variable-length records:

  RECORD [CONTAINS] [integer-2] TO integer-3 [CHARACTERS]

Variable-length records:

  RECORD [IS] VARYING [IN SIZE]
      [FROM] integer-4 [TO integer-5] [CHARACTERS]
      DEPENDING [ON] data-name
```

● Description

The RECORD clause, an optional entry in the FILE SECTION of the DATA DIVISION, specifies the number of characters in a logical record of a file. There are three different types of records: fixed length, fixed- or variable-length, and variable-length. The format for each type of record is different.

integer-1 through *integer-5* must be unsigned nonzero values.

integer-1 is the number of character positions in each record.

integer-2 is the minimum number of character positions in each record.

integer-3 is the maximum number of character positions in each record.

integer-4 is the minimum number of character positions in each record.

integer-5 is the maximum number of character positions in each record.

data-name is the number of table elements to be included in a record.

If the RECORD CONTAINS clause is omitted, the compiler calculates the length of the record from the record descriptions.

◘ RECORDING MODE clause

- General format

```
RECORDING [MODE IS] mode
```

- Description

The RECORDING MODE clause, an optional entry in the FILE SECTION of the DATA DIVISION, specifies the format type of a sequential file.

mode is in the following format:

```
F  Fixed
V  Variable
U  Undefined (variable or fixed)
S  Spanned
FIXED
VARIABLE
```

◘ REDEFINES clause

- General format

```
level-number <data-name1 or FILLER>
        REDEFINES data-name2
```

- Description

The REDEFINES clause, an optional entry in the WORKING-STORAGE SECTION of the DATA DIVISION, changes the definition of an existing data area and gives it a different name. A redefinition may alter the length and data type of the subfields.

data-name1 is the data area that already exists.

data-name2 is the new name of the redefined data area *data-name1*.

FILLER specifies that the data area does not have a name.

◘ RENAMES clause

● General format

```
66 data-name1 RENAMES data-name2
   <THROUGH or THRU> data-name3
```

● Description

The RENAMES clause, an optional entry in the WORKING-STORAGE SECTION of the DATA DIVISION, changes the grouping of elementary data areas. It allows overlapping of data areas.

data-name1 is the name of the new grouping.

data-name2 is a defined data area to be regrouped. If *data-names* is specified, then *data-name2* is the starting data area to be renamed. It cannot be level 01, 77, 88, or another 66.

data-name3 is the last data area in a group of data areas.

◘ SIGN clause

● General format

```
SIGN [IS] <LEADING or TRAILING> [SEPARATE CHARACTER]
```

● Description

The SIGN clause, an optional entry in the WORKING-STORAGE SECTION of the DATA DIVISION, specifies the position and format of the sign for numeric data.

If SEPARATE CHARACTER is not specified, then the operational sign is associated with the first digit position if LEADING is specified and with the last digit position if TRAILING is specified.

If SEPARATE CHARACTER is specified, then the operational sign is placed in a separate TRAILING or LEADING byte position.

◘ SYNCHRONIZED clause

● General format

```
<SYNCHRONIZED or SYNC> [LEFT or RIGHT]
```

● Description

The SYNCHRONIZED clause, an optional entry in the WORKING-STORAGE SECTION of the DATA DIVISION, aligns an elementary data item on either the halfword or fullword storage boundary. Proper alignment improves the performance of arithmetic computations.

LEFT specifies that the item begins at the left character position.

RIGHT specifies that the item begins at the right character position.

◘ USAGE clause

● General format

```
USAGE [IS] < DISPLAY                              or
             INDEX                                or
             POINTER                              or
             BINARY                               or
             PACKED-DECIMAL                       or
             <COMPUTATIONAL or COMP               or
             <COMPUTATIONAL-1 or COMP-1>          or
             <COMPUTATIONAL-2 or COMP-2>          or
             <COMPUTATIONAL-3 or COMP-3>          or
             <COMPUTATIONAL-4 or COMP-4>
          >
```

● Description

The USAGE clause, an optional entry in the WORKING-STORAGE SECTION of the DATA DIVISION, specifies the format for internal storage of a group or elementary item of data. The USAGE clause can be used with all level numbers except 66 and 88.

DISPLAY specifies storing one character of data in 1 byte, corresponding to the print format. This phrase can be used with the following types of data:

● Alphanumeric
● Alphabetic

- Alphanumeric—edited
- Numeric—edited
- External decimal (numeric)
- External floating-point

INDEX specifies that the data area is an index; therefore, it is used to store index name values. An elementary data area is 4 bytes long.

POINTER specifies that the data area is a pointer; therefore, it is used to store limited base addresses. An elementary data area is 4 bytes long.

BINARY specifies that the data area is for binary values, and its size depends on the number of digits.

Digits	Size in bytes
1-4	2 (halfword)
5-9	4 (fullword)
10-18	8 (doubleword)

PACKED-DECIMAL specifies internal decimal items. Each item contains up to 18 decimal digits stored, and two items are stored in 1 byte.

COMPUTATIONAL or **COMP** specifies a binary data item.

COMPUTATIONAL-1 or **COMP-1** specifies a single-precision internal floating-point data item.

COMPUTATIONAL-2 or **COMP-2** specifies a double-precision internal floating-point data item.

COMPUTATIONAL-3 or **COMP-3** specifies a packed-decimal data item.

COMPUTATIONAL-4 or **COMP-4** specifies a binary data item.

◘ VALUE clause

- General format

```
Format 1:
  VALUE [IS] literal

Format 2:
  88 condition-name <VALUE or VALUES> [IS or ARE]
           literal1 <THROUGH or THRU> literal2
```

- Description

The VALUE clause, an optional entry in the WORKING-STORAGE
SECTION of the DATA DIVISION, specifies the initial value of a data
area or value(s) for a condition name.

literal is a value assigned to a data area.

condition-name is the name of the condition to which a single value, a
set of values, a range of values, and/or combinations of sets and ranges
of values are assigned.

literal1 specifies a single value for a condition name.

literal1 THRU *literal2* specifies a range of values for a condition name.

◘ VALUE OF clause

- General format

```
VALUE OF <data-name1 [IS] <data-name2 or literal>
```

- Description

The VALUE OF clause, an optional entry in the FILE SECTION of the
DATA DIVISION, specifies an item in the label record of a file.

data-name1 is a data area containing the item and is defined in the
WORKING-STORAGE SECTION.

data-name2 is a data area containing the item and is defined in the
WORKING-STORAGE SECTION.

literal is a numeric or nonnumeric value.

4.6 PROCEDURE DIVISION

The PROCEDURE DIVISION is the part of the source program that contains the logic. It consists of declaratives, sentences, and statements that are executed during the run time of a program. The sentences and statements are grouped into paragraphs and sections of a COBOL program.

The general format of the PROCEDURE DIVISION is

```
PROCEDURE DIVISION
    USING data-name

DECLARATIVES. section-name SECTION priority-no.
    USE statement.
    paragraph-name. sentence...
END-DECLARATIVES.

section-name SECTION priority-no.
paragraph-name. sentence...
```

USING is an optional phrase as part of the PROCEDURE DIVISION header. It is used only if the program is called by another program and data are passed using *data-name*.

data-name is the name of a data area which is used to receive data from a calling program. It must be defined as level number 01 or 77 in the LINKAGE SECTION of the called program.

section-name is the name of a section, it is followed by the keyword SECTION. A section consists of one or more paragraphs.

priority-no is an optional entry in a section header. It follows the keyword **SECTION**. It is a number in the range 0 to 99.

paragraph-name is the name of a paragraph; it is followed by a period and one or more sentences. In a program, there may be zero to many paragraphs.

sentence is one or more COBOL sentences followed by a period.

In the rest of this section we describe all the statements, in alphabetical order, belonging to the PROCEDURE DIVISION.

● Example

```
/*****************************************
*                                       *
* Mainline                              *
*                                       *
*****************************************

     PROCEDURE DIVISION.

     MAINLINE.

         ACCEPT WS-CURRENT-DATE  FROM DATE.
         ADD 19000000              TO WS-CURRENT-DATE
         MOVE WS-CURRENT-DATE      TO WS-DATE
         MOVE WS-YEAR              OF WS-DATE
            TO YEAR-OF-DATE        OF WS-FORMATTED-DATE
         MOVE WS-MONTH             OF WS-DATE
            TO MONTH-OF-DATE       OF WS-FORMATTED-DATE
         MOVE WS-DAY               OF WS-DATE
            TO DAY-OF-DATE         OF WS-FORMATTED-DATE

         DISPLAY " DATE IS "
         DISPLAY WS-FORMATTED-DATE

            EXIT PROGRAM
              .
     END PROGRAM sample.
```

◘ ACCEPT statement

● General format

Format 1:

```
ACCEPT identifier FROM mnemonic-name
```

Format 2:

```
ACCEPT identifier FROM <DATE or DAY or
                   DAY-OF-WEEK, TIME>
```

● Description

The **ACCEPT** statement transfers data from an input device or system information, such as date and time, into a defined data area. There are two formats for the **ACCEPT** statment. Format 1 transfers data from a device. In this case, if the FROM phrase is omitted, a system input device is assumed. This format is used to receive data from the operator. Format 2 moves the date, day, day of the week, or time into an identifier.

identifier is a data area, which may be any group or elementary item. For format 1, the data type of the *identifier* can be alphabetic, alphanumeric, alphanumeric—edited, numeric—edited, or external decimal. For format 2, the data type of the *identifier* can be alphanumeric, alphanumeric—edited, numeric—edited, decimal, binary, or floating-point.

mnemonic-name is a name associated with an I/O device: a system input device or a console. The name must be defined in the SPECIAL-NAMES paragraph of the ENVIRONMENT DIVISION.

DATE specifies moving the current date to the identifier. The information is, from left to right: two digits for the year, two digits for the month, and two digits for the day.

DAY specifies moving the current Julian date to the identifier. The information is, from left to right, two digits for the year and three digits for the day.

DAY-OF-WEEK specifies moving the day of the week to the identifier. The following lists the resulting values and the corresponding day of the week.

Value	Day of the week
1	Monday
2	Tuesday
3	Wednesday
4	Thursday
5	Friday
6	Saturday
7	Sunday

TIME specifies moving the current time of day to the identifier. The information, from left to right, is

    two digits for the hour
    two digits for the minute
    two digits for the second
    two digits for the hundredths of a second

● Example

```
      WORKING-STORAGE SECTION.

      01 WS-TIME.
         05 WS-HRS               PIC 9(02).
         05 WS-MINS              PIC 9(02).
         05 WS-SECS              PIC 9(02).
         05 WS-HDTH              PIC 9(02).

      01 WS-DATE.
         05 WS-RUN-DATE          PIC 9(08).
         05 WS-PROCESS-DATE      PIC 9(08).


      PROCEDURE DIVISION.

      *  GET SYSTEM TIME AND DATE
         ACCEPT WS-TIME   FROM TIME.
         ACCEPT WS-RUN-DATE   FROM DATE.

      * GET PROCESS DATE FROM USER

         ACCEPT WS-PROCESS-DATE.

                   .
                   .
                   .
```

◘ ADD statement

● General format

```
Format 1:

  ADD <identifier1 or literal> TO identifier2 ROUNDED
     [ON] [SIZE ERROR statement1]
     [NOT [ON] SIZE ERROR statement2]
  [END-ADD]

Format 2:

  ADD <identifier1 or literal> TO identifier3
     GIVING identifier4 ROUNDED
     [ON] [SIZE ERROR statement1]
     [NOT [ON] SIZE ERROR statement2]
  [END-ADD]

Format 3:

  ADD <CORRESPONDING or CORR> identifier5 TO identifier6
     ROUNDED
     [ON] [SIZE ERROR statement1]
     [NOT [ON] SIZE ERROR statement2]
  [END-ADD]
```

- Description

The ADD statement adds one or more numeric operands and stores the result.

identifier1 must be an elementary numeric data area.

identifier2 must be an elementary numeric data area. It receives the sum.

identifier3 must be an elementary numeric data area.

identifier4 must be either an elementary numeric data area or a numeric—edited data area. It receives the sum.

identifier5 and *identifier6* must be group data areas. The elementary elements of *identifier5* are added and stored in the elements of *identifer6*.

literal is a numeric literal.

ROUNDED specifies that any fractional result is to be rounded to the nearest decimal position.

statement1 is the statement to which control is transferred when an ON SIZE ERROR condition occurs.

statement2 is the statement to which control is transferred when a NOT ON SIZE ERROR condition occurs.

CORRESPONDING specifies two group operands. The operation is to be performed on all corresponding elementary data items of both groups.

END-ADD is an optional phrase to terminate the ADD statement.

- Example

```
WORKING-STORAGE SECTION.
01  WS-CURRENT-DATE              PIC S9(08).
PROCEDURE DIVISION.
    ADD 19000000                      TO WS-CURRENT-DATE
        .
        .
        .
```

◧ ALTER statement

● General format

```
ALTER <procedure-name1 TO [PROCEED TO] procedure-name2>...
```

● Description

The **ALTER** statement changes the name of the procedure to which control is transferred in a **GO TO** statement. The change occurs during execution.

procedure-name1 is the name of the old paragraph.

procedure-name2 is the name of the new paragraph.

◧ CALL statement

● General format

```
Format 1:
  CALL <identifier1 or literal1>
  USING <identifier2                        or
      [BY] REFERENCE identifier2            or
      [BY] REFERENCE ADDRESS OF identifier2    or
      [BY]  CONTENT <identifier2 or literal2 or LENGTH>
        OF identifier2
        >
  [ON] OVERFLOW statement1
  [END-CALL]

Format 2:
  CALL <identifier1 or literal1>
  USING <identifier2                        or
      [BY] REFERENCE identifier2            or
      [BY] REFERENCE ADDRESS OF identifier2    or
      [BY] CONTENT <identifier2 or literal2 or LENGTH>
        OF identifier2
        >
  [ON] EXCEPTION statement1
  NOT [ON] EXCEPTION statement2
  [END-CALL]
```

- Description

The **CALL** statement transfers control from one program to another during execution. When the execution of the called program is terminated, the control goes back to the calling program.

identifier1 is an alphanumeric data area which contains the name of a program.

literal1 is the literal name of a program.

USING is used to pass parameters to the called program.

BY REFERENCE applies to all parameters that follow it. It specifies that the data area in the called program occupies the same storage area as in the calling program.

BY CONTENT applies to all parameters that follow it. It specifies that the value of each parameter is assigned to the corresponding parameter of the called program.

identifier2 is a data area.

literal2 may be a nonnumeric literal, a figurative constant, or a DBCS literal.

ON EXCEPTION specifies that if an exception condition occurs, program control must be transferred to *statement1*.

NOT ON EXCEPTION specifies that if no exception condition occurs, program control must be transferred to *statement2*.

ON OVERFLOW specifies that if an exception condition occurs, program control must be transferred to *statement1*. The ON OVERFLOW phrase has the same effect as the ON EXCEPTION phrase.

END-CALL is an optional clause to terminate the **CALL** statement.

- Example

```
WORKING-STORAGE SECTION.

01  WS-CURRENT-DATE            PIC S9(08).
```

```
LINKAGE SECTION.

01 LOGERRORSU-LINKAGE.
   05  WS-DATE.

       10 WS-YEAR              PIC X(04) VALUES SPACES.

       10 WS-MONTH             PIC X(02) VALUES SPACES.

       10 WS-DAY               PIC X(02) VALUES SPACES.

   05  ERROR-CODE              PIC x(1).


   PROCEDURE DIVISION.

       ADD 19000000                   TO WS-CURRENT-DATE
              .
              .
              .


       CALL "logErrorSU" USING LOGERRORSU-LINKAGE
              .
              .
              .
```

◘ CANCEL statement

- General format

```
CANCEL <identifier1 or literal1>
```

- Description

The **CANCEL** statement ensures that every time a program is called, a fresh copy, with all its initial values set, is loaded for execution.

identifier1 is a data area which contains the name of a program.

literal1 is the literal name of a program.

◘ CLOSE statement

● General format

```
Sequential file

  CLOSE filename
     [ <REEL or UNIT> [WITH] LOCK              or
       [WITH] <NO REWIND                       or
                        LOCK        or
                        DISP
                    >                          or
       <UNIT or REEL> [WITH] NO REWIND         or
       <UNIT or REEL> [FOR] REMOVAL
     ]

Indexed or relative file

  CLOSE filename [WITH] LOCK
```

● Description

The **CLOSE** statement closes a sequential file for processing.

filename is the name of the file to be closed.

UNIT or REEL specifies a medium with a multivolume file.

WITH LOCK ensures that the file cannot be opened again while this program is executing.

WITH NO REWIND specifies that the current volume is to be left in its current position.

● Example

```
      INPUT-OUTPUT SECTION.
      FILE-CONTROL.

      SELECT INPUT-TEST
          ASSIGN TO "tip.input.test"
          ORGANIZATION IS LINE SEQUENTIAL
          ACCESS MODE IS SEQUENTIAL
          FILE STATUS IS WS-FILE-STATUS.

      DATA DIVISION.
      FILE SECTION.

      FD  INPUT-TEST.
      01  INPUT-LINE                  PIC X(512).
```

```
WORKING-STORAGE SECTION.

01  WS-CURRENT-DATE                    PIC S9(08).


PROCEDURE DIVISION.
    ADD 19000000                       TO WS-CURRENT-DATE

    OPEN INPUT INPUT-TEST
        .
        .
        .

    CLOSE INPUT-TEST
        .
        .
        .
```

◘ COMPUTE statement

● General format

```
COMPUTE identifier1 ROUNDED
   < EQUAL OR = > arithmetic-expression
   [ON] SIZE ERROR statement1
   NOT [ON] SIZE ERROR statement2
[END-COMPUTE]
```

● Description

The **COMPUTE** statement evaluates an arithmetic expression and moves the result into one or more data areas.

identifier1 must be an elementary numeric item, an elementary numeric—edited item, or a floating-point item. It can be one or more of these items.

arithmetic-expression is made up of one or more arithmetic binary operators and numeric items.

statement1 is the statement to which control is transferred when an ON SIZE ERROR condition occurs.

statement2 is the statement to which control is transferred when a NOT ON SIZE ERROR condition occurs.

ROUNDED specifies that any fractional result is to be rounded to the nearest decimal position.

END-COMPUTE is an optional clause to terminate the **COMPUTE** statement.

- Example

```
WORKING-STORAGE SECTION.

01   WS-CURRENT-DATE                PIC S9(08).
01   WS-NEW-DATE                    PIC S9(08).

PROCEDURE DIVISION.

     COMPUTE  WS-NEW-DATE =
              19000000 + WS-CURRENT-DATE
         .
         .
         .
```

◘ CONTINUE statement

- General format

```
CONTINUE
```

- Description

The **CONTINUE** statement is a no-operation statement. It has no effect during the execution of a program.

- Example

```
WORKING-STORAGE SECTION.

01   WS-CURRENT-DATE                PIC S9(08).
01   WS-RESPONSE-STATUS             PIC S9(09) COMP.
     88   SUCCESSFUL                     VALUE 0.
     88   SEVERE-ERROR                   VALUE 100.

LINKAGE SECTION.
01   DOSAGE-LINKAGE.
     05 WS-NEW-DATE                 PIC S9(08).
     05 WS-RESPONSE                 PIC S9(09) COMP.
     88   SUCCESSFUL                     VALUE 0.
     88   NOT-FOUND                      VALUE 100, 1403.
```

```
PROCEDURE DIVISION.

COMPUTE  WS-NEW-DATE =
         19000000 + WS-CURRENT-DATE


CALL "Dosage" USING DOSAGE-LINKAGE


EVALUATE TRUE

    WHEN  SUCCESSFUL                OF DOSAGE-LINKAGE
       CONTINUE

    WHEN OTHER
       SET SEVERE-ERROR             OF RESPONSE-STATUS
          TO TRUE
       GO TO 0101-EXIT
END-EVALUATE
    .
    .
    .

IF NOT-FOUND                        OF DOSAGE-LINKAGE
   CONTINUE
ELSE
   DISPLAY      WS-NEW-DATE
END-IF
```

◘ DELETE statement

● General format

```
DELETE filename RECORD
   INVALID [KEY] statement1
   NOT INVALID [KEY] statement2
END-DELETE
```

● Description

The **DELETE** statement deletes a record in an indexed or relative file. After the record has been removed, the space is available for a record addition or a new record in indexed and relative files, respectively.

filename is the name of an indexed or relative file, defined as an FD entry in the DATA DIVISION.

statement1 is the statement to which control is transferred when an INVALID KEY condition occurs.

statement2 is the statement to which control is transferred when a NOT

INVALID KEY condition occurs.

END-DELETE is an optional phrase to terminate the DELETE statement.

◙ DISPLAY statement

● General format

```
DISPLAY <identifier or literal>
   UPON mnemonic-name
   [WITH] NO ADVANCING
```

● Description

The **DISPLAY** statement sends the content of one or more of its operands to an output device.

identifier is a data area which contains the data to be printed to an output device.

literal is a literal operand.

UPON is an optional clause specifying that a device or *mnemonic-name* must be associated with an output device described in the SPECIAL-NAMES paragraph of the ENVIRONMENT DIVISION.

WITH NO ADVANCING specifies that the positioning of the output device is not to be reset.

● Example

```
WORKING-STORAGE SECTION.

01  WS-CURRENT-DATE            PIC S9(08).

PROCEDURE DIVISION.

MAINLINE.

    ACCEPT WS-CURRENT-DATE FROM DATE.

    DISPLAY " DATE IS "
    DISPLAY WS-CURRENT-DATE
        :
        :
        :
```

◘ DIVIDE statement

● General format

Format 1:

```
DIVIDE <identifier1 or literal1> INTO identifier2 ROUNDED
    ON SIZE ERROR statement1
    NOT [ON] SIZE ERROR statement2
[END-DIVIDE]
```

Format 2:

```
DIVIDE <identifier1 or literal1> <INTO or BY>
        <identifier2 or literal2>
    GIVING identifier3 ROUNDED
    ON SIZE ERROR statement1
    NOT [ON] SIZE ERROR statement2
[END-DIVIDE]
```

Format 3:

```
DIVIDE <identifier1 or literal1> <INTO or BY>
        <identifier2 or literal2>
    GIVING identifier3 ROUNDED
    REMAINDER identifier4
    ON SIZE ERROR statement1
    NOT [ON] SIZE ERROR statement2
[END-DIVIDE]
```

● Description

The **DIVIDE** statement divides one numeric data item by or into another.

identifier1 and *identifier2* are elementary numeric data areas.

identifier3 and *identifier4* are elementary numeric or numeric—edited data areas.

literal1 and *literal2* are numeric literals.

statement1 is the statement to which control is transferred when an ON SIZE ERROR condition occurs.

statement2 is the statement to which control is transferred when a NOT ON SIZE ERROR condition occurs.

ROUNDED specifies that any fractional result is to be rounded to the nearest decimal position.

REMAINDER specifies that the remainder of the division is to be stored in *identifier4*.

END-DIVIDE is an optional phrase to terminate the DIVIDE statement.

◘ ENTER statement

● General format

```
ENTER language-name routine-name
```

● Description

The **ENTER** statement allows more than one language to be used in a source program.

language-name must be COBOL.

routine-name is a user-defined word that contains at least one alphanumeric character.

◘ ENTRY statement

● General format

```
ENTRY literal [USING] identifier
```

● Description

The **ENTRY** statement establishes an alternative entry point into a called COBOL program, other than at the start of the PROCEDURE DIVISION.

literal is nonnumeric and follows the rules for forming program names.

USING is used to pass parameters to the called program.

identifier is a data area.

◘ EVALUATE statement

- General format

```
EVALUATE < identifier1 or literal1 or
      expression1 or TRUE or FALSE
      >
    ALSO < identifier2 or literal2 or
      expression2 or TRUE or FALSE
      >
    WHEN phrase1 ALSO phrase2 statement1
    WHEN OTHER statement2
END-EVALUATE

where phrase1 is

    <ANY or condition1 or TRUE or FALSE or subphrase1>

where subphrase1 is

    <identifier3 or literal3      or
      arithmetic-expression1       or
     NOT identifier3 or NOT literal3  or
     NOT arithmetic-expression1
    > <THROUGH or THRU>
       <identifier4 or literal4 or
         arithmetic-expression2>
```

- Description

The **EVALUATE** statement evaluates a series of conditions and takes actions depending on the results of the evaluation. It is like an expanded **IF** statement.

Operands before the **WHEN** phrase are individually called *selection subjects* and collectively a *set of selection subjects*. Operands after the **WHEN** phrase are individually called *selection objects* and collectively a *set of selection objects*.

ALSO separates selection subjects within a set of selection subjects and selection objects within a set of selection objects.

END-EVALUATE is an optional clause to terminate the **EVALUATE** statement.

- Example

```
WORKING-STORAGE SECTION.

01  WS-CURRENT-DATE                    PIC S9(08).
```

```
01   WS-RESPONSE-STATUS                PIC S9(09) COMP.
     88  SUCCESSFUL                             VALUE 0.
     88  SEVERE-ERROR                           VALUE 100.


LINKAGE SECTION.

01   DOSAGE-LINKAGE.
     05 WS-NEW-DATE                     PIC S9(08).
     05 WS-RESPONSE                     PIC S9(09) COMP.
     88  SUCCESSFUL                      VALUE 0.
     88  NOT-FOUND                       VALUE 100, 1403.


PROCEDURE DIVISION.

   COMPUTE   WS-NEW-DATE =
             19000000 + WS-CURRENT-DATE

   CALL "Dosage" USING DOSAGE-LINKAGE

   EVALUATE TRUE

      WHEN   SUCCESSFUL              OF DOSAGE-LINKAGE
         CONTINUE

      WHEN   NOT-FOUND              OF DOSAGE-LINKAGE
         DISPLAY "DOSAGE NOT FOUND"

      WHEN OTHER
         SET SEVERE-ERROR           OF RESPONSE-STATUS
            TO TRUE
         GO TO 0101-EXIT
   END-EVALUATE
          .
          .
          .


   IF SUCCESSFUL              OF DOSAGE-LINKAGE

      CONTINUE

   ELSE

         SET SEVERE-ERROR     OF RESPONSE-STATUS
            TO TRUE
         GO TO 0101-EXIT

   END-IF
```

◻ EXIT statement

● General format

paragraph-name. EXIT.

● Description

The **EXIT** statement provides a common exit point for a series of paragraphs. It is also used to document the end of a paragraph.

paragraph-name is the name of a COBOL paragraph.

● Example

```
PROCEDURE DIVISION.

        .
        .
        .

    PERFORM 2400-GET-PIRATE-INFO
        THRU 2400-EXIT
        .
        .
        .

2400-GET-PIRATE-INFO.

    PERFORM 8360-OPEN-CR-PIRATE
        THRU 8360-EXIT

    PERFORM 8370-FETCH-CR-PIRATE
        THRU 8370-EXIT

    PERFORM 8380-CLOSE-CR-PIRATE
        THRU 8380-EXIT
        .
2400-EXIT. EXIT.
```

◻ EXIT PROGRAM statement

● General format

```
EXIT PROGRAM
```

● Description

The **EXIT PROGRAM** statement terminates the execution of a program and passes control to the calling program.

- Example

```
PROCEDURE DIVISION.

MAINLINE.

    ACCEPT WS-CURRENT-DATE  FROM DATE.
    ADD 19000000            TO WS-CURRENT-DATE
    MOVE WS-CURRENT-DATE    TO WS-DATE
    MOVE WS-YEAR            OF WS-DATE
       TO YEAR-OF-DATE      OF WS-FORMATTED-DATE
    MOVE WS-MONTH           OF WS-DATE
       TO MONTH-OF-DATE     OF WS-FORMATTED-DATE
    MOVE WS-DAY             OF WS-DATE
       TO DAY-OF-DATE       OF WS-FORMATTED-DATE


    DISPLAY " DATE IS "
    DISPLAY WS-FORMATTED-DATE


    EXIT PROGRAM
       .

END PROGRAM sample.
```

◘ GOBACK statement

- General format

```
GOBACK
```

- Description

The **GOBACK** statement terminates the execution of a program and passes control to the calling program.

◘ GO TO statement

- General format

```
Unconditional:

  GO [TO]  procedure-name1
```

```
Conditional:

  GO [TO] procedure-name2 DEPENDING [ON] identifier1
```

● Description

The **GO TO** statement transfers control from one procedure of a program to another.

procedure-name1 is the name of a paragraph or section to which control is unconditionally transferred.

procedure-name2 is the name of a paragraph or section; optionally one or more names may be specified.

identifier1 is a value that corresponds to a procedure name. If it is 1, control goes to the first procedure; if it is 2, control goes to the second procedure; and so on.

◻ IF statement

● General format

```
IF condition [THEN]

    <statement1 or NEXT SENTENCE>...

ELSE

    <statement2 or NEXT SENTENCE>...

END-IF
```

● Description

The **IF** statement first evaluates a condition and then, depending on the result of the evaluation, executes alternative logical parts of a program. If the result of the condition is TRUE, then only *statement1* is executed. If the result is FALSE, then only *statement2* is executed. Only one or the other is executed, never both. Both *statement1* and *statement2* are optional, but at least one should be specified within the **IF** statement. Within the **IF** statement, many levels of **IF** statement nesting can be used.

condition may be a simple or a compound condition.

statement1 is one or more statements.

statement2 is one or more statements.

ELSE is the clause that divides the two alternative actions if both are specified.

NEXT SENTENCE means to go to the next statement.

END-IF terminates the IF statement.

● Example

```
WORKING-STORAGE SECTION.

01   WS-CURRENT-DATE                PIC S9(08).

01   WS-RESPONSE-STATUS            PIC S9(09) COMP.
     88   SUCCESSFUL                            VALUE 0.
     88   SEVERE-ERROR                          VALUE 100.

LINKAGE SECTION.

01   DOSAGE-LINKAGE.
     05 WS-NEW-DATE                PIC S9(08).
     05 WS-RESPONSE                PIC S9(09) COMP.
     88   SUCCESSFUL               VALUE 0.
     88   NOT-FOUND                VALUE 100, 1403.


PROCEDURE DIVISION.

    COMPUTE   WS-NEW-DATE =
            19000000 + WS-CURRENT-DATE

    CALL "Dosage" USING DOSAGE-LINKAGE

    IF   SUCCESSFUL                OF DOSAGE-LINKAGE

        CONTINUE

    ELSE

        SET SEVERE-ERROR           OF RESPONSE-STATUS
          TO TRUE

        GO TO 0101-EXIT

    END-IF
         .
         .
         .
```

◘ INITIALIZE statement

● General format

```
INITIALIZE identifier1
   REPLACING <ALPHABETIC          or
           ALPHANUMERIC          or
           ALPHANUMERIC-EDITED   or
           NUMERIC-EDITED
              >
   [DATA] BY <identifier2 or literal1>
```

● Description

The **INITIALIZE** statement moves values to the specified data areas. The numeric data is set to zeros and alphanumeric to spaces.

identifier1 is the data area that receives the values.

identifier2 is the data area that contains the value to be moved to *identifier1*.

literal1 is the literal value to be moved to *identifier2*.

REPLACING specifies the data type of *identifier2* and *literal1*. The data types are alphabetic, alphnumeric, alphanumeric—edited, and numeric—edited.

● Example

```
WORKING-STORAGE SECTION.

01  WS-CURRENT-DATE              PIC S9(08).

PROCEDURE DIVISION.

MAINLINE.

    INITIALIZE WS-CURRENT-DATE

    ACCEPT WS-CURRENT-DATE FROM DATE.

    DISPLAY " DATE IS "
    DISPLAY WS-CURRENT-DATE
        .
        .
        .
```

▣ INSPECT statement

● General format

Format 1:

```
INSPECT identifier1
   TALLYING identifier2
   FOR <CHARACTERS phrase1 <ALL or LEADING>
        <identifier3 or literal1> phrase1
        >
```

Format 2:

```
INSPECT identifier1
   REPLACING
   <CHARACTERS BY <identifier5 or literal3> phrase1> or
             < <ALL or LEADING or FIRST>
                  <identifier3 or literal1>
     BY <identifier5 or  literal3>
     phrase1
     >
```

Format 3:

```
INSPECT identifier1
   TALLYING identifier2
   FOR <CHARACTERS phrase1
        <ALL or LEADING> <identifier3 or literal1>
        phrase1
        >
   REPLACING
   <CHARACTERS BY <identifier5 or literal3> phrase1> or
       < <ALL or LEADING or FIRST>
     <identifier3 or literal3>
     BY <identifier5 or  literal3>
   phrase1
   >
```

Format 4:

```
INSPECT identifier1
CONVERTING <identifier6 or literal4>
   TO <identifier7 or  literal5> phrase1
```

```
where phrase1 is
   <BEFORE or AFTER> [INITIAL] <identifier4 or literal2>
```

● Description

The **INSPECT** statement counts or replaces characters in a data area.

identifier1 is the data area to be inspected; it must be an elementary data item or a group of data items with USAGE DISPLAY.

identifier2 is the data area that holds the count (or tally). It receives the number of matches when the TALLYING clause is specified. It must be an elementary data item.

identifier3 is a data area and the tallying operand. It must be an elementary data item with USAGE DISPLAY.

literal1 is a literal value and the tallying operand.

literal2 is a literal value that is not counted during the execution of the **INSPECT** statement.

identifier4 is a data item that holds characters that are not counted during the execution of the **INSPECT** statement.

literal3 is a literal value and the replacing operand.

identifier5 is a data area and holds the replacing operand.

literal4 and *literal5* are strings of replacement values, and both must have the same size.

identifier6 and *identifier7* are data areas, each containing a string of replacement values. Both must have the same size.

◘ MERGE statement

● General format

```
MERGE filename1
    [ON] <ASCENDING  or DESCENDING> [KEY] data-name1
    [COLLATING] SEQUENCE [IS] alphabet-name1
    USING filename2 filename3
    GIVING filename4
    OUTPUT PROCEDURE [IS] proc-name1
        <THROUGH or THRU> proc-name2
```


● Description

The **MERGE** statement takes two files, based on some common keys, and writes the output records to an output file or makes them available to an output procedure.

filename1 describes the records to be merged; it must be defined in the SD entry of the DATA DIVISION.

data-name1 is a data area which specifies the KEY and is associated with *filename1*.

alphabet-name1 is specified in the ALPHABET clause of the SPECIAL-NAMES paragraph of the ENVIRONMENT DIVISION and is used in the collating sequence.

ASCENDING or DESCENDING specifies that the records are merged in ascending or descending order, based on the specified keys.

COLLATING SEQUENCE specifies the collating sequence to be used during the merge operation.

USING specifies the input files, namely, *filename2* and *filename3*.

filename2 and *filename3* are the files to be merged. They should be defined as FD entries of the DATA DIVISION. They are operands of the USING phrase.

GIVING specifies the output file, namely, *filename4*.

filename4 is the name of the output file. It must be defined as an FD entry of the DATA DIVISION. It is an operand of the GIVING phrase.

OUTPUT PROCEDURE specifies the procedure for selecting or modifying output records during the merge operation.

proc-name1 is the first section or paragraph in the OUTPUT PROCEDURE phrase.

proc-name2 is the last section or paragraph in the OUTPUT PROCEDURE phrase.

◼ MOVE statement

● General format

Format 1

```
  MOVE <identifier1 or literal1> TO identifier2...
```

Format 2

```
  MOVE <CORRESPONDING or CORR> identifier1 TO identifier2
```

● Description

The **MOVE** statement copies data from one data area to one or more data areas.

identifier1 is the data area that contains the data to be moved.

litereal1 is the literal value to be moved.

identifier2 is the data area which receives the data.

CORRESPONDING specifies two group operands. The operation is to be performed on all corresponding elementary data items of both groups. If specified, the elementary data items of *identifier1* are moved to *identifier2*.

● Example

```
    WORKING-STORAGE SECTION.

    01  WS-CURRENT-DATE              PIC S9(08).

    01  WS-DATE.
        10 WS-YEAR                   PIC X(04) VALUES SPACES.
        10 WS-MONTH                  PIC X(02) VALUES SPACES.
        10 WS-DAY                    PIC X(02) VALUES SPACES.

    01  WS-FORMATTED-DATE.
        05 YEAR-OF-DATE              PIC X(04) VALUES SPACES.
        05 FILLER                    PIC X(01) VALUES "/".
        05 MONTH-OF-DATE             PIC X(02) VALUES SPACES.
        05 FILLER                    PIC X(01) VALUES "/".
        05 DAY-OF-DATE               PIC X(02) VALUES SPACES.
```

```
/***********************************************
 *
 * Mainline
 *
 *
 ************************************************
    PROCEDURE DIVISION.

    MAINLINE.

        ACCEPT WS-CURRENT-DATE FROM DATE.

        ADD 19000000              TO WS-CURRENT-DATE

        MOVE WS-CURRENT-DATE      TO WS-DATE

        MOVE  WS-YEAR             OF WS-DATE
           TO YEAR-OF-DATE        OF WS-FORMATTED-DATE

        MOVE  WS-MONTH            OF WS-DATE
           TO MONTH-OF-DATE       OF WS-FORMATTED-DATE

        MOVE  WS-DAY              OF WS-DATE
           TO DAY-OF-DATE         OF WS-FORMATTED-DATE
      .
      .
      .
```

◘ MULTIPLY statement

● General format

Format 1:

```
  MULTIPLY <identifier1 or literal1>
     BY identifier2 ROUNDED
     [ON] SIZE ERROR statement1
     NOT [ON] SIZE ERROR statement2
  [END-MULTIPLY]
```

Format 2:

```
  MULTIPLY <identifier1 or literal1>
     BY <identifier2 or literal2>
       GIVING identifier3 ROUNDED
     [ON] SIZE ERROR statement1
     NOT [ON] SIZE ERROR statement2
  [END-MULTIPLY]
```

● Description

The **MULTIPLY** statement multiplies two numeric data items and stores
the result in a data area.

identifier1 is the name of a numeric data area which is multiplied by *identifier2*.

literal1 is the literal value that is multiplied by *literal2*.

identifier2 is the name of a numeric data area that receives the result in format 1.

identifier3 is the name of a numeric data area that receives the result of the multiplication in format 2.

statement1 is the statement to which control is transferred when an ON SIZE ERROR condition occurs.

statement2 is the statement to which control is transferred when a NOT ON SIZE ERROR condition occurs.

ROUNDED specifies that any fractional result is to be rounded to the nearest decimal position.

END-MULTIPLY is an optional clause to terminate the MULTIPLY clause.

◻ OPEN statement

● General format

```
Sequential file:
  OPEN INPUT filename1 <REVERSED or [WITH] NO REWIND>
     OUTPUT filename2... [WITH] NO REWIND
     I-O filename3...
     EXTEND filename4...

Relative and indexed file:
  OPEN INPUT filename1...
     OUTPUT filename2...
     I-O filename3...
     EXTEND filename4...
```

● Description

The **OPEN** statement opens a sequential, relative, or indexed file for processing. All the filenames must be defined in an FD entry in the DATA DIVISION.

INPUT opens *filename1* as an input file.

OUTPUT opens *filename2* as an output file.

I-O opens *filename3* as both an input and an output file.

EXTEND opens *filename4* as an output file. It must not be specified for a multiple-reel file.

REVERSED is valid for a sequential single-reel file.

NO REWIND is valid for a sequential single-reel file.

● Example

```
      INPUT-OUTPUT SECTION.
      FILE-CONTROL.

      SELECT INPUT-TEST
          ASSIGN TO "tip.input.test"
          ORGANIZATION IS LINE SEQUENTIAL
          ACCESS MODE IS SEQUENTIAL
          FILE STATUS IS WS-FILE-STATUS.

      DATA DIVISION.
      FILE SECTION.

      FD  INPUT-TEST.
      01  INPUT-LINE                     PIC X(512).


      WORKING-STORAGE SECTION.

      01  WS-CURRENT-DATE                PIC S9(08).


      PROCEDURE DIVISION.

         ADD 19000000                       TO WS-CURRENT-DATE

         OPEN INPUT INPUT-TEST
              .
              .
              .

         CLOSE INPUT-TEST
              .
              .
              .
```

◘ PERFORM statement

- General format

```
Basic PERFORM format:

  PERFORM <procedure-name1 [<THROUGH or THRU>
                 procedure-name2]            or
         statement1 [END-PERFORM]
         >

PERFORM TIMES format:

  PERFORM <procedure-name1 [<THROUGH or THRU>
              procedure-name2] <identifier1 or integer1>
              TIMES
                  or
         <identifier1 or integer1> TIMES statement1
              [END-PERFORM]
         >

PERFORM UNTIL format:

  PERFORM <procedure-name1 [<THROUGH or THRU>]
           procedure-name2 [WITH] TEST
           <BEFORE or AFTER> UNTIL condition1>
                   or
           [WITH] TEST <BEFORE or AFTER>
           UNTIL condition1
           statement1 [END-PERFORM]
         >

PERFORM VARYING format:

  PERFORM <procedure-name1 <THROUGH or THRU>
              procedure-name2 phrase1
              or
         phrase1 statement1 [END-PERFORM]
         >
  where phrase1 is
    [[WITH] TEST <BEFORE or AFTER>]
    VARYING <identifier1 or index-name1>
    FROM <identifier2 or index-name2 or literal1>
    BY <identifier3 or literal2>
    UNTIL condition1
```

- Description

The **PERFORM** statement transfers control to one or more procedures
and controls the number of times they are executed. After the execution
of the specified procedures, control goes to the next statement after the
PERFORM statement. There are four types of **PERFORM** statements:

- Basic **PERFORM**
- TIMES phrase **PERFORM**

- UNTIL phrase **PERFORM**
- VARYING phrase **PERFORM**

The basic **PERFORM** executes a procedure only once; however, the other types specify conditions which determine the number of times a procedure is executed.

procedure-name1 and *procedure-name2* are names of sections or paragraphs in the PROCEDURE DIVISION.

condition1 is a conditional expression.

identifier1, *identifier2*, and *identifier3* are data areas that contain values to control the number of execution of procedures.

statement1 is the last statement in an in-line PERFORM statement.

The TIMES phrase specifies the number of times that procedures are executed.

The UNTIL phrase specifies that execution of procedures continues until a specified condition is true.

The VARYING phrase specifies that the procedures executed as certain identifiers, subscripts, or indexes are initialized and incremented, and until a certain condition is true.

END-PERFORM is an optional phrase to terminate the **PERFORM** statement.

- Example

```
PERFORM 8020-FETCH-CR-DOSAGE
    THRU 8020-EXIT


PERFORM
    UNTIL (NOT IO-OK         OF WS-DOSAGE-STATUS)
        PERFORM 8020-FETCH-CR-DOSAGE
           THRU 8020-EXIT
        SET IDX-DOSAGE            UP BY 1
        IF  IDX-DOSAGE > WS-MAX-DOSAGE-CDS
            MOVE "DOSAGE-CD-TABLE"
              TO WS-TABLE-NAME
            PERFORM 9996-HANDLE-TABLE-OVERFLOW
            SET SEVERE-ERROR
            OF GETDOSAGESU-LINKAGE
```

```
              TO   TRUE
         GO TO 2200-EXIT
      END-IF
END-PERFORM
```

◘ READ statement

● General format

```
Sequential access:

  READ filename1 NEXT RECORD INTO identifier1
    [[AT] END statement1]
    [NOT [AT] END statement2]
  [END-READ]

Random access:

  READ filename1 [RECORD] INTO [identifier1]
    [KEY [IS] data-name1]
    [INVALID [KEY] statement3]
    [NOT INVALID [KEY] statement4]
  [END-READ]
```

● Description

The **READ** statement reads a record from an external file and places the data in a specified data area. There are two types of files: sequential-access and random-access. For sequential-access files, the next logical record is read. For random-access files, a specific record with a key is read. Before a file is read, it must be opened with an INPUT or I-O phrase.

filename1 is the name of the file to be accessed. It must be defined in an FD entry in the DATA DIVISION.

identifier1 is the data area that receives the read record. It must be defined in the WORKING-STORAGE SECTION as a group or elementary data item. It must be long enough to hold all the data in the record.

statement1 is the statement to execute when an AT END condition occurs.

statement2 is the statement to execute when a NOT AT END condition occurs.

statement3 is the statement to execute when an INVALID KEY condition occurs.

statement4 is the statement to execute when a NOT INVALID KEY condition occurs.

KEY IS specifies the key to retrieve a record from a file.

data-name1 is the data area, defined in the WORKING-STORAGE SECTION, which holds the key to retrieve a record from a file.

END-READ is an optional phrase to terminate the READ statement.

● Example

```
INPUT-OUTPUT SECTION.
FILE-CONTROL.

SELECT INPUT-TEST
    ASSIGN TO "tip.input.test"
    ORGANIZATION IS LINE SEQUENTIAL
    ACCESS MODE IS SEQUENTIAL
    FILE STATUS IS WS-FILE-STATUS.

DATA DIVISION.
FILE SECTION.

FD  INPUT-TEST.
01  INPUT-LINE                     PIC X(512).


WORKING-STORAGE SECTION.

01  WS-CURRENT-DATE                PIC S9(08).


PROCEDURE DIVISION.

   ADD 19000000                        TO WS-CURRENT-DATE

   OPEN INPUT INPUT-TEST

   READ INPUT-TEST NEXT RECORD

   CLOSE INPUT-TEST
       .
       .
       .
```

◘ RELEASE statement

● General format

```
RELEASE record-name [FROM identifier]
```

● Description

The **RELEASE** statement makes a record available for sorting and is used within the INPUT PROCEDURE of an internal sort.

record-name is defined as an SD entry in the FILE SECTION of the DATA DIVISION. Its content is placed in the sort file each time the RELEASE statement is executed.

identifier is a data area defined in the WORKING-STORAGE SECTION. Its content is moved to *record-name*.

◘ RETURN statement

● General format

```
RETURN filename [RECORD]
   [INTO identifier]
   [AT] END statement1
   [NOT [AT] END statement2]
[END-RETURN]
```

● Description

The **RETURN** statement retrieves the next record during an internal sort (or merge) operation. It is used within the OUTPUT PROCEDURE of a **MERGE** or **SORT** statement.

filename is the name of a file described as an SD entry in the DATA DIVISION.

identifier is the name of a data area which receives the record being retrieved from *filename*.

statement1 is the statement to execute when an AT END condition occurs.

statement2 is the statement to execute when a NOT AT END condition occurs.

END-RETURN is an optional phrase to terminate the RETURN statement.

◘ REWRITE statement

● General format

```
Sequential file:

  REWRITE record-name [FROM identifier]
  [END-REWRITE]


Relative and indexed files:

  REWRITE record-name [FROM identifier]
     [INVALID [KEY] statement1]
     [NOT INVALID [KEY] statement2]
  [END-REWRITE]
```

● Description

The **REWRITE** statement updates a record in a file. The file must be open to execute the rewrite operation.

record-name is the name of a logical record described as an FD entry of the DATA DIVISION.

identifier is the name of the data area from which the data is written.

statement1 is the statement to execute when an INVALID KEY condition occurs.

statement2 is the statement to execute when a NOT INVALID KEY condition occurs.

END-REWRITE is an optional phrase to terminate the **REWRITE** statement.

◻ SEARCH statement

● General format

```
Serial search:

  SEARCH identifier1
     [VARYING <identifier2 or index-name>]
     [[AT] END statement1]
     [WHEN condition1 <statement2 or NEXT SENTENCE>]...
  [END-SEARCH]

Binary search:

  SEARCH ALL identifier1
     [AT] END statement1
     WHEN <condition1                 or
       <data-name1  [IS] EQUAL [TO]
             <identifier3 or literal1 or expression1>
       [AND <data-name2  [IS]   EQUAL [TO]
             <identifier4 or literal2 or expression2>]
       <statement2 [END-SEARCH] or NEXT SENTENCE>
```

● Description

The **SEARCH** statement searches a data area (table) until a certain condition is satisfied. There are two kinds of searches: serial and binary.

identifier1 is the name of a data area, defined as a table with an OCCURS clause.

VARYING is used for a serial search which increments *index-name* or *identifier2*, the subscript to the table *identifier1*. The search starts from the current settings of the index.

identifier2 is a data area which holds a subscript to the table *identifier1*.

index-name is an index to table *identifier1*.

WHEN specifies the conditions for the search.

condition1 and *condition2* are conditional expressions.

identifier3 and *identifier4* are names of data areas.

statement1 is the statement to execute when an AT END condition occurs.

statement2 is the statement to execute that is associated with the WHEN clause.

literal1 and *literal2* are literal values.

expression1 and *expression2* are arithmetic expressions.

data-name1 and *data-name2* are associated with the WHEN clause. Both must specify a data item (ASCENDING/DESCENDING KEY) in the *identifier1* table element.

END-SEARCH is an optional phrase to terminate the SEARCH statement.

◘ SET statement

● General format

```
TO phrase:

   SET <index-name1 or identifier1> TO
       <index-name2 or identifier2  or integer1>

UP/DOWN phrase:

   SET index-name3... <UP or DOWN> BY
       <identifier3 or integer2>

ON/OFF phrase:

   SET mnemonic-name1... TO <ON or OFF>

TO TRUE phrase:
   SET condition-name1... TO TRUE

Pointer data item phrase:
   SET <identifier4 or ADDRESS OF identifier5>...
       TO <identifier6 or ADDRESS OF identifier7 or
               NULL or NULLS>
```

● Description

The **SET** statement does the following:

- Changes table indexes
- Sets status codes to external switches
- Sets values of conditional variables
- Sets values to pointer data areas

The TO phrase sets the value of *index-name2* or *identifier2* or *integer1* to the current value of *index-name1* or *identifier1*.

The UP/DOWN phrase increases or decreases the value of *index-name3* by *identifier3* or *integer2*.

The ON/OFF phrase sets *mnemonic-name1* to ON or OFF status.

The TO TRUE phrase sets *condition-name1* to its true value.

The ADDRESS OF phrase sets the value of *identifier6* or ADDRESS OF *identifier7* or NULL or NULLS to *identifier4* or ADDRESS OF *identifier5*.

● Example

```
          WORKING-STORAGE SECTION.

          01   WS-CURRENT-DATE          PIC S9(08).
          01   WS-RESPONSE-STATUS       PIC S9(09) COMP.
               88   SUCCESSFUL                       VALUE 0.
               88   SEVERE-ERROR                     VALUE 100.

          LINKAGE SECTION.

          01   DOSAGE-LINKAGE.

               05 WS-NEW-DATE           PIC S9(08).

               05 WS-RESPONSE           PIC S9(09) COMP.
                  88   SUCCESSFUL                    VALUE 0.
                  88   NOT-FOUND                     VALUE 100, 1403.

          PROCEDURE DIVISION.

              COMPUTE  WS-NEW-DATE =
                       19000000 + WS-CURRENT-DATE

              CALL "Dosage" USING DOSAGE-LINKAGE

              IF  SUCCESSFUL              OF DOSAGE-LINKAGE

                  CONTINUE

              ELSE

                  SET SEVERE-ERROR           OF RESPONSE-STATUS
                      TO TRUE

                  GO TO 0101-EXIT

              END-IF
                  .
                  .
                  .
```

◘ SORT statement

● General format

```
SORT filename1 [ON] <ASCENDING or DESCENDING>
   [KEY] data-name1...
   [[WITH] DUPLICATES IN ERROR]
   [[COLLATING] SEQUENCE [IS] alphabet-name1]
   < <USING filename2> or
         <INPUT PROCEDURE [IS] proc-name1
            <THRU or THROUGH> proc-name2
     >
   >
   < <GIVING filename3> or
         <OUTPUT PROCEDURE [IS] proc-name3
            <THRU or THROUGH> proc-name4
     >
   >

where filename1 is
   <ASCENDING or DESCENDING> KEY PHRASE
```

● Description

The **SORT** statement sorts input records in ascending or descending order specified by one or more keys. The input records can be made available to the **SORT** statement either from one or more input files or through a procedure specified in the INPUT PROCEDURE phrase. The sorted records can be either written to an external file or passed on for further processing to a procedure specified in the OUTPUT PROCEDURE phrase.

filename1 describes the records to be sorted; it must be defined in an SD entry in the DATA DIVISION.

data-name1 is a data area which specifies the KEY and is associated with *filename1*.

ASCENDING or DESCENDING specifies that the records are to be sorted in ascending or descending order, based on the specified keys.

COLLATING SEQUENCE specifies the collating sequence to be used during the merge operation.

alphabet-name1 is specified in the ALPHABET clause of the SPECIAL-NAMES paragraph of the ENVIRONMENT DIVISION and is used in the collating sequence.

USING specifies the input files, namely, *filename2*.

filename2 contains the files to be merged. They should be defined as FD entries in the DATA DIVISION. They are operands of the USING phrase.

GIVING specifies the output file, namely, *filename3*.

filename3 is the name of the output file. It must be defined as an FD entry in the DATA DIVISION. It is an operand of the GIVING phrase.

INPUT PROCEDURE specifies the procedures for selecting or modifying input records before the sort operation starts.

proc-name1 is the first section or paragraph in the INPUT PROCEDURE phrase.

proc-name2 is the last section or paragraph in the INPUT PROCEDURE phrase.

OUTPUT PROCEDURE specifies the procedure for selecting or modifying output records during the sort operation.

proc-name3 is the first section or paragraph in the OUTPUT PROCEDURE phrase.

proc-name4 is the last section or paragraph in the OUTPUT PROCEDURE phrase.

◘ START statement

● General format

```
START filename1
   KEY [IS] < EQUAL [TO]                              or
            =                                         or
            GREATER [THAN]                            or
            >                                         or
            NOT LESS                                  or
            NOT <                                     or
            GREATER [THAN] OR EQUAL [TO] or
            >=
         > data-name1
   [INVALID [KEY] statement1]
   [NOT INVALID [KEY] statement2]
[END-START]
```

● Description

The **START** statement establishes the position for retrieving a record of an indexed or relative file. Before this statement is executed, the file must be opened in INPUT or I-O mode.

filename1 is the name of the file for which the position of a record is sought. It must be described as an FD entry in the DATA DIVISION.

KEY specifies that the file indicator is to be positioned at the first logical record whose key field satisfies a comparison with the value in *data-name1*. The default is to position the file indicator at the logical record whose key field is equal to the current value of the prime record key.

statement1 is the statement to execute when an INVALID KEY condition occurs.

statement2 is the statement to execute when a NOT INVALID KEY condition occurs.

END-START is an optional phrase that terminates the START statement.

◘ STOP statement

● General format

```
STOP <RUN or literal>
```

● Description

The **STOP** statement terminates the execution of a program. All files are closed, and control is transferred to the calling program.

● Example

```
WORKING-STORAGE SECTION.

01  WS-CURRENT-DATE              PIC S9(08).
```

```
    PROCEDURE DIVISION.

    MAINLINE.

        INITIALIZE WS-CURRENT-DATE

        ACCEPT WS-CURRENT-DATE FROM DATE

        DISPLAY " DATE IS "

        DISPLAY WS-CURRENT-DATE
                    .
                    .
                    .
        STOP RUN.
```

◻ STRING statement

- General format

```
STRING <identifier1 or literal1>...
    DELIMITED [BY] <identifier2 or literal2 or SIZE>
    INTO identifier3
    [WITH] [POINTER identifier4]
    [ON] [OVERFLOW statement1]
    [NOT [ON] OVERFLOW statement2]
[END-STRING]
```

- Description

The **STRING** statement is used to concatenate several fields of data into one form. All the data areas must be defined with the USAGE DISPLAY phrase. There may be one or more input fields.

identifier1 is a data area that holds the input field.

literal1 is a nonnumeric value that is the input field.

DELIMITED BY specifies the limit of each input field with a delimiter.

identifier2 is a data area that holds one or more characters as the delimiters.

literal2 is a nonnumeric value that is the delimiter.

identifier3 is a data area that receives the output string.

POINTER specifies that the output is a pointer field.

identifier4 is a data area defined as a pointer data type.

statement1 is the statement to execute when an ON OVERFLOW condition occurs.

statement2 is the statement to execute when a NOT ON OVERFLOW condition occurs.

END-STRING is an optional phrase that terminates the STRING statement.

◘ SUBTRACT statement

- General format

Format 1:

```
SUBTRACT <identifier1 or literal1> FROM identifier2
   [ROUNDED]
   [ON] [SIZE ERROR statement1]
   [NOT [ON] SIZE ERROR statement2]
[END-SUBTRACT]
```

Format 2:

```
SUBTRACT <identifier1 or literal1> FROM
         <identifier2 or literal2>
   GIVING identifier4 [ROUNDED]
   [ON] [SIZE ERROR statement1]
   [NOT [ON] SIZE ERROR statement2]
[END-SUBTRACT]
```

Format 3:

```
SUBTRACT <CORRESPONDING or CORR> identifier5
   FROM identifier6 [ROUNDED]
   [ON] [SIZE ERROR statement1]
   [NOT [ON] SIZE ERROR statement2]
[END-SUBTRACT]
```


- Description

The **SUBTRACT** statement subtracts one or more numeric operands from one or more numeric operands and stores the result.

identifier1, *identifier2*, and *identifier3* must be elementary numeric data areas.

identifier4 must be either an elementary numeric data area or numeric—edited data area. It receives the sum.

CORRESPONDING specifies two group operands. The operation is to be performed on all corresponding elementary data items of both groups.

identifier5 and *identifier6* must be group data areas. The elementary elements of *identifier5* are subtracted from, and stored in, elements of *identifier6*.

literal1 is a numeric literal.

statement1 is the statement to which control is transferred when an ON SIZE ERROR condition occurs.

statement2 is the statement to which control is transferred when a NOT ON SIZE ERROR condition occurs.

ROUNDED specifies that any fractional result is to be rounded to the nearest decimal position.

END-SUBTRACT is an optional phrase to terminate the **SUBTRACT** statement.

◘ UNSTRING statement

● General format

```
UNSTRING identifier1
   [DELIMITED [BY] [ALL] <identifier2 or literal1>
     OR ALL <identifier3 or literal2>]
   [INTO identifier4 DELIMITER [IN] identifier5
            COUNT [IN] identifier6]
   [WITH] [POINTER identifier7]
   [TALLYING [IN] identifier8]
   [ON] OVERFLOW statement1
   NOT [ON] OVERFLOW statement2
[END-UNSTRING]
```

● Description

The **UNSTRING** statement takes contiguous data fields, separates them, and stores them into several data fields. Depending on the processing, it can replace several **MOVE** statements.

identifier1 is a data area that holds the input field.

DELIMITED BY specifies the limit of each input field with a delimiter.

identifier2 and *identifier3* are data areas that hold one or more characters as the delimiters.

literal1 and *literal2* are nonnumeric values that are the delimiters.

identifier4 is the data area that receives the output fields. It must be defined with the USAGE DISPLAY phrase.

DELIMITER IN specifies the delimiter for the output fields.

identifier5 is the data area that hold the output field delimiter.

COUNT IN specifies the data area of the count for the input fields.

identifier6 is the data area that holds the count of examined characters for the input fields.

POINTER specifies that the ouput is a pointer field.

identifier7 is a data area defined as a pointer data type.

TALLYING IN specifies the data area of the count for the output fields.

identifier8 is a data area that holds the number of output fields during the execution of the UNSTRING statement.

statement1 is the statement to execute when an ON OVERFLOW condition occurs.

statement2 is the statement to execute when a NOT ON OVERFLOW condition occurs.

END-UNSTRING is an optional phrase that terminates the **UN-STRING** statement.

◼ WRITE statement

● General format

Sequential file:

```
WRITE record-name1
   [FROM identifier1]
   [<BEFORE or AFTER> ADVANCING
     <mnemonic-name1 or PAGE> or
               [<identifier2 or literal>
                 <LINE or LINES>]]
   [<INVALID [KEY] statement1> or
    <[AT] END-OF-PAGE statement3>]
   [<NOT INVALID [KEY] statement2> or
            <NOT [AT] END-OF-PAGE statement4>]
 [END-WRITE]
```

Indexed and relative file:

```
WRITE record-name1
   [FROM identifier1]
   [INVALID [KEY] statement1]
   [NOT INVALID [KEY] statement2]
 [END-WRITE]
```

● Description

The **WRITE** statement causes a logical record to be written to a file. Before this operation, the file must be open in OUTPUT, I-O, or EXTEND mode. After the **WRITE** statement is executed, the FILE STATUS is updated. There are three types of files to which records are written:

●   Sequential files
●   Indexed and relative files

record-name1 is defined as an FD entry in the DATA DIVISION; its current content is written to the file.

identifier1, if specified, is a data area from which the record is written to the file.

identifier2 is a data area and must contain an integer value.

ADVANCING controls the positioning of the current output record on the page of a sequential file.

statement1 is the statement to execute when an INVALID KEY condition occurs.

statement2 is the statement to execute when a NOT INVALID KEY condition occurs.

statement3 is the statement to execute when an END-OF-PAGE condition occurs.

statement4 is the statement to execute when a NOT END-OF-PAGE condition occurs.

END-WRITE is an optional phrase to terminate the WRITE statement.

4.7 Compiler Directives

This section describes the compiler directive statements which are used in a COBOL source program.

◨ BASIC statement

● General format

```
[sequence-number] BASIS basis-name
```

● Description

The **BASIC** statement provides a way to include a complete COBOL program during compilation.

sequence-number is a number in columns 1 through 6.

basis-name is a program name.

■ CONTROL statement

● General format

```
Source code:

  <*CONTROL or *CBL> <SOURCE or NOSOURCE>

Object code:

  <*CONTROL or *CBL> <LIST or NOLIST>

Storage maps:

  <*CONTROL or *CBL> <MAP OR NOMAP>
```

● Description

The **CONTROL** statement displays or suppresses listing of source code, object code, or storage maps.

■ COPY statement

● General format

```
COPY text-name <OF or IN> library-name SUPPRESS
    REPLACING operand1 BY operand2
```

● Description

The **COPY** statement is used to include the text of a COBOL program during compilation. The text is commonly known as the *copy book*.

text-name is the name of a member of a library.

library-name is the name of the library where *text-name* is found.

operand1 and *operand2* are either pseudotext, identifiers, literals, or COBOL words.

◘ DELETE statement

- General format

```
[sequence-number] DELETE sequence-number-field
```

- Description

The **DELETE** statement removes COBOL statements from the BASIS source program.

sequence-number is a number in columns 1 through 6.

sequence-number-field is a number equal to a sequence number in the BASIS source program.

◘ EJECT statement

- General format

```
EJECT
```

- Description

The **EJECT** statement specifies that the next line of the source program is to be printed at the top of the page.

◘ INSERT statement

- General format

```
[sequence-number] INSERT sequence-number-field
```

- Description

The **INSERT** statement adds COBOL statements from the BASIS source program.

sequence-number is a number in columns 1 through 6.

sequence-number-field is a number equal to a sequence number in the BASIS source program.

◧ REPLACE statement

- General format

```
Format 1:

  REPLACE text1 by text2

Format 2:

  REPLACE OFF
```

- Description

The **REPLACE** statement replaces the source program.

text1 must contain one or more text words.

text2 may contain no word, one word, or many words.

◧ SKIP1/2/3 statements

- General format

```
<SKIP1 or SKIP2 or SKIP3> [.]
```

- Description

The **SKIP** statements insert one, two, or three blank lines in the source listing.

SKIP1 inserts one blank line.

SKIP2 inserts two blank lines.

SKIP3 inserts three blank lines.

◼ TITLE statement

- General format

```
TITLE literal [.]
```

- Description

The **TITLE** statement specifies that a title is to be printed at the top of each page of the source listing.

literal is the title.

DB2/2 Commands and Utilities

This chapter is a reference guide for programmers using DB2/2. DB2/2 is a relational database for OS/2. The subjects covered here can be grouped into these categories:

- System commands
- DOS and Windows database client application enabler commands
- DBM command line processor commands

For each command and utility, this chapter provides the syntax and a description of the function and its parameters. In some cases you will also find examples of how the functions use these parameters. Information on the privileges and authority needed to execute some of these commands is also presented.

5.1 System Commands

The system commands are issued at the OS/2 command line or from a command file (.CMD). These commands are generally used to maintain the DB2/2 database. The general format is

```
[drive] [path] system-commands parameters
```

drive is a two-character (A:, B:, etc.) drive indicating where the command is to be found.

path is the directory containing the command to be executed.

system-commands are **DBM** commands, **MIGRATE1, SQLSQLARWS, SQLBIND, SQLDRWS, SQLPREP, SQLQMF, SQLSAMPL, SQLVCFG, STARTDBM,** and **STOPDBM.**

parameters are options and keywords.

(**Note**: Both drive and path are optional, and if they are not specified, the system searches in the current drive and current directory for the command. If the command is not found, the path listed in the **PATH** environment variable is used.)

◖ DBM—command line processor

- General format

```
[drive] [path] DBM [-C or -O or -R ([path] filename)]...
        <command or statement> [\]]
              or
    [drive] [path] DBM ? [?phrase or ?message_number]
```

- Authorizations

Authority	Privilege
None required	None required

● Description

The DBM command is an interface between DB2/2 and OS/2 command line or batch file (.CMD).

drive is a two-character (A:, B:, etc.) drive indicating where the DBM command is to be found.

path is the directory containing the DBM command to be executed.

? is used to obtain general help (assistance) information.

?phrase is used to obtain help information on a specific command, such as a SQL statement or topic.

?message_number is used to get a description of a specific message number. A message number is prefixed with one of the following three-character codes.

● DBA—messages for the database administrator
● DBM—DB2/2 messages
● SQL—SQL messages
● QRW—query manager message

-C means to disallow a change or insert to the database to take effect unless a **DBM COMMIT** is issued. You can set an automatic-commit option in an environment variable in your CONFIG.SYS file. When automatic commit is enabled, all changes or insertions to the database become permanent.

-O means to direct messages or report data to a standard device instead of to the workstation screen.

-R   is used to send a report to a file.

path is the drive letter and directory name of the file to which the report is written.

filename is the name of the file to which the report is written.

.ext is the extension of the file, if any.

command is used to specify the DBM command you want to execute.

All the commands are listed and explained later in this chapter.

statement is used to specify the SQL statements. These statements are discussed in Chap. 6.

\ is the line continuation character. It is used when a DBM command or SQL statement is long and you want to type it in more than one line. When DBM reads \ as the last character of a line it automatically displays a new prompt (=>) and you can enter more characters to complete a command or statement.

● Example

In the next example, the SQL statement is used to insert a row in the CLIENTS table. Since there is a -C (suppress commit option), this addition to the database will not become permanent.

```
DBM -C INSERT INTO RBA.CLIENTS              \
    (NAME, CITY, POSTAL_C, PROV)   \
    VALUES ('RBC','NEWMARKET','L3X1F0','ONTARIO');
```

In the following command, the report data which results from executing the **SELECT** statement is written to the C:\BOOK\OS2REF\CLIENTS file.

```
DBM -R (C:\BOOK\OS2REF\CLIENTS) SELECT *  \
                FROM RBA.CLIENTS
```

DBM also allows redirection of data using the redirection symbol (>). The previous example can be rewritten, replacing the -R option with >.

```
DBM SELECT * FROM RBA.CLIENTS >      \
                C:\BOOK\OS2REF\CLIENTS
```

◘ MIGRATE1—migrate database

● General format

```
[drive] [path] MIGRATE1 database
```

- Authorizations

Authority	Privilege
None required	None required

- Description

The **MIGRATE1** system command is used to migrate a database created in EE (Extended Edition) 1.3 or ES (Extended Series) 1.0 to DB2/2.

drive is two-character (A:, B:, etc.) drive indicating where the **MIGRATE1** command is to be found.

path is the directory listing the **MIGRATE1** command to be executed.

database specifies the name of the database to be migrated from EE or ES to DB2/2.

- Example

The following command is used to migrate the CLIENTS database.

```
MIGRATE1 CLIENTS
```


◘ SQLARWS—add remote workstation

- General format

```
[drive] [path]  SQLRWS
                machine-id modetype
                   [/W=workstation or /R]
```

- Authorizations

Authority	Privilege
SYSADM LAN administration	Appropriate

• Description

The **SQLARWS** command allows a workstation to access and use DB2/2 programs residing on a LAN (local area network) server. This command makes the program appear to have been installed on the workstation.

drive is a two-character (A:, B:, etc.) drive indicating where the **SQLARWS** command is to be found.

path is the directory containing the **SQLARWS** command to be executed.

machine-id is a LAN machine ID for the workstation that must use the DB2/2 programs on a LAN server. It cannot be longer than eight characters.

modetype is used to specify the type of workstation and can be one of the following:

0 = local workstation
1 = database server workstation
2 = database client workstation
3 = database client workstation with local database

/W=*workstation*
This parameter is used to specify the node name of a workstation. This name must be defined in the DB2/2 configuration file. This parameter is required for client or server workstations but not for local workstations.

/R is used to replace an existing workstation configuration file.

• Example

The following command grants a client workstation access to a DB2/2 program. The workstation is known to the LAN as KINGFISH and as CRAYFISH to DB2/2.

```
SQLARWS KINGFISH 2 /W=CRAYFISH
```

◙ SQLBIND—bind the application to the database

● General format

```
[drive] [path] SQLBIND <program-name or
                       @list-file>
              database [option...]
```

● Authorizations

Authority	Privilege
SYSADM	BINDADD
DBADM	

● Description

The **SQLBIND** command is used to prepare SQL statements. The input is a file generated by the precompiler, and its extension is .BND. After the SQL statement is prepared, **SQLBIND** creates a package that is stored in the database.

drive is two-character (A:, B:, etc.) drive indicating where the **SQLBIND** command is to be found.

path is the directory contaning the **SQLBIND** command to be executed.

program-name specifies the bind files generated by the precompiler from a source program. If needed, you must give the pathname of this file.

@list-file is used to specify a list file. This file contains a number of the bind files in separate lines. If you list many files in one line, they must be separated by plus sign (+).

database is used to specify the alias of a database to bind the program.

option is used to specify special processing. There are several options and you can list none or many of these options. They are

/F=format
This option is used to specify the date and time formats used when binding a program.

format is one of the codes shown in Figure 5.1.

Code Date format	Time format	Description
ISO yyyy-mm-dd	hh.mm.ss	International Standards Organization
USA mm/dd/yyyy	hh:mm AM or PM	USA Standard
EUR dd.mm.yyyy	hh.mm.ss	European Standard
JIS yyyy-mm-dd	hh:mm:ss	Japanese Industrial Standard

DEF	The date and time formats used with the country code; this is the default
LOC	Special date and time formats depending on the country code

Figure 5.1 International date and time formats.

/G=grantspec
This option is used to grant execution and bind privileges to a user ID, group ID, or PUBLIC.

/I=isolation
This option is used to specify the isolation level. This tells DB2/2 how to isolate data in the database from other processing which may occur while the application is accessing the database.

isolation is one of the following:

   RR—repeatable read
   CS—cursor stability
   UR—uncommitted read

/K=blocking
This option is used to specify the type of record blocking and explains how to deal with ambiguous cursors.

   blocking is one of the following

   • ALL means to block for
      • FETCH-only cursors
      • Cursors not specified as **FOR UPDATE OF**
      • Cursors for which there are no static **DELETE WHERE CURRENT OF** statements
      • Any ambiguous cursors are treated as FETCH-only.

- UNAMBIG means to block for
  - FETCH-only cursors
  - Cursors not specified as **FOR UPDATE OF**
  - Cursors that do not have static **DELETE WHERE CURRENT OF** statements
  - Cursors that do not have dynamic statements
  - Any ambiguous cursors are treated UPDATE-only.

- NO means not to block any cursors. Any ambiguous cursors are treated as UPDATE-only.

The default is /K=UNAMBIG.

/M=destination
This option is used to specify a destination to which warning or error messages are written.

destination can be any one of the following:

- A name of a file
- LPT1 for a printer
- CON for the console
- NUL to suppress messages

- Example

The following statement creates a package for the TIP program from the TIP.BND bind file in the PRESCRIBER database.

```
SQLBIND TIP.BND PRESCRIBER
```

The next example is the same as the previous one, except two options are added. The /F=EUR option specifies European data and time format, and /M=LPT1 is used to send the messages to the printer.

```
SQLBIND TIP.BND PRESCRIBER   \
   /F=EUR /M=LPT1
```

◘ SQLDRWS—drop remote workstation

- General format

```
[drive] [path] SQLDRWS machine-id
```

- Authorizations

Authority	Privilege
SYSADM LAN administrator	LAN server

- Description

The **SQLDRWS** command describes a workstation that accesses DB2/2 programs located on the LAN server. The access is granted by the **SQLARWS** command, discussed previously.

drive is a two-character (A:, B:, etc.) drive indicating where the **SQLDRWS** command is to be found.

path is the directory containing the **SQLDRWS** command to be executed.

machine-id is used to specify a machine-id already defined in the LAN. The name cannot be more than eight characters in length.

- Example

In the following command, the KINGFISH workstation is denied access to DB2/2 program installed in the LAN server.

```
SQLDRWS KINGFISH
```

◘ SQLPREP—precompile a source file

- General format
```
[drive] [path] SQLPREP program-name
     database [option...]
```

- Authorizations

Authority	Privilege
SYSADM, DBADM, or BIND	None required

● Description

The **SQLPREP** command is used to precompile a program. *Precompilation*, as the name suggests, is a step preceding compilation and is needed when there are embedded SQL statements in a source program file. During this process, many tasks are accomplished; some of the most important ones are

● The validity of SQL statements is checked.
● Table names and column names are verified against a database.
● SQL statemens are translated into program language statements for compilation.
● A modified version of the program source file is created with the default extensions, for example, .C for C programs or .CBL for COBOL. Subsequently, this file, which includes your code and translated SQL statements, can be compiled.
● A bind file, with extension .BND is generated that contains the access path to the database.

drive is a two-character (A:, B:, etc.) drive indicating where the **SQLPREP** command is to be found.

path is the directory containing the **SQLPREP** command to be executed.

program-name is the name of the source file that is to be precompiled. The extensions for such a file are

    .SQC for C programs
    .SQB for COBOL programs

database is the alias of the database accessed by the SQL statements of the source program.

option is used to specify special processing. In one command you can list none to many options. They are as follows:

/B=[*filename*]
This option is used to specify the filename for the bind file with extension (.BND). If you omitted the filename, the precompiler used the program filename.

/C=None required or SAA
This option is used to specify whether the generated code should

conform to SAA (Systems Application Architecture) standards.

SAA means that the modified code is compatible with SAA standards.

None required means that the modified code is not compatible with SAA standards.

/F=format
This option is used to specify the date and time formats used when binding a program.

format is of one of the codes listed in Figure 5.1.

/I=isolation
This option is used to specify the isolation level. This tells DB2/2 how to isolate data in the database from other processing which may occur while the application is accessing the database.

isolation is one of the following:

    RR—repeatable read
    CS—cursor stability
    UR—uncommitted read

/K=blocking
This option is used to specify the type of record blocking and it tells how to deal with ambiguous cursors.

  blocking is one of the following:

- ALL means to block for
  - FETCH-only cursors
  - Cursors not specified as **FOR UPDATE OF**
  - Cursors for which there are no static **DELETE WHERE CURRENT OF** statements
  - Any ambiguous cursors are are treated as FETCH-only.

- UNAMBIG means to block for
  - FETCH-only cursors
  - Cursors not specified as **FOR UPDATE OF**
  - Cursors that do not have static **DELETE WHERE CURRENT OF** statements

- Cursors that do not have dynamic statements
- Any ambiguous cursors are treated as UPDATE-only.

- NO means not to block any cursors. Any ambiguous cursors are treated as UPDATE-only.

The default is /K=UNAMBIG.

/L=level
This option is used to specify the level of compliance to SAA standards.

level is 0 or 1.

0 means compatible with database common programming interface only.

1 means compatible with multivendor integrated architecture (MIA).

/M=destination
This option is used to specify a destination to which warning or error messages are written.

destination can be any one of the following:

- A name of a file
- LPT1 for a printer
- CON for the console
- NUL to suppress messages.

/#
This option is used to suppress generation of line macros in modified C programs only.

/O=optimize
This option is used to optimize the initialization code of the SQLDA structure. This optimization applies only to SQL statements using host variables.

/P=package
This option is used to create a package.

package is the name of the package.

/S

This option is used to suppress creation of the bind or package file.

- Example

In the following command, TIP.SQB is a COBOL source file. This file is precompiled to create a modified source file called TIP.CBL. The CUSTOMER database is used to validate table and column names found in the SQL statements of the source program.

```
SQLPREP TIP.SQB CUSTOMER /B /P
   /M=C:\TIP\ERROR.OUT
```

The /B option is used to generate a TIP.BND bind file, /P is used to create a package, and the messages are written to C:\TIP\ERROR.OUT.

◻ SQLQMF—Import a QMF file

- General format

```
[drive] [path] SQLQMF host-filename
        [drive1] [path1] filename
        [/S:host-session-id] [/M or /V]
        [/D:database [/I:import-option or
                        /T:table-name]...]
```

- Authorizations

Authority	Privilege
None required	None required

- Description

The SQLQMF command is used to download files from the MVS (multiple virtual storage) or VM (virtual machine) host system. Subsequently, the data in these files can be imported to DB2/2 tables. Before you can use this command make sure the following tasks have taken place:

- Start Communication Manager programs
- Start DB2/2

● Log on to the host system (VM or MVS) where the data resides

drive is two-character (A:, B:, etc.) drive indicating where the command is to be found.

path is the directory containing the command to be executed.

host-filename is the name of the data file in the host system to be downloaded. In MVS, the name should conform to dataset naming convention: fully or partially qualified dataset name, or a partitioned dataset (PDS) with a member name. In VM, the name must have a filename, filetype, and filemode, separated by spaces. If you omit filetype or filemode, the default is 'DATA A'.

drive1 is the letter of the drive where the data of the host file is downloaded to.

path1 is the directory and the filename where the data of the host file is stored.

filename is the name of the file in the workstation where the data of the host file is received. Depending on the type of information, **SQLQMF** will automatically add a file extension. The possible file extensions are:

.DEL   Data is in ASCII delimited format to be used by import command.
.COL   Table definition in ASCII text format.
.CRE   **CREATE TABLE** statements in ASCII text.
.IML   A file containing messages generated during the downloading of the data in the host files.
.TMP   A temporary file used by **SQLQMF** during the downloading; it is erased after the transfer of the data is completed.

/S:*host-session-id*
This option is used to specify a host session ID and consists of one character, such as A, B, or C. This identification is shown on the window of the host session. If none is specified, the **SQLQMF** assumes character A.

/M
This option is used to specify the MVS system. This is the default value.

/V
This option is used to specify the VM system.

/D:*database*
This option is used to specify a database name to which the host data is written. If this option is omitted, the data is stored in an ASCII delimited file.

/I:*import-option*
This option is used if the data is written to a database.

import-option is one of the following:

R   Replace data in all rows of an existing table
C   Create a table
A   Add data to an existing table
O   Overlay data to an existing table

/T:*table-name*
This option is used to specify the name of a table to which data is written.

table-name is the name of a table, and if it is not specified, the workstation filename is used.

- Example

The following command is used to download a file called 'CLIENTS.HOST.B' from MVS. This data is imported to the CLIENTS table of the CUSTOMER database.

```
SQLQMF     'CLIENTS.HOST.B'            \
              C:\CLIENTS    /S:B   /M  \
        D:\CUSTOMER   /I:C /T:CLIENTS
```

◘ SQLSAMPL—create sample database

- General format

```
[drive] [path] SQLSAMPL [drive1]
```

- Authorizations

Authority	Privilege
SYSADM	None required

- Description

The **SQLSAMPL** command creates a sample database with the following tables: ORG, STAFF, and STAFFG.

drive is two-character (A:, B:, etc.) drive indicating where the **SQLSAMPL** command is to be found.

path is the directory containing the **SQLSAMPL** command to be executed.

drive1 is to name the drive where the database is to be created. If you omit this parameter, the database is created in the drive where the **SQLLIB** subdirectory is found.

◻ SQLVCFG—view configuration

- General format

```
[drive] [path] SQLVCFG
```

- Authorizations

Authority	Privilege
None required	None required

- Description

The **SQLVCFG** command is used to view the names of all the return workstations granted access to the DB2/2 program on the LAN server. This command also shows the node type of each workstation. The information is sent to the standard output device of the LAN server.

drive is a two-character (A:, B:, etc.) drive indicating where the **SQLVCFG** command is to be found.

path is the directory containing the **SQLVCFG** command to be executed.

◻ STARTDBM—start DB2/2

● General format

```
[drive] [path] STARTDBM
```

● Authorizations

Authority	Privilege
None required	None required

● Description

The **STARTDBM** command starts the DB2/2 and also initiates the necessary resources. Before you can precompile a program or build a package to a particular database, the database must be running.

drive is a two-character (A:, B:, etc.) drive indicating where the **STARTDBM** command is to be found.

path is the directory containing the STARTDBM command to be executed.

◻ STOPDBM—stop DB2/2

● General format

```
[drive] [path] STOPDBM
```

● Authorizations

Authority	Privilege
None required	None required

● Description

The **STOPDBM** command is used to stop DB2/2 and release all the resources. DB2/2 will not stop if there is any programs connected to the database.

drive is a two-character (A:, B:, etc.) drive indicating where the STOPDBM command is to be found.

path is the directory containing the STOPDBM command to be executed.

5.2 DOS and Windows Database Client Application Enabler Commands

This section gives the syntax and a brief description of a few commonly used commands to access DOS or Windows clients—SQLLOGN2, STARTDRQ, STOPDRQ, and SQLLOGF2—used. These commands are entered at the DOS command line or batch file (.BAT). With Windows, these commands must be issued before entering the Windows environment.

◘ SQLLOGN2—log on DOS or Windows database client

● General format

```
SQLLOGN2 [userid [/P=password or *]]
```

● Authorizations

Authority	Privilege
None required	None required

● Description

The **SQLLOGN2** command is used to log on to DB2/2 DOS or Windows database client.

userid is used to specify a valid user ID on the DOS or Windows database client.

There are a few restrictions on this user ID:

- It must be unique and no longer than eight characters.
- It must not start with IBM, SQL, or SYS keywords.
- It cannot end with the $ character.

/P=*password*
This parameter is used to enter the password belonging to the user ID.

password is made up of 4 to 8 characters.

◘ STARTDRQ—Start DOS or Windows database client

- General format

```
STARTDRQ
```

- Authorizations

Authority	Privilege
None required	None required

- Description

The **STARTDRO** command is used to start a DOS or Windows database client.

◘ STOPDRQ—stop DOS or Windows database client

- General format

```
STOPDRQ
```

- Authorizations

Authority	Privilege
None required	None required

- Description

  The **STOPDRQ** command is used to stop a DOS or Windows database client.

◻ SQLLOGF2—log off DOS or Windows database client

- General format

```
SQLLOGF2
```

- Authorizations

Authority	Privilege
None required	None required

- Description

  The **SQLLOGF2** command is used to log off a DB2/2 DOS or Windows database client.

5.3 DBM Command Line Processor Commands

The DBM command is an interface between the DB2/2 and OS/2 command line or the batch file (.CMD). This command is used to maintain the operation of the database manager. Some of the operations you can perform are

- Maintain DB/2 databases
- Issue SQL statement
- Request help information

The general format of DBM is

```
[drive] [path] DBM [ -C or -O or -R ([path] filename) ]...
           <command or statement> [\]]
                     or
[drive] [path] DBM ? [?phrase or ?message_number]
```

drive is a two-character (A:, B:, etc.) drive indicating where the DBM command is to be found.

path is the directory containing the DBM command to be executed.

? means to contain general help information.

?phrase is used to obtain help information on a specific command: SQL statement or topic.

?message_number is used to obtain a description of a specific message number. A message number is prefixed with one of the following three-character codes:

- DBA—messages for the database administrator
- DBM—DB2/2 messages
- SQL—SQL messages
- QRW—query manager message

-C means to disallow a change or insert to the database to take effect unless a **DBM COMMIT** is issued. You can set the automatic commit option in an environment variable in your CONFIG.SYS file. When automatic commit is enabled, all changes or insertions to the database become permanent.

-O means to direct messages or report data to a standard device instead of to the workstation screen.

-R is used to write a report to a file.

path is the drive letter and directory name of the file to which the report is written.

filename is the name of the file to which the report is written.

.ext is the extension of the file, if any.

command is used to specify the DBM command you want to execute. All the commands are listed and explained in this chapter.

statement is used to specify the SQL statements. These statement are discussed in Chap. 6.

\ is the line continuation character. It is used when a DBM command or SQL statement is long and you want to type it in more than one line.

When DBM reads \ as the last character of a line; it automatically displays a new prompt (=>), and you can enter more characters to complete a command or statement.

This section describes all the commands used to manage the databases. The SQL statements are discussed Chap. 6.

◘ BACKUP DATABASE-copy local database

● General format

```
DBM BACKUP DATABASE database-name [ALL or CHANGES]
               TO drive
```

● Authorizations

Authority	Privilege
SYSADM or DBADM	None required

● Description

The **BACKUP DATABASE** command is used to make a backup copy of the local database. For the first time the entire database must be copied to the files. In subsequent times, you back up only the files that have changed since the last backup. This way you don't have to copy the database each time.

database-name is the alias of the database to be backed up.

ALL means to back up the entire database. This is the default value.

CHANGES means to copy the files that have changed since the last backup of the database.

drive is used to specify the drive letter where the backup files are stored. (Enter one character only, without the colon.)

- Example

In the following command, the CLIENTS database is backed up in drive A.

```
BACKUP DATABASE CLIENTS TO A
```

◘ BIND—bind the application program to the database

- General format

```
BIND filename TO DATABASE database-name
    [USING [MESSAGES msgfile] [ISOLATION isolation]]
    [BLOCKING blocking]
    [DATETIME format]
    [GRANT <PUBLIC or authority-id>]
```

- Authorizations

Authority	Privilege
SYSADM or DBADM BIND	BINDADD

- Description

The **BIND** command takes a bind created by the precompiler and generates a package which is used to access DB2/2 data during the execution of a program. During a bind processing, the following happens:

- Validation of the rules, structure, and syntax of SQL statements used in a program
- Verification of authority to access DB2/2 data
- Choice of an access path to data
- Creation of a package which is used to allocate resources during program execution

filename is used to specify the name of the bind file, previously generated when the application program was precompiled. This file can also consist of a list of bind files. If it is a list file, it must be preceded

by an "at" character (@). The bind files are separated by a plus sign (+).
The extension of the bind file or list file is .BND.

database-name is used to name the alias of the database to which an
application program is bound.

MESSAGES *msgfile*
This option is used to specify a destination to which warning or error
messages are written.

msgfile can be any one of the following:

- A name of a file
- LPT1 for a printer
- CON for the console
- NUL to suppress messages.

ISOLATION *isolation*
This option is used to specify the isolation level. This tells DB2/2 how
to isolate data in the database from other processing which may occur
while the application is accessing the database.

isolation is one of the following:

    RR—repeatable read
    CS—cursor stability
    UR—uncommitted read

BLOCKING *blocking*
This option is used to specify the type of record blocking and it tells
how to deal with ambiguous cursors.

  blocking is one of the following:

- ALL means to block for
    - FETCH-only cursors
    - Cursors not specified as **FOR UPDATE OF**
    - Cursors for which there are no static **DELETE WHERE
      CURRENT OF** statements
    - Any ambiguous cursors are treated as FETCH-only.

- UNAMBIG means to block for
  - FETCH-only cursors
  - Cursors not specified as **FOR UPDATE OF**
  - Cursors that do not have static **DELETE WHERE CURRENT OF** statements
  - Cursors that do not have dynamic statements
  - Any ambiguous cursors are treated as UPDATE-only.

- NO means not to block any cursors. Any ambiguous cursors are treated as UPDATE-only.

The default is UNAMBIG.

DATETIME *format*
This option is used to specify the date and time formats used when binding a program.

format is a code listed in Figure 5.1.

GRANT <PUBLIC or *authority-id*>
This specifies who gets the privilege: individual users or all users.

PUBLIC means to grant the privilege to all users.

authorization-id is a user ID or group name. You can specify one or more IDs, and it must not include the user ID that is issuing the command.

- Example

In the following command, TIP.BND is a bind file. This file is generated by the precompiler. The CUSTOMER database is used to validate table and column names found in the SQL statements of the source program.

```
BIND TIP.BND TO DATABASE CUSTOMER
   MESSAGES=C:\TIP\ERROR.OUT
```

The MESSAGES option is used to write the messages during the bind process to C:\TIP\ERROR.OUT.

◻ CATALOG APPN NODE—write information to the node directory

● General format

```
CATALOG APPN NODE node-name
   [NETWORKID netid]
   REMOTE partner-lu
   [LOCAL local-lu]
   [MODE mode]
   [IN codepage]
   [WITH "comment-string"]
```

● Authorizations

Authority	Privilege
SYSADM	None required

● Description

The **CATALOG APPN** is used to add an entry to the node directory. An entry contains information about a remote workstation that uses APPN (Advanced Peer-to-Peer Network) communication protocols. This information is used by DB2/2 to connect an application program to a remote database cataloged in this node.

node-name is used to specify the name of the remote workstation to the catalog. This name is the same as the one used to catalog a database with the **CATALOG DATABASE** command. The node name must conform to DB2/2 naming conventions.

NETWORKID *netid*
This parameter is used to specify the SNA (Systems Network Architecture) network ID where the remote LU (logical unit) is to be found.

netid is a string no longer than eight characters and it must conform to SNA naming conventions.

REMOTE *partner-lu*
This required parameter is used to specify the SNA partner LU (logical unit) that is needed for connection.

partner-lu is an LU name of the remote node. The length of this name cannot exceed eight characters.

LOCAL *local-lu*
This option parameter is used to specify the alias of the SNA local LU that is used for connection.

local-lu is an LU name in the local node. The length of this name cannot exceed eight characters.

MODE *mode*
This paramater is used to specify the SNA transmission mode used in the connection.

node is the name of the node, and it must be longer than eight characters. If you omit this parameter, DB2/2 places the default value of eight blank characters.

codepage is used to specify the code page of the characters found in the comment string.

comment-string is used to describe the APPN node entry found in the node directory. It must be enclosed in quotes (").

● Example

The following command is used to catalog an APPN node called XYZNODE.

```
CATALOG APPN NODE XYZNODE
   REMOTE XYZLU
   WITH "Catalog APPN NODE XYZNODE"
```

◨ **CATALOG DATABASE—write information to the database directory**

● General format

```
CATALOG DATABASE database-name
   [AS alias]
   <ON drive or AT NODE nodename>
   [IN codepage] [WITH "comment-string"]
```

- Authorizations

Authority	Privilege
SYSADM	None required

- Description

The CATALOG DATABASE command is used to add information about a database into the database directory.

database-name is used to specify the name of the database being cataloged to the directory.

alias is used to specify an alternate name of the database being cataloged.

drive is used to specify the drive where the database being cataloged is found. This should consist of one character without the colon.

nodename is used to specify the name of the remote workstation where the database is found.

codepage is used to specify the code page of the characters found in the comment string.

comment-string is used to describe the entry found in the database directory. It must be enclosed in quotes (").

- Example

The following statement is used to catalog the CLIENTS database which resides in the NODEXYZ remote workstation.

```
CATALOG DATABASE CLIENTS AT NODE
  NODEXYZ WITH "CLIENTS database"
```

◻ CATALOG DCS DATABASE—write an entry to the DCS directory

- General format

```
CATALOG DCS DATABASE database-name
```

```
[AS tdb-name]
[AR dll-name]
[PARMS "parameter-string"]
[IN codepage]
[WITH "comment-string"]
```

- Authorizations

Authority	Privilege
SYSADM	None required

- Description

The CATALOG DCS DATABASE is used to write information about a host database to the Database Connection Services (DCS) directory. This catalog information is needed by a workstation to access the host database using the SAA Distributed Database Connection Series/2 facilities.

database-name is used to specify the alias of the database that is being cataloged.

tdb-name is used to specify the name of the database that is being cataloged.

dll-name is used to specify the name of the dynamic link library program to be used. It is one of the following:

SQLJRDR1	DRDA-1 database connections for Distributed Relational Database Architecture; this is the default program.
SQL_AR0	ASP-0 or OS/2 database connections
SQLESRVR	Local server

parameter-string is used to specify parameters used by the program named in the AR parameter. This is a string, enclosed in quotes, that contains the connection and operating environment information. The parameters that you can list in this string are

TPP	Transaction program prefix. This is a hex (hexidecimal) value that identifies the first byte of the transaction program name. The default is 07.

TPN   Transaction program name. This is a character string that is used as the name of the transaction program, run on the host.

MAP   SQLCODE mapping file. This is a character string to specify the name of the file that converts host SQL return codes to DCS return codes. It can be one of the following:

DCS0DSN   EE database and DB2 database
DCS1DSN   EE or DB2/2 database and DB2 database
DCS0ARI   EE database and SQL/DS database
DCS0QSQ   EE database and OS/400 database
DCS1QSQ   ES or DB2/2 database and OS/400 database

D Disconnect option; this is used to disconnect the host when -300xx is encountered.

V Verify option; this is used to verify a user ID and password before connecting th the host.

codepage is used to specify the code page of the characters found in the comment string.

comment-string is used to describe the entry found in the   DCS directory. It must be enclosed in quotes (").

◘ CATALOG NetBios NODE—write NetBios (Network Basic Input/Output System) information to the node directory

- General format

```
CATALOG NetBios NODE nodename
   REMOTE partner-lu
   ADAPTER number
   [IN codepage]
   [WITH "comment-string"]
```

- Authorizations

Authority	Privilege
SYSADM	None required

● Description

The **CATALOG NetBios NODE** command is used to write information to the node directory about a remote workstation that uses NetBios (a communication protocol). DB2/2 reads this information from the node directory to connect an application to a remote database cataloged on this node.

nodename is used to specify the node name of the workstation. This name should be the same as the one used when the workstation was cataloged.

partner-lu is used to specify the name of a workstation to which you are trying to connect. This name cannot be longer than eight characters.

number is used to specify the LAN adapter number, which is 0 or 1.

codepage is used to specify the code page of the characters found in the comment string.

comment-string is used to describe the entry found in the DCS directory. It must be enclosed in quotes (").

● Example

The following command is used to catalog a remote workstation as a NetBios node.

```
CATALOG NetBios NODE XYZWKST       \
    REMOTE XYZWKST                \
                        ADAPTER 0 WITH "XYZ is a NetBios NODE"
```

◘ CATALOG APPC NODE—write information to the node directory

● General format

```
CATALOG APPC NODE node-name
    [NETWORKID netid]
    REMOTE partner-lu
    [LOCAL local-lu]
    [MODE mode]
    [IN codepage]
    [WITH "comment-string"]
```

● Authorizations

Authority	Privilege
SYSADM	None required

● Description

The **CATALOG APPC** is used to add an entry to the node directory. An entry contains information about a remote workstation that uses APPC communication protocols. This information is used by DB2/2 to connect an application program to a remote database cataloged in this node.

node-name is used to specify the name of the remote workstation to be cataloged. This name is the same as the one used to catalog a database with the CATALOG DATABASE command. The node name must conform to the DB2/2 naming conventions.

NETWORKID *netid*
This parameter is used to specify the SNA network ID where the remote LU is to be found.

netid is a string no longer than eight characters and must conform to SNA naming conventions.

REMOTE *partner-lu*
This required parameter is used to specify the SNA partner LU that is needed for connection.

partner-lu is an LU name of the remote node. The length of this name cannot exceed eight characters.

LOCAL *local-lu*
This option parameter is used to specify the alias of the SNA local LU that is used for connection.

local-lu is an LU name in the local node. The length of this name cannot exceed eight characters.

MODE *mode*
This paramater is used to specify the SNA transmission mode used in the connection.

node is the name of the node, and it must be longer than 8 characters. If you omit this parameter, DB2/2 places the default value of eight blank characters.

codepage is used to specify the code page of the characters found in the comment string.

comment-string is used to describe the APPC node entry found in the node directory. It must be enclosed in quotes (").

● Example

The following command is used to catalog an APPC node called XYZNODE.

```
CATALOG APPC NODE XYZNODE
   REMOTE XYZLU
   WITH "Catalog APPN NODE XYZNODE"
```

◘ CHANGE DATABASE COMMENT—modify comment in directory

● General format

```
CHANGE DATABASE database-name
   COMMENT [ON drive]
            [IN codepage]
   [WITH "comment-string"]
```

● Authorizations

Authority	Privilege
None required	None required

● Description

The CHANGE DATABASE COMMENT command is used to modify a comment in the database directory that is associated with a database.

database-name is used to specify the alias name of a database already cataloged and whose comment in the directory is to be changed.

drive is used to specify the drive where the database resides. It must contain one character without a colon (:).

codepage is used to specify the code page of the characters found in the comment string.

comment-string is used to describe any change in the comment entry found in the database directory. It must be enclosed in quotes (").

● Example

The following command is used to change the comment of the CLIENTS database.

```
CHANGE DATABASE CLIENTS COMMENT    \
          WITH "Test data loaded"
```

◘ CHANGE SQLISL—change isolation

● General format

```
CHANGE SQLIST TO isolation
```

● Authorizations

Authority	Privilege
SYSADM DBADM	None required

● Description

The CHANGE SQLISL is used to modify the method used by DB2/2 to isolate data accessed by a program while other processes are using the same database.

isolation is one of the following:

    RR—repeatable read
    CS—cursor stability
    UR—uncommitted read

◘ CREATE DATABASE—make a new database

- General format

```
CREATE DATABASE database-name
  [ON drive]
  [IN codepage]
  [WITH "comment-string"]
```

- Authorizations

Authority	Privilege
SYSADM	None required

- Description

The **CREATE DATABASE** is used to create a new database. At the same time the database is cataloged with an alias. As there is no way of specifying the alias in this command, the default is the same as the database specified in this command. To change the alias name, use the **CATALOG DATABASE** command. The creator of the database automatically recieves the **DBADM** authority and **CREATEAB** and **BINDADD** privileges.

database-name is used to specify the name of the database that you want to create. A database by this name should not already exist, and in this case no action is taken by DB2/2.

drive is used to specify the drive where the database should be created. It must contain one character without a colon (:).

codepage is used to specify the code page of the characters found in the comment string.

comment-string is used to describe an entry found in the database directory. It must be enclosed in quotes (").

- Example

The following example creates the CLIENTS database.

```
CREATE DATABASE CLIENTS
```

◘ DROP DATABASE—delete a Database

- General format

```
DROP DATABASE database-name
```

- Authorizations

Authority	Privilege
SYSADM	None required

- Description

The **DROP DATABASE** command is used to delete a database; all associated data files, user files, and database definitions are removed. DB2/2 uncatalogs the database from the database directory and the volume directory.

database-name is used to specify the name of the database you want to delete.

- Example

The following command deletes the CLIENTS database from the catalogs.

```
DROP DATABASE CLIENTS
```

◘ EXPORT—copy database table to file

- General format

```
EXPORT FROM database-name TO filename
    OF filetype
    [MODIFIED BY filet-mod]
    MESSAGES msgfile
    select-statement
```

- Authorizations

Authority	Privilege
SYSADM	CONTROL or
DBADM	SELECT for the chosen tables

● Description

The **EXPORT** command is used to copy the content of one or many tables to a file.

database-name is used to specify the alias of the database from which data is exported to a file.

filename is used to specify the name of the file to which data is written from the database.

filetype is used to specify the format of the output file. The types of files are

DEL   Delimited ASCII format. This file can be used by other database managers or file managers such as dBaseII, dBaseIII, BASIC, or IBM Personal Decision Series.

WSF   Worksheet format. This file can be used by programs such as Lotus 1-2-3 and Lotus Symphony.

IXF   DB2/2 format. This file can be used to import data to a DB2/2 database.

filet-mod is used when file type is DEL or WSF file. This parameter tells DB2/2 how to format data written to these files. For the DEL file, the following file type mode can be chosen:

COLDEL   Column delimeter. A character (e.g., ; and :) follows this keyword. This character placed between columns. The default is comma (,).

CHARDEL   Character string delimeter. A character (such as ', !, or ") follows this keyword. A pair of these characters is used to enclose character strings.

DECPT   Decimal point. A character follows this keyword. This character is used to enclose a character string. The default is period (.).

DECPLUSBLANK   Plus sign character. This option tells EXPORT to prefix positive decimal numbers with a blank space instead of a plus (+) character.

For WSF file format, *filemod* is used to select the generation output of the export file. The generations are

- First generation WSF file is Lotus 1-2-3/1 or 1-2-3/1A. This is the default.
- Second generation WSF file is Lotus Symphony/1.0.

msgfile is used to specify a file to which error or warning messages are directed. It can be any one of the following:

- A name of a file
- LPT1 for a printer
- CON for the console
- NUL to suppress messages.

select-statement is used to specify a **SELECT** statement that retrieves data from one or more tables. For more details on the **SELECT** statement, refer to Chap. 6.

- Example

The following **EXPORT** command exports data from the SALES tables of the CLENTS database. The data is written to a DB2/2 file called SALES.IXF. The error or warning messages are directed to SALES.MSG.

```
EXPORT FROM CLIENTS            \
   TO A:\SALES.IXF OF IXF      \
   MESSAGES SALES.MSG          \
   SELECT * FROM SALES
```

◘ GET AUTHORIZATIONS—retrieve authorization information

- General format

```
GET AUTHORIZATIONS
```

- Authorizations

Authority	Privilege
None required	None required

- Description

  The **GET AUTHORIZATIONS** command is used to obtain information on authority and privileges granted to a user.

◘ GET DATABASE CONFIGURATION—retrieve configuration for database

- General format

```
GET DATABASE CONFIGURATION FOR database-name
```

- Authorizations

Authority	Privilege
SYSADM or DBADM	None required

- Description

  The **GET DATABASE CONFIGURATION** is used to retrieve information about a database. Normally, the information is shown on the screen, but you can redirect it to a file by using the -R option (see examples).

- Example

  In the next example, the configuration data for CLIENTS database is written to the DBM.RPT file.

```
DBM -R GET DATABASE CONFIGURATION FOR    \
   CLIENTS
```

  In the next example, the information is written to CLIENTS.CFG.

◘ GET DATABASE MANAGER CONFIGURATION—retrieve parameter values

- General format

```
GET DATABASE MANAGER CONFIGURATION
```

- Authorizations

Authority	Privilege
SYSADM or DBADM	None required

- Description

The **GET DATABASE MANAGER CONFIGURATION** command is used to retrieve parameter values from the DB2/2 configuration file. Normally, this information is shown on the screen, but it can be written to a file (see examples).

- Example

In the following command, the parameter value from the DB2/2 configuration file is written to the DBM.RPT file.

```
DBM -R GET DATABASE MANAGER CONFIGURATION
```

In the next example, the information is written to the MANAGER.CFG file.

```
DBM _R(MANAGER.CFG) GET DATABASE          \
   MANAGER CONFIGURATION
```

◘ GET DATABASE STATUS—retrieve information about the database current activity

- General format

```
GET DATABASE STATUS [FOR DATABASE database-name]
         [ON drive]
```

- Authorizations

Authority	Privilege
SYSADM or DBADM	None required

● Description

The GET DATABASE STATUS command is used to retrieve from DB2/2 a summary of the activities currently taking place against either one specific database or all the databases. Normally, the report goes to the screen; you can also redirect it to a file (see example).

database-name is used to specify the alias of the database for which the status report is needed.

drive is used to specify the drive letter where the database is found and for which you want the status information. It must contain one character without a colon (:).

● Example

In the following examples, the status report about activities of CLIENTS database is written to the DBM.RPT file.

```
DBM -R GET DATABASE STATUS FOR DATABASE CLIENTS
```

In the next command, the information is written to the STATUS.RPT file.

```
DBM -R(STATUS.RPT) GET DATABASE STATUS FOR DATABASE \
     CLIENTS
```

◘ GET SYSTEM STATUS—retrieve information about the system

● General format

```
GET SYSTEM STATUS
```

● Authorizations

Authority	Privilege
SYSADM or DBADM	None required

● Description

The **GET DATABASE STATUS** command is used to obtain information about the status. It gives the following:

- Current normalized time
- Time zone displacement
- Product name
- Component identification
- Release level
- Corrective service level

Normally, the report goes to the screen; you can also redirect it to a file (see example).

● Example

In the following examples, the system information is written to the DBM.RPT file.

```
DBM -R GET SYSTEM STATUS
```

In the next command, the information is written to the SYSZYX.RPT file.

```
DBM -R(SYSZYX.RPT) GET SYSTEM STATUS
```

◘ GET USER STATUS FOR DATABASE—get user information

● General format

```
GET USER STATUS FOR DATABASE database-name
```

● Authorizations

Authority	Privilege
None required	None required

● Description

The **GET STATUS FOR DATABASE** command extracts information about all users connected to a particular database. Normally, the report goes to the screen; you can also redirect it to a file (see example).

database-name is used to specify a name or alias of a database for which you want data to be collected and reported.

● **Example**

In the following examples, the user information connected to CLIENTS database is written to the DBM.RPT file.

```
DBM -R GET USER STATUS FOR DATABASE CLIENTS
```

In the next command, the information is written to the USERS.RPT file.

```
DBM -R(USERS.RPT) GET USER STATUS FOR DATABASE CLIENTS
```

◻ IMPORT—import file to database table

● General format

```
IMPORT To database FROM filename OF filetype
   [MODIFIED BY filet-mod]
   <INSERT or
    INSERT_UPDATE or
    REPLACE or
    CREATE or
    REPLACE_CREATE>
   INTO tblname
   MESSAGES msgfile
```

● Authorizations

Authority	Privilege
SYSADM	CONTROL
DBADM	INSERT
	SELECT
	CREATETAB

● Description

The **IMPORT** command is used to copy the content of a file to one table or many tables.

database-name is used to specify the alias of the database to which data is imported from a file.

filename is used to specify the name of the file from which data is written to the database.

filetype is used to specify the format of the input file. The types of files are

DEL   Delimited ASCII format. This file can be used by other database managers or file managers such as dBaseII, dBaseIII, BASIC, or IBM Personal Decision Series.

WSF   Worksheet format. This file can be used by programs such as: Lotus 1-2-3 and Lotus Symphony.

IXF   DB2/2 format. This file can be used to import data to a DB2/2 database.

filet-mod is used when file type is DEL or WSF file. This parameter tells DB2/2 how to format data written to these files. For DEL file format, the following file type mode can be chosen:

COLDEL   Column delimeter. A character (e.g., ; and :) follows this keyword. This character is placed between columns. The default is comma (,).

CHARDEL   Character string delimeter. A character (e.g., ', !, or ") follows this keyword. A pair of these characters is used to enclose character strings.

DECPT   Decimal point. A character follows this keyword. This character is used to enclose a character string. The default is a period (.).

DECPLUSBLANK   Plus sign character. This option tells IMPORT to prefix positive decimal numbers with a blank space instead of a plus (+) character.

For WSF file format, *filemod* is used to select the generation output of the export file. The generations are

- First generation WSF file is Lotus 1-2-3/1 or 1-2-3/1A. This is the default.
- Second generation WSF file is Lotus Symphony/1.0.

INSERT means to add data to a table without changing the existing rows.

INSERT_UPDATE means to add data to the table or update rows with matching primary keys.

REPLACE means to remove all existing rows and add the imported data.

CREATE means to create a new table and import the data.

REPLACE_CREATE means to delete the content of the table, if it exists, and then import the data to the table.

tblname is the name of the table to which the data is imported.

msgfile is used to specify a file to which error or warning messages are directed. It can be any one of the following:

- A name of a file
- LPT1 for a printer
- CON for the console
- NUL to suppress messages

- Example

The following **IMPORT** command imports data to the SALES tables of the CLENTS database. The data is written from a DB2/2 file called SALES.IXF. The error or warning messages are directed to SALES.MSG.

```
IMPORT TO CLIENTS                    \
   FROM A:\SALES.IXF OF IXF      \
                   INTO SALES     \
   MESSAGES SALES.MSG
```

◘ INVOKE PROCEDURE—allow execution of procedure

- General format

```
INVOKE program
  [USING server-input-data]
```

- Authorizations

Authority	Privilege
None required	CONNECT

- Description

The **INVOKE PROCEDURE** command is used to give permission to an application on a database client to execute a procedure or function found in the database server.

program is used to specify the function in the dynamic link library (DLL) or a REXX procedure to be executed. This parameter may include a directory to locate the function or procedure, or the path may be listed in the **PATH** or **LIBPATH** in the CONFIG.SYS.

server-input-data is used to pass any argument to the procedure that is being executed and stored on the database server.

◼ LIST DATABASE DIRECTORY—get items from the system database directory

- General format

```
LIST DATABSE DIRECTORY
  [ON drive]
```

- Authorizations

Authority	Privilege
None required	None required

- Description

The **LIST DATABASE DIRECTORY** command is used to obtain the information about each database defined in DB2/2.

drive is used to specify the drive where the database directory is found. It is one character without a colon (:).

◻ LIST DCS DIRECTORY—get the content of the DCS directory

- General format

```
LIST DCS DIRECTORY
```

- Authorizations

Authority	Privilege
None required	None required

- Description

The **LIST DCS DIRECTORY** command is used to get the content of the DCS directory. This command shows a list of host databases that a workstation can access. Normally, the information goes to the screen, but if needed, it can be directed to a file (see example).

- Example

In the following example, the content of the DCS directory is written to the default DBM.RPT file.

```
DBM LIST DCS DIRECTORY
```

In the next command, the data from the DCS directory goes to a specified DCSXS1.RPT file

```
DBM -R(DCSXS1.RPT) LIST DCS DIRECTORY
```

◻ LIST NODE DIRECTORY—get the content of the node directory

- General format

```
LIST NODE DIRECTORY
```

- Authorizations

Authority	Privilege
None required	None required

● Description

The **LIST NODE DIRECTORY** command is used to get the content of the node directory. The node types may be APPC, APPN, or NetBios. Normally, the information goes to the screen, but if needed, it can be directed to a file (see example).

● Example

In the following example, the content of the node directory is written to the DBM.RPT.

```
DBM -R LIST NODE DIRECTORY
```

In the next command, the content of the node directory is written to the NODEXYZ.RPT file

```
DBM -R(NODEXYZ.RPT) NODE DIRECTORY
```

◘ MIGRATE DATABASE—migrate from OS/2 databases to DB2/2 databases

● General format

```
MIGRATE DATABASE database
```

● Authorizations

Authority	Privilege
None required	None required

● Description

The **MIGRATE DATABASE** command is used to move a database from EE 1.3 or ES 1.0 to DB2/2.

database is used to specify the alias of the database to be migrated to DB2/2.

● Example

The following command migrates the CLIENTS database.

```
MIGRATE DATABASE CLIENTS
```

◻ REORG TABLE—reorganize Table

● General format

```
REORG TABLE table IN database
   [INDEX index-name]
   USE path]
```

● Authorizations

Authority   Privilege

SYSADM   CONTROL
DBADM

● Description

The **REORG TABLE** command is used to improve the efficiency of a DB2/2 table. This command reconstructs the rows such that the data is compact and not fragmented.

table is used to specify the name of the table that needs to be reorganized. This table can belong to either a local or a remote database.

database is used to specify the alias of the database where the table to be organized is defined.

index-name is used to specify the index that is used by the table to be reorganized.

path is used to specify a path and directory that is used by DB2/2 to create temporary files.

◨ REORGCHK—determine whether reorganization is needed

- General format

```
REORCHK database [UPDATE STATISTICS or
                  CURRENT STATISTICS]
   [ON TABLE <USER or
                 SYSTEM or
                 ALL or
                 table>
```

- Authorizations

Authority	Privilege
SYSADM or DBADM	CONTROL

- Description

The **REORGCHK** command is used to check whether a database needs reorganization.

database is used to specify the alias of a database that is to be checked for reorganization. The output goes to the screen, but, if required, you can direct to an output file (see example).

UPDATE STATISTICS means to issue the **RUNSTATS** command to update the statistical information. The statistic is used to determine whether a **REORG** command must be issued. This is the default.

CURRENT STATISTICS means to use the current statistics to determine whether the tables need to be reorganized.

USER means to check the tables created by the users. This is the default.

SYSTEM means to check the tables created for system maintenance, such as catalog and tables.

ALL means to check all tables.

table is used to specify the name of a table to be checked.

- Example

The following command is used to check whether all users of the PRESCRIBER database need reorganization. The output goes to the DBM.RPT.

```
DBM -R REORGCHK PRESCRIBER
```

In the next command, the output information is written to the REORPRES.RPT file.

```
DBM -R(REORPRES.RPT) REORGCHK PRESCRIBER
```

◘ RESET DATABASE CONFIGURATION—set parameter to system defaults

- General format

```
RESET DATABASE MANAGER CONFIGURATION FOR database
```

- Authorizations

Authority	Privilege
SYSADM	None required

- Description

The **RESET DATABASE MANAGER CONFIGURATION** command is issued to set the parameters in the configuration file to default values used when the system was configured.

database is used to specify the alias of the database for which the configuration parameters are reset.

The parameters are

Keywords	Description
AGENTHEAP	Application agent heap
APPLHEAPSZ	Default application heap

BUFFPAGE	Buffer pool
DBHEAP	Database heap
DBATTR	Database attribute
INDEXREC	When to recreate invalid indexes; one possible value is **SYSTEM, ACCESS,** or **RESTART**
DLCHKTIME	Time interval
LOCKLIST	Storage for lock list
LOGFILSIZ	Storage for log files
LOGPRIMARY	Number of primary log files
LOGSECOND	Number of secondary log files
MAXAPPLS	Maximum number of application programs connected
MAXFILOP	Maximum number of database files that an application program can have open
MAXLOCKS	Percentage of lock list a program can use
MAXTOTFILOP	Number of user or database files opened by an application program
NEWLOGPATH	Alternate path to the recovery log files

◙ RESET DATABASE CONFIGURATION—set parameter to system defaults

● General format

```
RESET DATABASE MANAGER CONFIGURATION
```

● Authorizations

Authority	Privilege
SYSADM	None required

● Description

The **RESET DATABASE CONFIGURATION** command is used to set the parameters in the DB2/2 configuration to the defaults values shipped with the product. The parameters are

COMHEAPSZ	Size of the communications heap
NUMRC	Maximum number of remote connections active at one time to or from this workstation
SHEAPTHRES	Amount of memory available for sorts, in 4k bytes

	pages
INDEXREC	Invalid indexes will be created and will be either ACCESS or RESTART
RQRIOBLK	Storage allocated from communication heap to the I/O block on the database client, in number of segments
RSHEAPSZ	The size of the remote data services heap, in segments
SQLENSEG	Maximum amount of shared storage, in segments
SVRIOBLK	Amount of storage allocated from the communication heap to the I/O block on the database server, in kilobyte segment
NNAME	The workstation name

◘ RESTART DATABASE—restart from uncommitted state

- General format

```
RESTART DATABASE database
```

- Authorizations

Authority	**Privilege**
None required	None required

- Description

The **RESTART DATABASE** command is used to restart a database that is in an uncommitted state. After you issue this command, a reconnect to the database is necessary.

◘ RESTORE DATABASE—rebuild a damaged database

- General format

```
RESTORE DATABASE database FROM backup-drive
   [To restore-drive]
   [WITHOUT ROLLING FORWARD]
```

- Authorizations

Authority	Privilege
SYSADM	None required

- Description

The **RESTORE DATABASE** command is used to rebuild a database from a copy previously created by the **BACKUP DATABASE** command. This operation is needed if a local database is corrupted or damaged; the restored database is in the same state as when the previous backup was done.

database is an alias of the database to be restored.

backup-drive is used to specify the drive where the backup files exist.

restore-drive is used to specify the drive where the database is restored.

WITHOUT ROLLING FORWARD means not to place the database into a roll-forward pending state after successfully restoring the database. To remove a roll-forward pending state, issue a **ROLLFORWARD DATABASE** command before it can be used.

ROLLFORWARD DATABASE—recover from last backup state

- General format

```
ROOLFORWARD DATABASE database
   [TO <isotime or END OF LOGS> [AND STOP] or
    STOP or
                QUERY STATUS]
```

- Authorizations

Authority	Privilege
SYSADM	None required

- Description

The **ROLLFORWARD DATABASE** command is used after a database is restored. After a successful restoration the database is in the roll-forward pending state. This command recovers a database from its last backup state. Also, all the transactions processed since the backup are reapplied.

database is used to specify the alias of the database.

isotime is used to specify the point to which all committed transactions are to be rolled forward. The format of this parameter is the timestamp (yyyy-mmm-ddd.hh.mm.ss.nnnnnn).

END OF LOGS means to apply all committed transactions from all online archive log files. These files are listed in the logpath directory.

AND STOP means to roll back any incomplete transactions, turn off the roll-forward pending state of the database, and allow access to the database.

STOP means to roll back any incomplete transactions and allow access to the database after the roll-forward process is completed.

QUERY STATUS is used to obtain the following information about the roll-forward state:

- Next archive log file
- Log files processed
- Last committed transactions

◘ RUNSTATS—update statics about tables and indexes

- General format

```
RUNSTATS ON TABLE table
   [AND INDEXES ALL or
               USING INDEXES ALL or
               FOR INDEXES ALL]
   [SHRLEVEL] [REFERENCE or CHANGE]
```

- Authorizations

Authority	Privilege
SYSADM or DBADM	CONTROL

- Description

The **RUNSTATS** command is used to update statistical information on tables and indexes. The affected statistics are

- Number of records
- Number of pages
- Average record length

This information is used by DB2/2 to determine the optimal access path to the database.

table is used to specify the name of the table for which statistical information is to be updated.

AND INDEXES ALL means to update information for both tables and indexes.

USING INDEXES ALL means to update information for indexes only.

FOR INDEXES ALL means to update information for the indexes only.

SHRLEVEL is used to specify the level of user access at the time the information is gathered.

REFERENCE allows other users to have read-only access to the tables at the time statistics are collected.

CHANGE allows other users to have read or write access to the table at the time statistics are gathered.

◻ START DATABASE MANAGER—start running DB2/2

- General format

```
START DATABASE MANAGER
              or
STARTDBM
```

- Authorizations

Authority	Privilege
None required	None required

- Description

The **START DATABASE MANAGER** or **STARTDBM** command starts the DB2/2 and allocates the necessary resources. You have to issue this command before you can connect to a database, precompile a program, or bind a package to a table or database.

◘ START USING DATABASE—connect to a database

- General format

```
START USING DATABASE database
   [IN SHARED MODE or
    IN EXCLUSIVE]
```

- Authorizations

Authority	Privilege
SYSADM or DBADM	CONNECT

- Description

The **START USING DATABASE** command is used to connect to a database. It performs the same function as the **CONNECT** command.

database is used to specify the alias of the database that you want to connect.

IN SHARED MODE means that other users can access the database while you are using it. This is the default.

IN EXCLUSIVE means that you have the exclusive use of the database.

◧ STOP DATABASE MANAGER—stop DB2/2

- General format

```
STOP DATABASE MANAGER
          or
STOPDBM
```

- Authorizations

Authority	Privilege
None required	None required

- Description

The **STOP DATABASE MANAGER** or **STOPDBM** stops DB2/2 on a workstation. It also releases all the resources needed by DB2/2. DB2/2 cannot be stopped if there is any application program connected to the databases of your workstation.

◧ STOP USING DATABASE—disconnect from database

- General format

```
STOP USING DATABASE
```

- Authorizations

Authority	Privilege
None required	None required

- Description

The **STOP USING DATABASE** command is used to disconnect a user from a database. This command is the same as the **CONNECT RESET** command.

◧ UNCATALOG DATABASE—remove entry from system database directory

- General format

```
UNCATALOG DATABASE database
```

- Authorizations

Authority	Privilege
SYSADM	None required

- Description

The **UNCATALOG DATABASE** command is used to delete an entry from the database directory. This entry, previously entered using the **CATALOG DATABASE** command, is either indirect or remote database.

database is the alias of the database to be uncataloged.

◘ UNCATALOG DCS DATABASE—remove entry from DCS directory

- General format

```
UNCATALOG DCS DATABASE database
```

- Authorizations

Authority	Privilege
None required	None required

- Description

The **UNCATALOG DCS DATABASE** command is used to delete an entry from the Database Connection Services (DCS) directory. This entry, previously entered using the **CATALOG DCS DATABASE** command, is about a host database that a workstation can access using the DDCS/2 software.

database is the alias of the database to be uncataloged.

◼ UNCATALOG NODE—remove entry from node directory

- General format

```
UNCATALOG NODE
```

- Authorizations

Authority	Privilege
SYSADM	None required

- Description

The **UNCATALOG NODE** command is used to delete an entry from
the node directory. This entry was previously added to the directory by
the following commands:

- CATALOG NODE or CATALOG APPC NODE
- CATALOG APPN NODE
- CATALOG NetBios NODE

◼ UPDATE DATABASE CONFIGURATION—change parameters in the configuration file

- General format

```
UPDATE DATABASE CONFIGURATION FOR database
   USING <configuration-keyword value>...
```

- Authorizations

Authority	Privilege
SYSADM	None required

- Description

The **UPDATE DATABASE CONFIGURATION** command is used to
change parameters in the configuration file of a database.

database is used to specify to the alias of a database for which the
configuration is to be updated.

configuration-keyword is used to specify the parameter name for which a *value* is also entered. You can enter one or many pairs of configuration keywords and their associated values. The keywords are

Keywords	Description
AGENTHEAP	Application agent heap
APPLHEAPSZ	Default application heap
BUFFPAGE	Buffer pool
DBHEAP	Database heap
DBATTR	Database attribute
INDEXREC	When to re-create invalid indexes; one possible value is SYSTEM, ACCESS, or RESTART
DLCHKTIME	Time interval
LOCKLIST	Storage for lock list
LOGFILSIZ	Storage for log files
LOGPRIMARY	Number of primary log files
LOGSECOND	Number of secondary log files
MAXAPPLS	Maximum number of application programs connected
MAXFILOP	Maximum number of database files that an application program can have open
MAXLOCKS	Percentage of lock list a program can use
MAXTOTFILOP	Number of users or database files opened by an application program
NEWLOGPATH	Alternate path to the recovery log files

◘ UPDATE DATABASE MANAGER CONFIGURATION—change DB2/2 parameters in the configuration file

● General format

```
UPDATE DATABASE MANAGER CONFIGURATION
   USING <configuration-keyword value>...
```

● Authorizations

Authority	Privilege
SYSADM	None required

● Description

The **UPDATE DATABASE MANAGER CONFIGURATION** command is used to change parameters in the configuration file of DB2/2.

configuration-keyword is used to specify the parameter name for which a *value* is also entered. You can enter one or many pairs of configuration keyword and associated value. The keywords are

Keywords	Description
COMHEAPSZ	Size of the communications heap
NUMRC	Maximum number of remote connection active at one time to or from this workstation
SHEAPTHRES	Amount of memory available for sorts, in 4kbyte pages
INDEXREC	Invalid indexes will be created and will be either ACCESS or RESTART
RQRIOBLK	Storage allocated from communication heap to the I/O block on the database client, in number of segments
RSHEAPSZ	The size of the Remote Data Services heap, in segments
SQLENSEG	Maximum amount of shared storage, in segments
SVRIOBLK	Amount of storage allocated from the communication heap to the I/O block on the database server, in kilobyte segment
NNAME	The workstation name

Structured Query Language (SQL)

This chapter is a reference guide for programmers using SQL (Structured Query Language). SQL is a language for managing data in a relational database such as DB2/2, Sybase, or Oracle. Like any computer language, it has elements such as operators, expressions, and data types. It has a rich collection of statements to define and manipulate data in a database. Also, it is available with many commonly used functions.

The subjects covered here are:

- Language Elements
- SQL Statements
- Functions
- Structures

For each statement and function, this chapter provides the syntax and a description of the function and its parameters. In some cases you will also find examples of how the functions use these parameters.

6.1 Language Elements

Before you can use SQL statements against a database, you must know the basic elements of the language.

Characters and tokens

Statements are made up of a sequence of characters. The following is a list of characters recognized as valid in SQL.

- Lower- and uppercase letters
  a b c d e f g h i j k l m n o p q r s t u v w x y z
  A B C D E F G H I J K L M N O P Q R S T U V W X Y Z
- Decimal digits
  0 1 2 3 4 5 6 7 8 9
- Special characters
  # @ $
- Space character

A sequence of these characters is called a *token*. Many tokens, separated by spaces, placed according to the following syntax rules make a statement. There are two kinds of tokens: ordinary and delimiter. An *ordinary token* is one of the following:
- Numeric constant
- Ordinary identifier
- Host identifier
- Keyword

A *delimeter token* is a string constant, an delimited identifier, or an operator.

Comments

You can place comments in a static SQL statement. A comment is introduced with two consecutive hyphens (--). The following SQL statement is an example of how to include comments:

```
EXEC SQL
   CLOSE BRANCH_C -- Close the cursor
END-EXEC
```

You can add a comment within a statement wherever there is a space, except between EXEC and SQL or within a token delimiter. A comment terminates when the end of the line is reached.

Identifiers

An *identifier* is a series of characters used to form a name. There are two kinds of identifiers: SQL identifier and host identifier.

SQL identifiers are further divided into two types: ordinary identifiers and delimited identifiers.

- An *ordinary identifier* is made up of letters, digits, and underscore characters; for example,

```
RED_003
```

  Such a name should always start with a letter, and all letters with it should be uppercase. Also, it should not be the same as a SQL reserved word.

- A *delimited identifier* is made up of one or more letters, digits, and underscore characters, all enclosed with a pair of quotes ("). An ordinary identifier, in the form of a delimited identifier, can be a SQL reserved word or consist of lowercase characters. The following are examples of a delimited identifier:

```
"Monthly rate"  "MONTHLY_RATE" "Monthly_rate"
```

The length of SQL identifiers depends on the maximum length for long or short names. For short names the maximum length is 8 bytes; for long names, 18 bytes.

A *host identifier* is a name defined in a program used with SQL statements. These names, which could be constants or variables, follow the rules of the language used with SQL statements. The maximum length for host variable names is 30 characters, and the names should not start with SQL.

Authorization ID

An *authorization ID* is a user name that is explicitly or implicitly used before the names of tables, views, and indexes. The maximum length of this name is eight characters. It applies to every SQL statement. It is implicitly used when binding an application program and the user name is logged at the time of binding. In the interactive mode the authorization ID must be explicitly added before data objects. In the example,

```
DROP TABLE SMITH.CUSTOMER
```

the statement drops a table called **CUSTOMER** and the authorization ID is **SMITH**.

The authorization ID must not be confused with the authorization name used in the **GRANT** or **REVOKE** statement. In fact, it is incorrect to have the authorization ID and the authorization name the same in **GRANT** and **REVOKE** statements; for example,

```
GRANT TABLE SMITH.CUSTOMER TO SMITH
```

However, it is correct to specify

```
GRANT TABLE SMITH.CUSTOMER TO GREENE
```

Data types

Basically, SQL is used to manipulate pieces of data, and there are some very specific types of data that SQL statements are designed to handle. These data types are integer, floating-point, decimal, character string, graphic string, data, time, and timestamp. These data types are manifest as values that found constants, columns, host variables, functions, expressions, and special registers.

Each data type has a null value, and it is specified with the keyword NULL when creating the columns of a table in a database. This does not mean that if a column is defined to contain numeric values, the null value is zero; or, does it mean spaces if a column is defined to hold character string. This null value is a special value, simply meaning that the value is unknown and no mathematical operations are performed on such a field. On the other hand, if a column is defined with NOT NULL, this means that when a row is added to the database, the value cannot be a null value.

Now, let's look at the different data types of SQL:

INTEGER or INT define data to hold a large binary integer. The range of values is -2147483648 to + +2147483647.

SMALLINT defines data used to hold a small integer. The range of values is -32768 to +32767.

FLOAT defines data to hold a floating-point number. The number can be zero or can range from -1.79769E+308 to -2.225E-307, or from 2.225E-307 to 1.79769E+308.

DECIMAL(x,y) or DEC(x,y) defines data used to hold decimal numbers: x is the total number of digits (not including y) used to specify the precision (the number of digits of x varies from 1 to 31); y determines the total number of digits to the right of the decimal point, and this number ranges from 0 to the precision of the number. The default values for x and y are 5 and 0, respectively.

CHARACTER or CHAR defines data used to hold fixed-length character strings. The length you can specify must be in the range 0 to 254 bytes; if the length is 0, this means an empty string (this must not be confused with null string).

VARCHAR defines data used to hold variable-length character strings. The maximum size is 4000 bytes.

LONG VARCHAR defines data to hold variable-length character strings. The maximum size cab be 23,700 bytes.

GRAPHIC defines data to hold fixed-length graphic strings. The length you can specify must be in the range 1 to 127 bytes.

VARGRAPHIC defines data used to hold variable-length graphic strings. The maximum length of the string that you can specify is 2000 double-byte characters.

LONG VARGRAPHIC defines data used to hold variable-length graphic strings. The maximum length of the string that you can specify is 16,350 double-byte characters.

DATE defines data used to hold year, month, and day. There are various formats for the data strings, as shown in Figure 6.1.

Date format	Example	Type
yyyy-mm-dd	1993-12-10	International Standards Organization (ISO)
mm/dd/yyyy	12/10/1993	USA Standard (USA)
dd.mm.yyyy	10.12.1993	European Standard (EUR)
yyyy-mm-dd	1993-12-10	Japanese Industrial Standard (JIS)

Figure 6.1 Date string formats.

TIME defines data used to hold hours, minutes, and seconds. There are sevaral formats for time strings, as shown in Figure 6.2

Time format	Example	Type
hh.mm.ss	13.12.45	International Standards Organization (ISO)
hh:mm AM or PM	1:12 PM	USA Standard (USA)
hh.mm.ss	13.12.45	European Standard (EUR)
hh:mm:ss	13:12:45	Japanese Industrial Standard (JIS)

Figure 6.2 Time string formats.

TIMESTAMP defines data used to hold both date and time. It also contains time in microseconds at the end. The format is *yyyy-mm-dd-hh.mm.ss.nnnnnn*, where

yyyy	=	year
mm	=	month
dd	=	days
hh	=	hours
mm	=	minutes
ss	=	seconds
nnnnnn	=	microseconds

BIT DATA defines data as binary values. Usually such data is for exchange with other systems.

WITH DEFAULT defines the default values for data types just described. These values are shown in Figure 6.3.

Data type	Default values
INTEGER or INT	0
SMALLINT	0
FLOAT	0
DECIMAL	0
CHARACTER or CHAR	Blanks
VARCHAR	A string of length 0
LONG VARCHAR	A string of length 0
GRAPHIC	Double-byte blanks
VARGRAPHIC	A string of length 0
LONG VARGRAPHIC	A string of length 0
DATE	January 1, 0001
TIME	hours=0, minutes=0, seconds=0
TIMESTAMP	January 1, 0001, hours=0, minutes=0, seconds=0, microseconds=0

Figure 6.3 Default values for data types.

NOT NULL WITH DEFAULT means when a row is added to the database, a column with such a characteristic cannot contain null values; instead, it can have a default value.

Operators

As any other language, SQL has operators that expand its power. There are three main types: arithmetic, comparison, and boolean (see Figure 6.4).

Arithmetic operators allow the use of addition, subtraction, multiplication, and division. These operations are done only on numeric data; it is invalid to do arithmetic operations on characters or graphic strings.

Comparision operators are used to compare two numeric or nonnumeric data items. These operators determine whether a variable is equal to, not equal to, less than, or greater than an other variable or constant.

Boolean operators are used to perform logical comparison between predicates in a WHERE clause. These operators, such as **AND, OR**, and **NOT**, determine whether an expression is false or true.

Type	Operator	Meaning
Comparison	=	Equal to
	¬ = or < >	Not equal to
	>	Greater than
	¬ > or < =	Not greater than
	¬ < or > =	Not less than
Arithmetic	+	Addition
	-	Subtraction
	*	Multiplication
	/	Division
Boolean	**AND**	Logical **AND**
	OR	Logical **OR**

Figure 6.4 SQL operators.

Predicates

BETWEEN is a predicate; it compares a value that is equal to or intermediate between two other values. The general format is

```
expression [NOT] BETWEEN expression AND expression
```

The NULL predicate test for null values; the format is

```
expression IS [NOT] NULL
```

The IN predicate compares a value with one or more values; the format is

```
expression [NOT] IN < fullselect or
          expression>
```

The LIKE predicate searches for strings that have a certain pattern; the format is

```
column-name [NOT] LIKE <USER or host-variable or
            string-constant>
```

The EXISTS predicate tests for the existence of certain rows; the format is

```
EXISTS (fullselect)
```

Special registers

A *special register* is a storage area where special information is kept accessible by an application program. Examples of special registers are

Register	Description
CURRENT DATE	Holds current local time
CURRENT SERVER	Contains the name of the current application server
CURRENT TIME	Holds the current local time
CURRENT TIMESTAMP	Holds the current local date and time
USER	Holds the user ID that was passed to DB2/2 when the application connected to the database

6.2 SQL Statements

This section describes the SQL statements. For each statement, the syntax is given, followed by an explanation of the statement and its parameters. Also, there is a brief note on how a statement can be executed. The examples will help you understand how the SQL statement is used.

First, let's look at two important aspects of SQL statements: invocation and return codes. A SQL statement can be executed in one of three ways:

- Embedded in an application program
- Dynamically prepared and executed
- Issued interactively

Embedded SQL: This simply means that SQL statements are found in a program. These statements, found anywhere in the source code, must start with keywords EXEC and SQL; for example,

```
EXEC SQL SELECT * FROM DEPT_TABLE
```

To execute the SQL statement *embedded* in the program, first you have to precompile and subsequently compile and link to create an executable file. Next, when the whole program is run, the SQL statements will be executed in a logical manner.

Dynamic SQL: In a program it is possible to build SQL statements and execute them rather than hard-coding them. Usually, an application program will dynamically build an SQL statement in a host variable using data fed to it (e.g., input from a user). Once the statement is constructed with a character string, it is executed with an embedded statement, namely, **PREPARE** or **EXECUTE**.

Interactive SQL: All database managers have a facility to execute SQL statements entered at the terminal. For example, DB2/2 for OS/2 has Visualizer Query. There are a few things to remember when issuing statements interactively. First, the statement should not contain any reference to host variables and second, the syntax should be pure, without the keywords EXEC SQL; for example,

```
SELECT * FROM DEPT_TABLE
```

Return codes: Every time a SQL statement is executed, the database manager returns a code, which indicates the success of the operation. In the interactive mode, you see the code and a brief explanation on the screen. However, this code is passed to a program through an integer variable called **SQLCODE**. This variable is a field in the **SQLCA** structure which is used as a means of communication between the program and the database manager. (The **SQLCA** structure is given with the **INCLUDE** statement.)

An application program checks **SQLCODE** to decide on the next logical move; for example, **SQLCODE=0** means that the execution is successful and **SQLCODE=100** means that "no data" was found. There are too many such return codes to list all of them here.

There is another field in **SQLCA** structure, called **SQLSTATE**, indicating the outcome of the most recently executed SQL statement. A program can check this variable instead of **SQLCODE** because it can used to test for specific errors and classes of errors. One point to remember is that it is a string variable.

Next, we'll look at all the SQL statements.

◘ ALTER TABLE—add a column to a table and maintain keys

● General format

```
ALTER TABLE table-name
   <<ADD col-name data-type
    <NOT NULL WITH DEFAULT   or
       FOR BIT DATA>         or
    .
    .
    .
        col-name data-type
       <NOT NULL WITH DEFAULT  or
     FOR BIT DATA> >           or
PRIMARY KEY(col-name)          or
DROP KEY>
```

● Description

The **ALTER TABLE** statement is used primarily to add one or more columns to an existing table. The column is always added to the end of the table.

table-name is the name of the table you want to change. It must exist in the DB2/2 catalog.

ADD *col-name data-type* specifies the name of the column that you want to add to the table and its data type.

col-name is a unique name for the column.

data-type is one of the data types found in the following list:

INTEGER	SMALLINT	FLOAT
DECIMAL	CHAR	VARCHAR
GRAPHIC	VARGRAPHIC	LONG VARGRAPHIC
LONG VARCHAR	DATE	TIME
TIMESTAMP		

NOT NULL WITH DEFAULT allows default values but not null values.

FOR BIT DATA defines data as binary values.

PRIMARY KEY(*col-name*,...) specifies that primary keys are made of the column names to be used as indexes.

col-name is the name of an existing column of the table. You can list one or more columns.

DROP PRIMARY KEY means to remove the definition of the primary key as index. This only happens if the table has a primary key. If an existing index was previously used for the primary index, then the **ALTER TABLE** statement will not drop the index.

- Usage

Embedded in an application program, and dynamically prepared and executed.

- Example

The following example adds the column CONTACT_2 to the table RBA.CLIENTS.

```
ALTER TABLE RBA.CLIENTS
   ADD CONTACT_2 CHAR(20);
```

◘ BEGIN DECLARE SECTION—mark the beginning of a host variable declare section

- General format

```
BEGIN DECLARE SECTION
```

- Description

The **BEGIN DECLARE SECTION** statement is used in an application program to mark a section where host variables are defined. These definitions are done according to the rules of the host language. This section must terminate with the keywords **END DECLARE SECTION**.

- Usage

Embedded in an application program.

● Example

The following is an example of how to use the **BEGIN DECLARE SECTION** statement in a C program.

```
EXEC SQL BEGIN DECLARE SECTION;
     .
     .
     (host variable definitions)
     .
     .
EXEC SQL END DECLARE SECTION;
```

The following segment of a COBOL program demonstrates the use of the **BEGIN DECLARE SECTION** statement.

```
DATA DIVISION.
WORKING-STORAGE SECTION.
EXEC SQL BEGIN DECLARE SECTION END-EXEC.

EXEC SQL
     INCLUDE PATIENT.TBL
END-EXEC.

01   WS-PROGRAM-HOST-VARIABLES.
     05 DATABASE-USERNAME      PIC X(10) VALUE "GOPAULM".
         05 DATABASE-PASSWORD  PIC X(10) VALUE "GOPAULM".
         05 CURRENT-DATE                  PIC X(08).
         05 FIRST-NAME                    PIC X(25).
         05 LAST-NAME                     PIC X(25).

         EXEC SQL END SECTION END-EXEC.
```

◘ CLOSE—close a cursor

● General format

```
CLOSE cursor-name
```

● Description

A *cursor* is a pointer to the current row of a result table. After you have completed processing a result table, the cursor must be **CLOSE**d. But a cursor must first be **DECLARE**d and **OPEN**ed before it is used or closed. A **COMMIT** statement automatically closes all cursors.

cursor-name is the name of a cursor that was previously used in the **DECLARE CURSOR** statement.

- Usage

  Embedded in an application program.

- Example

  In the following C program fragment, a cursor called BRANCH_C is first declared, followed by an **OPEN** statement to open the cursor. Subsequently, this cursor is used to retrieve data from the database using the **FETCH** statement. Finally, the cursor is closed with the **CLOSE** statement.

```
EXEC SQL DECLARE BRANCH_C CURSOR FOR
   SELECT NAME, ADDRESS
    FROM CLIENTS
    WHERE BRANCH='E101';

EXEC SQL OPEN BRANCH_C;

while (SQLCODE==0)
{
   EXEC SQL FETCH BRANCH_C INTO :name, :address;
     .
     .
     .

}

EXEC SQL CLOSE BRANCH_C;
```

◘ COMMENT ON—add or replace comments on tables, views, or columns

- General format

```
COMMENT ON
   <TABLE <table-name or view-name>
       IS comment-string>    or
   <COLUMN <table-name.column-name or
      view-name.column-name>
       IS comment-string>
```

- Description

  The **COMMENT ON** statement adds or replaces comments in the catalogs of DB2/2.

  TABLE <*table-name* or *view-name*>
  This specifies what to comment on: a table or a view. In both cases the

comment is written to the REMARKS column of the SYSIBM.SYSTABLES catalog table for the row related to the specified table or view.

table-name is the name of a table already in SYSIBM.SYSTABLES.

view-name is the name of a view already in SYSIBM.SYSTABLES.

COLUMN *<table-name.column-name* or
     view-name.column-name>
This specifies commenting on a column.

column-name is the name of the column that already exists in a table or view.

IS *comment-string*
This is a keyword which precedes the comment you want to specify.

comment-string can be any SQL string constant, up to 254 bytes.

- Usage

Embedded in an application program, and dynamically prepared and executed.

- Example

The following example updates a comment on the table RBA.CLIENTS.

```
COMMENT ON TABLE RBA.CLIENTS
    IS 'LAST BACKUP Dec 12, 1993'
```

◘ COMMIT—make a change permanent

- General format

```
COMMIT [WORK]
```

- Description

The **COMMIT** statement is used to make changes in data permanent after they have been successfully completed. If you do not use **COMMIT** within your program and the execution of the program ends successfully, then DB2/2 will issue a **COMMIT**. It is highly recommended that you use **COMMIT** in your program, say every 100 updates of rows. **COMMIT** frees resources, allowing other programs to use them. Also, it saves you from having to rerun the whole job when only part of it failed. All changes made by the execution of **ALTER, COMMENT ON, CREATE, DELETE, DROP, GRANT, INSERT, REVOKE,** and **UPDATE** statements are committed to the database.

- Usage

Embedded in an application program, and dynamically prepared and executed .

- Example

The following command issues a **COMMIT** statement:

```
EXEC SQL COMMIT;
```

◘ CONNECT—connect to the application server

- General format

```
CONNECT [RESET]    or
                [TO <server-name or host-variable>
                  [IN [SHARE or EXCLUSIVE] MODE]
```

- Description

The **CONNECT** statement is used to connect an application process or a user, or both, to an application server. The connection is to one server at a time. If you issue CONNECT without any operand, the statement returns information about the current server, found in the **SQLERRMC** field of the **SQLCA** structure.

RESET means to disconnect the application process from the current server.

TO *<server-name* or *host-variable>*
This specifies the application server to which connection is made.

server-name is the name of the application server.

host-variable is a variable that contains the name of the application server.

IN SHARE MODE means that concurrent application processes can execute *only* read-only operation at the application server.

IN EXCLUSIVE MODE means that concurrent application processes *cannot* execute any operation at the application server.

● Usage

Embedded in an application program and issued interactively.

● Example

In the following statement, **CONNECT** is issued to connect a user to an application server TOROLABM:

```
CONNECT TO TOROLABM
```

In the next C program fragment, an application process is connected using a host variable SEC_SERVER to an application server SECD. After a successful connection, the product name of the application server is copied to the variable PRODUCT.

```
strcpy(CICS_SERVER,'SECD')
EXEC SQL CONNECT TO :SEC_SERVER;
if (strncmp(SQLSTATE,'00000',5)
   strncpy(PRODUCT,sqlca,sqlerrp,3);
```

◘ CREATE INDEX—create an index on a table

● General format

```
CREATE [UNIQUE] INDEX index-name
   ON table-name
   [(column-name <ASC or DESC>,...)]
```

● Description

The **CREATE INDEX** statement creates an index on an existing table of the DB2/2 database.

UNIQUE
This optional keyword is used to create only unique index keys.

INDEX *index-name*
This specifies the name of an index for which an index space is created.

index-name is the name of the index, which does not exist in the DB2/2 catalog.

ON *table-name*
This specifies the name of the table on which the index is to be created.

table-name is the name of a table already described in the DB2/2 catalog.

column-name is the name of a column that is to be part of the index key. You can enter one or more column names that are part of a table definition. The maximum number of columns you can enter in this statement is 16. Following each name you can specify the order of index entries.

ASC means to store the index entries in ascending order. ASC is the default.

DESC means to store the index entries in descending order.

● Usage

Embedded in an application program, and dynamically prepared and executed.

● Example

The following example creates an index IXCLIENTS on the table CLIENTS. Also, it specifies having only unique index keys. In this case, the column name is CLIENTID and the index entries are to be stored in descending order.

```
CREATE UNIQUE INDEX IXCLIENTS
    ON CLIENTS

    (CLIENTID DESC)
```

◼ CREATE TABLE—create a table for a database

● General format

```
CREATE TABLE table-name
   (col-name data-type
      <NOT NULL [WITH DEFAULT] [PRIMARY KEY] or
        FOR BIT DATA>,
      .
      .
      .
   col-name data-type
     <NOT NULL [WITH DEFAULT] [PRIMARY KEY] or
       FOR BIT DATA> )
   or
   PRIMARY KEY(col-name,...)
```

● Description

The **CREATE TABLE** statement creates a table within a DB2/2 database. Also, this statement lets you create one or more columns with specific data types for each column.

table-name is the name of the table you want to create. It must not exist in the DB2/2 catalog. The creator of the table has all the privileges.

col-name is a unique name for a column with the table.

data-type is one of the data types found in the following list:

INTEGER	SMALLINT	FLOAT
DECIMAL	CHAR	VARCHAR
GRAPHIC	VARGRAPHIC	LONG VARGRAPHIC
LONG VARCHAR	DATE	TIME
TIMESTAMP		

NOT NULL prevents columns from having null values but does not specify a default.

FOR BIT DATA defines data as binary values. It may be used for data exchange between systems.

PRIMARY KEY(*col-name*,...) specifies that primary keys are made of the column names to be used as indexes.

col-name is the name of an existing column of the table. You can list one or more columns, and these specified columns must not be defined with NOT NULL.

NOT NULL WITH DEFAULT allows columns to have default values instead of null values. The DB2/2 default values for data types are as follows:

Data type	Default value
Numeric	0
Fixed-length character string	Blanks
Variable-length character string	A string of length 0
Date	January 1, 0001
Time	0 hour, 0 minute, and 0 second
Timestamp	January 1, 0001, 0 hour, 0 minute, 0 second, and 0 microsecond

- Usage

Embedded in an application program, dynamically prepared and executed, and issued interactively.

- Example

The following creates a table of CLIENTS. The table will have four columns: CLIENTS_ID, CLIENTS_ADDR, CLIENTS_CITY, and CLIENTS_C. Each column allows default values. The primary key consists of the content of column CLIENTS_ID.

```
CREATE TABLE CLIENTS
   (CLIENTS_ID    SMALLINT      NOT NULL WITH DEFAULT,
    CLIENTS_ADDR CHAR (20)     NOT NULL WITH DEFAULT,
    CLIENTS_CITY CHAR (25)     NOT NULL WITH DEFAULT,
    CLIENTS_C     VARCHAR (25) NOT NULL WITH DEFAULT,
    PRIMARY KEY (CLIENTS_ID) )
```

◘ CREATE VIEW—create a view from a table or view

- General format

```
CREATE VIEW view-name [(column-name,...)]
     AS subselect-statement
     [WITH-CHECK-OPTION]
```

● Description

The **CREATE VIEW** statement derives a virtual table from one or more tables or views.

view-name is the view you want to create.

column-name is a unique name of a column already defined in a table. You can have one or more columns in this statement.

AS *subselect-statement*
This defines the view in association with the **SELECT** statement.

subselect-statement is a **SELECT** statement. This statement is described in more detail later in this chapter.

WITH CHECK OPTION
This option checks all inserts and updates against view definitions.

● Usage

Embedded in an application program, dynamically prepared and executed, and issued interactively.

● Example

The following example creates a view called CUSTNAME through a **SELECT** statement. The view consists of two columns, SOC_SEC and FIRST_AND_LAST, from the CUSTOMER table. The WITH CHECK OPTION verifies all inserts and updates against view definitions.

```
CREATE VIEW CUSTNAME
   (SOC_SEC,FIRST_AND_LAST)
   AS SELECT CUST_SOC_SEC, CUST_NAME
     FROM CUSTOMER
     WHERE CUST_SOC_SEC < 7000000
            WITH CHECK OPTION
```

◘ DECLARE CURSOR—define a cursor

● General format

```
DECLARE cursor-name CURSOR [WITH HOLD] FOR select-statement
```

- Description

The **DECLARE CURSOR** statement defines a cursor, which points to many rows of a table. It consists of a cursor name and a **SELECT** statement used to define the selection of rows. This statement is used in a program to access many rows in a table. A cursor can be considered a file and should be treated as such. Therefore, a declared cursor must be **OPEN**ed, **FETCH**ed (or read), or **CLOSE**d.

cursor-name is the name of the cursor you want to define.

select-statement is a **SELECT** statement; this statement is described in detail later in this chapter.

WITH HOLD means to maintain resources across multiple units of work. For units of work ending with **COMMIT**, the cursor is placed before the next logical row of the result table. For **ROLLBACK**, all open cursors are closed.

- Usage

  Embedded in an application program.

- Example

In the following example, a cursor called CLIENTS_C is defined in a COBOL program. It will point to each row in the table CLIENTS that is returned as a result of the **SELECT** statement.

```
EXEC SQL
   DECLARE CLIENT_C CURSOR FOR
   SELECT CLIENTS_ID, CLIENTS_ADDR, CLIENTS_CITY
     FROM CLIENTS
     WHERE CLIENTS_ID = :TRANS-BRANCH-ID
END-EXEC.
```

◨ DELETE—delete rows from a table or view

- General format

```
Not using cursor:

  DELETE FROM <table-name or view-name>
     WHERE search-condition
```

```
Using cursor:

  DELETE FROM <table-name or view-name>
     WHERE CURRENT OF cursor-name
```

- Description

  The **DELETE** statement removes a varying number of rows from a table or view depending on the search condition. The deletion of rows can be done with or without the cursor.

  FROM *table-name* or *view-name*
  This specifies the table or view from which the rows are to be removed.

  table-name is the name of a table already defined in a DB2/2 catalog.

  view-name is the name of a view already defined in a DB2/2 catalog.

  WHERE *search-condition*
  This clause determines how many rows will be deleted. If it is omitted, all the rows will be removed.

  search-condition is the same as the search condition used in the WHERE clause of the **SELECT** statement. Depending on the condition, many rows or no rows may be deleted.

  WHERE CURRENT OF *cursor-name*
  This clause determines how many rows will be deleted using a cursor.

  cursor-name is the name of a cursor, defined before using it in the **DELETE** statement. The **DECLARE CURSOR** statement defines the cursor. Before using it, the cursor must be opened with the **OPEN** statement. When the **DELETE** statement is executed, it removes the row where the cursor is positioned. After the deletion, the cursor points to the next row.

- Usage

  Embedded in an application program, dynamically prepared and executed, and issued interactively.

- Example

  The following example deletes all rows from the table CLIENTS where the column CL_CL_NAME is 'SMITH'.

```
DELETE
   FROM CLIENTS
   WHERE CL_CL_NAME = 'SMITH';
```

◘ DESCRIBE—get information about a prepared statement

- General format

```
DESCRIBE statement-name INTO descriptor-name
```

- Description

The **DESCRIBE** statement is used to obtain information about a statement that was dynamically prepared by the PREPARE statement.

statement-name is the name for which the information is sought. It must be a prepared statement.

INTO *descriptor-name*
This clause is used to specify where the information is to be placed.

descriptor-name is the name of a data structure such as **SQLDA**. Before using the **DESCRIBE** statement, you must set **SQLN** field of **SQLDA** to the number of variables represented by **SQLVAR**.

After the execution of **DESCRIBE**, the database manager updates the following fields of **SQLDA**:

Fields	Values
SQLDAID	'SQLDA'
SQLDABC	Length of the SQLDA data structure.
SQLD	Number of columns in the result table of a **SELECT** statement; otherwise it is 0.
SQLVAR	This field is not updated if SQLD is 0 or is greater than the value found in SQLN; otherwise, if SQLD has a value, say, n, where n is greater than 0 but less than or equal to the value of SQLN, then the values are assigned to the first n occurrences of SQLVAR. To further clarify this point, the first SQLVAR will have the description of the first column of the result table, the second occurence will contain the information about the second column, and so on.

SQLTYPE   This field contains a code that indicates the data type of the column. It also shows whether the column has a null value.
SQLLEN   This field has the length of the result columns.
SQLNAME   This field has the name of the column.

- Usage

  Embedded in an application program.

- Example

  In the following example there are three C statements. The first one is to copy a statement string into a string variable *s*. The second one contains a **PREPARE** statement. Next is a **DESCRIBE** staement that gets the information about this **SELECT** prepared statement and places it into the data structure **sqlda**.

```
strcpy(s,"SELECT CLIENTS_ID FROM CLIENTS");
EXEC SQL PREPARE select_clients FROM :s;
EXEC SQL DESCRIBE select_clients INTO :sqlda;
```

◘ DROP—remove an object

- General format

```
DROP  INDEX index-name          or
   PACKAGE package-name          or
   TABLE table-name              or
   VIEW view-name
```

- Description

  The **DROP** statement deletes a specific DB2/2 object, such as a particular view, index, and tables. It removes from the DB2/2 catalog the named object entry and any associated objects below it. It also deletes any packages that reference the object.

  INDEX *index-name*
  This specifies the index to be deleted.

  index-name is a name of an unpartitioned and user-created index already defined in the DB2/2 catalog.

PACKAGE *package-name*
This specifies the package to be invalidated.

package-name is the name of a package already defined in the DB2/2 catalog.

TABLE *table-name*
This specifies the table to be removed from a database. This will also drop all the indexes and primary keys associated with the table.

table-name is the name of a table already defined in the DB2/2 catalog. You cannot enter a catalog table that belongs to DB2/2.

VIEW *view-name*
This specifies the view to be deleted.

view-name is the name of a view already defined.

- Usage

Embedded in an application program, dynamically prepared and executed, and issued interactively.

- Example

The following example drops table RBA.CLIENTS.

```
DROP TABLE RBA.CLIENTS;
```

◘ END DECLARE SECTION—end the host variable declaration

- General format

```
END DECLARE SECTION
```

- Description

The **END DECLARE SECTION** statement is used in an application program to mark the end of host variable declaration section. Note that this section starts with **BEGIN DECLARE SECTION** and ends with **END DECLARE SECTION**, and in between are definitions of host variables used in SQL statements, such as **SELECT, FETCH, INSERT,** and **DECLARE CURSOR.**

● Usage

Embedded in an application program.

● Example

The following is an example of how to use **END DECLARE SECTION** in a C program.

```
EXEC SQL BEGIN DECLARE SECTION;
/* host variable definitions */
char database_name[11];
char database_password[11];
int  transit_number;
float base_price;
char first_name[26];
EXEC SQL END DECLARE SECTION;
```

The following segment of a COBOL program demonstrates the use of the END DECLARE SECTION statement.

```
DATA DIVISION.
WORKING-STORAGE SECTION.
EXEC SQL BEGIN DECLARE SECTION END-EXEC.

EXEC SQL
     INCLUDE PATIENT.TBL
END-EXEC.

01  WS-PROGRAM-HOST-VARIABLES.
    05 DATABASE-USERNAME          PIC X(10) VALUE "GOPAULM".
       05 DATABASE-PASSWORD PIC X(10) VALUE "GOPAULM".
       05 CURRENT-DATE                     PIC X(08).
       05 FIRST-NAME                       PIC X(25).
       05 LAST-NAME                        PIC X(25).

    EXEC SQL END SECTION END-EXEC.
```

◘ FETCH—get a row using the cursor

● General format

```
FETCH cursor-name < INTO host-variable,... or
                  USING DESCRIPTION description-name>
```

● Description

The **FETCH** statement positions the cursor on the next row of its results table and assigns the column values to variables of your program.

cursor-name is the name of the cursor, which must be **DECLARE**d and **OPEN**ed before use.

INTO *host-variable*
This specifies the variables of your program. The INTO clause follows the same rules as the INTO clause of the **SELECT** statement. You can have one or more variables. The first value of the row is placed in the first variable, the second value of the row in the second variable, and so on.

host-variable is the name of a structure or variable.

USING DESCRIPTION *description-name*
This parameter is used to name a **SQLDA** structure that holds a valid description of host variables. Before executing the **FETCH** statement you must initialize the following fields of **SQLDA**:

SQLN	The number of **SQLVAR** occurrences provided in the SQLDA
SQLDABC	The number of bytes of storage allocated for this SQLDA
SQLD	The number of variables used in the **SQLDA** while processing the **FETCH** statement
SQLVAR	Occurrences to indicate the attributes of variables

description-name is the name of a SQLDA structure.

● Usage

Embedded in an application program.

● Example

In the following example, a CR_PATIENT cursor is first declared, followed by an **OPEN** statement to open the cursor. Next data from each row is fetched from the **PATIENT** table into *patient_id*, *l_name*, and *f_name* host variables, until all the rows from the result table are processed. Finally, the cursor is closed.

```
EXEC SQL DECLARE CR_PATIENT CURSOR FOR
   SELECT PATIENT_ID,
          LAST_NAME,
          FIRST_NAME
   FROM PATIENT
   WHERE PATIENT_ID = "A1234";
```

```
EXEC SQL OPEN CR_PATIENT;

while (SQLCODE==0)
{
   EXEC SQL FETCH CR_PATIENT INTO :patient_id,
                                  :l_name,
                                  :f_name;
}

EXEC SQL CLOSE CR_PATIENT;
```

◘ GRANT—grant index privileges

● General format

```
GRANT CONTROL ON INDEX index-name
   TO <PUBLIC or authorization-id,...>
```

● Description

This **GRANT CONTROL ON INDEX** statement is used to give an ID or group name the CONTROL privileges on indexes of a database.

CONTROL
This parameter gives the privilege to drop the indexes of a table; this privilege is the same as the one given to the creator of the index.

ON INDEX *index-name*
This parameter is used to name the index for which CONTROL privilege is to be granted.

index-name is the name of an index already defined for a database.

TO <PUBLIC or *authorization-id,...*>
This specifies who gets the privilege: individual users or all users.

PUBLIC means to grant the privilege to all users.

authorization-id is a user ID or group name. You can specify one or more IDs, and it must not include the user ID that is issuing the command.

● Usage

Embedded in an application program, dynamically prepared and executed, and issued interactively.

● Example

In the following interactive command, the user TSMGOPA is granted **CONTROL** privilege on CLIENIDX.

```
GRANT CONTROL ON INDEX CLIENIDX TO TSMGOPAU
```

◘ GRANT—grant database privileges

● General format

```
GRANT database-privilege,...
   ON DATABASE
   TO <PUBLIC or authorization-id,...>
```

● Description

This **GRANT** statement gives one or more users privileges to use a resource at the database level of DB2/2. With this statement you can grant privileges against the entire database.

database-privilege is one or more of the following keywords:

Keyword	Privilege
DBADM	Administer a database
BINDADD	Create packages
CONNECT	Access the database

ON DATABASE
This specifies the entire database for which privileges are to be given with the **GRANT** statement.

TO <PUBLIC or *authorization-id,...*>
This specifies who gets the priviledge: individual users or all users.

PUBLIC means to grant the privilege to all users.

authorization-id is a user ID or group name. You can specify one or more IDs, and it must not include the user ID that is issuing the command.

- Usage

Embedded in an application program, dynamically prepared and executed, and issued interactively.

- Example

In the following interactive command, the users LAILA and SANJIV are granted the BINDADD privilege on the entire database.

```
GRANT BINDADD ON DATABASE
       TO LAILA, SANJIV;
```

◘ GRANT—grant package privileges

- General format

```
GRANT package-privilege,...
   ON PACKAGE package-name
   TO <PUBLIC or authorization-id,...>
```

- Description

This **GRANT** statement gives one or more users privileges against packages in the database. With this statement you can specify one or more privileges or packages.

package-privilege is one of the following keywords:

Keyword	Privilege
BIND	Issue the **BIND**, **REBIND**, and **FREE** commands against the packages named in this statement
EXECUTE	Run programs belonging to the package named in this statement
CONTROL	Grant **BIND**, **REBIND**, and **FREE** privileges to other users

ON PLAN *package-name*
This specifies an application plan for which privileges are to be given with the **GRANT** statement.

package-name is the name of the package for which the privileges are given.

TO <PUBLIC or *authorization-id,...*>
This specifies who gets the privilege: individual users or all users.

PUBLIC means to grant the privilege to all users.

authorization-id is a user ID or group name. You can specify one or more IDs, and it must not include the user ID that is issuing the command.

● Usage

Embedded in an application program, dynamically prepared and executed, and issued interactively.

● Example

In the following example, the interactive command is used to grant the **BIND** privilege to users ABBY and THOMASLO on the BIND01 package.

```
GRANT BIND
   ON PACKAGE BIND01
   TO ABBY, THOMASLO;
```

◘ GRANT—grant table or view privileges

● General format

```
GRANT < ALL or
      ALL PRIVILEGES or
      table-privilege,...>
  ON [TABLE] <table-name or view-name>
  TO <PUBLIC or authorization-id,...>
```

● Description

This **GRANT** statement gives one or more users privileges to use a resource at the table level of DB2/2. With this statement you can specify one or more privileges and tables or views.

ALL or ALL PRIVILEGES means to grant all privileges on tables or views mentioned with the ON clause.

table-privilege is one of the following keywords:

Keyword	Privilege
ALTER	Issue the **ALTER** statement
DELETE	Issue the **DELETE** statement
INDEX	Issue the **INDEX** statement
INSERT	Issue the **INSERT** statement
SELECT	Issue the **SELECT** statement
UPDATE	Issue the **UPDATE** statement
CONTROL	Grant all the privileges listed here as well as the ability to drop the table or view
REFERENCE	To create and drop a foreign key referencing a table as the parent

ON TABLE <*table-name* or *view-name*>
This specifies a table or view for which privileges are granted to users.

table-name is the name of an existing table.

view-name is the name of an existing view.

TO <PUBLIC or *authorization-id,...*>
This specifies who gets the privilege: individual users or all users.

PUBLIC means to grant the privilege to all users.

authorization-id is a user ID or group name. You can specify one or more IDs and it must not include the user ID that is issuing the command.

● Usage

Embedded in an application program, dynamically prepared and executed, issued interactively.

● Example

In the following example, the interactive command is used to grant all table privileges to users Z1335MG and ABBY.

```
GRANT ALL PRIVILGES
   ON TABLE RBA.CLIENTS
   TO Z1335MG, ABBY;
```

◘ INCLUDE—insert code or declarations into a source program

- General format

```
INCLUDE < SQLCA or
          SQLDA or
          name>
```

- Description

The **INCLUDE** statement causes the precompiler to get a named member and merge it into a source program during the precompile time.

SQLCA

This is required to access DB2/2 from a program. It's a set of fields that DB2/2 updates after each SQL statement is executed. These fields are described later in this chapter. For example, in COBOL the **INCLUDE SQLCA** statement specifies

```
01   SQLCA.
     05  SQLCAID             PIC X(8).
     05  SQLCABC             PIC S9(9) COMP-4.
     05  SQLCODE             PIC S9(9) COMP-4.
     05  SQLERRM.
       49  SQLERRML            PIC S9(4) COMP-4.
       49  SQLERRMC            PIC X(70).
     05  SQLERRP             PIC X(8).
     05  SQLERRD      OCCURS 6 TIMES PIC S9(9) COMP-4.
     05  SQLWARN.
       10  SQLWARN0            PIC X(1).
       10  SQLWARN1            PIC X(1).
       10  SQLWARN2            PIC X(1).
       10  SQLWARN3            PIC X(1).
       10  SQLWARN4            PIC X(1).
       10  SQLWARN5            PIC X(1).
       10  SQLWARN6            PIC X(1).
       10  SQLWARN7            PIC X(1).
     05 SQLEXT              PIC X(8).
```

SQLDA

This keyword specifies the SQL descriptor area (**SQLDA**) to be included. It is a data structure with many fields; it is discussed later in detail.

name is the name of a file whose content is to be included where the INCLUDE statement is found. This can be any relevant file, such as a copy book for a COBOL program or an include file for a C or C++ program.

● Usage

Embedded in an application program, dynamically prepared and executed, issued interactively.

● Example

In the following fragment program, there are are two **INCLUDE** statements. The first statement is used to include the SQL communication area. The next is used to include the **clients.tbl** file, which has a structure definition corresponding to the columns of the CLIENTS table. The structure is called **clients,** and two of the fields are **name** and **address**.

```
EXEC SQL INCLUDE SQLCA;
EXEC SQL INCLUDE clients.tbl;

EXEC SQL DECLARE BRANCH_C CURSOR FOR
   SELECT NAME, ADDRESS
    FROM CLIENTS
    WHERE BRANCH='E101';

EXEC SQL OPEN BRANCH_C;

while (SQLCODE==0)
{
   EXEC SQL FETCH BRANCH_C
            INTO :clients.name,
                 :clients.address;

      .
      .
      .

}

EXEC SQL CLOSE BRANCH_C;
```

◻ INSERT—Insert a row into a table or view

● General format

```
INSERT INTO <table-name or view-name>
   [column-name,...]
   VALUES (constant        or
            host-variable or
           NULL            or
                     special-register)...
   fullselect statement
```

- Description

  The **INSERT** statement inserts a row into a view or table. If the row is inserted into a view, it is also added to the table which is the basis for the view.

  table-name is the name of a table already described in the DB2/2 catalog.

  view-name is the name of a view already described in the DB2/2 catalog.

  column-name is the name of a row of a table or view. You can have one or more columns, in any order. The column list is optional; if it is omitted, the columns defined in the named view or table are used.

  VALUES specifies the values for the row you are inserting. Each value must correspond to the column name; for example, if you list five columns, you must also provide five corresponding values, separated by commas. The values can be keywords, constants, variables, NULL, or special register.

  constant is a specific value; it can be one of the following: integer, floating-point value, decimal, character string, or graphic string.

  host-variable is the name of a structure or variable that follows the rules of the host program.

  NULL is a keyword that represents a null value.

  special-register is one of the following: CURRENT DATE, CURRENT TIME, CURRENT SERVER, CURRENT TIMESTAMP, or USER.

  fullselect statement
  This is a **SELECT** statement, and the result of this statement is an insert to the table or view. This statement is discussed later in this chapter.

- Usage

  Embedded in an application program, dynamically prepared and executed, and issued interactively.

● Example

In the following example, the **INSERT** statement is used to add a row into a table RBA.CLIENTS. The columns are NAME, CITY, POSTAL_C, and PROV, and the values are RBC, NEWMARKET, L3X1F0, and ONTARIO.

```
INSERT INTO RBA.CLIENTS
    (NAME, CITY, POSTAL_C, PROV)
    VALUES ('RBC','NEWMARKET','L3X1F0','ONTARIO');
```

◘ LOCK TABLE—lock a table space

● General format

```
LOCK TABLE table-name
    IN <SHARE MODE or EXCLUSIVE MODE>
```

● Description

The **LOCK TABLE** command locks the table space, in either shared mode or exclusive mode. The lock can be released with a BIND command and an **SQL RELEASE** statement.

table-name is the name of the table for which the table space is locked.

IN <SHARE MODE or EXCLUSIVE MODE>
This specifies the type of locking.

SHARE MODE means to acquire a lock on the table for the unit of work (program) where this statement is executed that will allow other programs to access the table in read-only mode.

EXCLUSIVE MODE means to acquire a lock on the table for the unit of work (program) where this statement is executed that will not allow any other program to access the table.

● Usage

Embedded in an application program, dynamically prepared and executed, and issued interactively.

- Example

In the following example, the **LOCK TABLE** statement is used to acquire an exclusive lock on the RBA.CLIENTS table.

```
LOCK TABLE  RBA.CLIENTS IN EXCLUSIVE MODE;
```

◘ OPEN—open a cursor

- General format

```
OPEN cursor-name
   [USING host-variable,... or
                USING DESCRIPTOR description-name]
```

- Description

The **OPEN** statement is used after a cursor has been declared. This statement executes the **SELECT** statement associated with the **DECLARE CURSOR** statement; it creates the result table to which the cursor points. Subsequent to the **OPEN** statement, the cursor is initialized to point to a row with a **FETCH** statement.

cursor-name is the name of a cursor already **DECLARE**d.

USING *host-variable,...*
This specifies user-defined variables.

host-variable is the name of a structure or variable that follows the rules of the host program.

USING DESCRIPTION *description-name*
This parameter is used to name a **SQLDA** structure that holds a valid description of host variables. Before executing the **OPEN** statement you must initialize the following fields of **SQLDA**:

SQLN   The number of **SQLVAR** occurrences provided in the **SQLDA**

SQLDABC   The number of bytes of storage allocated for this **SQLDA**

SQLD   The number of variables used in the **SQLDA** while processing the **OPEN** statement

SQLVAR   Occurrences to indicate the attributes of variables

description-name is the name of a **SQLDA** structure.

- Usage

Embedded in an application program, dynamically prepared and executed, and issued interactively.

- Example

In the following fragment program, there are is an **OPEN** statement to open the BRANCH_C, and this statement is preceded by a statement to declare the cursor. After the cursor is opened, data is retrieved from the CLIENTS table using a **FETCH** statement. Finally, the cursor is closed.

```
EXEC SQL INCLUDE SQLCA;
EXEC SQL INCLUDE clients.tbl;

EXEC SQL DECLARE BRANCH_C CURSOR FOR
   SELECT NAME, ADDRESS
    FROM CLIENTS
    WHERE BRANCH='E101';

EXEC SQL OPEN BRANCH_C;

while (SQLCODE==0)
{
    EXEC SQL FETCH BRANCH_C INTO :clients.name,
                                 :clients.address;

      .
      .
      .

}

EXEC SQL CLOSE BRANCH_C;
```

◘ PREPARE—prepare an SQL statement for execution

- General format

```
PREPARE statement-name [INTO descriptor-name]
              FROM host-variable
```

- Description

This **PREPARE** statement is used to dynamically prepare a SQL statement for execution. This statement takes a string statement, which contains a SQL statement and converts it into an executable form, called a *prepared statement*. As seen earlier, the prepared statement is used before issuing an **EXECUTE** statement.

With the PREAPRE statement you can use only the following statements: **ALTER TABLE, COMMENT ON, COMMIT, CREATE INDEX, CREATE TABLE, CREATE VIEW, DELETE, DROP, GRANT, INSERT, LOCK TABLE, REVOKE, ROLLBACK, SELECT** statement, and **UPDATE**.

Also, when composing the string statement you have to keep in mind the following restrictions:

- A **SELECT** statement must not have the **INTO** clause; instead use a cursor and **FETCH** statement.
- The statement should not have the EXEC SQL keywords and a statement termination.
- The statement must not have host variables; instead you use parameter markers (?) and place corresponding host variables in the **EXECUTE** statement.
- The statement should not have any comments.

statement-name is the name of the prepared statement.

INTO *descriptor-name*
This parameter is used to identify a descriptor name where information is written after a successful execution of the **PREPARE** statement. As we saw earlier, the **DESCRIBE** statement can be used to accomplish the same function.

description-name is the name of a **SQLDA** structure.

FROM *host-variable*
This parameter is used to supply statement string to the SQL statement.

host-variable contains the statement string and is defined in a program according to the rules of the host language.

- Usage

Embedded in an application program.

- Example

In the following example there are three C statements. The first one is to copy a statement string into a string variable *s*. The second one contains a **PREPARE** statement. Next is a **DESCRIBE** statement that obtains the information about this **SELECT** prepared statement and places it into the data structure **sqlda**.

```
strcpy(s,"SELECT CLIENTS_ID FROM CLIENTS");
EXEC SQL PREPARE select_clients FROM :s;
EXEC SQL DESCRIBE select_clients INTO :sqlda;
```

◘ REVOKE—revoke index privileges

● General format

```
REVOKE CONTROL ON INDEX index-name
        FROM <PUBLIC or authorization-id,...>
```

● Description

This **REVOKE** statement takes away from users the **CONTROL** privileges on indexes of a database.

CONTROL
This parameter revokes the privileges to drop indexes of the database. This privilege is automatically granted to the creator of the index.

ON INDEX *index-name*
This parameter is used to specify the name of the index for which control privilege is removed.

index-name is the name of a database index that already exists.

FROM <PUBLIC or *authorization-id,...*>
This specifies the users whose privileges are revoked: individual users or all users.

PUBLIC means to revoke the privilege of all users.

authorization-id is a user ID or group name. You can specify one or more IDs, and it must not include the user ID that is issuing the command.

● Usage

Embedded in an application program, dynamically prepared and executed, and issued interactively.

● Example

The following interactive command is used to revoke the privileges to drop index INX001 from MIKHAIL and GABRIEL.

```
REVOKE CONTROL ON INDEX INX001
    FROM MIKHAIL, GABRIEL;
```

◻ REVOKE—revoke database privileges

● General format

```
REVOKE database-privilege,...
    ON DATABASE
    FROM <PUBLIC or authorization-id,...>
```

● Description

This **REVOKE** statement removes from one or all users privileges to use a resource at the database level of DB2/2. You can list one or more privileges.

database-privilege is one of the following keywords:

Keyword	Privilege
DBADM	Administer a database
BINDADD	Create packages
CONNECT	Access the database
CREATEAB	Create tables

FROM <PUBLIC or *authorization-id*,...>
This specifies the users whose privileges are revoked: individual users or all users.

PUBLIC means to revoke privileges of all users.

authorization-id is a user ID or group name. You can specify one or more IDs, and it must not include the user ID that is issuing the command.

● Usage

Embedded in an application program, dynamically prepared and executed, and issued interactively.

● Example

The following example revokes the BINDADD privilege of users ABBY01 and ABBY02 on database.

```
REVOKE BINDADD ON DATABASE
    FROM ABBY01, ABBY02;
```

◘ REVOKE—revoke package privileges

● General format

```
REVOKE package-privilege,...
   ON PACKAGE package-name
   FROM <PUBLIC or authorization-id,...>
```

● Description

This **REVOKE** statement revokes from one or all users privileges to use **CONTROL, BIND**, and **EXECUTE** statements against a package. With this statement you can specify one or more privileges but only one plan.

plan-privilege is one of the following keywords:

Keyword	Privilege
BIND	Issue the **BIND, REBIND,** and **FREE** commands against the plans named in this statement
EXECUTE	Run programs belonging to the plan named in this statement
CONTROL	Drop packages and grant package privileges to others

ON PACKAGE *package-name*
This specifies one package for which privileges are revoked.

package-name is the name of a package used to remove privileges.

FROM <PUBLIC or *authorization-id,...*>
This specifies the users whose privileges are revoked: individual users or all users.

PUBLIC means to revoke privileges of all users.

authorization-id is a user ID or group name. You can specify one or more IDs, and it must not include the user ID that is issuing the command.

- Usage

Embedded in an application program, dynamically prepared and executed, and issued interactively.

- Example

The following example revokes the **BIND** privilege of users ABBY and THOMASLO on package BIND01.

```
REVOKE BIND ON BIND01
    FROM ABBY, THOMASLO;
```

◘ REVOKE—revoke table or view privileges

- General format

```
REVOKE < ALL or  ALL PRIVILEGES or
      table-privilege,...>
  ON [TABLE] <table-name or view-name>
  FROM <PUBLIC or authorization-id,...>
```

- Description

This **REVOKE** statement revokes from one or more users privileges to use a resource at the table level of DB2/2. With this statement you can specify one or more privileges but only one table or view.

ALL or ALL PRIVILEGES means grant all privileges on tables or views mentioned with the ON clause.

table-privilege is one of the following keywords:

Keyword	Privilege
ALTER	Issue the **ALTER** statement
DELETE	Issue the **DELETE** statement
INDEX	Issue the **INDEX** statement
INSERT	Issue the **INSERT** statement
SELECT	Issue the **SELECT** statement

Keyword	Privilege
UPDATE	Issue the **UPDATE** statement
CONTROL	Grant all the privileges listed here as well as the ability to drop the table or view
REFERENCE	Create and drop a foreign key referencing a table as the parent

ON TABLE <*table-name* or *view-name*>
This specifies one or more tables or one or more views.

table-name is the name of a table.

view-name is the name of a view.

FROM <PUBLIC or *authorization-id,...*>
This specifies the users whose privileges are revoked: individual users or all users.

PUBLIC means to revoke privileges of all users.

authorization-id is a user ID or group name. You can specify one or more IDs, and it must not include the user ID that is issuing the command.

● Usage

Embedded in an application program, dynamically prepared and executed, and issued interactively.

● Example

The following example revokes all table privileges from users Z1335MG and ABBY.

```
REVOKE ALL PRIVILEGES
   ON TABLE RBA.CLIENTS
   FROM Z1335MG, ABBY;
```

◻ ROLLBACK—back out database changes

● General format

```
ROLLBACK [WORK]
```

- Description

The **ROLLBACK** statement backs out all changes to the database up to the point of the last execution of a **COMMIT** statement. If the **COMMIT** statement was not issued in a program and **ROLLBACK** is executed, then all changes will be backed out. DB2/2 issues a **ROLLBACK** if a program abends or if a timeout or lock occurs.

The **ROLLBACK** statement backs out the work of the following statements: **ALTER, COMMENT ON, CREATE, DELETE, DROP, GRANT, INSERT** and **UPDATE**.

- Usage

Embedded in an application program, dynamically prepared and executed, and issued interactively.

- Example

The following is an example of how to issue the **ROLLBACK** statement.

```
EXEC SQL
   ROLLBACK
END-EXEC.
```

◘ SELECT—retrieve data

- General format

```
1 - subselect:
  select-clause from-clause [where-clause]
                            [group-clause] [having-clause]

    select-clause is:
    SELECT [ALL or DISTINCT]
      < * or column-name,...>

    from-clause is:
    FROM <table-name,... or view-name,...>

  where-clause is :
    WHERE search-condition

  group-clause is:
    GROUP BY column-name,...

   having-clause is:
```

```
     HAVING search-condition
```

2 – fullselect is

```
<subselect or fullselect> <UNION or
                               UNION ALL or
                               EXCEPT or
                               EXCEPT ALL or
                               INTERSECT or
                               INTERSECT>
                    <subselect or (fullselect)>
```

3 – select-statement is

```
fullselect [order-by-clause [fetch-clause] or
                  update-clause                        or
                  fetch-clause]
```

4 – Embedded SELECT is

```
SELECT [ALL or DISTINCT]<* or column-name,...>
     from-clause [where-clause]
                      [group-clause] [having-clause]
```

● Description

The **SELECT** statement is used to retrieve rows of data from a database. There are two types of **SELECT** statement—interactive and embedded—and both are complete statements.

fullselect is part of an interactive **SELECT** statement or a **DECLARE CURSOR** statement.

subselect is part of *fullselect*, a **CREATE VIEW** statement, or an **INSERT** statement.

ORDER BY <*column-name* or *integer*>
          <ASC or DESC>,...

This clause specifies the sequence in which the rows are presented. If this clause is not used, the rows are returned in the order in which they are stored physically. With this clause you can specify a column name or column number and the order of presentation. This specification can be repeated many times.

column-name is the name of the column according to which the result table is ordered.

integer is the number which identifies the position of a column. This number should be greater than zero and not greater than the number of columns in the result table.

ASC is the keyword for ordering the column in an ascending sequence. ASC is the default.

DESC is the keyword for ordering the column in a descending sequence.

FOR UPDATE OF
This clause is effective only in application programs and is used with the **DECLARE CURSOR** statement.

ALL
This keyword is used in the **SELECT** clause to return all rows, including duplicate ones.

DISTINCT
This keyword is used in the **SELECT** clause to return only unique rows and discard any duplicate ones.

FROM <*table-name* or *view-name,...*>
This clause specifies one or more tables or views from which the data is extracted. In processing a **SELECT** statement, a result table is created, although the actual data is stored in the objects called *tables*. This result table exists temporarily and is only a conceptual file. It contains all the possible rows.

table-name is the name of a table already defined in the catalog.

view-name is the name of a view already defined in the catalog.

WHERE *search-condition*
This clause determines the number of rows that the result table will have.

search-condition is made up of columns, operators, and constants, composed in a logical manner. Each row that satisfies the search condition is found in the result table. The following operators, conditions, and keywords may be used as part of the search condition.

Type	Operator	Meaning
Comparison	=	Equal to
	¬ = or < >	Not equal to
	>	Greater than
	¬ > or < =	Not greater than
	¬ < or > =	Not less than
Arithmetic	+	Addition
	-	Subtraction
	*	Multiplication
	/	Division

Type	Operator	Meaning
Boolean	**AND**	Logical **AND**
	OR	Logical **OR**
Keyword	**BETWEEN**	A value is equal to or between two other values
	IN	Combine one or more **OR** operators
	NOT or ¬	Negative search condition
	LIKE	Compare similar values

GROUP BY *column-name,...*
This clause causes the rows in the intermediate result set to be grouped according to the values of one or more columns named in the GROUP BY clause. It is commonly used when there are one or more column functions in the **SELECT** clause.

column-name is the name of a column of the table or view.

HAVING *search-condition*
This specifies a search condition which each group of rows must satisfy in order to be passed to the column function.

search-condition is made up of columns, operators, and constants, composed in a logical manner. Each row that satisfies the search condition is found in the result table. The operators AND, OR, BETWEEN, IN, and LIKE may be used as part of the search condition.

UNION

This clause merges two results of two or more **SELECT** statements into one result table. With this clause, each **SELECT** statement is processed individually; they are then combined into one result table. All duplicate rows are discarded except when UNION ALL is used.

INTO *host-variable,...*

This clause specifies one or more host variables into which DB2/2 is to place the data retrieved by an embedded **SELECT** statement. **SELECT...INTO** works only if no rows or one row is retrieved. If SELECT...INTO results in more than one row, it will fail with a negative code (-811), and it will retrieve no data.

host-variable is the name of a structure or variable declared in your program. The variable is referenced by DB2/2 when SQL statements are executed. It is a good programming practice to provide variables that are compatible in data type and scale with the columns they receive. The following is a list of DB2/2 data types that correspond to COBOL data types.

DB2/2   **COBOL**

```
FIELD_A   CHAR(n)        01 FIELD-A   PIC X(n)
FIELD_A   VARCHAR(n)     01 FIELD-A
                            10 FIELD-A-LEN PIC S9(4) COMP
                            10 FIELD-A-TEXT  PIC X(n)
FIELD_A   SMALLINT       01 FIELD-A   PIC S9(4) COMP
FIELD_A   INTEGER        01 FIELD-A   PIC S9(9) COMP
FIELD_A   DECIMAL(p,q)   01 FIELD-A   PIC S9(a)V9(q) COMP-3
FIELD_A   DATE           01 FIELD-A   PIC X(10)
FIELD_A   TIME           01 FIELD-A   PIC X(8)
FIELD_A   TIMESTAMP      01 FIELD-A   PIC X(26)
```

Column functions

The following is a list of built-in column functions supplied by SQL. They operate on the entire column to produce one value in the result table.

Function	Description	Restrictions
SUM	Sum of values in column	Numeric data only
AVG	Average of values in column	Numeric data only
MIN	Minimum value within column	
COUNT	Count of the number of rows	

Scalar functions

The following is a list of built-in scalar functions supplied by SQL (all these functions are described in the next section):

CHAR, DATE, DAY, DAYS, DECIMAL, FLOAT, HOUR, INTEGER, LENGTH, MICROSECOND, MINUTE, MONTH, SECOND, SUBSTR, TIME, TIMESTAMP, TRANSLATE, VARGRAPHIC, and **YEAR.**

Concatenation

The concatenation operator (| |) combines character values into one string.

- Usage

Embedded in an application program, dynamically prepared and executed, and issued interactively.

- Example

The following example returns all unique rows with values for the CL_NAME and CL_LANG columns.

```
SELECT DISTINCT CL_NAME, CL_LANG
   FROM RBA.CLIENTS
```

The following example returns rows with values for the CL_NAME and CL_LANG columns according to a search condition. The condition is that the value of the CL_CITY column is 'TORONTO' and the first character of the CL_LANG column is 'E'.

```
SELECT CL_NAME, CL_LANG
   FROM RBA.CLIENTS
   WHERE CL_CITY='TORONTO' AND SUBSTR(CL_LANG,1,1)='E';
```

In the following example, two **SELECT** statements are executed using the UNION clause.

```
SELECT CL_NAME, 'CLIENT NAME'
   FROM RBA.CLIENTS
   WHERE CL_CITY='TORONTO' AND SUBSTR(CL_LANG,1,1)='E'
UNION
SELECT CL_NAME, 'CLIENT LANGUAGE'
   FROM RBA.CLIENTS
   WHERE CL_CITY='TORONTO' AND SUBSTR(CL_LANG,1,1)='E';
```

In the following example, all the rows of the CLIENTS table are first grouped together according to the values in CL_BRANCH. Then the highest CL_RATING of each group is found.

```
SELECT MAX(CL_RATING)
   FROM RBA.CLIENTS
   GROUP BY CL_BRANCH;
```

◘ UPDATE—update columns of a table or view

● General format

```
Not using cursor:

  UPDATE  <table-name or view-name> [correlation-name]
     SET column-name = <expression or NULL>
     WHERE search-condition

Using cursor:

  UPDATE <table-name or view-name>
     SET column-name = <expression or NULL>
     WHERE CURRENT OF cursor-name
```

● Description

The **UPDATE** statement updates the values of one or more columns of a table or view. The update can be done by using either a search condition or using the cursor.

table-name is the name of a table already defined in the DB2/2 catalog.

view-name is the name of a view already defined in the DB2/2 catalog.

correclation-name is used to designate a table or view.

SET *column-name* = <expression or NULL>
This specifies a list of columns and values. If there are more than one columns and values, each pair is separated by a comma.

column-name is the name of a column already defined in the table or view.

expression is any valid SQL expression.

NULL means a null value.

WHERE *search-condition*
This clause determines how many rows will be updated.

search-condition is the same as the search condition used in the WHERE clause of the **SELECT** statement. Depending on the condition, no rows or many rows may be updated.

WHERE CURRENT OF *cursor-name*
This clause determines how many rows will be updated using a cursor.

cursor-name is the name of a cursor, defined before using it in the **UPDATE** statement. The **DECLARE CURSOR** statement defines the cursor. When this statement is executed, it updates the row where the cursor is positioned. After the update, the cursor points to the next row.

● Usage

Embedded in an application program, dynamically prepared and executed, and issued interactively.

● Example

The following example updates columns of the table RBA.CLIENTS. The columns are NAME, CITY, and POSTAL_C, and the values are RBC, NEWMARKET, and L3X1F0.

For all the rows that have column ADDRESS equal to '330 MAIN ST', the update will take place.

```
UPDATE INTO RBA.CLIENTS
  SET  NAME='RBC', CITY='NEWMARKET', POSTAL_C='L3X1F0'
    WHERE ADDRESS='330 MAIN ST';
```

◘ WHENEVER—conditional processing

● General format

```
WHENEVER <NOT FOUND or
          SQLERROR or
         SQLWARNING>
     <CONTINUE or
          GOTO[:]host-label
```

● Description

The **WHENEVER** statement causes the DB2/2 translator to generate the code needed to check **SQLCODE** and/or **SQLWARN0** after each SQL statement is executed. If a certain condition is met, a specific action is taken. The condition may be an error, an exception, or a warning that exists in **SQLCA**. The following describes the conditions triggered after a statement is executed and the actions that can be taken.

NOT FOUND is a condition where **SQLCODE** is +100 or with a **SQLSTATE** of '02000'.

SQLERROR is a condition where **SQLCODE** is negative.

SQLWARNING is a condition where **SQLCODE** is greater than zero but not equal to 100 or where **SQLWARN0** is 'W'.

CONTINUE means to ignore the exception and continue processing.

GOTO *host-label*
This means to branch to a label in a program and begin processing the statements found there. In COBOL it is a paragraph or section, and a function in C.

host-label is a paragraph or section.

● Usage

Embedded in an application program, dynamically prepared and executed, and issued interactively.

● Example
The following is part of a COBOL program. It causes control to branch to paragraph 9999-SEVERE-ERROR if the condition SQLERROR occurs after any SQL statement is executed.

```
PROCEDURE DIVISION.

MAINLINE.
   EXEC SQL
     WHENEVER SQLERROR GOTO 9999-SEVERE-ERROR
   END-EXEC.
   .
   .
   .

STOP RUN.

9999-SEVERE-ERROR.
   DISPLAY "SEVERE ERROR ENCOUNTERED, SQLCODE = " AT 2001
```

```
DISPLAY SQLCODE AT 2035
DISPLAY SQLERRMC AT 2101
   END PROGRAM
                       .
9999-EXIT. EXIT.
```

6.3 Functions

DB2/2 has a number of built-in functions. Each one performs a specific operation. They are different from SQL statements; they are distinguished from statements because each function name is followed by a pair of parentheses, as in C. These functions take one or more operands called *arguments*, placed within the parentheses. There are two types of functions: column and scalar.

6.3.1 Column functions

There are five column functions: **AVG, COUNT, MAX, MIN,** and **SUM.** The argument of each of these functions is a set of values derived from one or more columns.

◘ AVG—calculate the avarage of numbers

● General format

AVG ([DISTINCT] *column-name*)

● Description

The **AVG** function returns the average of a set of numbers. The returned value depends on the data type of the column. The return value for an integer column is integer, for a floating-point column is floating-point, and so on. And, of course the result should be within the range of the data type; otherwise, the operation will result in error.

DISTINCT means that duplicate values are eliminated. If this keyword is omitted, then all values are used to calculate the average.

column-name is the name of an existing table whose values are used to calculate the average.

● Example

In the next **SELECT** statement, **AVG** is used to calculate the avarage of staff in department DX01. By omitting **DISTINCT** parameter, duplicate values are not ignored. The column STAFF_AGE of the table DEPARTMENT is the argument to the **AVG** function. The result is placed in AVG_AGE.

```
SELECT AVG(STAFF_AGE)
   INTO :AVE_AGE
   FROM DEPARTMENT
   WHERE DEPNO='DX01'
```

In the next statement the **DISTINCT** keyword is used with STAFF_AGE. This means that the averages of only unique values are used to calculate the average.

```
SELECT AVG(DISTINCT STAFF_AGE)
   INTO :AVE_AGE
   FROM DEPARTMENT
   WHERE DEPNO='DX01'
```

◘ COUNT—calculate the number of rows

● General format

```
COUNT(*)
   or
COUNT(DINCTINCT column-name)
```

● Description

The **COUNT** function returns the number of rows in a table or the number of values in a set of rows.

COUNT(*) returns a number of rows in a table. Rows where all the columns have NULL values are counted.

DISTINCT *column-name*
This parameter is used to specify distinct values of a column.

column-name is the name of a column in a table.

● Example

In the next **SELECT** statement, COUNT( ) returns the number of rows in the DEPARTMENT table, which has the department number 'DX01'. The value is placed in STAFF_CNT host variable.

```
SELECT COUNT(*)
   INTO :STAFF_CNT
   FROM DEPARTMENT
   WHERE DEPNO='DX01'
```

In the next **SELECT** statement, the argument of COUNT is DISTINCT STAFF_LEVEL. DISTINCT means that any duplicate values of STAFF_LEVEL will not be counted. Also, the rows that are counted must have DEPNO='DX01'. The count is placed in the STAFF_LVL host variable.

```
SELECT COUNT(DISTINCT STAFFF_LEVEL)
   INTO :STAFF_LVL
   FROM DEPARTMENT
   WHERE DEPNO='DX01'
```

◻ MAX—calculate the maximum of a set of values

● General format

```
MAX (column-name)
```

● Description

The **MAX** function calculates the maximum value in a set of values of a column. The data type of the returned value is the same as that of the argument.

column-name is the name of a column in a table for which maximum value is to be calculated.

● Example

The following **MAX** function within the **SELECT** statement is used to find the maximum value of STAFF_AGE from the DEPARTMENT where DEPNO='DX01'.

```
SELECT MAX(STAFF_AGE)
INTO :MAX_AGE
FROM DEPARTMENT
WHERE DEPNO='DX01'
```

◘ MIN—calculate the minimum of a set of values

- General format

```
MIN (column-name)
```

- Description

The **MIN** function calculates the minimum value in a set of values of a column. The data type of the returned value is the same as the data type of the argument.

column-name is the name of a column in a table for which mimimum value is to be calculated.

- Example

The following **MIN** function within the **SELECT** statement is used to find the minimum value of STAFF_AGE from the DEPARTMENT where DEPNO='DX01'.

```
SELECT MIN(STAFF_AGE)
INTO :MAX_AGE
FROM DEPARTMENT
WHERE DEPNO='DX01'
```

◘ SUM—calculate the sum of a set of numbers

- General format

SUM ([DISTINCT] *column-name*)

- Description

The **SUM** function returns the sum of a set of numbers. The returned value depends on the data type of the column. The return value for an integer column is integer, for a floating-point column it is floating-point and so on. And, of course, the result should be within the range of the data type; otherwise, the operation will result in error.

DISTINCT means that duplicate values are eliminated. If this keyword is omitted, then all values are used to calculate the sum of numbers.

column-name is the name of an existing table whose values are used to calculate the sum.

- Example

In the next **SELECT** statement, **SUM** is used to calculate the sum of staff in department DX01. By omitting the DISTINCT parameter, duplicate values are not ignored. The column STAFF_AGE of the table DEPARTMENT is the argument to the **SUM** function. The result is placed in SUM_AVG.

```
SELECT AVG(STAFF_AGE)
   INTO :SUM_AGE
   FROM DEPARTMENT
   WHERE DEPNO='DX01'
```

In the next statement the DISTINCT keyword is used with STAFF_AGE. This means that only unique values are used to calculate the sum.

```
SELECT SUM(DISTINCT STAFF_AGE)
   INTO :SUM_AGE
   FROM DEPARTMENT
   WHERE DEPNO='DX01'
```

6.3.2 Scalar functions

The main distinction of a scalar function is that its argument can be an expression. An expression can include a function (scalar or column), a constant, column names, host variables, and special registers. All these possible components of an expression must conform to the rules of SQL. In DB2/2 there are 19 scalar functions. The following paragraphs give the format, description, and examples of each of them.

◘ CHAR—Converts a datetime value to a string

- General format

```
CHAR (expression [,date-format])
```

- Description

The **CHAR** function converts a datetime value into a string.

expression must evaluate to a date, time, or a timestamp.

date-format determines the format of the datetime value. If it used, it is one of the following: ISO, USA, EUR, JIS, or LOCAL. These formats were discussed earlier.

● Example

In the next example, let's say the host variable CURRENT-DATE has 1994-01-10 in the internal format. The **CHAR** function will return '01/10/1994' in USA format.

```
CHAR (:CURRENT-DATE, USA)
```

In the next example, the expression is a bit more complicated. It adds the time value of a host variable ELAPSE-TIME and column START_TIME. Assume that START_TIME is 10.20.30 and ELAPSE-TIME is 050000 (5 hours). The return value will be be '15:20 PM'.

```
CHAR (START_TIME + :ELAPSE-TIME, USA)
```

◘ DATE—convert value to date format

● General format

DATE (*expression*)

● Description

The **DATE** function value returns the date portion of a value.

expression must evaluate to a date, timestamp, a positive number less than or equal to 3,652,059, or a string holding a date or a timestamp.

● Example

In the next example, the expression is TIMESTAMP, a register that holds the current time and date. The **DATE** function is used to extract the date portion. Let's say the timestamp is equivalent to '1994-01-11-10.20.30.000000'. The result of

```
DATE(TIMESTAMP)
```

will be '1994-01-11'.

◘ DAY—get the day part of a value

- General format

```
DAY(expression)
```

- Description

The **DAY** function returns the day part of a date or timestamp.

expression can be a date, timestamp, date duration, timestamp duration, or a valid string holding a date or a timestamp.

- Example

The following **SELECT** statement is used to retrieve a date from the CLIENT_ID column of the CLIENTS table. The search clause of this statement uses the **DAY** function twice. The first time it calculates the day of the current date; and next time, the day of the START_DATE column. Both return a day value, and if the difference is greater thamn 15, the CLIENT_ID for that row is placed into the WS-CLIENT host variable.

```
SELECT CLIENT_ID
  INTO :WS-CLIENT
    FROM CLIENTS
    WHERE DAY(TIMESTAMP) - DAY(START_DATE) > 15
```

In the next **SELECT** statement, the **DAY** function is used to get the day portion of the START_DATE column whose data type is date.

```
SELECT DAY(START_DATE)
    INTO :DATE
    FROM CLIENTS
    WHERE CLIENT_ID = 'ICM'
```

The selected row(s) must have CLIENT_ID = ICM. If START_DATE has '1994-01-30', the 30 will be placed in the DATE host variable.

◘ DAYS—get integer value of day from date

- General format

```
DAYS (expression)
```

- Description

  The **DAYS** function returns the integer value of a date.

  expression must be a date, timestamp, or a string holding a date or a timestamp.

- Example
  The following **SELECT** statement is used to calculate the difference in days between the current day and time, and the value retrieved from the CLIENT_ID column of the CLIENTS table. The returned number of days is placed into the :WS-DAYS host variable.

```
SELECT DAYS(TIMESTAMP) - DAYS(START_DATE)
   INTO :WS-CLIENT
     FROM CLIENTS
     WHERE DEPTNO = 'DEP001'
```

◑ DECIMAL—convert a number to a decimal

- General format

```
DECIMAL (numeric-expression
            [,precision-integer, scale-integer])
```

- Description

  The **DECIMAL** function is used to convert any types of numbers into its decimal representation.

  numeric-expression must evaluate to a numeric data type.

  precision-integer is an operational integer that specifies the precision of the result. Its value must be in the range 1 to 31. The default precision integer for a floating-point or decimal value is 15; for large integers, 11; and for small integers, 5.

  scale-integer is a value in the range 0 to the value of *precision-integer*.

- Example

  In the next interactive **SELECT** command, the decimal representation of SALES is returned. The SALE column is of SMALLINT data type and is converted to DECIMAL data type in this **SELECT** statement, which gets two columns of all rows where DEPNO = 'DX01'.

```
SELECT CLIENT_ID, DECIMAL(SALES,5,2)
   FROM CLIENTS
   WHERE DEPNO = 'DX01'
```

◖ FLOAT—convert a number to a floating-point value

- General format

```
FLOAT (numeric-expression)
```

- Description

The **FLOAT** function is used to convert any numeric value to a double precision floating-point number.

numeric-expression must evaluate to any numeric data type. If this value is null, the result from the **FLOAT** function is null.

- Example

In the next **SELECT** statement, the **FLOAT** function is used to convert the value of AMOUNT column from decimal to floating-point.

```
SELECT CLIENT_ID,
          FLOAT(AMOUNT)
   FROM CLIENTS
   WHERE DEPNO = 'DX01'
```

◖ HOUR—get the hour part of a value

- General format

```
HOUR(expression)
```

- Description

The **HOUR** function returns the hour part of a date or timestamp. The return value is in the range 0 to 24.

expression can be a date, timestamp, date duration, timestamp duration, or a valid string holding a date or a timestamp.

- Example

The following **SELECT** statement is used to retrieve a date from the

CLIENT_ID column of CLIENTS table. The search clause of this statement uses the **HOUR** function twice. The first time it calculates the hour of the current date; and the next time the hour of the START_DATE column. Both return a hour value, and if the difference is greater than 15, the value of the CLIENT_ID column for that row is placed into the WS-CLIENT host variable.

```
SELECT CLIENT_ID
   INTO :WS-CLIENT
     FROM CLIENTS
       WHERE HOUR(TIMESTAMP) - HOUR(START_DATE) > 15
```

◘ INTEGER—convert a number to an integer

- General format

```
INTEGER(numeric-expression)
```

- Description

The **INTEGER** function returns the integer part of a number. The result is a large integer.

numeric-expression must evaluate to any numeric data type. If this value is null, then the result from the **INTEGER** function is null.

- Example
In the next **SELECT** statement, the **INTEGER** function is used to obtain the integer part when AMOUNT is divided by EDLEVEL.

```
SELECT CLIENT_ID,
         EDLEVEL,
         (AMOUNT/EDLEVEL)
    FROM CLIENTS
   WHERE DEPNO = 'DX01'
```

◘ LENGTH—calculate the length of a value

- General format

```
LENGTH(expression)
```

- Description

The **LENGTH** function caluclates the length of a value.

The argument can be any data type. The return length is a large integer in the number of bytes. If the argument is graphic, the return value is half the length in bytes of the argument. If the argument is a null, the result is a null value.

The following shows the length in bytes and data types.

Length	Data types
2	Small integer
4	Large integer
$p/2 + 1$	For decimal number with precision p
8	Float
4	Date
3	Time
10	Timestamp
length of string	Character string

expression can evaluate to any data type.

● Example

Let's say the NAME host variable contains 'John Smith'.

```
LENGTH(:NAME) returns 10.
```

Assume that the START_DATE column is a DATE data type,

```
LENGTH (START_DATE) returns 4.
```

◘ MICROSECOND—get the microsecond part of a time value

● General format

```
MICROSECOND(expression)
```

● Description

The **MICROSECOND** function returns the microsecond part of a date or timestamp. The return value is in the range 0 to 999999.

expression can be a date, timestamp, date duration, timestamp duration, or a valid string holding a date or a timestamp.

● Example

The following **SELECT** statement is used to retrieve a date from the CLIENT_ID column of the CLIENTS table. The search clause of this statement uses the **MICROSECOND** function to determine whether the microsecond of the START_DATE column is greater that 0. If this evaluation is valid the value of the CLIENT_ID column for that row is placed into the WS-CLIENT host variable.

```
SELECT CLIENT_ID
   INTO :WS-CLIENT
     FROM CLIENTS
     WHERE MICROSECOND(START_DATE) > 0
```

◘ MINUTE—get the minute part of a time value

● General format

```
MINUTE(expression)
```

● Description

The **MINUTE** function returns the minute part of a date or timestamp. The return value is an integer in the range 0 to 59.

expression can be a date, timestamp, date duration, timestamp duration, or a valid string holding a date or a timestamp.

● Example

The following **SELECT** statement is used to retrieve a date from the CLIENT_ID column of the CLIENTS table. The search clause of this statement uses the MINUTE function to determine whether the minute of the START_DATE column is greater than 0. If this evaluation is valid, the value of the CLIENT_ID column for that row is placed into the WS-CLIENT host variable.

```
SELECT CLIENT_ID
   INTO :WS-CLIENT
     FROM CLIENTS
     WHERE MINUTE(START_DATE) > 0
```

◘ MONTH—get the minute part of a time value

● General format

```
MONTH(expression)
```

● Description

The **MONTH** function returns the month part of a date or timestamp. The return value is an integer in the range 1 to 12.

expression can be a date, timestamp, date duration, timestamp duration, or a valid string holding a date or a timestamp.

● Example

The following **SELECT** statement is used to retrieve a date from the CLIENT_ID column of the CLIENTS table. The search clause of this statement uses the **MONTH** function to determine whether the month of the START_DATE column is equal to 1. If this evaluation ia valid, the value of the CLIENT_ID column for that row is placed into the WS-CLIENT host variable.

```
SELECT CLIENT_ID
   INTO :WS-CLIENT
     FROM CLIENTS
     WHERE MINUTE(START_DATE) = 1
```

◘ SECOND—get the second part of a time value

● General format

```
SECOND(expression)
```

● Description

The **SECOND** function returns the second part of a date or timestamp. The return value is an integer in the range 0 to 59.

expression can be a date, timestamp, date duration, timestamp duration, or a valid string holding a date or a timestamp.

● Example

The following **SELECT** statement is used to retrieve a date from the

CLIENT_ID column of the CLIENTS table. The search clause of this statement uses the **SECOND** function to determine whether the minute of the START_DATE column is greater than 0. If this evaluation is valid, the value of the CLIENT_ID column for that row is placed into the WS-CLIENT host variable.

```
SELECT CLIENT_ID
   INTO :WS-CLIENT
     FROM CLIENTS
     WHERE SECOND(START_DATE) > 0
```

◻ SUBSTR—get a substring of a string

● General format

```
SUBSTR (string, start [,length])
```

● Description

The **SUBSTR** function returns a substring of a string.

string is a character or graphic string from which the substring is returned.

start is the starting position of the first byte of the substring.

length is the number of bytes from the starting position.

● Example

In the following example, the SUBSTR(F_NAME,1,1) returns the first character of the F_NAME column.

```
SELECT SUBSTR(F_NAME,1,1),
         L_NAME
     FROM CUSTOMER
```

◻ TIME—get a time from a value

● General format

```
TIME(expression)
```

● Description

The **TIME** function returns the time from the time value. The return value is the same as the argument, it returns timestamp for timestamp, time for time, string for string, and null for null.

expression can be a date, timestamp, date duration, timestamp duration, or a valid string holding a date or a timestamp.

● Example

In the search condition of the following **SELECT** statement, the TIME function is used to extract the time part of the START_TIME column. Next, it is determined whether it is equal to or greater than one hour after the current time.

```
SELECT NAME
    FROM COURSES
    WHERE TIME(START_TIME) >= CURRENTTIME + 1 HOUR
```

◘ TIMESTAMP—get a timestamp from a value

● General format

```
TIMESTAMP(expression1 [,expression2])
```

● Description

The **TIMESTAMP** function returns a timestamp value from one or two arguments. If the arguments are null, then the result is also a null value.

expression1 must be a timestamp or a string holding a valid timestamp, if *expression2* is not specified. If both expressions are entered, then *expression1* must be a date or a string holding a valid date.

expression2 is optional, and if specified, it must be a time or a string holding a valid time.

● Example

Assume that START_DATE = 1994-01-12 and START_TIME = 10.20.30.

```
TIMESTAMP(START_DATE,START_TIME
```

returns '1994-01-12-10.20.30.000000'.

◘ TRANSLATE—translate characters

- General format

Character string format:

```
TRANSLATE( char-string-expression
           [,to-string-expression, from-string-expression
           [,' ' or ,pad-char]])
```

Graphic string format:

```
TRANSLATE( graphic-string-expression,
           to-string-expression, from-string-expression
           [,' ' or ,pad-char] )
```

- Description

The TRANSLATE function is used to convert characters in a character string or a graphic string.

char-string-expression or *graphic-string-expression* is the string where the translation occurs.

to-string-expression contains a set of characters that are translated to or from the source string.

from-string-expression is a set of characters that are searched for in *char-string-expression* or *graphic-string-expression*. If found, they are translated to *to-string-expression*.

pad-char is a single character that is used to pad *to-string-expression*, if the length of *to-string-expression* is shorter than *from-string-expression*.

- Example

Let's say that the DISNEY host variable contains 'HANA BARBARA'. The following shows the operands and return values of the TRANSLATE function.

```
TRANSLATE(:DISNEY) returns 'HANA BARBARA'.
TRANSLATE(:DISNEY,I,A) returns 'HINI BIRBIRI'.
TRANSLATE(:DISNEY,ei,aa) returns 'HeNe BeRBeRe'.
TRANSLATE(:DISNEY,'i',ar) returns 'HiNi Bi Bi A'.
```

◘ VARGRAPHIC-convert to double-byte character string

- General format

```
VARGRAPHIC(expression)
```

- Description

The **VARGRAPHIC** function converts a string that has both single-byte and double-byte characters to pure double-byte character strings.

expression must evaluate to the character string data type, except LONG VARCHAR. The length of the string cannot exceed 2000 bytes.

◘ YEAR—calculate the year part of a time value

- General format

```
YEAR(expression)
```

- Description

The **YEAR** function returns the year part of a date or timestamp. The return value is an integer in the range 1 to 9999.

expression can be a date, timestamp, date duration, timestamp duration, or a valid string holding a date or a timestamp.

- Example

The following **SELECT** statement is used to retrieve a date from the CLIENT_ID column of the CLIENTS table. The search clause of this statement uses the YEAR function where the year of the REQUEST_DT column is compared with the year of the timestamp register. If both are equal, then the value of the CLIENT_ID column for that row is placed into the WS-CLIENT host variable.

```
SELECT CLIENT_ID
   INTO :WS-CLIENT
    FROM CLIENTS
    WHERE YEAR(REQUEST_DT) = YEAR(TIMESTAMP)
```

6.4 Structures

6.4.1 SQLCA—SQL communication area

The **SQLCA**, the SQL communication area, is the memory area that interfaces between your program and DB2/2. A program that executes an SQL statement (except **DECLARE**, **INCLUDE**, and **WHENEVER**) must include this structure, which is supplied with the precompiler of the language (C, C++, REXX, or COBOL); for example,

```
EXEC SQL INCLUDE SQLCA;
```

or

```
EXEC SQL INCLUDE SQLCA END-EXEC
```

The following lists the name of the fields of **SQLCA**, the data type, and a brief description of the data in each field.

Field type	Data type	Description
sqlcaid	CHAR(8)	Contains identifier 'SQLCA'.
sqlcabc	INTEGER	The length of the **SQLCA** structure.
sqlcode	INTEGER	The return code after executing an SQL statement. If it is zero, the execution is successful. If the return code is a positive value, the statement was executed successfully, but with a warning condition. If it is a negative value, the execution resulted in an error condition.
sqlerrml	SMALLINT	The length of **sqlerrmc** which is in the range 0 to 70.
sqlerrmc	VARCHAR(70)	This field must contain one or more tokens, separated by a hexadecimal value 'FF'. Each token is substituted by variables in the descriptions of error conditions.
sqlerrp	CHAR(8)	The first three characters of this field is 'SQL', followed by the name of the module that returned an error code, if any.
sqlerrd	Array	The array contains six **INTEGER** elements:
SQLERRD(1)		Reserved for internal use
SQLERRD(2)		Reserved for internal use
SQLERRD(3)		The number of rows affected by **INSERT**, **UPDATE** and **DELETE** statements
SQLERRD(4)		Reserved for future use
SQLERRD(5)		The number of rows updated or deleted
SQLERRD(6)		Reserved for future use
sqlwarn	Array	It is an array of CHAR(1), each containing a W if there is a warning

		return code; otherwise it is a blank.
sqlwarn0		Contains a blank if all other elements of this array contain blanks
sqlwarn1		Contains W if a truncation occurred when assigning value of a column to a host variable.
sqlwarn2		Contains W if null values were not given on the argument of a function
sqlwarn3		Contains W if the number of columns is not the same as the number of host variables
sqlwarn4		Contains W if a prepared **UPDATE** or **DELETE** statement does not have a WHERE clause
sqlwarn5		Reserved for future use
sqlwarn6		Contains W if the result of a date calculation was changed to avoid an impossible date
sqlstate	CHAR(5)	The return code of the most recently executed SQL statement.

6.4.2 SQLDA—SQL descriptor area

The **SQLDA**, the SQL descriptor area, is required when executing the **SQL DESCRIBE** statement. The **SQLDA** contains variables that are used when executing the **PREPARE, OPEN, FETCH,** and **EXECUTE** statements. If SQLDA is used with a **PREPARE** or **DESCRIBE** statement, then it provides information to your program about a prepared statement. And, if it is used with an **OPEN, EXECUTE,** or **FETCH** statement, it describes the host variables.

Fields	Data Type	Used in PREPARE or DESCRIBE	Used in FETCH, OPEN, or EXECUTE
sqlaid	CHAR(8)	Contains 'SQLDA'	Not used
sqldabc	INTEGER	Length of SQLDA	Length of SQLDA
sqln	SMALLINT	Number of occurrences of SQLVAR	Number of occurrences of SQLVAR
sqld	SMALLINT	Number of columns in SQLVAR	Number of host variables in SQLVAR

Figure 6.5 Description of **SQLDA**.

In a program if a **SQLDA**, which has four variables, is followed by an arbitrary number of occurrences of a five-variable sequence, then collectively this arrangement is called **SQLVAR**. In an **OPEN**, **FETCH**, or **EXECUTE** statement, each occurrence of **SQLVAR** describes a host variable. However, in the **DESCRIBE** or **PREPARE** statement, each occurrence of **SQLVAR** is for a column of a result table. Figures 6.5 and 6.6 describe the fields of **SQLDA** and **SQLVAR**.

Fields	Data Type	Used in PREPARE or DESCRIBE	Used in FETCH, OPEN, or EXECUTE
sqltype	SMALLINT	The data type of column	The data type for host variable
sqldlen	SMALLINT	Defines the external length of a value	Defines the external length of a value
sqldata	pointer	0 if the FOR BIT DATA option is used, and if the data type of the of the column is CHAR, VARCHAR, or VARCHAR	The address of the host variable
sqllnd	pointer	0 if the FOR BIT DATA option is used, and if the data type of the of the column is CHAR, VARCHAR, or VARCHAR	The address of an associated indicator variable
sqlname	VARCHAR (30)	Name of the column	Not used

Figure 6.6 Description of **SQLVAR**.

Toolkit Utility Programs

Toolkit is a collection of utility programs for programmers; it is supplied with C Set++ Tools from IBM. As we'll see, these programs are very appropriate for many programming situations. For each of these utility programs this chapter gives the format for usage, descriptions of function and parameters, and examples where needed. The programs covered here are

NMAKE	PACK
EXEHDR	UNPACK
FWDSTAMP	MAPSYM
IMPLIB	MSGBIND
MARKEXE	Resource compiler
MKMSGF	

7.1 NMAKE—Automate Development

● General format

```
NMAKE [option...] [macro-definition...] [target...]
        [/F description-file]
        or
NMAKE @command-file
```

● Description

The NMAKE program is very useful and it is an integral part of daily development tools for OS/2 programmers. It is used mainly to automate compiling, linking, or other processing based on date changes of files. NMAKE works on the basis of two sets of files: target files and dependent files. The target file timestamps are checked against the dependent files timestamps. If any dependent-file timestamps is more recent than the target files, NMAKE executes a series of commands that update the target files.

This tool is commonly used, especially when many sources, objects, and executable files are part of a large development project. Routinely, a few source files are changed at a time and the compiling and linking processes have repeated entirely. With NMAKE, you don't have to be concerned about which source files need to be compiled. NMAKE compiles the programs with the recent changes and then links them into an executable file. Also, NMAKE can be programmed to automatically execute any command such as

● Resource compiler
● Backups
● Configure data files

You can run the NMAKE program from the OS/2 command line or a command file. Once NMAKE is running you can halt it by pressing CTRL+C, and it will return to the operating system.

option directs the processing of NMAKE. You can specify zero to many options from the options listed below.

/a	Build **all** targets, ignoring the timestamp of dependencies.
/c	**C**ryptic mode. Do not display warning messages and sign-on banner.
/d	**D**isplay modification dates.
/i	**I**gnore exit codes of commands invoked.
/n	Do **n**ot execute any command; display them only.
/p	**P**rint macro definitions and target descriptions.

/q   Query date of the target file; you can use this option in a batch file.

/r   Ignore the inference rules from the 'tools.ini' file.

/s   Silent execution of commands.

/t   Touch target files so that the timestamps are current.

/?   Show help message.

/help Show help message.

/nologo Do not show logo.

macro-definition is zero to many macro definitions for NMAKE to use. If you specify a macro definition with spaces, you must enclose it with quotes ("). The macro definitions should be included in the description file.

target is the name of a file that needs to be updated, usually by a command. On a command line a target file is optional, and you can list zero to many such files. If none is listed, then NMAKE will update the first target in the description file.

command-file is a name of the file that contains commands fed to NMAKE.

/F *description-file* is an option that names a description file, other than MAKEFILE, where you build the relationship between the target files and dependent files. In this file you also tell NMAKE which command to execute to update the target files. If you omit this optional parameter, NMAKE will search for MAKEFILE in the current directory.

There are many aspects to a description file. Understanding them will make you more aware of how you can make NMAKE most functional. It will do some of the tedious and repetitive tasks for you during software development. It will let you concentrate on the real issues of programming, rather than wonder which files need to be compiled and linked, or which help file must be rebuilt.

Usually, a description file consists of a combination of the following:

- Description block
- Macros
- Directives
- Inference rules
- Pseudotargets

Description block: A *description block* tells the NMAKE about the targets, dependents, and commands. You have to list one command for one or more target or dependent files. Also, one file can contain one or more description block. The general form of the description block looks like this:

```
target...: dependent...
  command
  .
  .
  .
target...: dependent...;
  command
```

In the example,

```
PRTLABEL.OBJ: PRTLABEL.C
  ICC /C
```

PRTLABEL.OBJ is the target file, and the dependent is PRTLABEL.C. The

```
ICC /C
```

is the command to compile. In this case, if the data and time of PRTLABEL.C are more recent than PRTLABEL.OBJ, then NMAKE will compile the source file and update the object file. In the example

```
*.OBJ: *.C
  ICC /C
```

NMAKE will check the date and time of all the object files in the current directory and compile only those that were changed recently. You will see later that you can use inference rules and avoid the command.

Macros: A macro, as in the C and C++ languages, is a convenient way to replace a string with another string in the description file. In the last two examples, we saw ICC /C as a command. We can define a macro

```
ICC = ICC /C
```

and use it thus:

```
*.OBJ: *.C $(ICC)
```

When NMAKE processes this description block, it replaces ICC with
ICC /C. Macros become really practical when a number of strings such
as

```
ICC /C /Gd- /Se /Re /Ms /Gm+
```

are found in many places in a description file. If you have to change,
add, or delete these strings, you have to edit only at one occurrence.
Similarly, you can define macros for flags, libraries, options, and
commands. Some useful examples in OS/2 software development are

```
AFCLASS = /Mx -t -z
ASM     = /Ml /C /Zm
LFLAGS  = /NOE /NOD /ALIGN:16 /EXEPACK /M /BASE:0x10000
LINK    = LINK386 $(LFLAGS)
LIBS    = DDE4MBS + OS2386
```

When using a macro, after you have defined it, you must enclose it in
parentheses with a dollar ($) prefix. You can use a macro within a
macro, as shown in the third line in the preceding examples.

Inference rules: We saw earlier that the heart of the input file is the
description block, consisting of targets, dependencies, and commands. In
a description file, you can have many description blocks of different
categories. For example, the description files involves steps to compile,
link, create a help file, and so on. With inference rules, you don't need
to give a command.

Inference rules can be seen as templates indicating to NMAKE what to
do when a description block has no commands. The key is the
extensions of files. We know that C or C++ development files have
certain standard file extensions; for example, source files are C or CPP,
objects have OBJ, and so on. The first thing you do with inference rules
is to define all the extensions that will be used with the keyword
.SUFFIXES; for example,

```
.SUFFIXES: .rc .res .obj .lst .c .asm .hlp .ill .ipf
```

The extensions are preceded by a period (.), as in a filename and are
separated by space.

The next step is to define the inference rule. It consists of three parts:

- Files with 'from' extension
- File with 'to' extension
- Command

The general principle of the inference rule is

```
.from-ext .to-ext:
  commands
```

.from-ext corresponds to the dependent files.

.to-ext corresponds to the target files.

commands are executed to build the target from the dependents.

For example, in

```
.C .OBJ: $(CC) -Fo$*.obj $*.C
  CC = ICC /C /Gd-
```

the dependent files have extension C, the target files have OBJ, and the command is to run the compiler.

When NMAKE is working with a description block with commands, it refers to an inference rule, based on the given two types of extensions, that indicates how to build a target from dependent files. In the specification

```
PRTLABEL.OBJ: PRTLABEL.C PRTLABEL.h
```

this will match the preceding inference rule. The target-file extension matches the 'to' extension and the dependent-file extension matches the 'from' extension.

The inference rules eliminate the need to list the same command repeatedly in the many description blocks. In using the inference rules, you can give a path for both target and dependent files. Rules for compiling, linking, and assembling programs have already been defined. You can refer to these NMAKE program rules as well as any rule not found in a description file in the TOOLS.INI file.

Pseudotargets: The term pseudotarget refers to a special target in a description block and serves as a "handle" for building a group of files or executing a group of commands. In this case, the dependent files are treated as being obsolete. In the example

```
BACKUP: *.*
  COPY $*.* B:\ARCHIVE
```

BACKUP is the pseudotarget, NAMAKE copies all the files to drive B:
in directory ARCHIVE.

- Example

In the command line example

```
NMAKE /S "LINK=LINK386 /NOD /M" PRT.EXE CUSTOMER.EXE
```

NMAKE is invoked with

- /S option
- Macro definition "LINK=LINK386 /NOD /M"
- Two target files PRT.EXE and CUSTOMER.EXE
- Using default decription file MAKEFILE

The next example is a makefile to build an application called **CI**. The
name of the makefile is CIMAKE.MAK. The command to invoke the
NMAKE program is

```
nmake /F CIMAKE.MAK
```

```
#  Makefile
#
#     Filename : CIMAKE.MAK
#
#     Description:
#       This file is an input file to the nmake utility program.
#       It contains statements to produce output files, such as
#       object files, resource file, help file, and so on that are
#       needed to produce the CI executable file. This makefile
#       includes the following sections:
#       - Define variables for makefile
#       - Statements to link exe file
#       - Statements to add resources to exe file
#       - Statements to compile CiMainWindow Class
#       - Statements to compile dialog window classes
#       - Statements to create help resources for ci.exe
#
#-------------------------------------------------
#
#        Define variables for makefile
#
GCPPFLAGS=-Fd -c -Gm+ -O+

all:            ci

ci:             ci.exe cimain.hlp
#
#        Statements to link exe file
#
ci.exe:     cimain.obj cidialog.obj cimain.def cimain.res
            icc /Tdp /B" /PM:PM /MAP" \
            cimain.obj cidialog.obj \
```

```
                /Feci.exe /Fmcimain.map \
                dde4muii.lib dde4cci.lib dde4mbsi.lib cimain.def
#
#       Statements to add resources to exe file
#
        rc cimain.res ci.exe
#
#       Statements to compile CiMainWindow Class
#
cimain.obj:  cimain.cpp cimain.hpp cimain.h cidialog.hpp
        icc $(GCPPFLAGS) cimain.cpp
#
#       Statements to compile dialog window classes
#
cidialog.obj:  cidialog.cpp cidialog.hpp cimain.h
        icc $(GCPPFLAGS) cidialog.cpp
#
#       Statements to compile resources for hello5.exe
#
cimain.res:  cimain.rc cimain.h ci.ico cidialog.dlg
        rc -r cimain.rc
#
#       Statements to create help resources for ci.exe
#
cimain.hlp:  cimain.ipf
        ipfc cimain.ipf /x
```

7.2 EXEHDR—Display or Change Header Information of Executable File

- General format

```
EXEHDR [option...] filename
```

- Description

The EXEHDR (executable file header) utility program is used to look at or change header information of an executable file or dynamic-link library. The header, to be discussed in detail later, consists of characteristics of an executable file such as stack size, entry point of the code, number of objects (also called *segments*), and so on. This header information is used by the operating system during the execution of the file.

The EXEHDR program can be used by either displaying or changing the header information. You can view or modify attributes set by the linker related to the module definition file. Also, you can display the number and size of code and data segment.

EXEHDR displays two kinds of information: content of the file header and data about each object of a file. The listing goes to the standard output device, unless you use the redirection operator to send it to a file or printer. If EXEHDR is run with the "/Verbose" option (discussed later), it gives additional information.

Heading listing: The heading listing has seven fields. The names and brief descriptions of these fields are as follows:

Name	Description
Module	Name of application
Description	Description of the application
Data	Type of automatic data object
Initial CS:IP	Starting address of the program
Initial SS:SP	Initial stack pointer
Extra Stack Allocation	Extra stack allocation
DGROUP	Automactic data object number

Object listing: The *object listing* is the information about the object arranged in six colomns. The names and brief descriptions of these columns are as follows:

Column name	Description
No.	The object index number
type	Indication of whether object is code or data
Address	Location, with the file, of the contents of the file in hexadecimal
file	Size, in bytes, of the object as found in the file
mem	Size, in bytes, of the object as stored in memory.
flags	Object attributes

Verbose listing. If you specify the "/Verbose" option, the following information is shown:

- DOS header information
- OS/2 header information
- File addresses and lengths of the various tables in the file
- Object table with complete attributes
- Run-time relocation and fixups
- Exported entry points

filename is the name of the executable file whose information is to be shown or modified. You can enter one or more filenames.

option tells the program whether to display or change specific fields of the header record. You can enter one or more options. An option must start with a slash (/) followed by any of these keywords: ?, HEAP, HELP, MAX, MIN, NEWFILES, NOLOGO, PMTYPE, RESETERROR, STACK, or VERBOSE. In some cases a colon (:) and a value go after the option.

/? or /HELP means to display helpful information. When passing this option to EXEHDR, a list of options will be listed with possible values for some of them. The information looks like this:

```
Usage: EXEHDR [options] filename...
Valid options are:
/? Help
/HEAP:(0h-FFFFH)
/HELP
/MAX:(0H-FFFFH)
/MIN:(0H_FFFFH)
/NEWFILES
/NOLOGO
/PMTYPE:(PM      |     VIO     |    NOVIO    |    WINDOWAPI    |
        NOTWINDOWCOMPAT
/RESETERROR
/STACK:(0H-FFFFH)
/VERBOSE
```

/HEAp:*nnnn* is used to set the size of the local heap, with application to OS/2 programs only. The value for *nnnn*, in decimal, octal, or hexadecimal form, specifies the size in bytes.

/MAx:*nnnn* is used to set the maximum size of memory allocation for a program. This is the maximum storage space required to load and run a program. The value for *nnnn*, in decimal, octal, or hexadecimal form, is the maximum number of 16-byte paragraphs. This value must be greater than or equal to the minimum memory allocation (see /MIn option). The maximum memory allocation size can also be set with the LINK386 /Cp option.

/MIn:*nnnn* is used to set the minimum size of memory allocation for a program. The value for *nnnn*, in decimal, octal, or hexadecimal form, is the minimum number of 16-byte paragraphs. This value must be equal to or less than the maximum memory allocation (see /MAx option).

/NEwfiles is used to enable the use of long filenames for OS/2 16-bit files. OS/2 32-bit LINK386 already supports long filenames.

/NOlogo supresses product banner when the program starts execution.

/Pmtype:*type* is used to set the type of application, valid for OS/2 files only. This option is the same as the LINK386 /Pm option. Values for these application types are as follows:

Type	Equivalent keyword
PM	WINDOWAPI
VIO	WINDOWCOMPAT
NOVIO	NOTWINDOWCOMPAT

/Resererror resets the LINK386 error. During linking, if there is an error because of unresolved external reference or duplicate symbol definition, LINK386 will set an error flag in an executable file. OS/2 will not run a program with errors. The /R option lets you reset any linkage error, allowing such a program to be run. This is useful during the development and testing stage.

/Stack:*nnnn* is used to set the size of the stack. The value for *nnnn*, in decimal, octal, or hexadecimal form, specifies the size of bytes. This option is equivalent to the LINK386 /St option.

/Verbose is used to show the executable file header in verbose mode.

● Example

Display information. Let's look at the information for LINK386.EXE. To run EXEHDR, at command line, you type

```
EXEHDR LINK386.EXE
```

The first part is the header information. This is followed by data on the four objects of the link file.

```
Module:                     LINK386
Description:                Operating system/2 32-bit 2x Linker
Data:                       NONSHARED
Initial CS:IP               Seg 2 offset 6C78
Extra stack allocation:     4000 bytes
DGROUP:                     Seg 4
No. type    address file mem flags
1   CODE    00006000 0f7d6 0f7d7
2   CODE    00015a00 08e40 08e40
3   DATA    0001ea00 02865 02865
4   DATA    00021400 02337 08bd0
```

Change data: In the example,

```
EXEHDR /S:5000 /NE MYPROG.EXE
```

there are two options followed by the executable file MYPROG.EXE. The /S:5000 sets the stack allocation to 5000 bytes, and /Ne enables long filenames.

7.3 FWDSTAMP—Add Entry Point to DLL File

● General format

```
FWDSTAMPS [option...] input-dll def-file out-dll
```

● Description

The FWDSTAMP utility program is used to add entry points to DLL files. These entry points, also called *forwarders*, point to API (application program interface) functions or other exported code or data.

option is an optional parameter and can be one of the following:

/?   means to display information on how to use FWDSTAMP.

/V   means verbose mode, giving more information as FWDSTAMP is processing.

input-dll is the name of the dynamic-link library already created by LINK386. You must include the extension as part of the DLL filename.

def-file is the name of the module definition file (.DEF) that has the forwarders.

out-dll is the name of a dynamic-link library where FWDSTAMP puts the added forwarders.

7.4 IMPLIB—Create Import Library

● General format

```
IMPLIB [option...] implib-name
    <def-file... or dll-file...>
```

● Description

The IMPLIB utility program is used to create import libraries. An import library is created from dynamic-link libraries and the module definition file. An import library is similar to a regular library, except that it does not hold executable code. It holds all the necessary information for the linker to link dynamic-link libraries with the application. It is also used to resolve all the external reference during link time. The default extension of an import library is .LIB, the same as the standard library name. When running the linker, an import library can be listed instead of or in addition to standard library. for these three main reasons, creating and using import libraries, it is recommended that you use them with all dynamic-link libraries.

● It will save you the effort of creating an .DEF file that exeplicitly defines all the needed functions in the dynamic-link library.

● Although an extra step is wanted, IMPLIB automates the linking process.

● The task of writing DLL and the application can be separated, with distinct groups of developers performing these two tasks. The DLL files with associated import libraries can be produced by the DLL developers and handed over to the application programmers. Therefore, the application team need not worry about module definition files.

option is a parameter for controling the output of IMPLIB. The option characters are not case-sensitive; for example, /HELP is equivalent to /help. Also, the options can be abbreviated; in the following list, the significant characters are in uppercase. When running IMPLIB, you can list zero to many of these options:

/?	Shows the syntax summary of IMPLIB
/Help	Shows the syntax summary of IMPLIB
/Ignorecase	Turns case sensitivity off or on; the default state is off
/Nolog	Suppresses the banner when IMPLIB is invoked

implib-name is the import library.

def-file is one or more module definition files.

dll-file is one or more dynamic-link libraries containing exported routines.

7.5 MARKEXE—Change or Display Information of an Executable File

* General format

```
MARKEXE [/?] [FORCE] [option...] filename...
```

* Description

The MARKEXE program is used first to display the program type of an executable file. You can also use it to change the program type. A program type points to OS/2 sessions in which a program, whether it is an application or utility, can run.

We will see shortly all the information that MARKEXE can change in an executable file. Some of the tasks that MARKEXE can perform are

* View and change initialization for DLL

* View and change termination for DLL

* Set long filename support

In the MARKEXE syntax, the optional parameters are enclosed in brackets ([]); therefore, they are not part of the syntax.

/? is used to display all the options for MARKEXE.

FORCE makes a program executable in OS/2.

NO is used to set commands to the opposite condition. The NO is not effective with the DISPLAY UNSPECIFIED and WINDOWAPI options.

option is used to specify whether you want to view or set a program type. You can list one or many options with the MARKEXE command from the following list:

DISPLAY	Displays application type.
DLLINIT	Sets per-process initialization for the DLL. This applies to LINK386 executable files only.
DLLTERM	Sets per-process termination for DLL. This option applies to LINK executable files only.
LFNS	Enables support of long filenames. This option applies to LINK executable files only.
WINDOWAPI	Sets the application program to run in the PM (Presentation Manager) session only.
WINDOWCOMPAT	Sets the application program to run in a PM window or full-screen session.
NOTWINDOWCOMPAT	Sets the application to run in the OS/2 full-screen session.
UNSPECIED	Means that the application does not have an aaplication type. Such an application can be run in a full-screen session by default.

● Example

```
VIEW
   MARKEXE myprog.exe
```

```
Displays
```

```
   myprog.exe; OS/2 - 2.1, WINDOWCOMDAT
```

```
Set
   MARKEXE WINDOWAPI   myprog.exe
             yourprog.exe
```

7.6 MKMSGF—Convert Text to Binary

● General format

```
MKMSGF infile outfile [option...]
```

```
   or
```

```
MKMSGF @controlfile
```

● Description

The MKMSGF is an important program, if you are developing a PM application. In fact, the output from this utility is used by the MSGBIND (discussed later) program to bind messages to an executable file.

You may code your program with the **DosGetMessage** function, which uses the output message created by MKMSGF. Basically, MKMSGF takes a text file and converts it into a binary form that can be accessed faster by MSGBIND or **DosGetMessage**.

To get a message text, an application program makes a request by specifying a message number. The logic is to test whether a message segment is bound with the executable file. If this is true, then the system looks for the code-page number of the current session in all message segments. If a matching code-page number with a matching segment is found, the specified message number in **DosGetMessage** is searched for. If the right message is found, it returns to the calling application program. If the message is not found in the message segments of the executable file, **DosGetMessage** will look for a message file generated by MKMSGF. MKMSGF will find the file if one of the following conditions is met:

● The message file is in the current directory.

● The message file is found in the DPATH or APPEND environment variable.

● **DosGetMessage** is called with a fully qualified filename as the parameter.

infile is the name of the input file containing comments and codes to identify the messages. The extension of this file is .TXT. The message file contains the messages that are processed by MKMSGF. As explained earlier, these messages are eventually passed to an application program through the **DosGetMessage** function. The lines of this file must be formatted according to a few rules, and they can be categorized into three types: comment lines, component identifier lines, and component message lines. We'll have a look at these types next.

Comment lines: Comment lines allow you to add text to the message file which is not part of the messages you want to process; it may describe the purpose and usage of the messages. Such a line must start, in the first column, with a semicolon (;); for example,

```
; This message file is for
; component FAB
; and is used in PRTSAMP.C
```

are three comment lines.

The comment lines can appear anywhere in the file, except for the component identifier line and the first message line.

Component identifier line: The component identifier line specifies the group name of a number of message lines. This line simply consists of a three-character name, and it must precede all MKMSGF message numbers; for example,

```
FAB
```

is a component identifier line.

Component message line: Each component message line consists of two parts: a message header and a message text.

The message header is further divided into five parts:

- A three-character component identifier, discussed in the previous section

- A four-digit message number

- A one-character message type

- A colon (:)

- A space

The format of the message header looks like this:

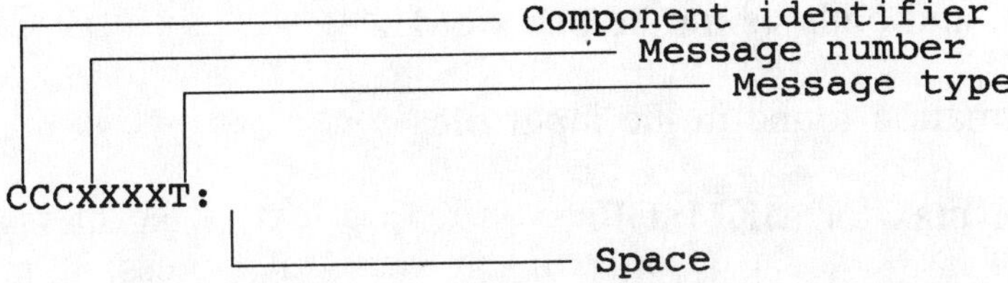

Type	Description
E	Error
H	Help
I	Information
P	Prompt
W	Warning
?	Empty message number

In preparing the message line you must follow the rules listed.

- The message header must start in the first column of the line.
- Multiple lines of message must use a message header for each line.
- The message number can start with any number, but subsequent lines must be numbered in sequential order.
- The symbol %0 at the end of a prompt text means not to add carriage return and linefeed at the end of a message.
- The symbols %1 to %9 can be used to start variable names within a message.

outfile is the name of the output file where MKMSGF writes the messages in binary form. Subsequently, it is used by the MSGBIND program and **DosGetMessage** function. The extension of this file is .MSG.

option is a keyword starting with a slash (/) to control output and specify various identifiers.

/P <code-page> specifies the code-page ID for the input message file. The default is no code-page value.

/D <DBCS range or country ID> specifies the DCBCS range or country identification. The valid DBCS range is $n_{10}, n_{11}, n_{20}, n_{21}, ..., nn_0, nn_1$. The default for the DBCS range is no value.

/L <language family id, sub id> specifies the language family ID and the language version, and both should be one word.

/V displays information found in the input file.

V? displays the syntax for MKMSGF.

controlfile contains multiple message files. As we saw earlier, there are two ways of running MKMSGF: specifying I/O files and options, or using a control file. In this section we'll discuss the control file, which is always followed by the "at" sign (@); for example,

MKMSGF *@controlfile*

A control file is used when creating a multi-code-page message file. The format of the line is

```
root.in root.out [option...]
sub-001 sub1.out [option...]
   .
   .
   .
sub-00n subn.out [option...]
```

● Example

In the following example, there are many instances of message lines associated with the component identifier FAB. Also, a few comment lines, starting with a semicolon (;), are added.

```
FAB0100E: Application FAB
;
;   File messages
;
FAB0101?:
FAB0102E: FILE NOT FOUND
FAB0103E: FILE NAME NOT CORRECT
;
;   Messages
;
FAB0104W: Warning! All files will be deleted!!!
FAB0105?:
FAB0106?:
FAB0107P: Do you want to replace (Y or N) ? %0
FAB0101I: File %1 replaced
FAB0101H: Usage: MYPROG [option...] infile outfile
```

7.7 PACK—Compress Data

● General format

```
Single-file:
  PACK source-file [packed-file]
     [/H:headerpath\ or
        /H:headerfile or
        /H:headerpath\header-file]
     [/D:headerdate]
     [/T:headertime]
```

```
    [/C]
    [/A]
    [/R]

Multiple-file:
  PACK list-file [packed-file] /L
    [/H:headerpath\ or
        /H:headerfile or
        /H:headerpath\header-file]
    [/D:headerdate]
    [/T:headertime]
    [/C]
```

● Description

The PACK utility program is used to compress a file. This file could be any kind of file—either data or executable. The advantage of using PACK is that it reduces the storage space occupied by a file on disk, thus giving you more room for something else. This program is useful when simply creating more space on a disk, for archiving files, or for preparing files for distribution. Of course, once compressed, the file cannot be used for processing; to restore the file to its original size there is another utility program called UNPACK, discussed later in this chapter.

PACK can be used in two ways: by specifying each file to be packed at the command line, one by one; or by listing all the files to be reduced in size in a list file and passing the list file to PACK. The formats of both methods are presented in the next section. You should use whichever method is most suitable for you.

In using PACK, there is no default file extension. It is mandatory to supply the filename and extension when invoking PACK. In cases where files are not found in the current directory, you must specify a full path and, perhaps, a drive if needed.

source-file is the name of the file to be compressed, and it is absolutely required in the single file format. When no other parameter is listed, the packed data is written to this file and the filename is changed to have the synbol @. The name of the source file is written in the header of the compressed file and is used as the destination file during the decompression. You can specify global filename characters.

packed-file is optional and is the name of the file where the source file is written to after the compression. It must have the @ symbol in the filename. As mentioned previously, if *packed-file* is not mentioned, the packed data is placed in *source-file*.

/H is used to specify the header file and path. Both pieces of information are written to the packed file and are later used during unpacking. This option can be entered in one of three ways:

/H:*headerpath*\ or
/H:*headerfile* or
/H:*headerpath**headerfile*

headerpath is the destination path where the header record of the compressed file is written. To the pathname you can add a drive letter, if needed. During the unpacking, the pathname can be overriden; otherwise UNPACK will use it as the destination.

headerfile is the name of the file to be placed in the header record of the packed file. This information is used by UNPACK and cannot be overriden.

/D:*headerdate* is used to specify a date that is written to the header record of the compressed file. The format is mm-dd-yyyy (month, day, and year); for example, /D:09-24-1993.

/T:*headertime* is used to specify a time that is written to the header record of the compressed file. The format is hh.mm (hour and minute), for example, /T:19.48.

/A means to add the source file to the packed file.

/C means that the current path be placed in the header record of the compressed file. During decompression, UNPACK will use this path as the destination for the file that contains uncompressed data. The /K option and *headerpath* are mutually exclusive.

/R means to remove the file specified by the source file from the file that contains only compressed data.

/L is needed for the multiple source file format and indicates that the filename is a list file.

filename is the name of a file containing many files to be compressed. You cannot use global filename characters.

● Example

```
PACK cds*.c  cdsprog.arc
PACK cdsmain.c cdsprog.arc /A
PACK cdsarc.lst cdsprog.arc
```

7.8 UNPACK—Unpack Data

● General format

```
UNPACK sourcefile
   [destination-drive:] [destination-path]
   [/SHOW] [/N:single-file] [/V] [/F]
```

● Description

The UNPACK OS/2 command is used to unpack a file that has previously been compressed by the PACK utility program. The PACK program changes the name of the compressed file to have the @ symbol. This program, discussed in the previous section, adds information such as filename and pathname, that can be used by UNPACK as default values. However, you can override them during the unpacking.

sourcefile is the name of the file that contains one or more compressed files.

destination-drive is the name of the drive where uncompressed files are written to.

destination-path is the name of the path where the uncompressed files are written to. If this parameter is not listed, UNPACK uses the path stored in the header record of the compressed file.

/SHOW tells the program to display the name of the files on which it is working.

/N:*single-file* means to unpack one file only from the packed file.

/V is used to verify that data is written to the destination file correctly.

/F specifies that files with extended attributes should not be be unpacked or copied if the destination files do not support extended attributes.

7.9 MAPSYM—Create a Symbolic File

- General format

```
MAPSYM [option...] input-file
```

- Description

The MAPSYM utility program creates a symbolic file from a map file, with the extension .MAP, is generated by the linker. The symbolic file, with the .SYM extension, is used by the kernel debugger.

input-file is the name of the input map file, with the extension .MAP. The output is a file with the same name as the input, but with the extension .SYM.

option can be one or more of the following:

/A omits alphabetical sorting of symbols.

/N includes source program line.

/L gives extra information during processing.

7.10 MSGBIND—Bind Messages

- General format

```
MSGBIND scriptfile
```

- Description
The MSGBIND utility program binds messages with an executable file. The result is that the messages are accessed faster although the executable file is larger.

The message segments (or objects) are placed together with the application code, and this may cause an error if the size exceeds 64 kbytes. If you want to separate the code from the message object, use the statement

```
SEGMENT '_MSGSEG32' CLASS 'CODE'
```

in the program definition file (.DEF).

As explained in the section MKMSGF, it is not necessary to bind messages and the executable files. The messages and the executable files can be separate, and the **DosGetMessage** function will be able to retrieve the messages from the file.

scriptfile is the name of the file that contains the executable files, message files, and message numbers. The script file contains lines that MSGBIND interprets as the following three types:

- > executable file

- < message file

- message numbers

MSGBIND takes the message numbers, finds them in the message file, and binds them to the executable file. It is possible to have any number of these files and message numbers. The important point to remember is that the input file is processed sequentially.

Executable file: An executable file is always preceded by the greater than symbol (>); for example,

```
> myprog.exe
```

is interpreted as a line with an executable file **myprog.exe.** You can have more than one executable file in an input file. All the message files and message numbers are associated with an executable file below it until another is encountered.

Message file: A message file is always preceded by the less-than symbol (<); for example,

```
< myfab.msg
```

is interpreted as a message file. It has an extension .MSG and is created by MKMSGF from the message text file. MSGBIND will bind all message numbers, found below it in this file, to the current executable file. If another message file is found, the message numbers below it will be searched in it.

Message numbers: A message number has a three-character component identifier followed by a four-digit number. This message number must be found in the current message file which is the first one above. When the message number is found in the message file, it is bound to the executable file.

● Example

This section shows how to run the MSGBIND program and explains the lines of an input file. To execute MSGBIND at the command line, type

```
MSGBIND CUSTOMER.BND
```

where **customer.bnd** is the script file.

The input file contains the following lines:

```
>CUSTMAIN.EXE
<CUSTMAIN.MSG
 CUS0001
 CUS0002
 CUS0003
<CUSTPM.MSG
 CUS0004
 CUS0005
 CUS0006
>CUSTFILE.EXE
>CUSTFILE.MSG
CUS0007
CUS0008
CUS0009
```

In this example, MSGBIND assumes **CUSTMAIN.EXE** to be the current executable file. Message numbers CUS0001 to CUS0003, which are first verified in message file **CUSTMAIN.MSG**, are bound to **CUSTMAIN.EXE**, followed by message numbers CUS004 to CUS006, but this time, these message numbers are searched in the **CUSTPM.MSG.**

Next, the executable file **CUSTFILE.EXE** becomes the current file and messages CUS0007 to CUS0009 are bound to it. These message numbers must be found in **CUSTFILE.MSG** for successful processing.

7.11 Resource Compiler

● General format

```
RC
```

```
or
```

```
RC [option...] resource-script-file [executable-file]

   or

RC [option...] resource-file [executable-file]

   or

RC -r resource-script-file [resource-file]
```

● Description

The resource compiler (RC) is a special OS/2 application development tool. Its main purpose is to prepare data that is used by the PM functions, such as **WinLoadString**, **WinLoadPointer**, **WinLoadMem**, and **WinLoadDlg**. Therefore, RC takes message strings, pointers, menus, and dialog boxes and converts them into a binary form that is added to an executable file of an application. Once processed and bound by the resource compiler, these window functions can load the resources as part of an application.

The resources can be bound to the executable files and changed subsequently without recompiling the application programs. This method is especially useful when an application is designed for different national languages. If you have to prepare the application for a specific language, you have to simply add all the new resources to the executable file.

The resource compiler can be run in several ways:

● Using a command line
● Using a command file
● Using the NMAKE utility program, as seen earlier in this chapter

Before invoking RC, make sure that the following environment variables are properly initialized:

```
DBCS       codepage, lead byte information, trail-byte information
TMP        temporary file path
TEMP       temporary file path
INCLUDE    include file path
```

Also, you have to make sure that RCPP.EXE is in the current directory or that its directory is listed in the environment variable **PATH**.

option is used to direct the processing or to provide input to RC. This parameter is not mandatory, and you can list as many as you need to.

The options are

-d *defname* This option is used to define a macro at runtime; for
example,

```
RC -dVERSION=1.0 MYPROG
```

will define the *defname* VERSION having the value 1.0 during
the processing of the resource script file **MYPROG**. With the -
d option, you can define one or many definition names.

-i   This option is used to specify a path where include files are
stored. Normally, you would specify the path for include files
in the environment variable **INCLUDE**. Cosequently, you will
use the -i option if a path is not listed in the variable
INCLUDE or the include file is not in the current directory.

-r   This option, seen before, is to create a binary resource file only.
In other words, the resources are not added to the executable
file.

-p   This is used to pack the code while not allowing the 386
resource to cross the 64-kbyte boundaries.

-cp   With this option you specify *cp*, *lb*, or *tb*, where *cp* is the
DBCS code page, *lb* is the lead byte information, and *tb* is
trail-byte information.

-k   This option specifies the code page.

The following is a list of code-page IDs, country codes, and country
names.

Codepage ID	Code	Name
932	81	Japan
934	82	South Korea
936	86	China
938	88	Taiwan

In the example,

```
RC -k938  MYPROG
```

the resource compiler takes the code page ID 938, which is Taiwan.

resource-script-file is the name of a file that consists of statements and directives, defining how resources ought to be handled. We'll examine the content in detail later. This parameter is required; its default extension is .RC. If you do not include this extension, .RC is assumed. Also, you must give the full path of the resource script file if it is not found in the current directory.

A resource script file consists of definitions of resources to be processed. They are all the resources valid for PM, such as message strings, pointers, names, dialog boxes, dialog templates, and icons. The resource script file is a text file that you create with an editor or it is generated, as we will see later, by the dialog editor.

The resources are defined by statements, and the processing can be logically directed with directives. Numerous statements and directives, listed in the next section, apply to resource definition.

For example, the statement

```
ICON 1 myicon.ico
```

defines an icon and tells the compiler that the file **myicon.ico** has the icons. On the other hand, the directive

```
#include <os2.h>
```

indicates that the header file **os2.h** should be included during processing.

The following lists an excerpt of a resource script file associated with the output of the dialog and icon editor.

For the dialog box

```
DLGINCLUDE 1 "C:\BOOK\OS2C\PGM\CIDLG.H"

DLGTEMPLATE CUSTINFO LOADONCALL MOVABLE DISCARDABLE
BEGIN
    DIALOG  "Customer Information", CUSTINFO, 35, 11, 327,
            157, WS_VISIBLE,
```

```
                FCF_SYSMENU | FCF_TITLEBAR
        BEGIN
            LTEXT               "Last Name: ", LNAME_T, 2,
                                144, 53, 8
            ENTRYFIELD          "", LNAME_F, 85, 144, 143,
                                8, ES_MARGIN
            LTEXT               "First Name:", FNAME_T, 3,
                                123, 51, 8
            ENTRYFIELD          "", FNAME_F, 86, 125, 141, 8,
                                ES_MARGIN
            LTEXT               "Address:", ADDRESS_T, 4, 108,
                                39, 8
            ENTRYFIELD          "", ADDRESS_F1, 87, 106, 171,
                                8, ES_MARGIN
            ENTRYFIELD          "", ADDRESS_F2, 88, 90, 169, 8,
                                ES_MARGIN
            LTEXT               "City:", CITY_T, 6, 71, 19, 8
            ENTRYFIELD          "", CITY_F, 34, 71, 172, 8,
                                ES_MARGIN
            LTEXT               "State/Prov:", STATE_PROV_T,
                                215, 71, 47, 8
            ENTRYFIELD          "", STATE_PROV_F, 272, 72, 32, 8,
                                ES_MARGIN
            ENTRYFIELD          "", POSTAL_ZIP_CODE_F, 87,
                                52, 62,
                                9, ES_MARGIN
            LTEXT               "Postal/Zip Code:",
                                POSTAL_ZIP_CODE_T, 7,
                                53, 70, 8
            ENTRYFIELD          "", TELEPHONE_F, 223, 53, 74, 8,
                                ES_MARGIN
            LTEXT               "Telephone:", TELEPHONE_T, 168,
                                53, 49, 8
            PUSHBUTTON          "Add", ADD_PB, 4, 26, 40, 14
            PUSHBUTTON          "Change", CHANGE_PB, 58, 25,
                                40, 14
            PUSHBUTTON          "Delete", DELETE_PB, 113, 25,
                                40, 14
            PUSHBUTTON          "Find", FIND_PB, 171, 25,
                                40, 14
            PUSHBUTTON          "Next", NEXT_PB, 225, 25,
                                40, 14
            PUSHBUTTON          "Previous", PREVIOUS_PB, 279,
                                24, 40, 14
            PUSHBUTTON          "EXIT", EXIT_PB, 144, 2,
                                40, 14
        END
    END
END
```

For the art work

```
    #include "icon.h"
    ICON        CI_ICON     CUSTINFO.ICO /* icon */
    POINTER     CI_PTR      CUSTINFO.PTR /* pointer */
    BITMAP      CI_BMP      CUSTINFO.BMP /* bitmap */
```

Statements: The *resource statements* define the resources that the compiler is to process and that are eventually used by an application program. The resource statements are definitions of PM items, strings, and files where information are to be found.

There are two types of resource statements: single-line and multiple-line. The *single-line* statement consists of a keyword indicating the kind of resource. Next, there is a constant or number associated with the resource, followed by a filename where resource data can be found. For example,

```
ICON 2 MYICON.ICO
```

is a single-line statement for an icon, followed by an icon identifier (or a tag) 2 and a file **MYICON.ICO**, where the icon data is found.

A *multiple-line* statement first contains a keyword for the resource type, followed by the resource identifier. In addition, it has other statements, grouped between the BEGIN and END keywords. You can use curly braces, { and }, instead of BEGIN and END. For example,

```
MENU 1
{
   MENUITEM  "File",101
   MENUITEM  "Action",102
   MENUITEM  "Help",103
}
```

has a resource type MENU, followed by a menu identifier 1. Between curly braces are defined two menu items with the strings "File", "Action", and "Help." You can have a nested loop as in

```
MENU MENU1
{
   SUBMENU  "File",SUB1
     BEGIN
        MENUITEM  "New",   ITEM_1
        MENUITEM  "Open",  ITEM_2
        MENUITEM  "Exit",  ITEM_3
     END
   SUBMENU  "Action",SUB2
     BEGIN
        MENUITEM  "List",  ITEM_4
        MENUITEM  "Print", ITEM_5
     END
   SUBMENU  "Help",SUB3
     BEGIN
        MENUITEM  "General Help", ITEM_6
        MENUITEM  "Product Information", ITEM_7
     END
}
```

Figures 7.1 and 7.2 respectively list statements and directives used by the resource compiler.

```
ACCELTABLE           ASSOCTABLE           AUTOCHECKBOX
AUTORADIOBUTTON      BITMAP               CHECKBOX
CODEOAGE             COMBOBOX             CONTROL
CTEXT                CTLDATA              DEFPUSHBUTTON
DIALOG               DLGINCLUDE           DLGTEMPLATE
ENTRYFIELD           FONT                 FRAME
GROUPBOX             HELPITEM             HELPSUBITEM
HELPSUBTABLE         HELPTABLE            ICON
LISTBOX              LTEXT                MENU
MENUITEM             MESSAGETABLE         MLE
POINTER              PRESPARAMS           PUSHBUTTON
RADIOBUTTON          RCDATA               RCINCLUDE
RESOURCE             RTEXT                STRINGTABLE
SUBITEMSIZE          SUBMENU              WINDOW
WINDOWTEMPLATE
```

Figure 7.1 Statements used by the resource compiler.

```
define      elif      else      endif
if          ifdef     ifndef    include
undef
```

Figure 7.2 Directives used by the resource compiler.

executable-file is the name of an executable file where the compiled resources are added. This option output file must be either .EXE or .DLL. If you omit this optional parameter, the RC will try to locate a file with extension .EXE with the same name as the resource script file or resource file, depending on the format. If it cannot find the proper output file, it will stop processing after generating an error message.

resource-file is the name of an input or output file, depending on the format. It is a binary file and its extension is .RES; if you do not specify it, then RC assumes by default .RES. In the third format, where you are adding resources to an executable file, this resource file is required. In cases where you are only creating a binary resouce file, and you do not list the resource file, RC will assume the filename the same as the resource script file and an extension .RES.

● Example

This section discusses a few examples to illustrate some of the points that were covered previously. In the command

```
RC MYPROG
```

the resource compiler will look for **MYPROG.RC** in the current directory. If found, it will process it and add it to **MYPROG.EXE**.

In the next example,

```
RC MYSCRIPT MYPROG
```

RC processes a resource script file **MYSCRIPT.RC** and adds it to **MYPROG.EXE.** However, in the command

```
RC -r MYPROG
```

RC will look for resource script file **MYPROG.RC** and after processing it, the binary output is placed in the resource file **MYPROG.RES.**

In the example

```
RC MYRES MYPROG.DLL
```

RC will take the binary resource file **MYRES.RES** and add it to **MYPROG.DLL**. But, if you type

```
RC MYRES
```

RC will add the resources to **MYRES.EXE,** and if it cannot find the executable file, it will display a message.

Online Information Programming

These days it is impossible for any software to succeed in the marketplace if it does not have online help information as part of the programs. Therefore, as creating a user-friendly product is the goal of designers, one way to achieve this is to make help information available at the fingertips of the user. In an Presentation Manager (PM) application, help must be available at various points of interfaces; some of these interfaces are

Menu bar	Windows
Dialog boxes	Pull-downs
Input fields	Push buttons

In OS/2 the Information Processing Facility (IPF) is a product used to incorporate help information in various critical parts of PM application programs. IPF, which is part of the Toolkit, has many capabilities, including building standalone information systems for reference and tutorials; however, in this chapter we'll only see how IPF can be used to provide online information in programs.

As a designer of online information, you need to know what IPF features support your design. IPF features include

- A tagging language that formats text, provides ways to connect information units, and customizes windows
- A compiler that creates online documents and help windows
- A viewing program that displays formatted online documents

Using IPF, you can develop a user interface that provides general help for application windows, and contextual help for fields within windows. Enabling help for applications requires programming code that communicates with IPF and the PM to help windows. An IPF window can be controlled by IPF or by an IPF communication object written by a programmer. The IPF communication object determines what is displayed in an application-controlled window.

This chapter gives information on the following topics:

- Before using IPF
- IPF compiler
- Data structure
- Using the help facility
- Communication between IPF and the application
- Window functions
- Tag reference

8.1 Before Using IPF

Before using IPF, there are a few things to keep in mind: the source file, the resource script file, and the include file.

◼ Source file

The IPF *source file* contains the information to be displayed within application programs. It also has instructions on how to present the text. The instructions are called the *tags* (a complete tag reference is given later in this chapter). IPF is flexible with respect to breaking down the information; you can have one source file for the whole application, or you can create several source files.

Within the file, the text must be distinguished from the corresponding tag. A tag always starts with a colon (:), followed by a name, and ends with a period (.). For example,

```
:h1.IPF source file
```

has both a tag and text. The tag **:h1.** tells the compiler that the text that follows is a heading and should be formatted in a particular way.

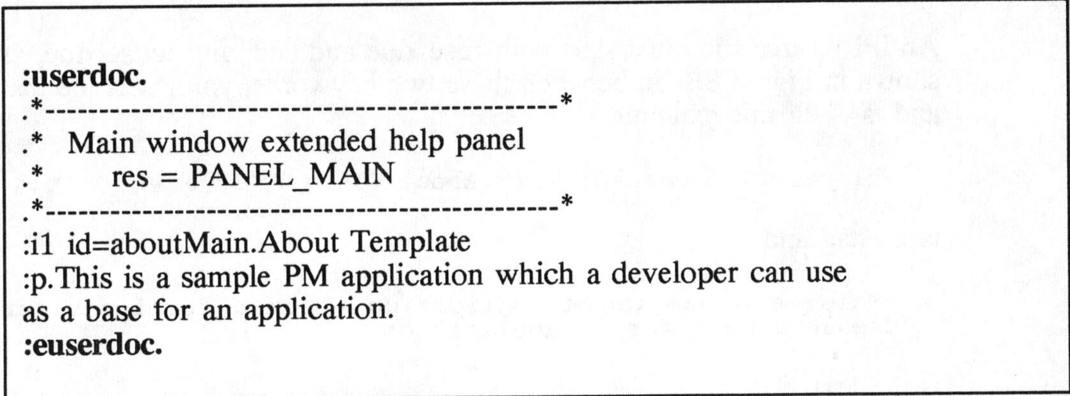

```
:userdoc.
.*--------------------------------------------------*
.*   Main window extended help panel
.*        res = PANEL_MAIN
.*--------------------------------------------------*
:i1 id=aboutMain.About Template
:p.This is a sample PM application which a developer can use
as a base for an application.
:euserdoc.
```

Figure 8.1   Sample IPF source file.

```
:userdoc.
.*------------------------------------------------------*
.*   Main window extended help panel
.*        res = PANEL_MAIN
.*------------------------------------------------------*
:h1 res=2100 name=CI_MAIN.About CI
:i1 id=aboutMain.About Template
:p.This is a sample PM application which application developers can use as
a base their own applications.
.*-- Import the File menu help file --*
.im cifile.ipf
:euserdoc.
```

Figure 8.2   Content of **cimain.ipf**.

As we will see later, the compiler that supplied with IPF converts the text source file to binary form. Subsequently, the output binary file is integrated with the executable file of the program with the help of the resource compiler. The compiler is discussed in Chap. 7.

An IPF source file must start with **:userdoc** and end with **:euserdoc**, as shown in Figure 8.1. In between these two keywords, you insert the text and tags. In this example,

```
:h1 res=2100 name=CI_MAIN.About CI
```

is the tag and

```
"This is a sample PM application which a developer can
use as a base for an application."
```

is the text.

In a source file you can include one or more other source files, as shown in Figure 8.2. This source file, called **cimain.ipf**, includes **cifile.ipf** with the tag

```
.im cifile.ipf
```

When processing **cimain.ipf**, the IPF compiler incorporates **cifile.ipf**, as shown in Figure 8.3, to produce a binary file.

```
.*----------------------------------------------------*\
.*   Main file menu:     res = CI_FILE                 *
.*----------------------------------------------------*/
:h1 res=2210 name=CI_FILE.File Menu
:i1 id=File.File Menu
:p.The File menu contains commands that you use to create
and open data files. In addition, it also contains the
command that you use to exit the Sample application. The
following commands appear in the File menu:
:parml tsize=15 break=none.
:pt.New
:pd.Creates a new untitled file
:pt.Open
:pd.Opens an existing file
:pt.Exit
:pd.Quits the Sample application
:eparml.
.*----------------------------------------------------*\
.*   File menu New command help panel                 *
.*        res = CI_FILENEW                             *
.*----------------------------------------------------*/
:h1 res=2220 name=CI_FILENEW.New
:i2 refid=File.New
:p. You can create a new file in the Sample application
window by using the New command. To create a new file, do
the following: :ul.
:li.Select the File menu and choose the New command.
:eul.
:p. The word "Untitled" appears in the title bar of the new
file.
.*----------------------------------------------------*\
.*   File menu Open command help panel                *
.*        res = CI_FILEOPEN                            *
.*----------------------------------------------------*/
:h1 res=2230 name=CI_FILEOPEN.Open
:i2 refid=File.Open
:p.You can open a file that exists on any drive or in any
directory by using the Open command. To open a file, do the
following: :ul.
:li.Select the File menu and choose the Open command.
:eul.
:p.A dialog box appears, showing you a list of files in the
current directory.
.*----------------------------------------------------*\
.*   File menu Exit command help panel                *
.*        res = CI_FILEEXIT                            *
.*----------------------------------------------------*/
:h1 res=2290 name=CI_FILEEXIT.Exit
:i2 refid=File.Exit
:p.You quit the Sample application by using the Exit
command. To quit the Sample application, do the following:
:ol.
:li.Select the File menu and choose the Exit command.
:eol.
```

Figure 8.3 Content of **cifile.ipf**.

◘ Resource script file

Previously we saw how to create an IPF source file, containing text and tags, that is processed by the IPF compiler and ready for use by the application program. The next step is to provide hooks to enable your program to use the output of the IPF compiler.

In this step you create a resource script file (see Figure 8.4). It contains definitions of help tables as resources which can be processed by the resource compiler (RC). The output from the resource compiler can be bound to an application executable file or written to a dynamic-link library (DLL). During runtime, the text of the source file is referenced in the program and is loaded and shown at the appropriate places.

```
#include <os2.h>
#include "cimain.h"
  /*
   *  Help table definition
   */
HELPTABLE    CI_HELP_TABLE
{
    HELPITEM      IDR_MAIN,  SUBTABLE_MAIN, CI_MAIN
    HELPITEM      IDD_PRODUCTINFO,
        SUBTABLE_PRODUCTINFODLG, CI_PRODUCTINFODLG
}

  /*
   *  Main window subtable, includes menu item help
   */
HELPSUBTABLE SUBTABLE_MAIN
SUBITEMSIZE      2
{
    HELPSUBITEM      IDM_FILE,              CI_FILE
    HELPSUBITEM      IDM_FILENEW,           CI_FILENEW
    HELPSUBITEM      IDM_FILEOPEN,          CI_FILEOPEN
    HELPSUBITEM      IDM_FILEEXIT,          CI_FILEEXIT
}
```

Figure 8.4 Resource script file.

We start by discussing two RC statements: **HELPTABLE** and **SUBHELPTABLE**. Both are needed to integrate help information in an application program. These two commands create data structures, as in C or C++, that are referenced when programming the online facilities.

HELPTABLE is used to define entries where help is provided in the application. Appropriate places would be the window, the dialog box, menus, and so on. Each entry consists of the following:

- **HELPITEM** keyword
- Application window ID
- ID of the **HELPSUBTABLE** resource
- Window ID of the extended help window

In the next segment,

```
HELPTABLE   CI_HELP_TABLE
{
    HELPITEM     IDR_MAIN,   SUBTABLE_MAIN, CI_MAIN
    HELPITEM     IDD_PRODUCTINFO,
                 SUBTABLE_PRODUCTINFODLG, CI_PRODUCTINFODLG
}
```

the **HELPTABLE** contains two **HELPITEM**s, which are also defined in the same file.

On the other hand, **HELPSUBTABLE** is used to define each item where the information is invoked in the application window. The item must have a child window of the application window identified in the **HELPTABLE** resource. Each **HELPSUBTABLE** must have one **SUBITEMSIZE**, and for each control, child window, and menu item, you have to specify a **HELPITEM**.

Each entry of **HELPSUBTABLE** must have the following:

- **HELPSUBITEM** keyword
- Field ID
- Window ID of the field's help window
- Optional integers defined in the application

For example, the HELPSUBTABLE **SUBTABLE_MAIN** has four **HELPITEM**s for one pull-down.

◻ Include file

So far we have discussed the source file used by the IPF compiler and the resource script file processed by the RC; we also need an include file to tie the IPF source file, script file, and program together. An include file contains a value for the symbolic names defined in these three files. Figure 8.5 shows a listing of the **cimain.h** include file. This include file is needed when you are compiling both the resource file and the program. To draw attention to the relationship, let's look at three lines taken from the help source file, resource file, and include file.

```
Help source file:    :h1 res=2210 name=CI_FILE.File Menu

Resource file:       HELPSUBITEM      IDM_FILE,    CI_FILE

Include file:        #define CI_FILE          2210
```

As you can see, the symbolic name CI_FILE is defined as value 2210. Both the value and the name are used in the help file while the name is part of the **HELPSUBITEM** statement in the resource file. Figure 8.5 is an example of an include file required for the resource file shown in Figure 8.4.

```
/*
 *   Help table and subtables
 */
#define  CUSTINFO_HELP_TABLE              1000
#define  SUBTABLE_MAIN                    2000
#define  SUBTABLE_PRODUCTINFODLG          3000
/*
 *   Main window help panels
 */
#define  CI_MAIN                          2100
#define  CI_PRODUCTINFODLG                3100
#define  CI_FILE                          2210
#define  CI_FILENEW                       2220
#define  CI_FILEOPEN                      2230
#define  CI_FILEEXIT                      2240
```

Figure 8.5 cimain.h include file.

◘ Output file

The IPF compiler processes a source file and produces two types of output: the standalone system file or the program online help file. They are distinguised by the type of extension; the standalone system file has the extension .INF, and the program online file has the extension .HLP. To produce one or the other you specify the /INF option when running the IPF compiler. If you include the /INF compiler option, the output goes to file with extension .INF; otherwise, the extension of the output file is .HLP. As discussed next, the path of the .HLP is added to the environment variable HELP and the filename is referenced in the initialization functions.

◉ Environment variables

Before you use the IPF compiler, make sure that the environment variables are initialized properly. There are three variables, **IPFC**, **HELP** and **BOOKSHELF**. The initialization is usually done when installing the Toolkit, and the place to do this is in CONFIG.SYS.

IPFC: The IPFC environment variable is used by the IPF compiler to identify the directory where data files are found; for example in

```
IPFC=C:\TOOLKT20\IPFC
```

the path is C:\TOOLKT20\IPFC, where the IPF compiler will search for the data files needed for processing.

HELP: The **HELP** environment variable contains the directories (or path) where all the help files (.HLP) are found. For example,

```
HELP=C:\OS2\HELP;\OS2C\PGM\CUSTINFO
```

contains two directories that are searched for help files when programs with help information are run.

BOOKSHELF: The **BOOKSHELF** environment variable contains directories (or path) for online documents used by VIEW. For example,

```
BOOKSHELF=C:\OS2\BOOK
```

specifies a path where document files are found.

8.2 IPF Compiler

● General format

```
IPFC source-file [/INF] [/S] [/Wn]
        [> message-output-file]
```

● Description

In the previous section, we saw how the IPF compiler converts a source file, holding the help information or online document, into binary form. Depending on the option given at the time of running the compiler, it creates a help file (.HLP) or online file (.INF). To see the content of the online file, you use the program VIEW.

source-file is the name of an IPF source file. As mentioned earlier, it contains information, intertwined with tags, to be presented to the user.

/INF is an option to compile an IPF source file that contains online information. With this option specified, the output file has an extension .INF. If this option is omitted, the input file is assumed to contain help information and the output file has the extension .HLP.

/S is an option to suppress the performance of the search function. If you use this option, the output data is compressed by 10 percent, thus saving storage space.

/X is an option to generate and display a cross-reference list.

/W*n* is an option to generate and display a list of error messages. *n* is the level of information generated. The valid values are 1, 2, and 3.

Value   Level of information

Value	Level of information
1	Returns warning level 1 messages that are most severe
2	Returns warning level 1 and 2 messages
3	Returns all three warning levels of messages; warning level 3 are the least severe messages

message-output-file is the name of the file where error and cross-reference messages are written to. If this parameter is omitted, the message and error, from /X and /W*n* options, are written to the screen.

● Example

In the next example, the **myprog.ipf** source file is processed by the IPF compiler. Note that the /INF option is missing; this means that the output is used by programs and will go to **myprog.hlp**. The /w3 option is used to return all three warning levels of messages.

As mentioned earlier, error messages are either displayed or written to a file. To redirect a message to a file, use the redirection symbol (>) and a filename to receive the message in the command line. In this case the messages are written to **myprog.err**.

```
IPFC myprog.ipf /w3 > myprog.err
```

8.3 Data Structure

Earlier, we saw how to create the help tables; this information has to be passed on to the IPF from a program. The communication between the help tables and the program is done by the data structure called **HELPINIT**. After the initialization is completed, one or many instances of help can be created. (The definition of the structure is found in **PMHELP.H**.) Next, you must associate the help instance with a window. This section first describes the **HELPINIT** structure, followed by an initialization of the structure.

```
typedef struct_HELPINIT /* init */
{
    ULONG           cb;
    ULONG           ulReturnCode;
    PSZ             pszTutorialName;
    PHELPTABLE      phtHelpTable;
    HMODULE         hmodAccelActionBarModule;
    HMODULE         hmodAccelActionBarModule;
    ULONG           idAccelTable;
    ULONG           idActionBar;
    PSZ             pszHelpWindowTitle;
    ULONG           fShowPanelId;
    PSZ             pszHelpLibraryName;
} HELPINIT;
```

The following describes each element of the **HELPINIT** structure.

Element name	Description
cb	The length of **HELPINIT** structure.
ulReturnCode	Return code from IPF.
pszTutorialName	A pointer to a tutorial name. If this field is NULL, then IPF does not provide a **Tutorial** choice in the **Help** pull-down menu; otherwise, it does include the tutorial choice. If the user selects **Tutorial**, IPF sends

<table>
<tr><td></td><td>the HM_TUTORIAL message to the application program associated with this structure.</td></tr>
<tr><td>phtHelpTable</td><td>A pointer to a help table.</td></tr>
<tr><td>hmodAccelActionBarModule</td><td>The name of the file where help table and subtables are to be found. If the value of this field is 0, the tables are found in the EXE file.</td></tr>
<tr><td>hmodAccelActionBarModule</td><td>The name of DLL containing a modified menu bar. This value is 0 if there is no modified menu bar.</td></tr>
<tr><td>idAccelTable</td><td>The name of the accelarator table if a modified menu bar is specified in the previous file; otherwise, the value is 0.</td></tr>
<tr><td>idActionBar</td><td>The name of the template if the modified menu bar is used; otherwise, this value is 0.</td></tr>
<tr><td>pszHelpWindowTitle</td><td>A pointer to the name of the title for the main window.</td></tr>
<tr><td>fShowPanelId</td><td>A flag that is used to show or hide the window IDs. The values are CMIC_SHOW_PANEL_ID and CMIC_HIDE_PANEL_ID. This flag can be used during the development stage for debugging purpose.</td></tr>
<tr><td>pszHelpLibraryName</td><td>The name of help files containing the help windows. These files are searched in directories listed in the HELP environment variable and the current directory.</td></tr>
</table>

● Example

In an application you have to provide a function to initialize the **HELPINIT** structure. The **CiHelpInit** function is an example of such a function which is used once during the initialization of the application. In this function, after initializing the structure, the **WinCreateHelpInstance** function creates a help instance. If this is successful, the **WinCreateHelpInstance** associates the help instance with a window. If everything goes well, the **fHelpEnabled** flag is set to **TRUE**.

```
static HWND   hwndHelpInstance;
static CHAR   szLibName[] = "CUSTINFO";
```

```
static CHAR   szWindowTitle[] = "Customer Information Help";
static BOOL   fHelpEnabled = FALSE;

/***********************************************
   Name:    CiHelpInit()
   Purpose:
   Usage:
   Method:
***********************************************/
void CiHelpInit(void)
{
   HELPINIT  hinit;       /* define initialization struture */

   fHelpEnabled = FALSE;       /* set to FALSE for now */

   /* initialize the HELPINIT structure  */
   hinit.cb  = sizeof(HELPINIT); /* set to size of hinit */
   hini.ulReturnCode = 0;
     hini.pszTutorialName = (PSZ)NULL;/* No tutorial */

     hini.phtHelpTable = CUSTINFO_HELP;
     hini.hmodHelpTableModule = (PSZ)NULL;
   hini.hmodAccelActionBarModule = (PSZ)NULL;
                               /* resource in EXE file*/
   hini.idAccelTable = 0; /* resource in EXE file */
   hini.idActionBar = 0; /* default menu bar */

   strcpy( hinit.pszHelpWindowTitle, szWindowTitle);

   /* if debugging, show panel ids, else don't */
#ifdef DEBUG
   hini.fShowPanelId = CMIC_SHOW_PANEL_ID;
#else
   hini.fShowPanelId = CMIC_HIDE_PANEL_ID;
#endif

   hini.pszHelpLibraryName = (PSZ)szLibName;

     /* creating help instance */
     hwndHelpInstance = WinCreateHelpInstance(hab, &hini);

   if(hwndHelpInstance == NULLHANDLE || hini.ulReturnCode)
   {
       MessageBox(hwndMainFrame,
           IDMSS_HELPLOADERROR,
           MB_OK | MB_ERROR,
           TRUE);
           return;
   }

   /* associate help instance with main frame */
   if(!WinAssociateHelpInstance(hwndHelpInstance,
                               hwndMainFrame))
   {
       MessageBox(hwndMainFrame,
           IDMSG_HELPLOADERROR,
           MB_OK | MB_ERROR,
           TRUE);
       return;
   }
```

```
    /* help manager is successfully initialized so  */
    /* set flag to TRUE */
  fHelpEnabled = TRUE;
}   /* End of CiInitHelp    */
```

When an application program that creates a help instance ends it should also terminate the instance. With the **EndHelpInstance** function, for example, a previously created help instance is destroyed.

```
/*********************************************
  Name:     CiDestroyHelpInstance()
  Purpose:
  Usage:
  Method:
*********************************************/
VOID CiDestroyHelpInstance(VOID)
{
  if(hwndHelpInstance != NULLHANDLE)
    WinDestroyHelpInstance(hwndHelpInstance);
}   /* End of DestroyHelpInstance   */
```

8.4 Using the Help Facility

When IPF is used within your program, the user requests help information in three ways:

- Hit the F1 key at any time.
- Click on the **Help** item of the menu bar or the pull-down menu.
- Press a **Help** push button found in a dialog box.

F1 key: When the user presses the F1 key, from any window maintained by the PM, a WM_HELP message will be generated and posted to the queue for the window.

Help menu bar item: The **Help** item, either in the menu bar or in a help pull-down, should be defined using the MIS_HELP style. Using this information will cause a WM_HELP message to be generated, instead of a WM_COMMAND message.

Help pushbutton. A **Help** push button in a dialog box should be defined with BS_HELP and BS_NOPOINERFOCUS types. This will cause a WM_HELP message to be passed to IPF. Subsequently, IPF determines the control window within the dialog box that is currently holding the input focus, and then displays the help panel for that control window.

8.5 Communication between IPF and the Application

IPF responds to a user's request for help information by sending messages to the application. After receiving a message, the application program may choose to respond with a message. This section describes the messages passed between IPF and application program. The communication is through the IPF window procedure found in the application program, which is required if you are using IPF. The prototype of this function is

```
MRESULT EXPENTRY IPFWinProc(HWND hwnd,
                            USHORT message,
                            MPARAM param1,
                            MPARAM param2)
```

The application program sends a message by calling the **WinSendMsg** function, whose prototype is

```
MRESULT WinSendMsg(HWND hwnd,
                   USHORT message,
                   MPARAM param1,
                   MPARAM param2)
```

In addition to the return value for each message, it also provides a description of *param1* and *param2* parameters, including the datatype and value.

◨ HM_ACTIONBAR_COMMAND

This message is sent by IPF to the application program to notify that the user selected an item from a customized menu bar item. This item belongs to the current active window.

● Parameters

param1 **idCommand** (USHORT) The identity of the menu bar item
                                that the user selected
param2 (ULONG)   NULL value

● Return

flreply (ULONG)   NULL value

◘ HM_CONTROL

This command is sent by IPF to the application or the communication object. This happens prior to the addition of controls. If an application wants to filter any of the controls, it can subclass the child of the coverpage window and intercept this message. If this message is not intercepted by the application program, IPF adds the control to the control area.

- Parameters

param1 (HIUSHORT) NULL
    controlres (LOUSHORT)　　　The **res** identification number of the control that was selected.

param2 (BIT32)　　　Reserved

- Return

flreply　(ULONG)　　　NULL value

◘ HM_CREATE_HELP_TABLE

This parameter is sent by the application to tell IPF to use the new help table.

- Parameters

param1 **HELPTABLE(pHelpTable)**　　　A pointer to the new help table structure

param2 (ULONG)　　　NULL value

- Return

flreply (ULONG), the return value is one of the following:

0　　　The request was completed successfully

Other　　　The request was not completed; for more information, see the value of **ulErrorCode** of the HM_ERROR message

◘ HM_DISMISS_WINDOW

This message is sent by the application to tell IPF to remove the active help window.

● **Parameters**

param1 (ULONG) NULL value
param2 (ULONG) NULL value

● **Return**

reply ulreturnValue (ULONG):

0	The request was completed successfully.
Other	Could find a help window. The request was not completed; for more information, see the value of **ulErrorCode** of the HM_ERROR message.

◘ HM_DISPLAY_HELP

This message sent by the application to tell IPF to show a specific help window. The help window must be associated with the currently active application window, which is usually sent to IPF with the HM_SET_ACTIVE_WINDOW message.

● Parameters

param1 **HelpPanelId (PIDENTITY)**	A pointer to a USHORT data type, which identifies the help window (**usTypeFlag** parameter of HM_RESOURCEID).
HelpPanelName (PSTRL)	A pointer to the PSZ datatype, which identifies the name of the help window. (**usTypeFlag** parameter of HM_PANELNAME).
param2 **usTypeFlag (USHORT)**	HM_RESOURCEID is used to indicate that *param1* is to point to the identity of the help window.

HM_PANELNAME is used to indicate that *param1* is to point to the name of the help window.

- Return

reply **ulreturnValue** (ULONG), the return value, is one of the following:

0   The request was completed successfully.

Other   Could find a help window. The request was not completed; for more information see the value of **ulErrorCode** of the HM_ERROR message.

◉ HM_ERROR

This message is received by the application when an error occurred during user interaction. This is the only way to communicate the error to the application when the user initiated the communication. Other errors caused when the application sends a message to IPF are returned as the *flreply* parameter of the message.

- Parameters

param1 **ulErrorCode** (ULONG)

The error codes are

HMERR_LOAD_DLL
The application cannot load the dynamic link library (DLL).

HMERR_NO_FRAME_WND_IN_CHAIN
The frame window is not in the window chain from which to find or set the associated help instance.

HMERR_INVALID_ASSOC_APP_WND
The application window handle named in the **WinAssociateHelpInstance** function call is an invalid window handle.

HMERR_INVALID_ASSOC_HELP_INST
The help instance handle named in the **WinAssociateHelpInstance** funtion call is an invalid window handle.

HMERR_INVALID_DESTROY_HELP_INST

The window handle named as the help instance to destroy is not of the help instance class.

HMERR_NO_HELP_INST_IN_CHAIN
The parent or owner chain of the application window does not have an associated help instance.

HMERR_INVALID_HELP_INSTANCE_HDL
The handle that is a help instance does not have the class name of an IPF help instance.

HMERR_INVALID_QUERY_APP_WND
The application window named in a **WinQueryHelpInstance** function call is not a valid window handle.

HMERR_HELP_INST_CALLED_INVALID
The handle of the help instance named in a function call to IPF does not have the class name of an IPF help instance.

HMERR_HELPTABLE_UNDEFINE
The application did not provide a help table for context-sensitive help.

HMERR_HELP_INSTANCE_UNDEFINE
The help instance handle is not valid.

HMERR_HELPITEM_NOT_FOUND
Context-sensitive help was requested but the ID of the named main help item was not found in the help table.

HMERR_INVALID_HELPSUBITEM_SIZE
The help subtable item size is less than 2 (<2).

HMERR_HELPSUBITEM_NOT_FOUND
Context-sensitive help was requested but the ID of the named help item was not found in the help subtable.

HMERR_INDEX_NOT_FOUND
The index is not found in the library file.

HMERR_CONTENT_NOT_FOUND
The library file does not have any content.

HMERR_OPEN_LIB_FILE
The library file cannot be opened.

HMERR_READ_LIB_FILE
The library file cannot be read.

HMERR_CLOSE_LIB_FILE
The library file cannot be closed.

HMERR_INVALID_LIB_FILE
The library file is not valid.

HMERR_NO_MEMORY
Unable to allocate the requested amount of memory.

HMERR_ALLOCATE_SEGMENT
Cannot allocate a segment of memory for memory allocation requests
from IPF.

HMERR_FREE_MEMORY
Cannot free allocated memory.

HMERR_PANEL_NOT_FOUND
Cannot find the requested help window.

HMERR_DATABASE_NOT_OPEN
Cannot read the unopened database.

param2 (ULONG) NULL value.

- Return

flreply (ULONG) NULL value.

◘ HM_EXIT_HELP

This message is sent by the application to tell IPF to show the extended
help window for the active application window.

- **Parameters**

param1 (ULONG) NULL value.
param2 (ULONG) NULL value.

- Return

  reply **ulreturnValue** (ULONG); the return value is one of the following:

  0   The request was completed successfully.
  Other   Could find a help window. The request was not completed; for more information, see the value of **ulErrorCode** of the HM_ERROR message.

◘ HM_EXT_HELP_UNDEFINED

This message is sent by IPF to the application when an extended help window is not defined. The application responds in one of the following ways:

- Ignores the request for help and does not display a help window
- Displays its own window
- Uses the HM_DISPLAY_HELP message to tell IPF to display a particular window

- Parameters

  param1 (ULONG) NULL value.
  param2 (ULONG) NULL value.

- Return

  flreply (ULONG) NULL value.

◘ HM_GENERAL_HELP

This message is sent by the application to tell IPF to show the general help window for the action application window.

- **Parameters**

  param1 (ULONG) NULL value.
  param2 (ULONG) NULL value.

- Return

  reply **ulreturnValue** (ULONG); the return value is one of the following:

0   The request was completed successfully.

Other   Could find a help window. The request was not completed; for more information, see the value of **ulErrorCode** of the HM_ERROR message.

�‍▣ HM_GENERAL_HELP_UNDEFINED

This message is sent by IPF to the application when the general help window is not defined. The application responds in one of the following ways:

- Ignores the request for help and does not display a help window
- Displays its own window
- Uses the HM_DISPLAY_HELP message to tell IPF to display a particular window

- Parameters

param1 (ULONG) NULL value.
param2 (ULONG) NULL value.

- Return

flreply (ULONG) NULL value.

▣ HM_HELP_CONTENTS

This message is sent by the application to tell IPF to show the content window.

- Parameters

param1 (ULONG) NULL value.

param2 (ULONG) NULL value.

- Return

reply **ulreturnValue** (ULONG); the return value is one of the following:

0   The request was completed successfully.

Other   Could find a help window. The request was not completed; for more information see the value of **ulErrorCode** of the HM_ERROR message.

◘ HM_HELP_INDEX

This message is sent by the application to tell IPF to show the help index window.

● Parameters

param1 (ULONG) NULL value.
param2 (ULONG) NULL value.

● Return

reply **ulreturnValue** (ULONG), the return value is one of the following:

0   The request was completed successfully.
Other   Could find a help window. The request was not completed; for more inform see the value of ulErrorCode of the HM_ERROR message.

◘ HM_HELPSUBITEM_NOT_FOUND

This message is sent by IPF to the application when a user requests help on a field but the related entry in the help subtable cannot be found. The application can respond in one of the following ways:

● Ignore the notification and not display help for that field or window
● Display its own window
● Use the HM_DISPLAY_HELP message to tell IPF to display a particular window

● Parameters

param1 **usContext** (USHORT); the types of windows are

HLPM_WINDOW An application window.
HLPM_FRAME   A frame window.
HLPM_MENU   A menu window.

param2 **sTopic** (USHORT)

This is the topic identifier; the values are

window   The window containing the field on which help is
requested.
menu   The submenu containing the field on which help is
requested.

sSubTopic (USHORT)
This is a subtopic identifier, the values are:

control The control of the cursored field where help is requested.
-1   No menu item is selected.
Other Menu item of the currently selected submenu item where
help was requested.

● Return

reply **fAction** (BOOL); the return values are

FALSE   Display the extended help window.
TRUE   Do nothing.

◘ HM_INFORM

This message is sent by IPF to the application when a user selects a
hypertext field that was specified with the **reftype=inform** attribute of
the **:link** tag.

● Parameters

param1 **idnum** (USHORT)   The identity that is associated with the
hypertext field.
param2 (ULONG)   NULL value.

● Return

flreply (ULONG)   NULL value.

◘ HM_INVALIDATE_DDF_DATA

This message is sent by the application to tell IPF that the previous dynamic data formatting (DDF) information is no longer valid. This message should be sent to the child of the coverpage window handle.

● **Parameters**

param1 (ULONG) **rescount**   The count of DDFs to be rendered invalid.

param2 (PUSHORT) **resarray**   The pointer to an array of USHORT data type, containing the values of the elements of the **res** numbers of DDFs to be invalidated.

● Return

reply **ulreturnValue** (ULONG); the return value is one of the following:

0   The request was completed successfully.
Other Could find a help window. The request was not completed; for more information see the value of **ulErrorCode** of the HM_ERROR message.

◘ HM_KEYS_HELP

This message is sent by the application to tell IPF to show the keys help window. On receiving this message, IPF sends an HM_QUERY_KEYS_HELP message to the active application window.

The active application window is the window that was specified when the last HM_SET_ACTIVE_WINDOW message was sent. If no HM_SET_ACTIVE_WINDOW message was issued, then the active application window is the window specified in the **WinAssociateHelpInstance** function call.

As a reply the application program sends one of the following:

● The identity of a keys help window in the **HelpPanel** parameter of the HM_QUERY_KEYS_HELP message.

● Zero, if no action is to be taken by IPF for keys help.

● Parameters

> *param1* (ULONG) Reserved value.
> *param2* (ULONG) Reserved value.

● Return

> *reply* **ulreturnValue** (ULONG); the return value is one of the following:

0   The request was completed successfully.
Other Could find a help window. The request was not completed; for more information, see the value of **ulErrorCode** of the HM_ERROR message.

◘ HM_LOAD_HELP_TABLE

The message is sent by the application IPF along with a module handle containing the help table, the help subtable, and the name of the help table.

● Parameters

> *param1* **idHelpTable** (USHORT)   Name of the help table.
> **fsidentityflag** (USHORT)   Help table name indicator.
> *param2* MODULE (HMODULE)   Handle of the module that holds the help table and help subtable.

● Return

> *reply* **ulreturnValue** (ULONG); the return value is one of the following:

0   The request was completed successfully.
Other Could find a help window. The request was not completed; for more information, see the value of **ulErrorCode** of the HM_ERROR message.

◘ HM_NOTIFY

This message is sent by IPF to the application or communication object when an application event has happened that the application wants to

control. It is used by the application to subclass and change the behavior
or appearance of the help window.

- Parameters

param1 **controlres** (HIUSHORT)	The **res** number of the control.
reserved (HIUSHORT)	NULL value.
event (LOUSHORT)	The type of event, which is one of the following:
CONTROL_SELECTED	A control was selected.
HELP_REQUESTED	Help was requested.
OPEN_COVERPAGE	The coverpage is shown.
OPEN_PAGE	The child window of the coverpage is opened.
SWAP_PAGE	The child window of the coverpage is swapped.
OPEN_INDEX	The index window is displayed.
OPEN_TOC	The table of contents window is displayed.
OPEN_HISTORY	The history window is displayed.
OPEN_LIBRARY	The new library is opened.
OPEN_SEARCH_HIT_LIST	The search list is displayed.

param2 (ULONG) Window handle of a relevant window.

- Return

reply **result** (BOOL); the return value is one of the following:

TRUE	The controls are not formatted and the window is not resized.
FALSE	IPF processes the request as normal.

◻ HM_QUERY

This message is sent by the application to IPF when the application
requires IPF-specific information. The types of information are

- The current instance handle

- The active communication object window
- The active window
- The group number of the current window

● Parameters

param1 **reserved** (USHORT)   NULL value.

usmessageid (USHORT)   The type of window to query. It is one of the following:

HMQW_INDEX   The handle of the index window.

HMQW_TOC   The handle of the Table of Contents window.

HMQW_SEARCH   The handle of the Search Hitlist window.

HMQW_VIEWEDPAGES   The handle of the Viewed Pages window.

HMQW_LIBRARY   The handle of the Library List window.

HMQW_OBJCOM_WINDOW   The handle of the active communication window.

HMQW_INSTANCE   The handle of the help instance.

HMQW_COVERPAGE   The handle of the IPF MDI parent window.

HMQW_VIEWPORT   The handle of the viewport window found in the low order word of *param1* and *param2* parameters.

HMQW_GROUP_VIEWPORT   The group number of the window whose handle is found in *param2* parameter.

HMQW_RES_VIEWPORT   The resource identification number of the window whose handle is found in *param2*.

HMQW_ACTIVEVIEWPORT   The handle of the currently active window.

USERDATA   The previously stored user data.

usselectionid (USHORT) is one of the following:
HMQVP_NUMBER   A pointer to a USHORT; it contains the **res** ID of the window.

HMQVP_NAME	A pointer to a string; it is the ID of the window.
HMQVP_GROUP	The group number of the window.

param2 (PVOID)   This parameter depends on the value of *param1*:
- If *param1* is HMQW_VIEWPORT, then *param2* is a pointer to the **res** number, ID, or group ID.
- If *param1* is HMQW_GROUP_VIEWPORT, then *param2* is the handle of the viewport window for which the group number is requested.
- If *param1* **messageid** is HMQW_RES_VIEWPORT, then *param2* is the handle of the viewport for which the **res** number is requested.

- Return

reply **ulreturnValue** (ULONG), the return value is one of the following:

0	The request was completed successfully.
Other	This value depends on *param1*. It is one of the following: the handle (HWND), group number (USHORT), or **res** number (USHORT) of the window, or the user data (USHORT).

◻ HM_QUERY_DDF_DATA

This message is sent by IPF to the communication object when IPF has encountered the DDF tag.

- Parameters

param1 (HWND) **pageclienthwnd**	The client handle of the page that holds the OBJCOM window.
param2 (ULONG) **resid**	The **res** ID for the DDF tag.

- Return

reply **hddfddfhandle** (HDDF); the return value is one of the following:

0	An error occurred during processing of the application's DDF.
Other	The DDF handle to be displayed.

◘ HM_QUERY_KEY_HELP

This message is sent by IPF to the application when a user has requested keys for a function.

- Parameters

param1 (ULONG) NULL value.
param2 (ULONG) NULL value.

- Return

reply **usHelpPanel** (USHORT); the return value is one of the following:

0   Do nothing.
Other   The identity of the keys help window that is to be displayed.

◘ HM_REPLACE_HELP_FOR_HELP

This message is sent by the application to tell IPF to show the application-defined 'Help for Help' window instead of the IPF 'Help for Help' window.

- Parameters

param1 **idUsingHelpPanel** (USHORT)

The ID of the application-defined Using Help window. This value is one of the following:

0   The IPF Using Help window.
Other   The ID of the application-defined Using Help window.

param2 (ULONG) NULL value.

- Return

flreply (ULONG)   NULL value.

◘ HM_SET_ACTIVE_WINDOW

This message is sent by the application, and this will allow the application to change the active application window with which the IPF help window is associated.

- Parameters

param1 **hwndActiveWindow** (HWND)   The handle of the window to be made active.

param2 **hwndRelativeWindow** (HWND)   The handle of the window next to which the help window is to be positioned.

- Return

reply **ulreturnValue** (ULONG), the return value is one of the following:

0   The request was completed successfully.
Other   Could find a help window. The request was not completed; for more information, see the value of **ulErrorCode** of the HM_ERROR message.

◖ HM_SET_COVERPAGE_SIZE

This message is sent by the application to tell IPF to set the size coverpage window.

- **Parameters**

param1 (PRECTL) **coverpagerectl**   The size of the coverpage.
param2 (ULONG)   NULL value.

- Return

reply **ulreturnValue** (ULONG); the return value is one of the following:

0   The request was completed successfully.
Other   Could find a help window. The request was not completed; for more information, see the value of **ulErrorCode** of the HM_ERROR message.

◘ HM_SET_HELP_LIBRARY_NAME

This message is sent by the application to tell IPF to replace the list of help libraries specified in the initialization structure with a new list.

● Parameters

param1 **HelpLibraryName** (PSTRL)	A pointer to a PSZ data type (a string) that holds a list of help window library names. These names will be searched by IPF for the requested help window.
param2 (ULONG)	NULL value.

● Return

reply **ulreturnValue** (ULONG); the return value is one of the following:

0	The request was completed successfully.
Other	Could find a help window. The request was not completed; for more information, see the value of **ulErrorCode** of the HM_ERROR message.

◘ MH_SET_HELP_WINDOW_TITLE

This message is sent by the application to tell IPF to change the text of a help window title.

● Parameters

param1 **HelpWindowTitle** (PSTRL)	A pointer to the Help window title.
param2 (ULONG)	NULL value.

● Return

reply **ulreturnValue** (ULONG); the return value is one of the following:

0	The request was completed successfully.
Other	Could find a help window. The request was not completed; for more information, see the value of **ulErrorCode** of the HM_ERROR message.

◘ HM_SET_OBJCOM_WINDOW

This message is sent by the application to tell IPF to identify the communication object to which the HM_INFORM and HM_QUERY_DDF_DATA messages are sent.

- Parameters

param1 (HWND) **objcomhwnd**   The handle of the communication object window to be set.

param2 (ULONG)   NULL value.

- Return

reply **hwndprevioushwnd** (HWND)   The handle of the previous communication object window.

◘ HM_SET_SHOW_PANEL_ID

This message is sent by the application to tell IPF to show or hide window IDs for each help window.

- Parameters

param1 **fsShowPanelId** (USHORT) The show window flag:

CMIC_HIDE_PANEL_ID	Hide a window.
CMIC_SHOW_PANEL_ID	Show a window.
CMIC_TOGGLE_PANEL_ID	Switch the display of the window identity.

param2 (ULONG)   NULL value.

- Return

reply ulreturnValue (ULONG); the return value is one of the following:

0   The request was completed successfully.
Other   Could find a help window. The request was not completed; for more information, see the value of ulErrorCode of the HM_ERROR message.

◘ HM_SET_USERDATA

This message is sent by the application to tell IPF to store data in the IPF data area.

- Parameters

param1 (ULONG) NULL value.
param2 (VOID)

- Return

reply **return-value** (ULONG); the value is one of the following:

TRUE   The user data was successfully stored.
FALSE   The request failed.

◘ HM_TUTORIAL

This parameter is sent by IPF to tell the appliation when the user selects **Tutorial** item from the **Help** pull-down.

- **Parameters**

param1 **TutorialName** (PSTRL) A pointer to the default tutorial name.
param2 (ULONG)   NULL value.

- Return

flreply (ULONG)   NULL value.

◘ HM_UPDATE_OBJCOM_WINDOW_CHAIN

This message is sent by the communication to the currently active communication object when the sending object wants to withdraw from the communication chain.

- Parameters

param1 (HWND) The handle of the object to be withdrawn from the communication chain.

param2 (HWND)	Window containing the handle of the object to be replaced.

- Return

flreply (ULONG)	NULL value.

8.6 Window Functions

This section lists six PM functions that are used to incorporate help information in an application program. Many of these functions have been mentioned earlier; this time we will look at a them in a bit more detail. They are

WinAssociateHelpInstance
WinCreateHelpInstance
WinCreateHelpTable
WinDestroyHelpInstance
WinLoadHelpTable
WinQueryHelpInstance

■ WinAssociateHelpInstance—connect a help instance to an appplication window chain

- Define macro and prototype

```
#define INCL_WINHELP

BOOL WinAssociateHelpInstance( HWND hwndHelpInstace,
                               HWND hwndApp)
```

- Description

hwndHelpInstace is a variable of type HWND that contains a handle placed by successful operation of the **WinCreateHelpInstance** function.

hwndApp contains the handle of the application window to which a previously created help instance is associated. The same association happens with any of the children or owned windows of the application window.

● Return

This function returns a boolean flag with the following conditions:

TRUE   If operation is completed successfully.
FALSE   If operation resulted in an error. In case of an error, you must check the **ulReturnCode** field of the **HELPINIT** structure for a more precise error code.

WinCreateHelpInstance—create a help instance

● Define macro and prototype

```
#define INCL_WINHELP

HWND WinCreateHelpInstance(HAB hab,
                           HELPINIT phinitHMInitStructure)
```

● Description

hab is the handle of the application anchor block, which is returned by the **WinInitialize** function.

phinitHMInitStructure is a pointer to the **HELPINIT** structure, holding information, such as help table, help window name, or help library, which are required to create the help instance.

● Return

This function returns a handle if a help instance is created; otherwise a NULL is returned in case there is an error. In case of an error, you must check the **ulReturnCode** field of the **HELPINIT** structure for a more precise error code.

WinDestroyHelpInstance—destroy help instance and remove its window from the parent window

● Define macro and prototype

```
#define INCL_WINHELP /* Or use INCL_WIN or INCL_PM */
BOOL WinDestroyHelpInstance( HWND hwndHelpInstance )
```

- Description

hwndHelpInstance is a handle previously returned by
WinCreateHelpInstance for the help instance to be destroyed.

- Return

This function returns a boolean flag with the following conditions:

TRUE   If the operation is completed successfully.

FALSE   If the operation results in an error. In case of an error, you
must check the **ulReturnCode** field of the **HELPINIT**
structure for a more precise error code.

◘ WinCreateHelpTable—indentify or change the help table

- Define macro and prototype

```
#define INCL_WINHELP /* or use INCL_WIN or INCL_PM */
BOOL WinCreateHelpTable( HWND hwndHelpinstance,
                         PHELPTABLE phthelpTable)
```

- Description

hwndHelpinstance is the handle of an instance of the help manager.

phthelpTable is the help allocated by the application.

- Return

This function returns a boolean flag with the following conditions

TRUE   If the operation is completed successfully.

FALSE   If the operation results in an error.

◘ WinLoadHelpTable—load a help table

- Define macro and prototype

```
#define INCL_WINHELP
BOOL WinLoadHelpTable( HWND hwndHelpinstance,
               USHORT idHelpTable,
                    HMODULE module)
```

- Description

  hwndHelpinstance holds the handle of the help instance, which is returned by the **WinCreateHelpInstance** function.

  idHelpTable holds the name of the help table to be loaded.

  module holds the handle of the module that contains the help table and associated help subtable.

- Return

  This function returns a boolean flag with the following conditions:

  TRUE   If the operation is completed successfully.
  FALSE   If the operation results in an error.

◘ WinQueryHelpInstance—get the help instance associated with a particular application window chain

- Define macro and prototype

```
#define INCL_WINHELP

HWND WinQueryHelpInstance(HWND hwndApp)
```

- Description

  hwndApp holds the handle of the application window.

- Return
  The function returns a handle for a help window. If no help instance is associated with the application, it returns a NULLHANDLE.

8.7 Tag Reference

The IPF tags direct the compiler as how the online data, whether it is part of a program or a standalone information system, is to be presented to the user. This section lists and describes all the tags used by the IPF compiler to create help windows and online documents.

The structure and syntax of the IPF tags are similar to those of the Generalized Markup Language (GML) which is also used in IBM's DCF document composition facility) product. With the IPF tag language you can do the following kinds of formatting:

- Highlight text
- Set margins
- Add lists, notes, and notices
- Create tables
- Incorporate graphic objects, such as art and graphs
- Change size, font, and color of text
- Customize the display window

As mentioned earlier, the tags are embedded in the text and the particular syntax description of each tag distinguishes itself from the text. The general format of the tag is

```
:tagname attribute.
```

where *tagname* is the name of a tag. There are a few things to remember about using tags:

- Tagname
- Element that the tag describes
- Attributes of the tag
- End tag

Some tags have attributes associated with them. An attribute is to give more control information for the tag. An attribute is followed by apostrophes or single quotation marks, for example,

```
:font facename='Tms Rmn'
```

An end tag is used to mark an end of a block, which starts with a tag with the same name, except for 'e'. For   example, the end tag for the **:userdoc.** tag is the **:euserdoc.** tag.

In a source file, the IPF compiler required a minimum number of tags in a specific order before the file can be compiled. For example,

```
:userdoc.
:h1 id=custinfo.Tag Customer Information Help
:p.This is an example of how to use IPF tags.
:euserdoc.
```

contains the minimum number of tags for an acceptable compilation.

The rest of the section gives the syntax, including an end tag if required, of the IPF tags, followed by attributes and a brief description, to be used to implement help information in an application or to create an online document system.

◨ Comment

- Tag general format

```
.*
```

- Description

This tag is used to add comments in a file. The text related to this tag is ignored by the compiler.

- Attribute

```
comment
```

◨ Application-controlled window

- Tag general format

```
:acviewport.
```

- Description

This tag enables an application to dynamically control the information displayed in an IPF window.

- Attribute

```
dll=' '
objectname=' '
objectinfo=' '
vpx=
vpy=
vpcx=
vpcy=
```

◨ Art link

- Tag general format

```
:artlink.
   .
   .
   .
:eartlink.
```

- Description

This tag identifies link definitions for hypergraphic areas of a bitmap.

- Attribute

None.

◘ Artwork

- Tag general format

```
:artwork.
```

- Description

This tag identifies a bitmap to be copied to the user's file.

- Attribute

```
name=' '
align=
linkfile=' '
runin
fit
```

◘ Break

- Tag general format

```
:br.
```

- Description

This tag causes a break in a line of a given text.

- Attribute

  None.

◘ Caution

- Tag general format

```
:caution.
   .
   .
:ecaution
```

- Description

  This tag alerts the user to risk of an action.

- Attribute

```
text=' '
```

◘ Character graphic

- Tag general format

```
:cgraphic.
   .
   .
:ecgraphic
```

- Description

  This tag defines a character graphic.

- Attribute

  None.

◘ Color

- Tag general format

  :color.

- Description

  This tag changes the colors of the text and text background.

- Attribute

  ```
  fc=
  bc=
  ```

◘ Define content

- Tag general format

  :ctrl.

- Description

  This tag defines the contents of the control area of a window.

- Attribute

  ```
  ctrlid=
  controls=
  page
  coverpage
  ```

◘ Define control

- Tag general format

  ```
  :ctrldef.
      .
      .
      .
  :ectrldef.
  ```

- Description

  This tag defines the control area of a window.

- Attribute

None.

◻ Dynamic data formatting

- Tag general format

```
:ddf.
```

- Description

This tag allows the display of dynamically formatted data in an application-controlled window.

- Attribute

```
res=
```

◻ Definition list

- Tag general format

```
:dl.
  .
  .
  .
:edl.
```

- Description

This tag identifies a list of terms and definitions.

- Attribute

```
compact
tsize=
break=
```

◻ Document profile

- Tag general format

```
:docprof.
```

- Description

  This tag specifies the heading-level entries to be displayed in the Table
  of Contents window.

- Attribute

```
toc=
dll=' '
objectname=' '
objectinfo=' '
ctrlarea=
```

◘ Figure

- Tag general format

```
:fig.
  .
  .
  .
:efig.
```

- Description

  This tag identifies a figure.

- Attribute

  None.

◘ Figure caption

- Tag general format

```
:figcap.
```

- Description

  This tag specifies a figure title.

- Attribute

  None.

◻ Font

- Tag general format

```
:font.
```

- Description

  This tag changes the font to the specified typeface, size, and code page.

- Attribute

```
facename=
size=
codepage=
```

◻ Footnote

- Tag general format

```
:fn.
 .
 .
 .
:efn.
```

- Description

  This tag identifies a pop-up window.

- Attribute

```
id=
```

◻ Headings

- Tag general format

```
:h1. through :h6.
```

- Description

  This tag defines window characteristics.

- Attribute

```
res=            id=             name=
global          tutorial=' '    x=
y=              width=          height=
group=          viewport        clear
titlebar=       scroll=         rules=
nosearch        noprint         hide
toc=            ctrlarea=       ctrlrefid=
```

◘ Hide

- Tag general format

```
:hide.
 .
 .
 .
:ehide.
```

- Description

This tag controls display of IPF text and graphics to meet conditions set
by the IPF_KEYS= environment variable.

- Attribute

```
key=
```

◘ Highlighted phrase

- Tag general format

```
:hp1. through :hp9.
 .
 .
 .
:ehpn.
```

- Description

This tag emphasizes text by changing the font style or foreground color.

- Attribute

```
None.
```

◘ Index

- Tag general format

```
:i1. and :i2.
```

- Description

  This tag places topics into the index.

- Attribute

```
for :i1.
    id=
    global
    roots=' '
    sortkey=' '
for :i2.
    refid=
    global
    sortkey=' '
```

◘ Index command

- Tag general format

```
:icmd.
```

- Description

  This tag identifies the help window that describes a command.

- Attribute

  external command
  string

◘ Index synonym

- Tag general format

```
:isyn.
```

- Description

  This tag identifies synonyms and word variations for the help keywords.

- Attribute

  ```
  root=
  ```

◘ List item

- Tag general format

  ```
  :li.
  ```

- Description

  This tag identifies an item within a list.

- Attribute

  None.

◘ Lines

- Tag general format

  ```
  :lines.
  .
  .
  :elines.
  ```

- Description

  This tag turns formatting off.

- Attribute

  ```
  align=
  ```

◘ Link

- Tag general format

  ```
  :link.
  .
  .
  :elink.
  ```

- Description

  This tag activates a link to additional information.

- Attribute

```
reftype=       res=         refid=
database=' '   object=' '   data=' '
auto           viewport     dependent
split          group=       vpx=
vpy=           vpcy=        vpcx=
titlebar=      scroll=      rules=
```

◻ Left margin

- Tag general format

  ```
  :lm.
  ```

- Description

  This tag sets the left margin of the text.

- Attribute

  ```
  margin=
  ```

◻ List part

- Tag general format

  ```
  :lp.
  ```

- Description

  This tag identifies an explanation within a list.

- Attribute

  None.

◨ Note

- Tag general format

  ```
  :note.
  ```

- Description

  This tag starts a note.

- Attribute

  ```
  text=' '
  ```

◨ Note

- Tag general format

  ```
  :nt.
  .
  .
  .
  :ent.
  ```

- Description

  This tag starts a note that can have multiple paragraphs.

- Attribute
  ```
  text=' '
  ```

◨ Order list

- Tag general format

  ```
  :ol.
  .
  .
  .
  :eol.
  ```

- Description

  This tag starts a sequential list of items or steps.

- Attribute

  compact

◻ Paragraph

- Tag general format

  `:p.`

- Description

  This tag starts a new paragraph.

- Attribute

  None.

◻ Parameter list

- Tag general format

  ```
  :parml.
    .
    .
    .
  :eparml.
  ```

- Description

  This tag starts a two-column list of parameter terms and descriptions.

- Attribute

  ```
  tsize=
  break=
  compact
  ```

◻ Push button

- Tag general format

  `:pbutton.`

- Description

  This tag defines author-controlled push buttons.

- Attribute

```
id=
res=
text=' '
```

◘ Parameter description

- Tag general format

```
:pd.
```

- Description

  This tag starts the description for a parameter term in a parameter list.

- Attribute

  None.

◘ Parameter term

- Tag general format

```
:pt.
```

- Description

  This tag identifies a term in a parameter list.

- Attribute

  None.

◘ Right margin

- Tag general format

```
:rm.
```

- Description

  This tag sets the right margin of the text.

- Attribute

  ```
  margin=
  ```

◻ Simple List

- Tag general format

  ```
  :sl.
   .
   .
   .
  :esl.
  ```

- Description

  This tag starts a nonsequential list of items.

- Attribute

  ```
  compact
  ```

◻ Table

- Tag general format

  ```
  :table.
   .
   .
   .
  :etable.
  ```

- Description

  This tag formats information as a table.

- Attribute

  ```
  cols=' '
  rules=
  frame=
  ```

◼ Title

- Tag general format

```
:title.
```

- Description

  This tag provides a name for the online document.

- Attribute

  None.

◼ Unordered list

- Tag general format

```
:ul.
   .
   .
   .
:eul.
```

- Description

  This tag starts a list of nonsequential items.

- Attribute

```
compact
```

◼ User Document

- Tag general format

```
:userdoc.
   .
   .
   .
:euserdoc.
```

- Description

  This tag identifies the source file that is to be compiled.

- Attribute

None.

◘ Warning

- Tag general format

```
:warning.
.
.
:ewarning.
```

- Description

This tag alerts the user of a potential risk or possible error condition.

- Attribute

```
text=' '
```

◘ Example

- Tag general format

```
:xmp.
.
.
:exmp.
```

- Description

This tag turns formatting off.

- Attribute

None.

Preprocessor Directives

During the compilation of a C or C++ program, a preprocessor step takes place. In this step several tasks may be performed:

- Tokens in the current file may be replaced by other tokens. Each token comprises a series of characters, and tokens are separated by white space. The only white space allowed on a preprocessor directive is the space, horizontal tab, and comments.
- Include files may occur within the current file.
- Conditional compilation of a program.
- The line number of the next line of source and the filename of the current file may be changed.
- Diagnostic messages may be produced.

The compiler looks for preprocessor directives on how to process this step. This chapter describes these directives by giving the general format, a description, and useful examples for each directive. The directives are:

#define	#undef	# operator	#error
#include	#if	#elif	#ifdef
#ifndef	#else	#endif	#line
#pragma			

Before delving into the directives, it is worth having a brief look at conditional compilation directives. A *conditional compilation* directive causes the preprocessor to select or discard portions of a source program for compilation. What should be passed on to the compiler depends on the conditions that the preprocessor evaluates.

There are many conditional compilation directives, and there are many ways of using them. One way is to write portions of program code that are applicable for different stages of the software life cycle: development, testing, and production. With conditional directives you can "turn on" only part of your source code and discard the rest, during a compilation. The preprocessor does the work of selecting the appropriate parts to suit each situation. The preprocessor allows the following conditional directives:

#if, **#else**, and **#endif**
#elif
#ifdef
#ifndef

As we will discuss the different preprocessor directives in detail, you will notice that they add power and flexibility to development of sofware.

◘ #define

● General format

```
Simple form:
  #define identifier token_string

Complex form:
  #define identifier(parameter1,...,parametern) token_string
```

● Description

The **#define** directive has two forms: simple and complex. In the simple form, this directive tells the preprocessor to replace all the occurrences of the *identifier* with the *token_string*.

The complex form is called a *macro*. A complex macro receives one to many parameters when it is invoked. There should be no space between the *identifier* and the left parenthesis. The parameters are separated by commas. The *token_string* is the replacement code. A macro looks like a function, and when it is invoked, it must have the same number of arguments as the corresponding macro definition has parameters.

The scope of a macro definition begins when it is defined and does not end until a corresponding **#undef** directive is found. If a corresponding **#undef** directive is not found at all during the preprocessing step, the scope of the macro definition lasts until the end of the compilation is reached. Once removed, the same identifier can be reused to define another macro. Macros are very useful in replacing function calls by inline code, which leads to efficient programs.

A recursive macro is not fully expanded. For example, the definition

```
#define x(a,b) x(a+1,b+1) + 4
```

would expand **x(20,10)** to **x(20+1,10+1) + 4** rather than trying to expand the macro **x** over and over within itself.

You can also use the /D compiler option to define macros on the command line, when the compiler is invoked. Macros defined on the command line override macros defined in the source code.

● Example

In the following example, COUNT is associated with the number 5. A **#define** directive does not use any storage area. The preprocessor substitutes every occurrence of COUNT with the value 5, only once in this case.

```
#define COUNT 5
main()
{
    int i;
    for( i = 0; i <= COUNT ; i++ )
      printf( "New World Order" );
}
```

In the example, **ADD** is a macro which has two parameters, **a** and **b**. The replacement code is **(a+b)**. In the **main** function, this **ADD** macro is used to add **x** and **y**.

```
/****************************************************************
This program illustrates the macro definition and its use.
****************************************************************/
#include <stdio.h>
#define ADD(a,b) (a+b) /* macro to add */
main()
{
    int x = 1, y = 5;

    printf( "Sum of x and y is %d \n", ADD(x,y));
}
```

The following are a few examples of efficient programming using macros.

```
/* find the minimum of two values */
#define min(a,b) ( ( (a) < (b) ) ? (a) : (b) )
/* find the minimum of two values */
#define max(a,b) ( ( (a) > (b) ) ? (a) : (b) )
/* check if a character is alpha */
#define ISALPHA(c) ( ( ('a') <= (c) ) && ( (c) <= 'z') ) \
        || ( ('A') <= (c) ) && ( (c) <= 'Z') ) )
/* copy string s to d */
#define Copy(d,s) strncpy( d, s, sizeof(d) )
/* fill an array with zeroes */
#define Zero_array(a) memset( a, 0, sizeof(a) )
```

◙ Predefined macros

Both C and C++ provide the following predefined macro names as specified in the ANSI language standard. The name of each of these macros has two leading and trailing underscore (__) characters. Although they are available to you, these macros cannot be undefined by your program.

Predefined macros	Return values
__DATE__	A character string containing the date when the source file was last compiled. The date format is Mnn dd yyyy, where Mnn is the month (Jan, Feb, etc.) dd is the day, and yyyy is the year.
__TIME__	A character string containing the time when the source file was last compiled. The time format is hh:mm:ss.
__FILE__	A character string containing the source filename.
__LINE__	An integer representing the current line number.
__STDC__	A nonzero integer value to indicate the implementation follows ANSI Standard C, otherwise it is zero.
__TIMESTAMP__	A character string literal containing the date and time when the source file was last modified. The date and time will be in the form Day Mmm dd hh:mm:ss yyyy where Day is the day of the week (Mon, Tue, Wed, Thu, Fri, Sat, or Sun),

	Mmm is the month in an abbreviated form (Jan, Feb, Mar, Apr, May, Jun, Jul, Aug, Sep, Oct, Nov, or Dec), dd is the day, hh is the hour. mm is the minutes, ss is the seconds, and yyyy is the year.
__ANSI__	Allows only language constructs that conform to ANSIC standards. It is defined by using the **#pragma langlvl** directive or /Sa option.
__SAA__	Allows only language constructs that conform to the most recent level of SAA C standards. It is defined by using the **#pragma langlvl** directive or /S2 option. This macro is not supported for C++.
__SAAL2__	Allows only language constructs that conform to SAA Level 2 C standards. It is defined by using the **#pragma langlvl** directive or /S2 option. This macro is not supported for C++.
__EXTENDED__	Allows additional language constructs provided by the implementation. It is defined using the **#pragma langlvl** directive or /S2 option.

The C/C++ Tools compiler offers several other predefined macros:

_CHAR_UNSIGNED	Means that the default character type is unsigned. It is defined using the **#pragma chars** directive or /J compiler option.
_CHAR_SIGNED	Means that the default character type is signed. Defined using the **#pragma chars** directive or /J compiler option.
__COMPAT__	Means that language constructs compatible with earlier versions of the C++ language are allowed. It is defined using the **#pragma langlvl(compat)** directive or /Sc compiler option. This macro can be used only in C++ programs.
__cplusplus	Means that the product is a C++ compiler. This macro can be used only in a C++ program.
__DBCS__	Means that DBCS support is enabled. It is defined by using the /Sn compiler option.
__DDNAMES__	Means that the ddnames are supported. It is defined by using the /Sh compiler option.
__DLL__	Means that the code for a DLL (dynamic-link library) is being compiled. It is defined using the /Ge- compiler option.

__FUNCTION__	Means the name of the function currently being compiled. For C++ programs, it expands to the actual function prototype.
__IBMC__	Means the version number of the C/C++ Tools C compiler.
__IBMCPP__	Means the version number of the C/C++ Tools C++ compiler.
_M_I386	Means that the code is being compiled for a 80386 chip or higher.
__MULTI__	Means that the multithread code is being generated. Defined using the /Gm compiler option.
__OS2__	Means the product is an OS/2 compiler.
__SPC__	Means the subsystem libraries are being used. It is defined using the /Rn compiler option.
__TEMPINC__	Means that the template-implementation file method of resolving template functions is being used. It is defined using the /Ft compiler option.
__TILED__	Means that the tiled memory is being used. It is defined using the /Gt compiler option.
__32BIT__	Means the product is a 32-bit compiler.

● Example

The following program prints the values of the predefined macros __LINE__, __FILE__, __DATE__, and __TIME__. It also prints the value of CONF, which is defined as "YES" or "NO" depending on whether __STDC__ is defined.

```
/*********************************************
This program illustrates predefined macros.
*********************************************/

#include <stdio.h>

#if __STDC__
# define CONF "YES"
#else
# define CONF "NO"
#endif

main()
{
   printf( "Line      File      Date      Time      ANSI\n");
   printf( "%d        %s        %s        %s        %s\n",
      __LINE__, __FILE__, __DATE__, __TIME__,
                       CONF );

}
```

◼ #undef

● General format

```
#undef identifier
```

● Description

As mentioned earlier, the scope of a **#define** identifier lasts until the end of a source file unless it is nullified with a **#undef** directive.

You can also use the /U compiler option to undefine macros. The /U option does not undefine macros defined in source code.

● Example

The directive

```
#define COUNT 100
```

defines COUNT. And, the next directive COUNT

```
#undef COUNT
```

removes the identifier. The same identifier (COUNT) can be used again to represent the same or another constant.

◼ # Operator

● Description

The preprocessor operator # causes a formal parameter of complex macro definition to become a string. When using the **#** operator in a complex macro definition, you have to remember the following rules:

- A parameter in a macro that is preceded by the # operator will be converted into a character string literal containing the argument passed to the macro.
- Leading and trailing white-space characters that appear before or after the argument passed to the macro are deleted.
- Multiple white-space characters found within the argument passed to the macro are reduced to single space character.
- If the argument passed to the macro has a string literal and if a \

(backslash) character appears within the literal, a second \ character will be inserted before the original \ when the macro is expanded.

- If the argument passed to the macro has a " (double quotation mark) character, a \ character will be inserted before the " when the macro is expanded.
- The conversion of an argument into a string literal occurs proir to macro expansion on that argument.
- If more than one ## operator or # operator appears in the replacement list of a macro definition, the order of evaluation of the operators is not defined.
- If the result of the replacement is not a valid character string literal, the behavior is undefined.

- Example

The following example illustrates the use of operator #. In the macro definition of **massage** the token **x** is preceded by #.

```
#define message(x)    #x

main()
{
    printf("Message is: %s\n", message(Peace has come));
}
```

When this program is run, the result is

```
    Message is: Peace has come
```

When the macro *message* is invoked, the # operator will enclose the argument with double quotes. After the execution of the preprocessor, the macro expansion will become

```
    printf("Message is: %s","Peace has come\n");
```

◨ #error—generate error message

- General format

```
#error character
```

- Description

The **#error** directive is used to generate an error message and stop the compilation. The **#error** directive is useful in detecting errors in conditional compilation. If the preprocessor passes a portion of your program when it should not have, this directive gives you an appropriate message and terminates the compilation.

- Example

In the following example, when the compiler reaches the **#error** directive, it will show the message associated with it and stop.

```
#error Program: LGLP701, this is test code, should \
            not be compiled
```

◘ #include—insert a file

- General format

```
#include "file_name" or
        <file_name> or
         characters
```

- Description

The **#include** directive causes the preprocessor to replace the line in a program with the content of a specified file. Generally, a header file contains other preprocessor directives, data definitions and declarations, function prototypes, macros, or other **#include** directives. There are two types of header files. One type is supplied with the C compiler, such as **stdio.h** and **stdlib.h**; these files should not be changed. The other type is header files used for your own programs, which multiply and grow depending on the needs of the software design.

The convention is to enclose the system include files that are supplied with the C or C++ compiler in brackets, such as

```
#include <stdio.h>
```

Files enclosed in brackets are searched in the following places in the order indicated:

- Any directories specified using the /I compiler option (that have not been removed by the /Xc option). Any directories listed in the **ICC** environment variable are searched before those specified on the command line.

- Any directories listed in the **INCLUDE** environment variable, provided the /Xi option is not in effect.

The double quotation marks are used for user defined include files; for example,

```
#include "mydef.h"
```

Files enclosed in double quotes are searched in the following places in the order indicated:

- The directory where the original **.c** source file are found.
- Any directories listed using the /I compiler option (that have not been removed by the /Xc option). Any directories listed in the **ICC** environment variable are searched before those specified on the command line.
- Any directories listed using the **INCLUDE** environment variable, provided the /Xi option is not in effect.

You can give a fully qualified filename and the preprocessor, searches only the directory that is part of the name.

So far we discussed at the first two types of parameters: filename enclosed in brackets and filename enclosed in double quotation marks. The third option is to place characters which represent a macro. The preprocessor resolves macros on an **#include** directive. After macro replacement, the resulting token sequence must have a filename enclosed in either double quotation marks or brackets; for example,

```
#define MONTH <july.h>
#include MONTH
```

- Example

The **mydef.h** file is an example of an include file, and it contains the following lines:

```
/*mydef.h*/
#include <stdio.h>
#include <stdlib.h>
#include <string.h>

#define RC_FAIL   -1  /* return for failure */
#define RC_SUCCESS 0 /* return code for success */
#define NULLPTR ( (MFILE *) 0) /* null pointer */
#define EOS '\0' /* end-of-string  */
```

```c
typedef    unsigned    char  UCHAR;

struct     mfile_struct
{
   struct mfile_struct *id;  /* memory file instance id */
   int     fmaxrows;       /* maximum number of rows  */
   int        fmaxcol;     /*  maximum  number  of  columns
                              */
   int    rows_full;       /* number of rows filled */
   UCHAR  *mf_data_ptr;   /* pointer to data storage */

};

typedef    struct mfile_struct MFILE;

/* function prototypes */

MFILE *mf_ist( int row, int col );
int mf_rls( MFILE *mfptr );
int mf_read( MFILE *mfptr, char *fptr );
int *mf_getrp( MFILE *mfptr, int row );
```

It has **#include** directives, other preprocessor directives (**#define**), structure definition, datatype definitions, and function prototypes. Next is an example of how to use this **mydef.h** header file.

```c
/*****************************************
This program illustrates the use of the
preprocessor #include directive.
******************************************/

#include "mydef.h"

main()
{


}
```

During compilation of the program, the preprocessor will replace **#include "mydef.h"** with the content of the **mydef.h** file. Notice that we used double quotation marks instead of angle brackets.

A **#define** directive is used to define a macro that represents the name of the C or C++ standard I/O include file. A **#include** directive is subsequently used to make the header file available to the C or C++ program; for example,

```c
 #define  IO_HEADER    <stdio.h>
        .
        .
        .
 #include IO_HEADER  /* equivalent to specifying #include
                    <stdio.h> */
```

◼ #if, #elif

● General format

```
#if constant-expression_1
   statements
#elif constant-expression_2
   statements
#elif constant-expression_3
   statements
#else
   statements
#endif
```

● Description

The **#if** and **#elif** directives are used to compare the value of the expression to zero. All macros are expanded, any defined expressions are processed, and all remaining identifiers are replaced with the token 0.

The **#elif** is an else-if control contruct. It is always preceded by the **#if** directive and followed by none or many **#elif** directives, and finally followed by the directive **#endif**.

The **#else** directive is optional and it must be placed just before the **#endif** directive. If the evaluation of *constant-expression* yields 1 (TRUE), then the next **#elif** or **#else** will be included for compilation.

The evaluation of expressions must follow these rules:

● No casts are performed.
● The expression can hold the defined unary operator.
● The expression can contain defined macros. If a macro is not defined, a value of 0 is assigned to it.
● Arithmetic operation is performed using **long int**.

● Example

In the following example identifier DEBUG and TEST are defined and conditional directives are used to select only one of the three definitions and initialization of the variable in_file[ ]. In this case, the preprocessor will send

```
static char in_file[] = "TEST.DAT" ;
```

to the compiler because expression TEST >= 1 yields value 1.

```
#define DEBUG 0
#define TEST  1
#if DEBUG >= 1
   static char in_file[] = "MY.DAT";
#if TEST >= 1
   static char in_file[] = "TEST.DAT";
#elif
   static char in_file[] = "PROD.DAT";
#endif
```

◻ #ifdef—check whether a macro is defined

- General format

```
#ifdef identifier
   statements
#endif
```

- Description

The **#ifdef** directive is used to check whether an identifier has been defined as a macro by the preprocessor. If it is defined, then the C statements immediately following the directive **#ifdef** are passed to the compiler.

- Example

In the following example, in_file is initialized to TEST.FIL if DEBUG is defined as a macro by the preprocessor. Otherwise, it will be initialized to PROD.FIL.

```
#ifdef DEBUG
   static char in_file[] = "TEST.FIL";
#else
   static char in_file[] = "PROD.FIL";
#endif
```

The **#ifdef** directive checks for the existence of macro definitions.

If the identifier specified is defined as a macro, the tokens that immediately follow the condition are passed on to the compiler.

◼ #ifndef—check whether a macro is not defined

● General format

```
#ifndef identifier
    statements
#endif
```

● Description

The **#ifndef** directive is used to check whether an identifier has not been defined as a macro by the preprocessor. If it is *not* defined, then the C or C++ statements immediately following the directive **#ifndef** are passed to the compiler.

● Example

In the following example, **in_file** is initialized to TEST.FIL if DEBUG is *not* defined as a macro by the preprocessor. Otherwise, it will be initialized to PROD.FIL.

```
#ifndef DEBUG
    static char in_file[] = "TEST.FIL";
#else
    static char in_file[] = "PROD.FIL";
#endif
```

The **#ifndef** directive checks for the existence of macro definitions.

If the identifier specified is not defined as a macro, the tokens that immediately follow the condition are passed on to the compiler.

The following example defines MAX_LEN to be 60 if EXTEND is not defined for the preprocessor. Otherwise, MAX_LEN is defined to be 65.

```
#ifndef EXTEND
    #    define MAX_LEN 50
    #else
    #    define MAX_LEN 65
    #endif
```

◼ #else

● General format

```
#else statement
```

● Description

The **#else** directive accompanies the **#if**, **#ifdef**, or **#ifndef** directive. If the condition found in these associated directives evaluates to 0, and the conditional compilation directive contains a preprocessor **#else** directive, the source text located between the preprocessor **#else** directive and the preprocessor **#endif** directive is passed to the compiler.

● Example

In the following example, **in_file** is initialized to TEST.FIL if DEBUG is *not* defined as a macro by the preprocessor. Otherwise, it will be initialized to PROD.FIL.

```
#ifndef DEBUG
    static char in_file[] = "TEST.FIL";
#else
    static char in_file[] = "PROD.FIL";
#endif
```

The **#ifndef** directive checks for the existence of macro definitions.

If the identifier specified is not defined as a macro, the tokens that immediately follow the condition are passed on to the compiler.

The following example defines MAX_LEN to be 60 if EXTEND is not defined for the preprocessor. Otherwise, MAX_LEN is defined to be 65.

```
#ifndef EXTEND
    #    define MAX_LEN 50
    #else
    #    define MAX_LEN 65
    #endif
```

In the following example, an **if-else-endif** construct is used for conditional compilation.

```
/*******************************************
This program illustrates #if #else #endif.
*******************************************/
#include <stdio.h>
#define TEST 1
#if TEST >= 1
    static char in_file[] = "TEST.DATA";
#else
    static char in_file[] = "PROD.DAT";
#endif
main()
{
    FILE *fh;
```

```
if ( ( fh = fopen ( in_file, "r" ) ) != NULL )
  return;
else
  printf ( "Input file is %s \n", in_file );
fclose ( fh );
}
```

◘ #endif

- General format

```
#endif
```

- Description

The **#end** directive ends a conditional directive such as **#if**, **#ifdef**, or **#ifndef**.

- Example

Here are a few examples of using the **#endif** directive.

```
#if TEST >= 1
   static char in_file[] = "TEST.DAT";
#elif
   static char in_file[] = "PROD.DAT";
#endif


#if TEST >= 1
   static char in_file[] = "TEST.DATA";
#else
   static char in_file[] = "PROD.DAT";
#endif


#ifndef EXTEND
#    define MAX_LEN 50
#else
#    define MAX_LEN 65
#endif
```

◘ #line

- General format

```
#line decimal-constant "filename"
```

● Description

The preprocessor *line control* directive is used to renumber the source lines. The preprocessor assigns the source line, following the **#line**, with the *decimal-constant* as the line number. The *filename* is optional; if it is omitted, the current source file is assumed. The line number and filename are available to your program through macros __LINE__ and __FILE__.

● Example

In **Function_1** and **Function_2** the current value of macro __LINE__ is printed. Note that the line number is set to 2000 and 3000 with the **#line** directive just before each function.

```
/*********************************************
This program illustrates the #line directive.
*********************************************/

#include <stdio.h>

#line 1000
main()
{
   Function_1();
   Function_2();
}

#line 2000
static void Function_1()
{
   printf("Function_1: line number is %d\n", __LINE__);
}

#line 3000
static void Function_2()
{
   printf("Function_2: line number is %d\n", __LINE__);
}
```

◘ #pragma character_sequence

● General format

```
#pragma token...
```

● Description

The **#pragma** directive allows you to pass intructions to the compiler.

token is specific to the implementation of the C compiler you are using.

It is a series of characters giving instructions and arguments to the compiler. You can pass such information as title, comments, and pagesize.

There are many programs available: alloc_text, chars, checkout, comment, data_seg, define, disjoint, entry, export, handler, implementation, import, info, isolated_call, langlvl, linkage, map, margins, pack, priority, page, pagesize, seg16, sequence, skip, stack16, strings, subtitle, and title .

◻ #pragma alloc_text

● General format

```
#pragma alloc_text(codesegment,function...)
```

● Description

The **#pragma alloc_text** directive is used to group functions into different 32-bit code segments. This allows you to organize functions in memory to achieve efficiency.

codesegment is the name of the code segment in which the functions are placed.

function is the name of the subroutine. You can specify any number of functions to be included in the named codesegment. If a function is not listed here, it is placed in the default 32-bit code segment called CODE32.

◻ #pragma chars

● General format

```
#pragma chars (signed—or unsigned)
```

● Description

The **#pragma chars** directive is used to specify that the compiler is to treat all character objects as signed or unsigned data type. This pragma must be placed before any statements in a file.

◘ #pragma checkout

● General format

```
#pragma checkout (resume or suspend)
```

● Description

The **#pragma checkout** directive is used to control the diagnostic messages produced by the /Kn compiler options and is used to suspend the diagnostics performed by the compiler when the /Kn option is given during specific portions of your program, and then resume the same level of diagnostics at some later point in the file.

● Example

The following line shows how nested **#pragma checkout** directives are allowed.

```
/*  Assume /Kpx has been specified  */
#pragma checkout(suspend)
                    /*  No diagnostics are performed */
    .
    .
    .
#pragma checkout(suspend)  /*  No effect  */
    .
    .
    .
#pragma checkout(resume)   /*  No effect  */
    .
    .
    .
#pragma checkout(resume)    /*  Diagnostics continue  */
```

◘ #pragma comment

● General format

```
#pragma comment ( compiler or
                  date      or
                  timestamp or
                  <copyright or user> [,"character"] )
```

● Description

The **#pragma comment** directive is used to add a comment to the object file.

compiler is the name and version of the compiler and is written to the end of the object file produced by the compiler.

date is the date and time of compilation and is added to the end of the object file produced by the compiler.

timestamp is the last modification date and time of the source and is added to the object file.

copyright indicates that the text specified in the *character* field is placed by the compiler into the object file and is loaded into memory when the program is run.

user indicates that the text specified in the *character* field is placed by the compiler into the object file, but it is not loaded into memory when the program is run.

◼ #pragma data_seg

- General format

```
#pragma data_seg(datasegment)
```

- Description

The **#pragma data_seg** directive lets you place static and external variables in different 32-bit data segments.

After this directive is encountered, all static and external variables are placed in the specified data segment either until another **#pragma data_seg** directive is found or at the end of the compilation.

When using **#pragma data_seg**, there are a few restriction to keep in mind:

- String literals used to initialize pointers are not placed in the specified data segment, but in the default 32-bit data segment (DATA32). To place a string in a particular data segment, use an array to initialize the string instead of a pointer; for example,

  ```
  char str[ ] = "fruits";
  ```

  instead of

```
char *str = "fruits";
```

- The **#pragma data_seg** directive affects only 32-bit data segments; it does not apply to data placed in 16-bit segments because of the /Gt option or **#pragma seg16**.

- Static and external variables declared previous to the first **#pragma data_seg** are placed in the default DATA32 segment, with the exception of uninitialized variables and variables explicitly initialized to zero (they are found in the BSS32 segment).

◘ #pragma define

- General format

```
#pragma define(template_class_name)
```

- Description

The **#pragma define** directive is used to force the definition of a template class, and you don't have to define an object of the class.

There are two main reasons to use the **#pragma define** pragma: (1) to organize your program for efficiency and (2) to generate template functions automatically.

◘ #pragma disjoint

- General format

```
#pragma disjoint(name [,name...]
```

- Description

The **#pragma disjoint** directive is used to list the identifiers (or names) that are not aliased to each other.
name of an expression. This expression can be an identifier, operator function, conversion function, destructor, or qualified name.

The **#pragma disjoint** directive tells the compiler that none of the identifiers listed share the same physical storage. This list can be used for optimizations. If any identifiers actually share physical storage, the pragma may give incorrect results.

This pragma can appear anywhere in the source file. Note that a name cannot make reference to any of the following:

- A member of a class, structure, or union
- A class, structure, or union tag
- An enumeration constant
- A label

The names must be declared before they appear in the **#pragma disjoint** directive. Also, a pointer in the name list must not have been dereferenced or be used as a function argument before appearing in the **#pragma disjoint** directive.

◻ #pragma entry

- General format

#pragma entry (*func_name*)

- Description

The **#pragma entry** directive tells the compiler that the name function is the entry point for the application that is being built. Normally, OS/2 starts at an application provided by a C or C++ library entry point. This entry function also performs initialization and termination. But if you provide a different entry point using the **#pragma entry**, OS/2 calls this entry point and does not execute any of the library initialization or termination functions. When using **#pragma entry**, you must ensure that, if your program requires initialization and termination functions, they are provided.

func_name is the name of the function, and it must be found in the same compilation unit as the **#pragma entry** directive. Also, the function must be a declared as an external function.

◻ #pragma export

- General format

```
#pragma export (function_name,
   ["export_name"] ,ordinal)
```

● Description

The **#pragma export** directive tells the compiler that a DLL function is to be exported, and it also lists the name of the function outside the DLL.

function_name is the name of the function within the DLL.

export_name is the name for the function outside the DLL. If no export name is specified, the default is the function name.

ordinal is the number of the function within the DLL. Another module can import the function using either the same export name or the ordinal number. For example, the statements

```
int abby(int);
#pragma export(abby, abbym, 4)
```

declare that the function called **abby** is to be exported. The directive statement also says that the function can be imported by another module using the name **abbym** or the ordinal number 4.

You must remember that there are two ways to create an import library for the DLL:

● Create it from the DLL itself
● Provide a .DEF file with an EXPORTS entry for every function, regardless of whether **#pragma export** is used.

For more information on DLLs and .DEF files, see Chap. 3.

◘ #pragma handler

● General format

```
#pragma handler(function)
```

● Description

The **#pragma handler** directive registers an exception handler code for a particular function.

With the **#pragma handler** directive, the compiler generates the code to install the C/C++ Tools exception handler _Exception before starting execution of the function. When function stops, the compiler execution also generates code to destroy the exception handler. It is advisable to use this directive whenever you change library environments or enter a user-created DLL.

function is the name of the function for which the exception handler is registered. You should declare this function before you use it in this directive.

◼ #pragma implementation

● General format

```
#pragma implementation(string_literal)
```

● Description

The **#pragma implementation** directive is used to tell the compiler the name of the file that contains the function template definitions. These definitions must correspond to the template declarations in the include file containing the pragma.

The main reason for using **#pragma implementation** is to organize your program for the efficient or automatic generation of template functions.

◼ #pragma import

● General format

```
#pragma import(function,
        ["external_name"] "mod_name",ordinal)
```

● Description

The **#pragma import** directive lets you import a function from a DLL using either an ordinal number or a function name different from the one that it has in the DLL.

function is the name of the function that you use in your source program.

external_name is the name of the function in the DLL. In a C++

program, *external_name* can also be a function   prototype. This parameter is optional and, if not specified, it is assumed to be the same as the function. Note that both *function* and *external_name* must be defined only once in the file where the **#pragma import** is found.

mod_name is the name of the DLL containing the function.

ordinal is the position of the function within the DLL. If *ordinal* is 0, then *external_name* is used to find the function. If *ordinal* is any other number, *external_name* is ignored and the function is located by number. Usually, it is faster to locate the function by number than by name.

One advatage of using **#pragma import** is to reduce the link time; the linker does not require an import library to resolve external names. This directive is also useful in C++ programming; you do not have to use the fully qualified function name to call an imported function.

◻ #pragma info

● General format

```
#pragma info(all        or
             none       or
             restore    or
                 <grp or nogrp>,... )
```

● Description

The **#pragma info** directive is used to control the diagnostic messages generated by the /Wgrp compiler options.

The **#pragma info** directive can be used instead of the /Wgrp option to turn groups of diagnostics on or off. When you use **#pragma info(grp)** it creates all messages associated with that diagnostic group. However, specifying **#pragma info(nogrp)** does not generate any message associated with that group.

◻ #pragma isolated_call

● General format

```
#pragma isolated_call(name [,name])
```

● Description

The **#pragma isolated_call** directive is used to list functions that do not change data objects that are visible at the time of the function call. This directive informs the compiler that none of the following functions has side effects:
● Accessing a volatile object
● Modifying an external object
● Modifying a file

name can be an identifier, operator function, conversion   function, or qualified name.

This pragma should appear before any of the functions, found in the identifier list, are called. All identifiers must be declared before they are used in the pragma.

◼ #pragma langlvl

● General format
```
#pragma langlvl (ansi        or
                 extended    or
                 compat      or
                 saa         or
                 saal2)
```

● Description

The **#pragma langlvl** directive is used to select elements of the C/C++ Tools implementation. It must appear before any C code and can be specified only once in a program file.

ansi is used to define the preprocessor variables __ANSI__ and __STDC__.

extended is used to define the preprocessor variable __EXTENDED__. The default language level is extended.

compat is used to define the preprocessor variable __COMPAT__.

saa is used to define the preprocessor variables __SAA__ and __SAA_L2__.

saal2 is to define the preprocessor variable __SAA_L2__.

◘ #pragma linkage

● General format

```
#pragma linkage (identifier,
                 <optlink              or
                  system               or
                  [far32] pascal  or
                  far16 [cdel           or
                 _cdecl                or
                 _pascal               or
                 _pascal               or
                 _fastcall             or
                 _fastcall> )
```

● Description

The **#pragma linkage** directive is used to identify the linkage or calling convention used in a function call.

identifier is the name of the function that will be given the particular linkage type or the name of a typedef that resolves to a function type. If identifier is a typedef, then any function defined using this name will be given the particular linkage type.

◘ #pragma map

● General format

#pragma map(*identifier*,"*name*")

● Description

The **#pragma map** directive is used to associate an external name with a C identifier. This directive is used primarily for compatibility with IBM C/370, but it can also be used with the C/C++ Tools debugger.

◘ #pragma margin

● General format

```
#pragma nomargins
   or
#pragma margins(l,r)
```

● Description

The **#pragma margins** directive is used to set the right and left columns in the input line that are to be scanned for input to the compiler.

Typically, the margin directive is used if there are characters outside a certain range of columns in the source file to be ignored. The compiler ignores any text in the source input that does not fall within the range specified in the directive.

l is the first column of the source input line that is to be scanned, and must be between 1 and 65,535, inclusive. The default value is 1, which is used when **nomargins** is specified.

r is the last column of the source input line that is to be scanned. It must be greater than or equal to 1 and less than or equal to 65,535. If this value is an asterisk (*), it indicates the last column of input. The default value is infinity, which is used when **nomargins** is specified.

◻ #pragma pack

● General format

```
#pragma pack([1 or
              2 or
              4])
```

● Description

The **#pragma pack** directive is used to set the byte alignment for the structures and unions. This directive causes all structures and unions that follow it in the program to be packed along a 1-byte, 2-byte, or 4-byte boundary. The alignment to a specific rule is effective until another **#pragma pack** directive changes the packing boundary.

If no value is give with this directive, packing is performed along the system default boundary, which is a 4-byte boundary, unless the /Sp compiler option was used. If this option is used, **#pragma pack** causes packing to be done along the boundary specified by /Sp. The /Sp option is described in Chap. 3.

The Figure 9.1 shows how each data type is packed for each **#pragma pack** option.

Data Type	#pragma pack value		
	1	**2**	**4**
char	1	1	1
short	1	2	2
int or long	1	2	4
float, double, or long double	1	2	4
pointer	1	2	4

Figure 9.1 Data alignments according to data types.

◻ #pragma page

● General format

```
#pragma page([n])
```

● Description

The **#pragma page** directive is used to skip a specified number of pages of the generated source listing.

n is the number of pages to skip; if it is omitted, the next page is started.

◻ #pragma pagesize

● General format

```
#pragma pagesize([n])
```

● Description

The **#pragma pagesize** directive is used to set the number of lines per page for the generated source listing. The listing pagesize can be set with the /Lp compiler option. This option is described in Chap. 3.

n is the number of lines per page. The value of n must be between 16 and 32,767, inclusive. The default page length is 66 lines.

#pragma priority

- General format

```
#pragma priority([n])
```

- Description

The priority pragma specifies the order in which static objects are to be initialized at run time.

n is an integer literal in the range of INT_MIN to INT_MAX. The default value is 0. A negative value indicates a higher priority; a positive value indicates a lower priority.

The first 1024 priorities (INT_MIN to INT_MIN + 1023) are reserved for use by the compiler and its libraries. The priority value specified applies to all run-time static initialization in the current compilation unit.

#pragma seg16

- General format

```
#pragma seg16(identifier)
```

- Description

The **#pragma seg16** directive specifies that a data object will be shared between 16-bit and 32-bit processes. This directive tells the compiler to lay out the identifier in memory so that it does not cross a 64-kbyte boundary.

identifier can then be used in a 16-bit program and it can be a typedef or a data object; for example:

```
typedef struct moo moostr;
#pragma seg16(moostr)
moostr  puux;
```

uses the typedef **moostr** to declare **puux** as an object addressable by a 16-bit program.

The equivalent of the **#pragma seg16** directive is the /Gt compiler option. The /Gt option is described in Chap. 3.

◘ #pragma sequence

● General format

```
#pragma nosequence
    or
#pragma sequence(l,r)
```

● Description

The **#pragma sequence** directive is used to define the section of the input line that is to contain sequence numbers. If a source file is used to produce a system that uses sequence numbers, you can use this option to have the sequence numbers ignored. The default is no sequence numbers, which is the same as specifying **#pragma nosequence**.

l is the column number of the left-hand margin. This value must be between 1 and 65,535 inclusive, and must also be less than or equal to the value of r.

r is the column number of the right-hand margin. This value must be greater than or equal to l and less than or equal to 65,535. An asterisk (*) can be assigned to r to indicate the last column of the line.

◘ #pragma skip

● General format

```
#pragma skip([n])
```

● Description

The **#pragma skip** directive is used to specify the number of lines of the generated source listing.

n is the number of lines that are skipped and must be a positive integer less than 255. If n is omitted, one line is skipped.

◘ #pragma stack16

- General format

```
#pragma stack16([size])
```

- Description

The **#pragma stack16** directive is used to specify the size of the stack to be allocated for calls to 16-bit functions.

size is the size of the stack in bytes, and must be in the range 512 to 65,532. The size applies to any 16-bit functions called from that point until the end of the compilation unit, or until another **#pragma stack16** directive is given.

If the size is omitted, the default value is 4096 bytes (4kbytes). Remember that a 16-bit stack is taken from the 32-bit stack allocated for the thread calling the 16-bit code. The 32-bit stack is therefore reduced by the amount you specify with the **#pragma stack16** directive. It is important to ensure that the 32-bit stack is large enough for both your 32-bit and 16-bit code.

◘ #pragma string

- General format

```
#pragma strings( writable or readonly)
```

- Description

The **#pragma strings** directive is used to indicate the access mode of memory where the compiler may place strings.

writable means the compiler may place string in read and write memory; this is the default.

readonly means the compiler may place the string into read-only memory.

◻ #pragma subtitle

- General format

```
#pragma subtitle("subtitle")
```

- Description

The **#pragma subtitle** directive places the text specified as the subtitle on all subsequent pages of the generated source listing.

To specify the subtitle in a program listing, you can also use the /Lu compiler option.

◻ #pragma title

- General format

```
#pragma title("title")
```

- Description

The **#pragma title** directive places the text specified as the title on all subsequent pages of the generated source listing.

To specify the title in a program listing, you can also use the /Lt compiler option.

OS/2 Commands

This chapter is a reference of OS/2 Commands. As in the rest of the book, for easy access, the information of each command is separated into four categories:

- General format
- Usage
- Description
- Return code

Before you begin to use this reference, it would be helpful to understand a few general, but important points, of each type of information presented regarding the OS/2 commands.

General format: This gives the syntax of a command. In OS/2, there are two types of commands: internal and external.

Internal: Internal commands run without any delay associated with loading the program from disk. These commands are part of the OS/2 command processor. Their names appear as the first item in syntax. In the example

```
TYPE MYFILE.DAT
```

TYPE is an internal command.

External: External commands are on the disk as program files. Some of these programs come with OS/2 and others you acquire by installing an application, such as in word processing, compilers, utilities, and databases. This chapter lists only external commands that accompany OS/2. When an external command is entered, the OS/2 operating system searches for it in the current directory of the default or specified drive. If it is not found, the operating system continues searching for it in the directories listed in the **PATH** statement. Their names are preceded by an optional drive and path parameter in a given syntax. For example, the ANSI is an external command:

```
[drive] [path] ANSI [ON or OFF]
```

In an OS/2 session, the combined length of a filename and path can be up to 259 bytes. In a DOS session, the maximum length for a filename and path is 80 bytes, of which 64 bytes is for the path, ensuring room for an 8.3 filename in the lowest subdirectory.

Parameters: After the command, you enter parameters. Parameters are classified as keywords, variables, or a combination of both. Include all punctuation shown in the general form, such as colons, semicolons, commas, quotation marks, and equal signs.

Generally, the parameters are path and filename, options, and other required or optional information needed to successfully process the command. Commands that allow you to enter filenames can accept a path (directory) name before the filename.

You can use a period (.) for the current directory or two periods (..) for the parent directory for any OS/2 command that allows you to enter a path. Do not put a space between the drive, path, filename, and optional extension. The colon, backslash, and period already serve as separators.

The current directory is the directory that the OS/2 operating system searches when a filename is entered with no pathname. You have a current directory for every drive in your system. For example, in the next command if the drive and path are omitted, the filename is searched in the current directory.

```
TYPE    [drive] [path] filename
```

Usage: This specifies how a command is used: CONFIG.SYS, command line or batch file.

CONFIG.SYS: This is a configuration file for your system. It contains many commands that are executed during the startup of the OS/2 system. Some commands are issued strictly for this file and cannot be issued otherwise, such as at the command line or in a batch file. The following are a few examples of commands found in CONFIG.SYS.

```
DEVICE=C:\IBMCOM\PROTOCOL\LANPDD.OS2
DEVICE=C:\IBMCOM\PROTOCOL\LANVDD.OS2
DEVICE=C:\OS2\INSTALL\PRELOAD\PREL_IMG.SYS
SET RESTARTOBJECTS=startupfoldersonly
RUN=C:\OS2\CMD.EXE /C C:\CDSLUTIL\CFGCDSL.CMD
IFS=C:\OS2\HPFS.IFS /CACHE:512 /CRECL:4 /AUTOCHECK:CD
PROTSHELL=C:\OS2\PMSHELL.EXE
SET USER_INI=C:\OS2\OS2.INI
SET SYSTEM_INI=C:\OS2\OS2SYS.INI
SET OS2_SHELL=C:\OS2\CMD.EXE
SET AUTOSTART=PROGRAMS,TASKLIST,FOLDERS
LIBPATH=C:\IBMCOM\DLL;C:\COBOL\EXEDLL;C:\IBMLAN\NETLIB;
```

Command line: When the OS/2 command processor is running, you will see a command prompt; for example,

```
[C:\MYWORK]
```

At this point the processor is ready to receive a command, and you enter the command on the command line. When a command has finished processing, a command prompt is again displayed on the screen. You can type commands in uppercase letters, lowercase letters, or a combination of both. From an OS/2 command prompt, you can type up to 299 characters (bytes) before you press Enter. From a DOS command prompt, you can type up to 127 bytes before you press **Enter**. You can process commands from the command prompt of a session while running your programs in other sessions. An example of a command issued at the command line is

```
[C:\MYWORK] TYPE mywork.day
```

Batch file: OS/2 allows you give put one or more commands in a file and pass them to the system for processing. A batch file has the extension .CMD, and this is what distinguishes it from other files. In a batch file, you can include internal and external commands. The following is the content of a batch file:

```
procob INAME=MISMM04.SQC HOST=COBOL  > MISMM04.MS1
MORE < MISMM04.MS1
```

```
PAUSE
COBOL  MISMM04.CBL LITLINK; >MISMM04.MS2
MORE < MISMM04.MS2
PAUSE
ANIMATE MISMM04
REM link and run
REM link @m04.lnk
REM MORE < MISMM04.MS2
REM PAUSE
REM mismm04
REM pause
REM MORE < MISMM04.LST
```

Description: For each command, there is a description of the main functions of the command.

Return codes: Some commands issue a return code. This code tells you the state of the processing. In a batch file, this code can be used to do conditional processing.

◘ ANSI— turn extended keyboard and display support on and off

- General format

    [*drive*] [*path*] ANSI [ON or OFF]

- Usage: CONFIG.SYS, command line, and batch file.

- Description

The **ANSI** command is used to allow or prevent extended display and keyboard support in the OS/2 environment. It turns on or off the ANSI control sequence processing in OS/2 sessions. You use ANSI control sequences to redefine keys, manipulate the cursor, and change display color attributes. You must keep in mind that when KEYS is ON, ANSI extended keyboard support is disabled.

ON means to turn on the extended display and keyboard support.

OFF means to turn off the extended display and keyboard support.

If you omit the parameter for this command, ANSI displays its current status.

☐ APPEND—set search path for data files outside the current directory

● General format

```
[ drive ] [ path ] APPEND [/E]
           [ drive ] [ path ] [/PATH:ON or /PATH:OFF]
```

● Usage: CONFIG.SYS, command line, and batch file.

● Description

The **APPEND** command is used to sets a search path for data files that are outside the current directory. Enter **APPEND** without a parameter to display the **APPEND** statement in your AUTOEXEC.BAT file. This statement can be set by system installation. Enter **APPEND** to cancel the **APPEND** command.

The first time you use **APPEND**, it is an external command, and you might need to specify a drive and path to locate it. Once **APPEND** is loaded, it becomes an internal command, and a drive and path are no longer needed.

APPEND is useful when you want to keep an application program and its associated data files in one directory and group information by category in other directories. If you specify a path with **APPEND** the first time you use it, this path is not stored in the environment, and you can view or change it only with the **APPEND** command. You can append as many directories as you can specify in a total of 128 characters.

The search sequence for a specified file is as follows: (1) search the specified directory, or the current directory if you do not specify the directory; then (2) search the directories indicated by the current **APPEND** command.

APPEND is similar to the PATH command, although the **PATH** command finds only startable files. You can look at or modify **APPEND** paths in the environment by using **APPEND**, or you can use the **SET** command.

◼ ASSIGN— assigns a drive letter to a different drive

● General format

> [*drive*] [*path*] ASSIGN [*x* = *y*]...

● Usage: Command line and batch file.

● Description

The **ASSIGN** command is used to assign a drive letter to another drive. If you enter this command without any parameter, it resets all drives to their original state. **ASSIGN** allows you to perform disk operations on drives other than A and B for programs that use only those two drives.

When using **ASSIGN**, remember that it hides the true device type from commands that require actual drive information. In DOS sessions, some commands do not work on drives that have **ASSIGN** in effect; they are **CHKDSK, DISKCOMP, DISKCOPY, FORMAT, JOIN, LABEL, PRINT, RECOVER, RESTORE**, and **SUBST**.

● Return code: 0 for normal completion.

◼ ATTRIB—turns file attributes on or off

● General format

```
[ drive ] [ path ] ATTRIB [[+R or -R] or
                           [+S or -S] or
                           [+H or -H] or
                           [+A or -A] ]...
        [ drive ] [ path ] filename [ /S ]
```

● Usage: Command line and batch file.

● Description

The **ATTRIB** command is used to either show or change the attribute(s) of a file.

+R or -R is used to turn on or off the read-only attribute.
+S or -S is used to turn on or off the system file attribute.
+H or -H is used to turn on or off the hidden file attribute.
+A or -A is used to turn on or off the archive bit flag.

filename is the name of the file for which the attribute is either displayed or changed.

/S means to find all occurrences of that file.

- Return code: 0 for normal completion

◘ AUTOFAIL—Display information about error conditions

- General format

```
AUTOFAIL [NO or YES]
```

- Usage: CONFIG.SYS.

- Description

The **AUTOFAIL** statement is used to tell the OS/2 system whether or not to display information about error conditions.

NO causes a window to appear that informs you of an error condition. This is the default value.

YES causes the appropriate error code to appear rather than a window.

◘ BACKUP—Store one or more files from one disk to another

- General format

```
[ drive ] [ path ] BACKUP
                  < source-drive or
                        path          or
                  filename >

      target-drive [ /L:filename      or
                     /D:mm-dd-yy       or
                     /T:hh:mm:ss       or
                     /M               or
                     /A               or
                     /F:xxx            or
                     /S    ]...
```

- Usage: Command line and batch file.

● Description

The **BACKUP** command is used to copy one or more files from one disk to another for the purpose of backup. **BACKUP** can back up files on disks of different types; however, there are a few exceptions. **BACKUP** does not back up the system files (COMMAND.COM and CMD.EXE), hidden system files, any open dynamic-link library files (.DLL), and files opened with Deny Read/Write.

In case where the target drive is a diskette, after **BACKUP** fills a diskette, it prompts the user to insert a new diskette. **BACKUP** also marks a label on each diskette in consecutive order, and records the date and diskette number.

When restoring the files with the **RESTORE** command, you will be prompted to insert in the order they were backed up.

When the backup is successful, **BACKUP** creates two files, called BACKUP.XXX and CONTROL.XXX, in the root directory on the target diskette. The BACKUP.XXX file contains the contents of all the backup files, and the CONTROL.XXX file has controlling information such as paths and filenames.

<source-drive or *path* or *filename>*
This parameter specifies the source of the file(s) to be backed up and it can be either a drive, a drive plus a directory, or a filename.

target-drive is the destination drive.

/L:filename is the option to specify the backup log file. If this option is omitted, the BACKUP.LOG file is used and placed in the root directory of the source drive.

/D:mm-dd-yy is used to back up those files that have changed on or after the specified date.

/T:hh:mm:ss is used to back up those files that have changed on or after the specified time. This option is usually recommended with the /D option.

/M means to back up the current directory on C drive those files that were changed since the last backup to A drive.

/A means to add files to the backup drive.

/F:*xxxx* means to format the destination diskette, where *xxxx* is the type: 360, 720, 1200, 1440, or 2880.

/S means to copy files in the source directory and in all directories below the starting source directory.

- Return code: 0 Successful completion
  - 1 Back up did not occur
  - 2 Because of file errors, some files or directories were not backed up
  - 3 Termianted by the user
  - 4 Terminated abnormally because of error
  - 5 Not defined
  - 6 **BACKUP** was unable to process the **FORMAT** command

◖ BASEDEV—Install base device driver

- General format

```
BASEDEV = filename [ arguments ]
```

- Usage: CONFIG.SYS.

- Description

The **BASEDEV** statement is used to load base device drivers. The driver supports devices such as a disk, diskette, printer.

filename is a file that contains the device-driver code that the OS/2 operating system needs to recognize a device and correctly process information received from or sent to that device. A *base device driver* is one that is needed when the OS/2 operating system is first started.

BASEDEV processes the device drivers according to the extension of the filename and not in the order in which they appear in your CONFIG.SYS file. The **BASEDEV** statements are then processed in the following order of filename extensions: .SYS, .BID, .VSD, .TSD, .ADD, .I13, .FLT, and .DMD.

Files with other filename extensions will not be loaded. The following base device drivers are included with your OS/2 diskettes:

IBM2ADSK.AD	Driver for non-SCSI disk drives on Micro Channel workstations
OS2DASD.DMD	General-purpose device support for disk drives.
IBM1FLPY.ADD	Driver for diskette drives on non-Micro Channel workstations
IBM2FLPY.ADD	Driver for diskette drives on Micro Channel workstations
IBM1S506.ADD	Driver for non-SCSI disk drives on non-Micro Channel workstations
IBMINT13.I13	General-purpose device support for non-Micro Channel SCSI adapters
PRINT01.SYS	Driver for locally attached printers on non-Micro Channel workstations
PRINT02.SYS	Driver for locally attached printers on Micro Channel workstations
IBM2SCSI.ADD	Driver for Micro Channel SCSI adapters
OS2SCSI.DMD	General-purpose device support for non-disk SCSI devices

◘ BOOT—switch between DOS and OS/2

● General format

```
[ drive ] [ path ]   BOOT </OS2 or /DOS >
```

● Usage: OS/2 or DOS command line.

● Description

The **BOOT** command is used to switch between the DOS and OS/2 operating systems that are on the same hard disk. Before using the **BOOT** command, ensure that all system operations are complete and all programs are terminated. **BOOT** checks whether the following files exist:

OS/2 files
    OS2LDR (hidden file)
    OS2KRNL (hidden file)
    OS2\SYSTEM\BOOT.OS2
    OS2\SYSTEM\CONFIG.OS2

DOS files
    IBMBIO.COM or MSDOS.SYS (hidden file)
    IBMDOS.COM or IO.SYS (hidden file)
    OS2\SYSTEM\BOOT.DOS
    OS2\SYSTEM\CONFIG.DOS

- Return code: BOOT displays the following:
    - 0 for normal completion
    - The appropriate error message

◘ BREAK—check Ctrl and Break keys

- General format

```
BREAK [ ON or OFF ]
```

- Usage: DOS command line, CONFIG.SYS, or batch file.

- Description

The **BREAK** command is used to tell DOS to check whether the Ctrl and Break keys have been pressed before carrying out a program request. Pressing and holding the Ctrl and Break keys together stops a command from completing its task.

The current status is shown by typing **BREAK** without any parameter.

◘ BUFFERS—sets the number of disk buffers for the system.

- General format

```
BUFFERS = x
```

- Usage: CONFIG.SYS.

- Description

The **BUFFERS** command is used to set the number of disk buffers that the system uses.

x is a number, and each number is a disk buffer. The buffer is a 512-byte block of storage the system uses to read and write blocks of data that does not occupy an entire sector. By increasing the value specified for **BUFFERS**, you can increase the speed of your system. However, when you increase the number of disk buffers, you decrease the available memory in your system.

◘ CACHE—specify parameters used by HPFS

● General format

```
CACHE   [ /LAZY:state ] [ /MAXAGE:time ]
        [ /DISKIDLE:time ] [ /BUFFERIDLE:time ]
```

● Usage: CONFIG.SYS (part of RUN command) or command line.

● Description

The **CACHE** command is used to specify the parameters that the High Performance File System (HPFS) uses to write information to a disk. To display the current value for **CACHE**, enter this command without a parameter.

◘ CALL—execute a batch file from another batch file

● General format

```
CALL   batchfile [ argument ]
```

● Usage: Batch file.

● Description

The **CALL** command is used to execute a batch file from within another batch file without ending the first one. A batch file can then be used for commands from within a master batch file.

When using this command, there are a few points to remember:

● Piping and redirection should not be used with the **CALL** command.
● You can use **CALL** from any line inside a batch file.
● The number of batch files is limited only by available memory. In an OS/2 session, a batch file should not call itself. If it does, it runs out of stack space and ends. In a DOS session, a batch file can call itself, but make sure that the batch file eventually ends.
● **CALL** causes the data structure and file pointer of the currently running batch file to be saved and a new data structure to be created. When the called batch file ends, the original batch file continues its

processing with the statement following **CALL**.
- You can use **CALL** to protect your INI files by having them automatically backed up each time you start your system.
- Batch-file parameters can be passed to another batch file with **CALL**.

◻ CHCP—alternate between code-page character sets

- General format

```
CHCP [nnn]
```

- Usage: Command line.

- Description

The **CHCP** command is used to alternate between two code-page character sets that are defined in your CONFIG.SYS file. If you enter this command without a parameter, it displays the current code page being used or to determine whether any are specified.

In the OS/2 environment, **CHCP** checks that the correct **DEVINFO=** statement is included in the CONFIG.SYS file for the code page being requested. If not, a message is displayed.

nnn is a number indicating which one of the two prepared system code pages is correct. If it is the number of a code page that has not been prepared for the system, you receive an error message. If no **CODEPAGE=** statement is included in the CONFIG.SYS file, **CHCP** returns the default code-page ID of the country.

- Return code: The current code page ID of the country.

◻ CD or CHDIR—changes the current directory

- General format

```
CHDIR or CD [ drive ] [ path ]
```

- Usage: Command line or batch file.

- Description

The **CD** or **CHDIR** command is used to change the current directory, allowing you to access any subdirectory you have created with the **MD** command. If the path in the directory you want to change to has a path different from the path in your current directory, you must enter its entire path, including the root directory.

If you are not sure of the path of the directory you want to change to, use the **DIR** or **TREE** commands to display the directories of the drive. If you type this command without a parameter, **CD** displays the name of the current directory.

◘ CHKDSK—scans a disk and checks it for errors

- General format

```
[ drive ] [ path ] CHKDSK [ drive ] [ path ] [ filename ]
              [/F or /V]... [/C or /F:n]...
```

- Usage: Command line or batch file.

- Description

The **CHKDSK** command is used to analyze directories and files. It determines the file system type and produces a disk status report. **CHKDSK** also displays the volume label and the volume serial number of the disk.

CHKDSK can detect lost clusters on your disk. These are parts of files that the system did not save completely, and this will take up space on your disk. If **CHKDSK** finds them, it prompts the user with a message asking whether to convert lost chains to files. If the answer is "yes" (type a Y), **CHKDSK** converts these parts into files that you can examine and delete to save space on your disk. If the answer is "no" (type an N), **CHKDSK** deletes these parts of files from your disk without warning. The files **CHKDSK** creates from lost chains follow this naming convention: FILE*nnnn*.CHK (*nnnn* is a sequential number starting with 0000).

- Return code: 0 Normal completion
            1 Not defined

2 Not defined
3 Ended by user
4 Ended because of error
5 Not defined
6 **CHKDSK** was unable to execute file system's **CHKDSK** program

◘ CLS—clear the screen

● General format

```
CLS
```

● Usage: Command line and batch file.

● Description

The **CLS** command is used to clear the window or entire display screen of any information.

◘ CMD—start the OS/2 command processor

● General format

```
[ drive ] [ path ]   CMD [ drive ] [ path ]
        [ /Q ] [ /S ] [ /K"string" or /C"string" ]
```

● Usage: Command line or batch file.

● Description

The **CMD** command is used to start the OS/2 command processor, CMD.EXE. This executable file is found in the C:\OS2 subdirectory. To return to the previous command processor, use the **EXIT** command. To start another command processor, type **CMD** without any parameter.

If any environment variable in the current command processor is altered, the change is known only to the current command processor.

The quotation marks are used to pass significant characters to the new CMD.EXE. To have a new CMD.EXE process the **DIR** command and then have the parent CMD.EXE display the word "HELLO," type the following:

```
CMD /C DIR & ECHO HELLO
```

To have the new CMD.EXE process the **DIR** command and display the word "HELLO," type the following:

```
CMD /C "DIR & ECHO HELLO"
```

◘ CODEPAGE—select the system code pages

- General format

```
CODEPAGE = xxx [ ,yyyy ]
```

- Usage: CONFIG.SYS.

- Description

The **CODEPAGE** command is used to select the system code pages to be prepared by the OS/2 operating system for code-page switching. The code pages are character sets for a particular language. You must include the appropriate **DEVINFO** statements (for keyboard and video display) for both code pages in the CONFIG.SYS file.

You have to remember that the keyboard and country information default to the national language code page supported by the country code specified in the **COUNTRY** statement. The English code page is 437, and the international code page, which contains a set of code common to many languages, is 850.

◘ COMMAND—start DOS command processor

- General format

```
[ drive ] [ path ] COMMAND [ drive ] [ path ]
                       [/P or /E:x]
                       [/C string or /K string]
```

- Usage: Command line.

- Description

The **COMMAND** command starts the DOS command processor, COMMAND.COM. The command processor is found in the

C:\OS2\MDOS subdirectory. Once DOS is running, to return to the previous command processor, use the **EXIT** command. If COMMAND.COM is not found in the specified directory, the OS/2 operating system searches the environment for the value of COMSPEC. This system variable, which is placed in the environment when a DOS session is started, describes the path the system uses to reload the command processor.

You can change the value for COMSPEC with the **SET** command. If you use the **SET** command to change any environment variables in the current command processor, the change is known only to the current command processor. Returning to the primary DOS command processor with the **EXIT** command causes a resumption of the environment that the primary DOS command processor knew before the secondary copy existed.

◘ COMP—Compares content of files

● General format

```
[ drive ] [ path ] COMP [ drive ] [ path ] [ filename-1 ]
                        [ drive ] [ path ] [ filename-2 ]
```

● Usage: Commmand line and batch file.

● Description

The **COMP** command is used to compare the contents of two files. You would type COMP without a parameter to start a step-by-step menu to compare files.

filename-1 and *filename-2* are the files to be compared; they can be on the same drive or different drives, or in the same directory or different directories. The two sets of files you want to compare can have the same path and filenames, provided they are on different drives. If you specify only a drive for the second file and do not specify a filename, **COMP** assumes that the second filename is the same as the first. If you specify a drive or path with no filename for either the primary or secondary path and filename, **COMP** assumes a filename of *..

After comparison of the two files, **COMP** proceeds with the next pair of files that match the two filenames. When **COMP** cannot find any more files that match the first parameter, it displays a message asking if you want to compare more files. Type a Y (yes) to compare two more files, or end **COMP** by entering an N (no).

If the file sizes are different, **COMP** displays a message informing you of this and asks if you want to continue. You now have the option to continue or end the comparison. If you choose to continue, **COMP** processes both files on the basis of the length of the smaller files.

- Return code: 0 Normal completion
         1 No files were found to compare
         2 Some files or directories were not processed because of file errors
         3 Ended by user
         4 Ended because of error
         5 Files comparison was not satisfactory.

◨ COPY—copies and combines files

- General format

```
COPY [ drive ] < filename or path [ filename ]>
            [/A or /B]
            [+]
            [,,]
            [ drive ] [ path ] [ filename ]
            [/V or /F or </A or /B>]...
```

- Usage: Command line and batch file.

- Description

The **COPY** command is used to copy one or more files. You can copy files from one diskette or hard disk to another or can copy files within directories. If you want to copy one or more files to a subdirectory, make sure that the subdirectory exists.

+ means to append files. This option is used when merging multiple files into one file, or when adding one file to the end of another.

+ ,, means to change the date and time. This option is used when you want to change the date and time of a file, or if you want to update the date and time of a file after it is copied. You can use global filename characters in the source file specification to change the dates and times of a group of files. If you do not include a target file specification, all files found that match the source file specification remain where they are, but their dates and times are changed.

Note: The destination can be a device name, such as console (CON) or printer (PRN).

◘ COUNTRY—specify information for a country

• General format

    COUNTRY = *nnn* [, [*drive*] [*path*] *filename*]

• Usage: CONFIG.SYS.

• Description

The **COUNTRY** command is used to specify country-dependent information to OS/2. OS/2 identifies the following information for a country:

• Date and time format
• Decimal separator
• Character-case map table
• Sequence by which data is sorted

◘ CREATEDD—create a dump diskette

• General format

    [*drive*] [*path*] CREATEDD *target-drive*

• Usage: Command line.

• Description

The **CREAREDD** command is used to make a dump diskette to be used with the standalone dump procedure. This utility program prepares a diskette for an OS/2 memory dump. If a dump requires more than one diskette, the first diskette must be prepared with **CREATEDD** while the rest can be any formatted diskette. This command is intended for those with advanced technical knowlege of OS/2. When you use **CREATEDD** to format a diskette, all the information on the diskette is erased.

◘ DATE—change or show system date

- General format

```
DATE [mm-dd-yy]
     [dd-mm-yy]
     [yy-mm-dd]
```

- Usage: Command line and batch file.

- Description

The **DATE** command is used to either show or change the date used by the system. It also resets the date on your computer's clock. This date is recorded in the directory when you create or change a file.

When entering a new date, the system accepts a slash (/), a period (.), and a dash (-), as the valid date separator for your country. You can change the format in which the date is displayed with the **COUNTRY** command in your CONFIG.SYS file. If you enter this command without a parameter, **DATE** displays the system date and prompts you to change it.

◘ DDINSTAL—install new device drivers

- General format

```
DDINSTAL
```

- Usage: Command line.

- Description

The **DDINSTAL** command provides an automated way to install new device drivers after the OS/2 has been installed. After you enter this command, **DDINSTAL** will show the device driver installation the window from which the device-driver files are installed.

These files are provided on a separate diskette called a *device support diskette*. This diskette contains a device-driver profile file (with extension .DDP) that controls the installation process. The **DDINSTAL** program uses the information from the device-driver profile to add the necessary statements to the CONFIG.SYS file and to copy all the support files into their appropriate directories on the hard disk.

◘ DEBUG—access DOS DEBUG environment

● General format

```
DEBUG [ drive ] [ path ] [ filename ]
```

● Usage: Command line.

● Description

The **DEBUG** command without a location and filename is used to access the DOS **DEBUG** environment and must be able to enter all **DEBUG** commands in response to the **DEBUG** prompt, a hyphen (-). **DEBUG** commands are

?	Shows a list of the **DEBUG** commands
A	Assembles 8086, 8087, and 8088 mnemonics
C	Compares two portions of memory
D	Shows the contents of memory
E	Enters data into memory starting at a specified address
F	Fills a range of memory with specified values
G	Runs the executable file that is in memory
H	Performs hexadecimal arithmetic
I	Shows one byte value from a specified port
L	Loads the contents of a file or disk sectors into memory
M	Copies the contents of a block of memory
N	Specifies a file for an L or W command, or specifies the parameters for the file that are being tested
O	Sends one byte value to an output port
P	Executes a loop, a repeated string instruction, a software interrupt, or a subroutine
Q	Stops the **DEBUG** session
R	Displays or alters the contents of one or more registers
S	Searches a portion of memory for a specified pattern of one or more byte values
T	Processes one instruction and then displays the contents of all registers, the status of all flags, and the decoded form of the instruction that **DEBUG** will process next
U	Disassembles bytes and displays the corresponding source statements
W	Writes the file being tested to a disk
XA	Allocates expanded memory

XD   Deallocates expanded memory
XM   Maps expanded memory pages
XS   Displays the status of expanded memory

◪ DETACH—detach OS/2 program

● General format

DETACH   *command*

● Usage: Command line and batch file.

● Description

The **DETACH** command is used to start a program, and when it is running, the program is detached from the command processor. Such a program must be able to process programs independently outside the control of the command processor, without issuing any input or output calls to the keyboard, the mouse, or the display.

You can detach any program, command, or file that does not require the use of a screen (e.g., internal commands and batch (.CMD) files). The OS/2 system detaches CMD.EXE when it runs the internal command or batch file. For example, if you type DETACH DIR, it is changed to the equivalent of DETACH CMD.EXE /C DIR.

With the **DETACH** command, you can use redirection sequences to redirect a program's standard input and output to devices other than the keyboard and the display. This allows the program to run without interaction with the keyboard, mouse, or display.

◪ DEVICE—install device driver

● General format

DEVICE= [*drive*] [*path*] *filename* [*argument...*]

● Usage: CONFIG.SYS.

● Description

This **DEVICE** command is used to load a device driver. It is used to load drivers to support standard default devices, such as standard system display terminals, keyboards, printers, diskette drives, hard disk drives, and serial devices. You can, however, replace these or add other devices by coding and loading a device driver using **DEVICE** statements in the CONFIG.SYS file. **DEVICE** statements are processed in the order in which they appear in the CONFIG.SYS file.

filename is a file that contains the code needed so that the OS/2 operating system can recognize the device and correctly process information received from or sent to that device.

Device drivers supplied with OS/2 diskettes are as follows:

Driver	Description
ANSI.SYS	Extended screen and keyboard support for DOS sessions
COM.SYS	OS/2 application programs or system programs, such as SPOOL, to use serial devices
EGA.SYS	DOS programs that require Enhanced Graphics Adapter (EGA) support to be run
EXTDSKDD.SYS	Access to an external diskette drive referencing a logical drive letter
LOG.SYS	System error logging using the SYSLOG utility program
MOUSE.SYS	Support for pointing devices
OS2CDROM.DMD	CD-ROM support for OS/2 sessions
PMDD.SYS	Draw support for OS/2 sessions
POINTDD.SYS	Mouse pointer draw support
TOUCH.SYS	Touch devices
VDISK.SYS	A simulated disk called a virtual disk
VEMM.SYS	DOS Expanded Memory Manager
VXMS.SYS	DOS Extended Memory Specification

◘ DEVICE—install serial port drivers

● General format

```
DEVICE= [ drive ] [ path ] COM.SYS
               [ (n,addr,IRQ,S) or
                 (n,addr,IRQ) ]
```

- Usage: CONFIG.SYS.

- Description

  This **DEVICE** command is used to support other devices attached to serial ports COM1 through COM4; the DEVICE command for these ports must be listed before the DEVICE=C:\OS2\COM.SYS statement in the CONFIG.SYS file, or the port will be unavailable to COM.SYS. The COM.SYS file supports ports COM1, COM2, COM3, and COM4.

◘ DEVICE—install EGA register interface device driver

- General format

  ```
  DEVICE = [ drive ] [ path ] EGA.SYS
  ```

- Usage: CONFIG.SYS.

- Description

  This **DEVICE** command is used to support the EGA register interface. The EGA.SYS device driver provides support for the EGA register interface in DOS sessions. EGA.SYS must be installed for those application programs that use the EGA register interface.

◘ DEVICE—access external disk drive

- General format

  ```
  DEVICE = [ drive ] [ path ] EXTDSKDD.SYS
                 </D:d  or
                 /T:t  or
                 /S:s  or
                 /H:h  or
                 /F:f >
  ```

- Usage: CONFIG.SYS.

- Description

  This **DEVICE** statement allows you to access a disk using a logical drive letter. More than one external device driver can be installed at the same time. The maximum   number is the total number of physical diskette drives installed in your system.

◘ DEVICE—install logging service device driver

- General format

```
DEVICE = [ drive ] [ path ] LOG.SYS
        [/E:x] [/A:x] [/OFF]
```

- Usage: CONFIG.SYS.

- Description

This **DEVICE** statement is used to activate the System Error Logging Service (SELS) device driver. Once activated, the SELS can be paused. When paused, no error logging is performed.

For the logging servece to work, You must also include a RUN=LOGDAEM.EXE command in the CONFIG.SYS file in addition to this DEVICE=LOG.SYS statement. Together, these two commands and their parameters allow the SELS to retrieve error data and keep that data in specific error-log files. LOG.SYS is the filename of the SELS device driver.

◘ DEVICE—install pointer device driver

- General format

```
Device Dependent Statement

DEVICE = [ drive ] [ path ] filename
            [SERIAL=COMn]

Device Independent Statement

DEVICE = [ drive ] [ path ] MOUSE.SYS
            [QSIZE=q] [TYPE=name] [RELAXED]
```

- Usage: CONFIG.SYS.

- Description

This **DEVICE** statement is used to install the pointing device driver, such as a mouse. In conjuction with the pointer device driver, you have to install the POINTDD.SYS device driver. To be able to use a mouse in programs running in a DOS window or full-screen session or a WIN-OS/2 session, the VMOUSE.SYS device driver must also be installed.

These device drivers are installed automatically at the time of OS/2 installation when the system detects the presence of a supported pointing device.

◨ DEVICE—install CD-ROM device driver

- General format

```
DEVICE = [ drive ] [ path ] OS2CDROM.DMD
                        [/V or
                         /Q ]
```

- Usage: CONFIG.SYS.

- Description

This **DEVICE** statement is used to install the driver for CD-ROM drives.

◨ DEVICE—install pointer draw device driver

- General format

```
DEVICE = [ drive ] [ path ] PMDD.SYS
```

- Usage: CONFIG.SYS.

- Description

This **DEVICE** statement is used to install the pointer draw device-driver for OS/2 sessions. The DEVICE=PMDD.SYS statement is added to your CONFIG.SYS file when you install the OS/2 operating system. When the system starts, it uses the PMDD.SYS device driver to provide pointer draw support for OS/2 sessions.

If the PMDD.SYS device statement is removed from your CONFIG.SYS file, your system will not restart. If this happens, take the following steps:

- Insert the OS/2 Installation Program diskette. When the logo screen appears, proceed to the Welcome screen and press Esc.
- Copy the file, CONFIG.BAK, into the root directory. You now have a generic backup CONFIG.SYS file that you can rename to be your CONFIG.SYS file.

- Use the System Editor to edit the CONFIG.SYS file.
- Restart the system.

◘ DEVICE—install mouse pointer

- General format

```
DEVICE = [ drive ] [ path ] POINTDD.SYS
```

```
Device Dependent Statement
```

```
DEVICE = [ drive ] [ path ] filename
           CODE INIT
```

```
Device Independent Statement
```

```
DEVICE = [ drive ] [ path ] TOUCH.SYS
           [ QSIZE=q  or  TYPE=name ]
```

- Usage: CONFIG.SYS.

- Description

This **DEVICE** command is used to install the mouse-pointer draw device. Before you can use a mouse, you must load this device driver, in addition to specifying the appropriate mouse device-driver statements in the CONFIG.SYS file.

POINTDD.SYS provides draw support in all text modes for OS/2 sessions; POINTDD.SYS tracks (provides mode information) for all advanced function modes on the 8514A. It tracks for CGA (Color Graphics Adapter), EGA, and VGA (Video Graphic Array) graphic modes in OS/2 sessions.

This statement is also used to install drivers for touch devices. For a touch device to be effectively used, the POINTDD.SYS device driver and appropriate mouse device-driver support must be loaded. In addition, these statements must be included in the CONFIG.SYS file in the following order:

- A device-dependent statement that gives the name of the file containing the information for the touch device you use

- A device-independent statement that identifies the touch device to TOUCH.SYS

◘ DEVINFO—prepare a device for code-page switching

- General format

```
DEVINFO [ drive ] [ path ] filename [ arguments ]
```

- Usage: CONFIG.SYS.

- Description

The **DEVINFO** command is used to prepare a device, such as your keyboard or display terminal, for code-page switching. For each device used for code-page switching, there must be a separate **DEVINFO** statement.

◘ DEVINFO—prepare display for system code-page switching

- General format

```
DEVINFO = SCR,device, [ drive ] [ path ] filename
```

- Usage: CONFIG.SYS.

- Description

This **DEVINFO** statement is used to prepare a display for system code-page switching. This statement is one of the interrelated CONFIG.SYS statements required for successful code-page switching. The other statements are **CODEPAGE** and **COUNTRY.**

To prepare a VGA display, type the following in the CONFIG.SYS file:

```
DEVINFO=SCR,VGA,C:\OS2\VIOTBL.DCP
```

◘ DEVINFO—prepare keyboard for system code-page switching

- General format

```
DEVINFO = KBD,layout, [ drive ] [ path ] filename
```

- Usage: CONFIG.SYS.

● Description

This **DEVINFO** command is used to prepare a keyboard for system code-page switching. This statement is one of the interrelated CONFIG.SYS statements required for successful code-page switching. The other statements are **CODEPAGE** and **COUNTRY.**

The **DEVINFO=KBD** statement specifies your keyboard layout and a file named KEYBOARD.DCP that contains a keyboard layout table for translating keystrokes into the characters of each code page supported by the system.

To prepare a U.S. keyboard using the keyboard layout, type the following in the CONFIG.SYS file:

```
DEVINFO=KBD,US,C:\OS2\KEYBOARD.DCP
```

◘ DIR—lists the files in a directory

● General format

```
DIR [ drive ] [ path ] [ filename ]
            [    /W      or
                 /F      or
                 /P      or
                 /N      or
                 /A      or
                 /B      or
                 /O      or
                 /R      or
                 /S      or
                 /L      ]...
```

● Usage: Command line and batch file.

● Description

The **DIR** command is used to list the files and subdirectories in a directory. If you type this command without a parameter, list the files in the current directory. **DIR** shows the name, size (in bytes), and the date and time of the file. **DIR** also displays the disk volume label and volume serial number. It also gives the total number of files, the number of bytes used in the files displayed, and the amount of free space (in bytes) remaining on the disk.

When using **DIR,** you must remember that directory entries for hidden system files are not listed, although they may exist. Also, if you do not specify a filename extension, adding an asterisk (*) after the filename indicates that all files with that filename (regardless of the extension) should be displayed. **DIR** shows files consecutively on the screen if you specify multiple filenames. You can include a drive and path when specifying multiple filenames and may also use the global filename characters * and ? in the filename you specify.

◘ DISKCACHE—memory allocation for control information

● General format

```
DISKCACHE = n [,LW] [,T] [,AC:x]
```

● Usage: CONFIG.SYS.

● Description

The **DISKCACHE** command is used to allocate a specific number of blocks of memory for control information and disk cache. Basically, what the disk cache does is allow a portion of the system storage to be used as an additional hard-disk buffer. Another advantage of **DISKCACHE** is to speed up application programs that read hard disks by keeping hard disk data frequently accessed in a cache buffer. When an application program requests hard-disk data that is already in the cache buffer, the disk cache sends the data directly to the application program. This method of accessing data is much faster than if the data had to be read from the disk each time.

◘ DISKCOMP—compare two diskettes

● General format

```
[drive] [path] DISKCOMP [source-drive] [target-drive]
```

● Usage: Command line and batch file.

● Description

The **DISKCOMP** command is used to compare the contents of the diskette in the source drive to the contents of the diskette in the target drive.

If you enter this command without a parameter, **DISCOMP** starts a step-by-step procedure to compare the contents of diskettes in different diskette drives.

Remember that **DISKCOMP** does not work in DOS sessions on drives that have an **ASSIGN, JOIN,** or **SUBST** command in effect. Also, **DISKCOMP** does not work on network drives.

- Return code: 0   for normal completion or displays the appropriate error message.

◘ DISKCOPY—copy one diskette to another

- General format

```
[ drive ] [ path ] DISKCOPY [ source-drive ] [ target-drive
]
```

- Usage: Command line and batch file.

- Description

The **DISKCOPY** command is used to copy the contents of the diskette in the source drive to the diskette in the target drive. If needed, the target diskette is formatted during the copy. Remember that neither the source nor the target drive can be a hard disk or a virtual drive. **DISKCOPY** also displays the volume serial number of the target diskette.

DISKCOPY does not work in DOS sessions on drives that have an **ASSIGN, JOIN,** or **SUBST** command in effect.

- Return code: 0   for normal completion or displays the appropriate error message.

◘ DOSKEY—retrive DOS command and create macros

- General format

```
[ drive ] [ path ] DOSKEY  [ Macroname=text ]
        [   /REINSTALL or
            /BUFSIZE=n or
                /M    or
                /H    or
            /OVERSTRIKE or
             /INSERT ]...
```

- Usage: DOS Command line or batch file

- Description

The **DOSKEY** command is used to recall DOS commands, edit command lines, and create macros. After the command is recalled, you can edit it and reissue it.

The following keys are used to recall the commands.

Key	Recall
Up Arrow	Recalls the DOS command you used before the one displayed
Down Arrow	Recalls the DOS command you used after the one displayed
Page Up	Recalls the first DOS command you used in the current session
Page Down	Recalls the most recent DOS command you used

◘ DOS—Specify memory for DOS kernel

- General format

```
DOS= <HIGH or LOW> , < UMB or  NOUMB >
```

- Usage: CONFIG.SYS.

- Description

The **DOS** command is used to specify whether the DOS kernel will reside in the high memory area (HMA) and whether the operating system or DOS applications will control upper memory blocks (UMBs).

◘ DPATH—specify search path for data files

- General format

```
DPATH <[ drive ] path> [; [ drive ] path]...
```

- Usage: CONFIG.SYS, command line, and batch file.

- Description

  The **DPATH** is an environment variable, and its values give application programs the search path to data files that are outside the current directory. The **DPATH** environment variable can be set only using the **SET** command in OS/2 sessions.

  If you type **DPATH** without a parameter, **DPATH** shows the current value of the **DPATH** environment variable. Also, if you type **DPATH**, followed by a semicolon (;), it clears the **DPATH** environment variable. **DPATH** indicates what directories applications should search for in their data files (if an application program uses the **DPATH** directory list).

◘ EAUTIL—split and join extended attributes

- General format

```
EAUTIL datafile [holdfile] [/S [/R]  or
                            /J [/O or /M]]
                    [ /P ]
```

- Usage: Command line and batch file.

- Description

  The **EAUTIL** command is used to remove and save extended attributes from a file and then rejoin the extended attributes to the file.

- Return code: 0 Normal completion
              1 File not found
              4 Ended because of error

◘ ECHO—turn display of commands on or off

- General format

```
ECHO [  ON      or
        OFF     or
      message ]
```

- Usage: Command line or batch file.

- Description

  The **ECHO** command is used to show or to prevent the screen output

of OS/2 commands as they are run from a batch file. You can control
(|) and redirect (>) output from a batch file. You can enter this command
at the command line without a parameter to display the current **ECHO**
state.

◻ DEL or ERASE—delete file

● General format

```
DEL or ERASE [ drive ] <filename or
                        path [ filename ] > [/P or /N]
```

● Usage: Command line and batch file.

● Description

The **DEL** or **ERASE** command is used to remove one or more files
from a drive. **ERASE** or **DEL** does not delete a subdirectory name. To
remove a directory, use the **RD** or **RMDIR** command; however, **ERASE**
or **DEL** will erase the contents of a subdirectory. In addition, read-only
and hidden files, such as the operating system files of IBMBIO.COM
and   IBMDOS.COM, cannot be deleted.

Before erasing all files in a directory, the system displays the name of
the directory, along with the message: Are you sure (Y/N)? If you enter
a Y (yes), it erases all the files of a directory; if you enter an N (no), the
DEL or **ERASE** command is aborted.

◻ EXIT—exit from the command processor

● General format

```
EXIT
```

● Usage: Command line.

● Description

The **EXIT** command is used to close the current command processor
(CMD.EXE or COMMAND.COM). Control is returned to the previous
command processor, or to the desktop if no previous session exists.

In case of a program, you must first end the program before typing
EXIT. If no previous command processor exists, typing **EXIT** returns
you to the desktop.

◘ EXTPROC—define external batch processor

● General format

```
EXTPROC [ drive ] [ path ] filename [ arguments ]
```

● Usage: Batch file.

● Description

The **EXTPROC** command is used to define an external batch processor for a batch file. With this command you can substitute your own batch processor for the OS/2 batch processor.

The **EXTPROC** command must be the first statement in any batch file you want processed by your batch processor. CMD.EXE calls your batch processor to process your batch-file statements.

◘ FCBS—define file control block

● General format

```
FCBS =  total,locked
```

● Usage: CONFIG.SYS (DOS only).

● Description

The **FCBS** command is used to define a file control block used by a program to store specific information about files currently used. This statement has no effect in OS/2 sessions.

If a program tries to open more than the number of files specified in the **FCBS** statement, the system closes the least-recently used file control block and opens the new file.

◘ FDISK—manage partition or logical drive

● General format

```
[ drive ] [ path ] FDISK [ drive ] [ path ]
                    < /QUERY   or
                      /CREATE or
                      /DELETE or
```

```
                    /SETNAME:name        or
                    /SETACCESS           or
                    /STARTABLE           or
                    /FILE:filename >
              [  /NAME:name or
                 /DISK:n      or
                 /FSTYPE:x or
                 /START:m    or
                 /SIZE:m      or
                 /VTYPE:n    or
                 /BOOTable:s   or
                 /BOOTMGR]
```

- Usage: Command line.

- Description

  The **FDISK** command is used to manage a primary partition or a logical drive in an extended partition. This command lets you create or delete a partition. **FDISK** can be used both interactively or from the command line.

  Interactive: The interactive (or full-screen) version of **FDISK** is used during installation of the operating system. It provides users with the same functions as the **FDISKPM** version. The full-screen version supports windows and looks and acts much the same as **FDISKPM** but without the mouse support.

  Command line: The **FDISK** command issued at the command prompt is used to establish or change partition values. The parameters and options with the **FDISK** command specify and limit the values and characteristics of the partitions.

- Return code: 0   for normal completion. Other code with appropriate error message.

◨ FDISKPM—PM facility to manage partition and logical drive

- General format

  ```
  [ drive ] [ path ] FDISKPM
  ```

- Usage: Command line.

- Description

  The **FDISKPM** command is a Presentation Manager application to manage a primary partition or a logical drive in an extended partition. As does the **FDISK** command, **FDISKPM** lets you create or delete partitions, except **FDISKPM** presents menus and displays to guide you through the tasks necessary to set up   your hard disks. Help is available for all selectable items and entry fields within **FDISKPM**.

◘ FILES—specify maximum number of files

- General format

```
FILES = n
```

- Usage: CONFIG.SYS (DOS only).

- Description

The **FILES** command is used to specify the maximum number of files available in DOS sessions. When a DOS session is started, 20 files are available for use by all programs running in that DOS session.

◘ FIND—Search string in file

- General format

```
[ drive ] [ path ] FIND [/V or /C or /I or N]
    "string" [ drive ] [ path ] filename
```

- Usage: Command line

- Description

The **FIND** command is used to search for a specific string in a file or files. The line(s) where the string is found are sent to the output device.

When specifying the string, remember to enclose the phrase or word in quotation marks in the exact format (uppercase or lowercase) in which it is written in the text.

Two single quotes in succession are not equivalent to quotation marks. When searching for strings that contain quotation marks, an extra set of quotation marks must be entered both before and after the string.

You must use a double backslash (\\) to find lines that contain the backslash (\) character.

You must explicitly name the filename; global characters such as the asterisk (*) or question mark (?) do not work.

- Return code: 0 for normal completion.

◘ FOR-Repetitive running of commands

- General format

```
To use FOR from the OS/2 command prompt:
 FOR % variable IN (set) DO command
To use FOR from a batch file:
 FOR %%c IN (set) DO command
```

- Usage: Batch file.

- Description

The **FOR** command is used for repetitive run of OS/2 commands. For OS/2 sessions, piping and redirection can be used with the FOR command.

set is one of many filenames and pathnames (if needed). An item in the set can contain the global filename characters * or ?.

% is placed before the variable if you are processing from the command prompt.

%% is placed before the variable if you are using the variable in a batch file.

In the following example, three source files are compiled and the compiler messages are being saved in three files that have an .OUT extension.

```
FOR %1 IN ( FILE1 FILE2 FILE3 )
   DO CL /C %1.C > %1.OUT 2>&1
```

◙ FORMAT—format disk

- General format

```
[ drive ] [ path ]  FORMAT   drive
                [   /ONCE      or
                    /4         or
                    /T:tracks  or
                    /N:sectors or
                    /F:xxxx    or
                    /FS:xxxxx  or
                    /L         or
                    /V [:label]  ]
```

- Usage: Command line and batch file.

- Description

  The **FORMAT** command is used to format a disk. **FORMAT** marks the directory and file allocation tables on the disk and checks the disk for defects.

  If you format a drive for the HPFS (High Performance File System), **FORMAT** checks the IFS statement in the CONFIG.SYS file to determine whether the drive is listed with the /AUTOCHECK parameter. If the drive is listed, **FORMAT** does not update the **IFS** (install file system) statement. If the drive is not listed, **FORMAT** adds the drive letter.

  When formatting a diskette or hard disk that already contains information, remember that all the information is erased. Also, be sure to specify a drive letter, followed by a colon (e.g., A:); otherwise, the system displays an error message indicating that you have not specified a target drive.

- Return code:
  - 0 Normal completion
  - 3 Ended by user
  - 4 Ended because of error
  - 5 Ended because of NO response when user was prompted to format a hard disk
  - 6 FORMAT was unable to process another file system's format program
  - 7 Volume not supported by another file system's format program

◘ FSACCESS—remap drive

- General format

```
FSACCESS [!] [ DOSletter or
               DOSletter - DOSletter  or
               DOSletter = OS2drive ]
```

- Usage: Command line.

- Description

The **FSACCESS** command is used to reassign drive letters, and it also makes the drive accessible or not accessible. It can be called multiple times to reassign drive letters, make new drives accessible, or remove access to drives. Drives cannot be in use (the current drive) when remapped.

◘ GOTO—transfer control to a label

- General format

```
GOTO label
```

- Usage: Batch file.

- Description

The **GOTO** command is used to transfer control to the line that has an appropriate label. A label is indicated by a colon (:), followed by the label name. With **GOTO**, if you use a label that is not found in the batch file, the current processing of the batch file ends.

◘ GRAFTABL—load addition characters

- General format

```
[ drive ] [ path ]   GRAFTABL [ nnn  or
                                ?    or
                                /STA ]
```

- Usage: Command line and batch file (DOS only).

● Description

The **GRAFTABL** command is used to provide additional characters for graphics. **GRAFTABL** loads a table of these additional characters into memory. **GRAFTABL** is effective only in a DOS session; it has no effect on OS/2 sessions.

If you enter this command without a parameter, **GRAFTABL** will show the current graphics code-page table that is loaded.

● Return code:
    0 No previously loaded character table exists and a code page is now resident
    1 A previously loaded character table exists; if a new table was requested, it replaces the previous table at its original location
    2 No previously loaded character table exists and no new table is loaded
    3 Incorrect parameter
    4 Incorrect DOS version

◘ HELP—Show command help information

● General format

```
[ drive ] [ path ]  HELP [  ON     or
                            OFF    or
                      message help or
                       [ book ] topic ]
```

● Usage: Command line

● Description

The **HELP** command is used to get online help of a command or information about a message generated after issuing a command. If you enter this command without a parameter, **HELP** will show the **HELP** options available for the current mode of operation. The options are

● Return to the desktop.
● Switch to the next session.
● Exit the current OS/2 session.
● Get additional help on error and warning messages.

◘ IF—conditional processing

- General format

```
IF [NOT] <ERRORLEVEL number or string1==string2
   [EXIST] [drive] [path ] filename
   command
```

- Usage: Batch file.

- Description

The **IF** command is used for conditional processing of OS/2 commands.
If a condition is true, the operating system processes the command. If it
is not true, it skips the command and processes the next one in the file.

◘ IFS—install file system

- General format

```
IFS = [ drive ] [ path ] filename [ arguments ]
```

- Usage: CONFIG.SYS.

- Description

The **IFS** command is used to install a file system, such as a HPFS.

filename is a file that contains the system driver, needed to manage disks
and diskettes formatted for file systems other than the file allocation
table (FAT), for example, HPFS.IFS.

◘ IFS—specify program for CD-ROM file system

- General format

```
IFS = [ drive ] [ path ] CDFS.IFS [ arguments ]
```

- Usage: CONFIG.SYS.

- Description

This **IFS** command is used to install the CD-ROM file system (CDFS).
The CD-ROM file system provides file-system functionality for the CD-

ROM devices that are supported by OS/2 2.1 and higher. The file that contains the driver is CDFS.IFS, which provides read-only access to data stored on CD-ROM media.

◘ IFS—specify program for HPFS

- General format

```
IFS = [ drive ] [ path ] filename [/C:nnnn]
        [/AUTOCHECK:xxx [/CRECL:x]
```

- Usage: CONFIG.SYS.

- Description

  This **IFS** statement is used to install the HPFS and to replace the default FAT file system.

  The features of HPFS are

  - Cache memory access
  - Long filenames
  - Contiguous file allocation
  - Extended attributes
  - "Lazy" writing
  - Balanced directory tree

◘ OPL—grant I/O privilege

- General format

```
IOPL = <NO or YES or list,...>
```

- Usage: CONFIG.SYS.

- Description

  The **IOPL** command is used to grant I/O privilege to requesting processes in OS/2 sessions.

  IOPL assigns a privilege level to a program, which determines what code segments and data segments it can access. The privilege level also limits the machine instructions a program can process.

The default is YES, and application programs are usually assigned privilege level 3. This means that they can call routines that run at any other privilege level. However, they can access only their own data segments and cannot issue any I/O instructions.

◻ JOIN—connect a drive to a directory of another drive

● General format

```
[ drive ] [ path ] JOIN drive
    drive\directory [/D]
```

● Usage: Command line.

● Description

The **JOIN** command is used to logically connect a drive to a directory on another drive. This allows you to access a drive by a directory name instead of a drive letter. Remember that you can join a drive only at the root directory. If the directory name does not exist, the OS/2 operating system creates a directory on the drive you specify. A directory that already exists must be empty for the **JOIN** to work.

If you enter this command without a parameter, **JOIN** will show the names of the drives currently joined.

◻ KEYB—specify keyboard layout

● General format

```
[ drive ] [ path ] KEYB [ layout ] [ subcountry ]
```

● Usage: Command line or batch file.

● Description

The **KEYB** command is used to replace the current keyboard layout with a specified keyboard layout for all OS/2 and DOS sessions.

If the CONFIG.SYS file of your system contains a keyboard **DEVINFO** statement, then you have the ability to switch keyboard layouts using KEYB. If a **DEVINFO** statement is not found in the CONFIG.SYS file, then typing **KEYB** with any layout returns an error message. Typing

KEYB without a layout parameter, regardless of whether there is a **DEVINFO** statement in your CONFIG.SYS file, causes the current keyboard code-page information to be displayed.

◘ KEYS—retrieve previous commands

● General format

```
KEYS [OFF or ON or list]
```

● Usage: Command line and batch file.

● Description

The **KEYS** command is used to allow or not allow previously issued commands to be retrieved. Once retrieved, the command can be reissued, with or without editing.

When **KEYS ON** is issued, it disables the ANSI extended keyboard support in a OS/2 session.

◘ LABEL—create or change volume label

● General format

```
[ drive ] [ path ] LABEL [ drive ] [ label ]
```

● Usage: Command line and batch file.

● Description

The **LABEL** command is used to either place or change the volume identification label on a disk.

If you enter this command without a parameter, **LABEL** shows the current label and volume serial number. **LABEL** prompts you if you want to change it. A volume label must not exceed 11 characters in length. If you press **ENTER** without entering a label, the volume label remains unchanged.

● Return codes: 0 for normal completion

◘ LASTDRIVE—specify last drive

● General format

```
LASTDRIVE = letter
```

● Usage: CONFIG.SYS (DOS).

● Description

The **LASTDRIVE** command is used to specify the last drive recognized in a DOS session; this statement has no effect in OS/2 sessions.

◘ LIBPATH—specify locations for dynamic link libraries (DLLs)

● General format

```
LIBPATH = [ drive ] path;...
```

● Usage: CONFIG.SYS.

● Description

The **LIBPATH** command is used to list a set of directories to be searched when the OS/2 operating system loads (DLLs). Because DLL modules are shared globally, this command allows path searching to be defined globally rather than on a per-process basis (as done by the **PATH** command).

(**Note:** the **LIBPATH** is not an environment variable; therefore it cannot be viewed with the SET command. Also, unlike the PATH environment variable, the current directory is not searched first.)

◘ LOADHIGH—load terminate and stay resident (TSR) programs

● General format

```
<LOADHIGH or LH> [ drive ] [ path ] filename [ arguments ]
```

● Usage: Command line (DOS).

● Description

The **LOADHIGH** or **LH** command is used to load TSR DOS programs into an available upper memory block (UMB) for a DOS session.

◘ MAKEINI—create a system setting file (OS2.INI)

● General format

`[ drive ] [ path ] MAKEINI [ user or system ]`

● Usage: Command line and batch file.

● Description

The **MAKEINI** command is used to initialize system settings, such as application defaults, display options, and file options, found in the OS2.INI startup file located in the C:\OS2 directory of your hard disk. There is also a system file called OS2SYS.INI, which contains information about installed fonts and printer drivers. You issue this command only when you receive a system error message and you suspect that the OS2.INI startup file must be re-created.

◘ MAXWAIT—set maximum wait time

● General format

`MAXWAIT = seconds`

● Usage: CONFIG.SYS.

● Description

The **MAXWAIT** command is used to set the amount of time a program waits before the system assigns it a higher priority. The system limits the time that a regular-class program waits to be processed. When the time limit is reached, the system raises the priority of the program to give it a chance to be processed.

The right amount of time depends on the number of applications that must run concurrently and the kinds of activities the applications perform. The system default is 3 s (three seconds). Experiment with this time to improve overall system performance.

◙ MEM—display memory usage

- General format

```
MEM   [/P or /D or /C]
```

- Usage: Command line (DOS only).

- Description

The **MEM** command shows the amount of used and available memory in the DOS environment.

◙ MEMMAN—select storage allocation options

- General format

```
MEMMAN = < <SWAP or NOSWAP> or
            <MOVE or NOMOVE> or
            <COMMIT or PROTECT> >
```

- Usage: CONFIG.SYS.

- Description

The **MEMMAN** command is used to configure the memory management for the OS/2 environment. Applications consist of groups of segments that can be either loaded into physical memory at the same time (simultaneously) or called when needed. If not enough memory is available to satisfy a request, the system attempts to provide more memory by writing the least-frequently used data segments to a temporary file on a disk. This file is called a "swap file."

The default for a system started from a hard disk is swapping (SWAP); if it booted from a diskette, the default is no swapping (NOSWAP).

◙ MD or MKDIR—create a new directory

- General format

```
MD or MKDIR   [ drive ] path...
```

- Usage: Command line and batch file.

- Description

The **MD** or **MKDIR** command is used to create one or more new subdirectories within the root directory (the directory you are in when the OS/2 operating system starts) or within another subdirectory. **MKDIR** makes a multilevel directory structure, which is helpful in keeping related program or data files together.

◩ MODE—set operation mode for devices

- General format

```
MODE device [ arguments ]
```

- Usage: Command line or batch file.

- Description

The **MODE** command is used to set operation modes for devices. The device modes are:

COM#	Asynchronous communications modes
DISPLAY	Display modes for video adapters
LPT#	Parallel printer modes
DSKT	Diskette input/output write verification

◩ MORE—read from or send to standard device

- General format

```
[ drive ] [ path ] MORE
```

- Usage: Command line and batch file.

- Description

The **MORE** command is used to send data to the standard output device (usually the display) one full screen at a time. The input can be a file or a device. After each screen, **MORE** pauses with the message **--More--** until you press any key to continue.

Generally, **MORE** is used for viewing long files or directories. To view the next screen, press any key. By pressing the CTRL and BREAK keys together, you abort the **MORE** program.

- Return code: 0 for normal completion.

◘ MOVE—Move file from one directory to another

- General format

```
MOVE    [ drive ] < filename or [ path ] filename>
        [ path ] [ filename ]
```

- Usage: Command line and batch file.

- Description

The **MOVE** command is used to copy one or more files from one directory to another directory on the same drive and remove them from the source directory.

With **MOVE**, you can use the global filename characters ? and * in the filename parameter of both the source and target files. When global characters are specified in the source filename, the names of the files will be shown as the files are being moved.

◘ PATCH—apply repairs to software

- General format

```
[ drive ] [ path ] PATCH [ drive ]
    [ path ] filename.ext [/A]
```

- Usage: Command line.

- Description

The **PATCH** command is used to apply IBM-supplied patches to software. These patches are used for repairs to programs, and the **PATCH** command should be used by those understanding the needs and effects of a patch.

If you enter the **PATCH** command without any options, you will have to supply an offset to indicate where the patch is to be made. **PATCH** displays the contents of the location specified by the offset and allows you to enter the patch. Make sure that both the offset and the patch contents are in hexadecimal notation.

If you issue **PATCH** with the /A option, it automatically applies patches shipped by IBM to make fixes to IBM-supplied code, and verification is performed before the patch is applied. Verification might not be done on non-IBM-supplied patches.

Return code: 0 for normal completion.

◘ PATH—specify search path for commands and programs

- General format

```
PATH   [ drive ] [ path ]
```

- Usage: CONFIG.SYS and Command line.

- Description

The **PATH** command is used to set one or many search paths for commands and programs. If you enter this command without a parameter, it shows the paths currently in effect. To delete the use of the **PATH** command, enter the command followed by a semicolon (;).

Generally, the setting of PATH is done in the CONFIG.SYS and AUTOEXEC.BAT files, thus circumventing the need to set **PATH** from the command prompt each time you turn on your system.

◘ PAUSE—suspend processing of a batch file

- General format

```
PAUSE
```

- Usage: Batch file.

- Description

The **PAUSE** command is used to suspend processing of the batch file and shows the following message:

Press any key when ready . . .
Enter this command to display the message:

Press any key when ready...

The **PAUSE** command is placed in a batch file at strategic points where you want the processing to be suspended. When the system stops, it gives you time to decide whether to stop the processing. Press and hold CTRL+BREAK, and type Y to stop a batch file from processing. In a DOS session, press any key to continue processing.

◘ PAUSEERROR—turn pausing off or on

- General format

```
PAUSEONERROR = [YES or NO]
```

- Usage: CONGIG.SYS.

- Description

The **PAUSEERROR** command is used to allow or prevent pausing when error messages are issued during the processing of the CONFIG.SYS file. The default is YES.

◘ PICVIEW—display a picture file

- General format

```
PICVIEW    [ drive ] [ path ] filename [/P or /S]
```

- Usage: Command line.

- Description

The **PICVIEW** command is used to view a picture file. This facility is also available from the Productivity folder.

If you issue **PICVIEW** without a parameter, the Picture Viewer window appears. **PICVIEW** lets you select the files to be displayed from the Picture Viewer window.

◘ PMREXX—display output from REXX procedures

● General format

```
[ drive ] [ path ] PMREXX
  [ drive ] [ path ] filename [ arguments ]
```

● Usage: Command line.

● **Description**

The **PMREXX** command is used to browse the output from REXX procedures and provide an input field for them.

PMREXX is a PM window application, and when invoking it you must enter a REXX batch file. By using **PMREXX,** you add the following features to REXX:

● A window for the display of the output of a REXX procedure, such as

  ● The **SAY** instruction output
  ● The **STDOUT** and **STDERR** outputs from secondary processes started from a REXX procedures file
  ● The REXX **TRACE** output (not to be confused with OS/2 tracing)

● An input window for

  ● The **PULL** instruction in all its forms
  ● The **STDIN** data for secondary processes started from a REXX procedures file

● A browsing, scrolling, and clipboard capability for REXX output.
● A selection of fonts for the output window.
● A simple environment for experimenting with REXX instructions through use of the REXXTRY.CMD program.   REXXTRY interactively interprets REXX instructions and can be started from an OS/2 command prompt.

◘ PRINT—send a file to the printer

● General format

```
[ drive ] [ path ] PRINT [/D:device or /B]...
[ drive ] [ path ] filename [/C or /T or /D:device]
```

- Usage: Command line and batch file.

- Description

The **PRINT** command is used to send one or many files to the printer. The files are placed in a print queue. This command is also used to cancel printing of one or more files.

The global filename characters (* and ?) are allowed. Also, the files are queued for printing in the order in which you enter them.

◻ PRINTMONBUFSIZE—set buffer size for parallel-port device driver

- General format

```
PRINTMONBUFSIZE = port_1_buffer_size, port_2_buffer_size...
```

- Usage: CONFIG.SYS.

- Description

The **PRINTMONBUFSIZE** is used to define parallel-port device-driver buffer size. The default is 134 bytes, and if you increase the size of the OS/2 parallel-port device-driver buffer, it will also increase performance of data transfer to devices connected to the parallel port.

◻ PRIORITY—select priority calculation

- General format

```
PRIORITY = [DYNAMIC or ABSOLUTE]
```

- Usage: CONFIG.SYS.

- Description

The **PRIORITY** command is used to select priority calculations in scheduling regular-class programs.

OS/2 regularly monitors the programs that are running and tries to give them the best possible overall performance. If the priority is set to DYNAMIC, the default value, the system changes the priority of programs frequently to ensure that the keyboard and mouse are responsive while programs are running in the background.

When the priority is set to ABSOLUTE, the system loses the ability to adjust the priority. And, this option must be used with care and complete understanding of how the programs are running. The advantage of the absolute priority is that it can help achieve predictable results by determining the order of priority strictly on the basis of class and level.

◘ PRIORITY_DISK_IO—set disk I/O priority

- General format

```
PRIORITY_DISK_IO = [YES or  NO ]
```

- Usage: CONFIG.SYS.

- Description

  The **PRIORITY_DISK_IO** command is used to give disk input/output a priority for applications running in the foreground.

  If the option is YES, the default value, an application running in the foreground will receive disk I/O priority over applications running in the background.   This means that the application in the foreground will have a better response time than applications running in the background.

◘ PROMPT—change the text of the system command prompt

- General format

  PROMPT [*text*]

- Usage: Command line and CONFIG.SYS.

- Description

  The **PROMPT** command is used to change the system command prompt. The default is the default drive letter followed by the > symbol. If you enter this command without the text, the current prompt is reset.

◻ PROTECTONLY—set operating environments

- General format

```
PROTECTONLY [ NO or YES ]
```

- Usage: CONFIG.SYS.

- Description

The **PROTECTONLY** is used to select one or two operating environments. The system requires this statement in the CONFIG.SYS file. A YES value for **PROTECTONLY** allows memory under 640 kbytes, which is normally used for DOS programs, to be available for OS/2 programs. When specifying **PROTECTONLY=YES**, you cannot run programs in DOS sessions. If you later decide that you want to run DOS programs in the lower 640 Kbytes of memory, specify **PROTECTONLY=NO**. This allows you to use both DOS and OS/2 programs.

◻ PROTSHELL—load user interface program and OS/2 command processor

- General format

```
PROTSHELL =  [ drive ] [ path ]  filename [ arguments ]
```

- Usage: CONFIG.SYS.

- Description

The **PROTSHELL** command is used to load the user interface program and OS/2 command processor. **PROTSHELL** also replaces the default OS/2 command processor, CMD.EXE, with another command processor.

◻ PSTAT—display processing status

- General format

```
[ drive ] [ path ] PSTAT [/S or
                          /L or
                          /M or
                          /P:pid ]
```

● Usage: Command line batch file.

● Description

The **PSTAT** command is used to show the process, thread, system-semaphore, shared-memory, and DDL information. **PSTAT** helps you determine which threads are running in the system, along with their current status and current priorities.

The **PSTAT** command is helpful in determining why a given thread is blocked (waiting for a system event), or why the thread's performance is slow (low priority compared to other threads). Moreover, it displays the process ID that has been assigned for each process. The process ID can then be used as input to the **TRACE** utility program for debugging on a per-process basis.

▣ RECOVER—recover files from disk

● General format

```
[ drive ] [ path ] RECOVER
            [ drive ] path filename
            [ drive ] [ path ] filename
```

● Usage: Command line batch file.

● Description

The **RECOVER** command is used to restore files from a disk that contains defective sectors. In OS/2 2.1 and above, this command reads the specified disk, sector by sector, and if **RECOVER** encounters a bad portion, the sector is marked and data is no longer allocated to it. All the files on the disk can be recovered if the directory has been damaged.

RECOVER locks the drive to be recovered so that no other applications or processes are allowed to access the drive. You cannot use the **RECOVER** command recover files on the disk that contains the RECOVER.EXE file or OS/2 message file OSO001.MSG, found in \OS2\SYSTEM directory. To restore a disk with these two files, copy them to a diskette and then issue this command against the drive.

● Return code: 0 Normal completion
              1 Undefined

2 Undefined
3 Ended by user
4 Ended because of error
5 Unable to read or write to one of the file allocation tables
6 Unable to execute another file system's recover program

◘ REM—add comments in a batch file or CONFIG.SYS

● General format

```
REM [ comment ]
```

● Usage: Batch file and CONFIG.SYS.

● Description

The **REM** command is used to add comment or line spacing in a batch file or a CONFIG.SYS file. The OS/2 operating system treats the preceding **REM** commands as comments and does not attempt to act on the comments. The main purpose of using **REM** is to improve the readability of your batch file.

◘ RENAME or REN—change name and extension of a file

● General format

```
RENAME or REN [ drive ] [ path ] filename1 filename2
```

● Usage: Command line and batch file.

● Description

The **RENAME** or **REN** command is used to change a filename or extension without changing the contents of the file. In OS/2 sessions, you can also change the name of a directory.

When using this command, you can use global filename characters (* or ?) in either filename. All files matching the first filename are renamed. If global filename characters appear in the second filename, the corresponding character positions are not changed.

◘ REPLACE—replace files

● General format

```
[ drive ] [ path ] REPLACE [ source-drive ]
[ path ] filename target-drive [ path ]
          [ /A   or
            /S   or
            /P   or
            /R   or
            /W   or
            /U   or
            /F ]
```

● Usage: Command line and batch file.

● Description

The **REPLACE** command is used to selectively replace files on the target drive with files of the same name from the source drive. This command is also used to add files from the source drive to the target drive.

REPLACE will copy the source file's extended attributes to the target file. When replacing files that have extended attributes, be sure to use OS/2 2.1 to ensure that all extended file attributes are replaced.

● Return code: 0 Normal completion
              1 No files were found to replace
              2 Some files not replaced (or added) because of file errors
              4 Ended because of error

◘ RESTORE—restore backup files

● General format

[*drive*] [*path*]   RESTORE source-drive
[target-drive] [*path*] [*filename*]

```
< /P or
  /M or
  /B:mm-dd-yy   or
  /A:mm-dd-yy   or
  /E:hh:mm:ss   or
  /L:hh:mm:ss   or
  /S            or
  /N            or
  /F            or
  /D >...
```

- Usage: Command line and batch file.

- Description

  The **RESTORE** command restores one or more files previously backed up using the **BACKUP** command. During the restore, the command prompts you to insert the source diskette; make sure that you insert the correct backup diskette. When you restore all your files, **RESTORE** prompts you to insert the backup diskettes in order. It will copy the extended attributes of the backed-up source file or directories.

  RESTORE works only within the source directory unless you specify the /S parameter. With this parameter, **RESTORE** copies files in the source directory and in all directories below the starting source directory.

  RESTORE will restore files to the same directory they were in when **BACKUP** copied them; otherwise, the system displays an error message.

  If you use wildcards, **RESTORE** prompts you to insert the next diskette after it has restored all files on the backup diskette that match the specified filename.

- Return code: 0 Normal completion
             1 No files were found to restore
             2 Some files were not processed because of file errors
             3 Ended by user
             4 Ended because of error

◘ RMDIR or RD—remove directory

- General format

```
RMDIR or RD   [ drive ] [ path ]
```

- Description

  The **RMDIR** or **RM** command is used to delete one or more empty directories. You cannot remove the root directory or the current directory. Also, make sure that all hidden files are deleted before using the **RD** command. To empty a directory of files, use the **DEL** or **ERASE** before using the **RD** or **RMDIR** command.

◘ RMSIZE—specify highest memory address

● General format

    RMSIZE = *number_of_k_bytes*

● Usage: CONFIG.SYS and command line.

● Description

The **RMSIZE** command is used to specify the highest storage address allowed for a DOS session.

If you do not have an **RMSIZE** command in your CONFIG.SYS file, the default is the total amount of low memory installed (either 512 kbytes or 640 kbytes). This is the largest usable size for DOS sessions at which your system can operate. If you enter a size that is too large for your system, the system displays an error message during startup and automatically calculates the largest default value possible.

◘ RUN—load and start a system program

● General format

    RUN [*drive*] [*path*] *filename* [*arguments*]

● Usage: CONFIG.SYS.

● Description

The **RUN** command is used to load and start a system program during system initialization, such as CACHE.EXE. This command is not meant to run a Presentation Manager application or any other application. In CONFIG.SYS, the **RUN** commands are processed in the order in which they appear in the file, but all **DEVICE** statements are processed before any **RUN** commands. If you want to start an application automatically during startup, it should be part of the System Startup folder on the desktop.

Because **RUN** programs are started before initialization of the user interface and disk error handling, the program must prevent the OS/2 operating system from performing disk handling or must perform its own.

A program started with a **RUN** statement can establish a keyboard or mouse monitor for any nondetached program. Also, it can issue I/O requests to the keyboard, mouse, or display only after it has established a window.

◘ RUN—start the logging daemon process

- General format

```
RUN = [ drive ] [ path ] LOGDAEM.EXE
              [/E:filename [/W:x]
```

- Usage: CONFIG.SYS.

- Description

This **RUN** command is used to start the Logging Daemon process for system error-log files. The   System Error Logging Service (SELS) supports software that detects errors and logs them in the system-error log file.

◘ SET—set values to environment variables

- General format

```
To use SET from the command prompt:
  SET [ variable=[value]...]
To use SET in your CONFIG.SYS file:
  SET  variable = value...
```

- Usage: Command line, batch file, and CONFIG.SYS.

- Description

The **SET** command is used to set one or more values to environment variables. You can use the **SET** command in your CONFIG.SYS file or batch files to set search paths and environment variables. If you enter this command without a parameter, **SET** will show the environment variables for the current mode of operation.

If the name specified by the first string of the **SET** command already exists in the environment, the command processor replaces its current value with the new value specified by the second string. If you enter the **SET** command with only the variable name and the equal sign (=), the command processor removes the environment variable or replaceable parameter name and its associated value from the environment, if the name exists.

The environment variables are stored in a special place that is used by the command processor to store and look up information, such as the values assigned to names. You can use **SET** to create a replaceable parameter or to set the value of a system variable, such as **PATH**. Application programs (particularly compilers and assemblers) and batch files can use the information stored in the environment to affect their processing.

You can use the **SET** command to set the value of OS/2 system variables. These system variables for OS/2 sessions are

Variable	Description
PATH	Sets a search path for executable files
DPATH	Sets a search path for data files
KEYS	Permits previously issued commands to be retrieved and edited
PROMPT	Sets a new command prompt

The system variables for DOS sessions are

Variable	Description
PATH	Sets a search path for executable files
PROMPT	Sets a new command prompt
APPEND	Sets the search path for data files if the **APPEND** command is entered with the /E option

The system variables for the Workplace Shell are

Variable	Description
USER_INI	Sets the INI file used by the Workplace Shell for system information about such

items as program defaults, display options, and file options.

SYSTEM_INI   Sets the INI file used by the Workplace Shell for system information about such items as installed fonts and printer drivers.

OS2_SHELL   Sets the command processor for OS/2 sessions.

RESTARTOBJECTS   Sets the objects that will be automatically started by the Workplace Shell. The YES and NO options determine whether objects running at the time of shutdown and objects in the Startup folder are to be started. The **STARTUPFOLDERSONLY** option is used if only objects in the Startup folder are to be started. The **REBOOTONLY** option is used if objects are to be started only when the Workplace Shell is started by pressing **CTRL+ALT+DEL** or turning on the computer.

AUTOSTART   Sets the parts of the Workplace Shell that are automatically started. Parts of the Workplace Shell that are started by default include **FOLDERS, PROGRAMS, TASKLIST** (the Window List), and **CONNECTIONS** (network connections). Deleting any of these options means that the deleted options will be disabled the next time the system is started. For example, deleting the **FOLDERS** option from the **AUTOSTART** statement means that all folders, including the desktop itself, will not start. Similarly, deleting the **TASKLIST** option means that no Window List will be displayed. Deleting the **PROGRAMS** option means that programs, except those in the Startup folder, cannot be started from the Workplace Shell even if **RESTARTOBJECTS=YES**. Deleting **CONNECTIONS** means that network connections will not be started. Modifying the **AUTOSTART** statement is not recommended for general use.

RUNWORKPLACE   Sets the interface that is started by the OS/2

operating system. PMSHELL.EXE is the
program for the Workplace Shell.

◻ SETBOOT—set up the Boot Manager

● General format

```
[ drive ] [ path ] SETBOOT [ /T:x  or
                             /T:NO or
                             /M:m  or
                             /Q    or
                             /B    or
                             IBA:n or
                             IBD:d or
                             /X:x  or
                             /N:name ]
```

● Usage: Command line.

● Description

The **SETBOOT** command gives you the ability to set up the Boot
Manager for a hard disk. This command lets you enter parameters at the
command prompt to enable you to take full advantage of the Boot
Manager. The Boot Manager operates in either attended or unattended
mode. In attended mode, the Boot Manager displays a list of startable
systems, enabling you to select the system to be started.

◻ SETLOCAL—define local drive, directory, and environment variables

● General format

```
SETLOCAL
```

● Usage: Batch file.

● Description

The **SETLOCAL** command is used to define the drive, directory, and
environment variables which are local to the current batch file.

When this command is issued, it saves the current drive, directory, and
environment variables. The previous drive, directory, and environment

variable values are restored by issuing a matching **ENDLOCAL** command or when the batch file ends.

◘ SHELL—load and start DOS command processor

● General format

```
SHELL = [ drive ] [ path ]  filename [ arguments ]
```

● Usage: CONFIG.SYS.

● Description

The **SHELL** command is used to load and start the DOS command processor. The default filename is COMMAND.COM. With this command you can replace the DOS command processor with another command processor.

If the **SHELL** command is not entered in the CONFIG.SYS file, the default DOS command processor is loaded and started with a /P parameter to retain COMMAND.COM in storage.

◘ SHIFT—expand the number of parameters in batch file

● General format

```
SHIFT
```

● Usage: Batch file.

● Description

The **SHIFT** command allows more than 10 replaceable parameters in batch file processing. When using this command, it is important to remember the following:

● Normally, batch files are limited to receive up to 10 parameters, %0 through %9. The use of **SHIFT** command lets you expand the number of parameters beyond 10.

● All parameters on the command line are shifted one position to the left, with the %1 parameter replacing the %0 parameter, the %2 parameter replacing the %1 parameter, and so on. Each following shift command causes all the parameters to be shifted to the left by one position.

- There is no backward shift. Once **SHIFT** is run, the %0 parameter that existed before the shift cannot be recovered.

◘ SORT—sort data read from the standard input

- General format

```
[ drive ] [ path ] SORT [/R] [/+n]
```

- Usage: Command line and batch file

- Description

The **SORT** command is used to read data from standard input, sort the data, and write it to standard output. The input and output devices can be redirected to files.

When using the **SORT** command, there are a few facts to remember:

- Large files take a few minutes before processing is completed. The maximum size of a file you can sort is approximately 63 kbytes bytes.
- The input and output files cannot be the same.
- Characters are sorted according to their ASCII values, except that lowercase characters are treated as uppercase characters.

- Return code: 0 for normal completion.

◘ SPOOL—redirect printer output

- General format

```
[ drive ] [ path ]   SPOOL [/Q or
                           /D:device or
                           /O:device]
```

- Usage: Command line and batch file.

● Description

The **SPOOL** command is used to redirect printer output from one device to another. In other words, output from one parallel printer can be sent to another, or from a parallel printer to a serial printer. Before using this command to spool to a serial port, make sure that the COM.SYS device driver is installed (found in CONFIG.SYS).

◘ START—start an OS/2 program in another session

● General format

```
START ["program title"]
         [/K or /C or /N]
         [/F or /B]
         [/PGM]
         [/FS or /WIN or /PM or /DOS]
         [/MAX or /MIN]
         [/I]
         command [command or inputs]
```

● Usage: Command line and batch file

● Description

The **START** command is used to start an OS/2 program in another session. Normally, this command is used to automatically start programs at system startup by invoking the special batch file called STARTUP.CMD.

You can also issue the **START** command without a parameter at the command line to invoke an OS/2 command processor. With **START**, If you enter the /WIN, /FS, or /PM parameter, the program is executed in the foreground session. You can use **START** to run full-screen applications or applications running in a window such as Presentation Manager programs. **START** determines the type of application and will run it in the appropriate window or full-screen session. You cannot start a batch file (.CMD) with the /PM parameter.

◘ SUBST—substitute drive letter

● General format

```
[ drive ] [ path ] SUBST [drive <drive\path or /D>]
```

● Usage: Command line.

● Description

The **SUBST** command is used to substitute a drive letter for another drive and path so that you can access that drive and path using only the drive letter. When the system finds a drive that was created with the **SUBST** command, it replaces the reference with the new path.

If you enter this command without a parameter, **SUBST** shows the names of the substitutions currently in effect on your system.

◻ SWAPPATH—specify the size and location of the swap file

● General format

```
SWAPPATH = drive [ path ] [ minfree ] [ initial ]
```

● Usage: Command line and CONFIG.SYS.

● Description

The **SWAPPATH** command is used to specify the location and size of the swap file. The name of the swap file is SWAPPER.DAT, and its default location is C:\OS2\SYSTEM. This file provides temporary storage for data segments that the system has removed from physical memory to satisfy a request for memory.

The swap file can become quite large, and isolating it in either a subdirectory or a separate partition on a hard disk is recommended. After relocating the swap file to a subdirectory or separate partition, you will have to shut down and restart the system, and erase the old swap file from its old location.

minfree specifies the minimum free space that can remain on the disk before you receive a warning that the swap file has increased to a size that leaves less than this amount of free space on the disk.

initial specifies the size of the swap file initially allocated by the operating system at the time of installation.

◘ SYSLEVEL—show service level

- General format

```
[ drive ] [ path ] SYSLEVEL
```

- Usage: Command line.

- Description

The **SYSLEVEL** command is used to show the system service level. This command may take a while to complete, and while it is processing the "Please wait..." message will be displayed. After the current corrective service level is determined, it is shown on the screen; for example,

```
C:\OS2\INSTALL\SYSLEVEL.OS2
IBM OS/2 Base Operating System
Version 2.10     Component ID 562107701
Type 0
Current CSD level: XR00000
Prior   CSD level: XR00000
```

◘ SYSLOG—view or print system error log file

- General format

```
SYSLOG [/S           or
        /R           or
        /P:pathname  or
        /W:x ]
```

- Usage: Command line.

- Description

The **SYSLOG** command is used to either view or print the formatted contents of the system error-log file.

The following is a list of the parameters:

/S Suspend system error logging
/R Resume system error logging
/P Redirect error logging data from one file to another
/W Specify the size of an error-log file

If this command is issued without any parameter, the **SYSLOG**, which is a Presentation Manager application and runs in a window, is started.

▢ THREADS—set maximum number of actions

- General format

```
THREADS =  number
```

- Usage: CONFIG.SYS.

- Description

The **THREADS** command is used to set the maximum number of threads that can be executed concurrently for OS/2 sessions. The default is 64, and the maximum setting is 4095.

▢ TIME—show or change system time

- General format

```
TIME [hh [:mm] [:ss] ]
```

- Usage: Command line and batch file.

- Description

The **TIME** command is used to either show or change the system time. It also resets the time on your computer's clock. This time is recorded in the directory when you create or change a file. If you enter this command without a parameter, **TIME** shows the system time and prompts you about changing it.

You can add time in hours and minutes, using a 24-h clock (military time), separated by a colon or period. If needed, you can also specify the seconds and hundredths of a second separated by a period or a comma, depending on the decimal separator shown on your screen.

▢ TIMESLICE—set amount of processing time

- General format

```
TIMESLICE = minimum [,maximum]
```

- Usage: CONFIG.SYS.

- Description

The **TIMESLICE** command is used to set the minimum and maximum amount of processor time given by the system to processes and programs for both OS/2 and DOS sessions.

The minimum amount of time is given to a thread before yielding the processor to a thread of the same priority level; this is also the maximum amount of time a thread can be processed before yielding processor time.

The default is dynamic time slicing based on system load and paging activity. Dynamic time slicing gives the best performance in all situations.

◘ TRACE—turn System Trace Facility on or off

- General format

```
[ drive ] [ path ] TRACE <OFF or ON>
                      [/S or /R or /C]
[< major_code_spec or (minor_code_spec) > or
 <tdf_spec or (minor_code_spec) or
 (event_type_spec) > or <tdf_keyword or
 (minor_code_spec) or (event_type_spec) >  or
 <  /P: or pid_spec > ]
```

- Usage: Command line.

- Description

The **TRACE** command is used to turn the System Trace Facility on or off. If turned on, the trace facility records a sequence of system events, function calls, or data. This information can be used for debugging programs and commands. After the recording is done, the data is retrieved with the System Trace Formatter (see **TRACEFMT** command). For the tracing to take effect, you must have the **TRACEBUF** command, which allocates the trace buffer, in the CONFIG.SYS. Alternatively, you can enter this in CONFIG.SYS, as we will see next.

This command must be issued with caution, and you must turn it on tracing only when needed as there is a lot of overhead associated with it. It may slow down the whole system. It is intended to be used with the assistance of your technical coordinator.

◘ TRACE—turn tracing of CONFIG.SYS ON or OFF

● General format

```
TRACE = <OFF or ON> event,...
```

● Usage: CONFIG.SYS.

● Description

This **TRACE** command is used to trace the processing of the CONFIG.SYS file. It keeps track of key events in the execution of the system. If turned on, the trace facility records a sequence of system events, function calls, or data. This information can be used for debugging programs and commands. After the recording is done, the data is retrieved with the System Trace Formatter, using the **TRACEFMT** command. To speed up this process, it is advisable to increase the trace buffer size using the **TRACEBUF** command (discussed next).

◘ TRACEBUF—set buffer size for trace

● General format

```
TRACEBUF= size
```

● Usage: CONFIG.SYS.

● Description

The **TRACEBUF** command is used to set the size of the trace buffer in the CONFIG.SYS file. In this buffer, the trace events are recorded. The default buffer size is 4 kbytes, and the maximum size is 63 kbytes.

If you do not specify a **TRACE** or **TRACEBUF** statement in the CONFIG.SYS file, OS/2 2.1 does not allocate a trace buffer, and system tracing is not available.

◨ TRACEFMT—show trace records

- General format

  [*drive*] [*path*] TRACEFMT

- Usage: Command line.

- Description

  The **TRACEFMT** command shows formatted trace data recorded while the system is running. The information is displayed in reverse timestamp order. **TRACEFMT** works only if you have the **TRACE** or the **TRACEBUF** statement in your CONFIG.SYS file.

  TRACEFMT is a Presentation Manager* application running in a window. It can perform the following tasks:

  - Open a file
  - Get a system trace buffer
  - Save As
  - Print
  - View formatted data
  - View summary by process ID
  - View summary by major code

◨ TREE—display directory structure of a drive

- General format

  [*drive*] [*path*] TREE [*drive*] [/F]

- Usage: Command line.

- Description

  The **TREE** command is used to show all the directory paths of a drive. With the /F option, this command also displays the files in the root directory and in each subdirectory.

- Return code: 0 for normal completion.

◼ TYPE—show content of a file

- General format

```
TYPE   [ drive ] [ path ] filename
```

- Usage: Command line.

- Description

The **TYPE** command is used to show the contents of one or more files on the screen. In a DOS session, only one file is specified with this command. In OS/2, **TYPE** displays files consecutively on the screen if multiple files are entered. You can include a drive and path when specifying multiple filenames and can also use the global filename characters * and ? as part of the filename.

The **TREE** command shows ASCII files, and the text appears in a legible format as it is found in the file, except tab characters are expanded to an eight-character boundary. However, other files, such as graphic or program files, may appear unreadable because of the presence of nonalphabetic or nonnumeric characters.

◼ UNDELETE—recover file previously deleted

- General format

```
UNDELETE   [ drive ] [ path ] [ filename ]
           [/L or /A or /S or /F]...
```

- Usage: Command line.

- Description

The **UNDELETE** command is used to recover files that have been previously erased from a drive. When files are erased, they are placed in a special directory, the location of which is set by the **DELDIR** statement found in CONFIG.SYS. The maximum size of the directory is set. If the number of deleted files exceeds this maximum number, the system automatically erases files in the first-in-first-out order.

The files that are recoverable are restored in their original path.

◘ UNPACK—decompress file

- General format

```
[ drive ] [ path ] UNPACK [ drive ] [ path ] filename
        [ drive ] [ path ] [/V] [/F] [/N:filename]

                        or

[ drive ] [ path ] UNPACK [ drive ] [ path ] filename
                    [/SHOW]
```

- Usage: Command line and batch file.

- Description

The **UNPACK** command is used to decompress files that were previously packed. It also copies files that are not compressed but are located on the OS/2 installation diskettes. Packed files have a @ ("at" symbol) as the last character in their filenames.

There is no need to specify an output filename; **UNPACK** uses the filename from the original unpacked file as the destination filename. It also preserves the date, time, and file attribute of the original uncompressed file. **UNPACK** also copies files; therefore, it can unpack diskettes that contain both compressed and uncompressed files.

- Return code: 0 Normal completion
                 1 No files were found to unpack or copy
                 2 Some files or directories were not unpacked or copied because of file errors
                 3 Ended by user
                 4 Ended because of error

◘ VER—show the OS/2 version number

- General format

VER

- Usage: Command line and batch file.

- Description

The **VER** command is used to display the OS/2 version number.

◘ VERIFY—check data written to disk

● General format

```
VERIFY [ ON or  OFF ]
```

● Usage: Command line batch file.

● Description

The **VERIFY** command is used to turn on or off checking of data; it confirms that data written to a disk has been written correctly. If you issue **VERIFY ON**, verification is done for file system I/O write actions for both hard disks and diskettes on a per session basis. The system does a **VERIFY** action each time you write data to a disk. You receive an error message only if the system is unable to write the data to the disk successfully. If you enter this command without a parameter, **VERIFY** displays the current **VERIFY** status.

This command has the same purpose as the /V parameter in the **COPY** and **XCOPY** commands.

◘ VIEW—display online document

● General format

```
[ drive ] [ path ] VIEW
            [ drive ] [ path ] filename [topic]
```

● Usage: Command line.

● Description

The **VIEW** command is used to look at online documents created with the Information Presentation Facility (IPF) compiler. **VIEW** displays IPF files that have a .INF extension.

◘ VMDISK—create DOS startup diskette

● General format

```
VMDISK sourcedrive [target-drive] [ path ] filename
```

● Usage: Command line.

- Description

The **VMDISK** command is used to create a file that contains the image of a DOS startup diskette. After creating this file, you can create a DOS session by starting from this image file.

◼ VOL—display volume label of a disk

- General format

```
VOL [drive...]
```

- Usage: Command line and batch file.

- Description

The **VOL** command is used to see the disk volume label and serial number if they exist. From a DOS session, **VOL** displays the label for only one disk. From OS/2, if you specify more than one drive, **VOL** displays the volume labels consecutively.

If you enter this command without a parameter, **VOL** displays the volume label and volume serial number of the current drive.

◼ XCOPY—copy files including directory

- General format

```
[ drive ] [ path ] XCOPY [ drive ]
    <filename or path [ filename ] [ drive ] [ path ]
                          filename
        [   /D:mm-dd-yy   or
            /S            or
            /E            or
            /P            or
            /V            or
            /A            or
            /M            or
            /H            or
            /T            or
            /R            or
            /O            or
            /F   ]
```

- Usage: Command line and batch file.

● Description

The **XCOPY** command is used to copy one or groups of files, which can include lower-level subdirectories. When using this command, remember the following important points:

- Specify the drive, path, and filename for the source and target drives. If you do not specify a path, **XCOPY** starts from the current directory. If you do not specify a filename, **XCOPY** uses *.* as the default value.
- **XCOPY** works only within the source directory unless you use the /S parameter, which copies files in the source directory and in all directories below the starting source directory.
- If you specify the /D parameter, the month, date, and year may be in different positions. This depends on your country.
- If you use the /M parameter, **XCOPY** copies files whose archive bit is set, and then turns off the archive bit of the source file. You can use the **ATTRIB** command to reset the archive bit for your files.
- If the target path does not exist on the target, you can use **XCOPY** to create the directories before copying. You can rename files on the target by specifying a new filename on the target.

- **XCOPY** will copy the extended attributes of a source file to the target file as indicated by the parameters in the syntax.

● Return code: 0   Normal completion
　　　　　　　　 1   No files were found to copy
　　　　　　　　 2   Some files or directories were not copied because of file or directory errors
　　　　　　　　 3   Ended by user
　　　　　　　　 4   Ended because of error

REXX

This chapter is a reference guide for programmers using REXX in the OS/2 environment. It contains statements that make up a program. The statements covered here are

- REXX instructions
- Command functions

This chapter also provides information on REXX built-in functions that can be used by statements.

REXX supports free-format statements, which can appear anywhere between columns 1 and 72. A statement can have any number of embedded blanks and can be terminated with either an end-of-line character or a semicolon (;).

Two or more statements can appear on same line, separated from each other with semicolons. Also, one statement can span more than one line, in which case a comma at the end of the line indicates a continuation of the statement.

Comments appear between the delimiters /* and */ and can span one or more lines.

This chapter also includes other useful information, such as

- Arithmetic operators
- Concatenation operators
- Operator precedence
- Logical operators
- Comparison operators
- Variable names
- Input/output streams

General format: The general form of a REXX statement is

```
[label:] term... [;]
```

where *term* is either a comment enclosed by the delimiters /* and */ or an expression. An expression can be either a character expression, a numeric expression, a comparison expression, or a logical expression.

11.1 Arithmetic Operations

The arithmetic operators used in REXX numeric expressions are as follows:

Operator	Operation
+	Addition
-	Subtraction
*	Multiplication
/	Division, returning decimal quotient
%	Division, returning integer quotient
//	Division, returning remainder
**	Exponential
-n	Negation
+n	Addition

11.2 Concatenation Operators

The following concatenation operators are supported by REXX.

Operator	Operation
blank	Concatenate two strings with a blank character in between
||	Concatenate two strings without a blank character in between

11.3 Operator Precedence

In REXX, if there is more than one operator in an expression, then operations are performed according to the following order of precedence:

Order	Operation	Operators
1	Expressions in parentheses	( )
2	Prefix operators	- + \
3	Exponential operators	**
4	Multiplication and division	* / % //
5	Addition and subtraction	+ -
6	Concatenation	||
7	Comparison	== = \== \= > < >< >= <= \< \>
8	Logical AND	&
9	Logical OR and Exclusive OR (XOR)	| &&

11.4 Logical Operation

A logical operator is used when a boolean operation is peformed on two binary operands. The following is a list of logical operators, including the operation and return code.

Operator	Operation	Returns
&	AND	1 if both comparisons are true; otherwise 0.
|	OR	1 if one of several comparisons is true; otherwise 0.
&&	XOR	1 if only one of a group of comparisons is true; otherwise 0.
\	NOT	The reverse of the logical value of the expression

11.5 Comparison Operators

A comparison operator is used when two operands are compared with each other. After a comparison expression is processed, from left to right, it yields 1 if the comparison condition is true and 0 if the comparison condition is false. The following is a list of REXX comparison operators.

Operator	Operation
=	Equal to
\=	Not equal to
>	Greater than
<	Less than
><	Greater than or less than (not equal to)
<>	Greater than or less than (not equal to)
>=	Greater than or equal to
<=	Less than or equal to
\<	Not less than
\>	Not greater than
>>=	Strictly greater than or equal to
<<=	Strictly less than or equal to
<>	Less than or greater than
>>	Strictly greater than
<<	Strictly less than

11.6 Variable Names

In REXX, variable names can be up to 250 characters long. A variable may consist of the following characters:

Uppercase characters A to Z
Lowercase characters a to z
Numbers 0 to 9
Special characters   @ # $! ? . — and '4A'x

11.7 Input and Output Streams

In REXX there two types of streams: transient and persistent. A *transient* stream is a dynamic stream where the data is sent or received over a serial interface. A *persistent* stream is a static form which can be a file or data object.

In OS/2 there are several streams associated with input and output devices. Some valid ones are

COM1:/COM2:	Communication posts
CON:	Display as output and keyboard as input
KBD:	Keyboard
LPT1:/LPT2:	Printer
PRN:	The current default printer output
STDERR:	Standard error output stream
STDIN:	Standard input stream
STDOUT:	Standard output stream
QUEUE:	REXX external data queue

The **STDIN** and **STDOUT** are the default streams.

11.8 Functions and Instructions

This section provides a description of the functionality and parameters of each REXX instruction or function as well as a list of return codes and practical examples.

◘ ABBREV function

- General format

```
ABBREV(string, prefix[,length])
```

- Description

The **ABBREV** function checks for a prefix in a character string.

string is a character string to be checked for a prefix.

prefix is a character string.

length is the maximum number of prefix characters that should match the leading characters of the string.

- Return

The **ABBREV** function returns 1 (TRUE) if *prefix* is found in *string*; otherwise it returns 0 (FALSE). The function returns a TRUE or FALSE code according to the following conditions:

Return code	Condition
1	*prefix* is equal to the leading characters of *string* and the number of characters matched is less than *length*
0	*prefix* is not equal to the leading characters of *string*
0	The number of characters matched is greater than *length*

● Example

```
ABBREV('Profile','Pro')          returns 1 (TRUE)
ABBREV('SUN','')                 returns 1 (TRUE)
ABBREV('SUNDAY','SUN',3)         returns 1 (TRUE)
ABBREV('Monday','day')           returns 0 (FALSE)
ABBREV('JOHN',Jo)                returns 0 (FALSE)
```

◘ ABS function

● General format

```
ABS(number)
```

● Description

The **ABS** function calculates the absolute value of a number.

number is a number for which the absolute value is returned.

● Return

The **ABS** function returns the value of *number* without considering the sign. The number of digits returned is determined by the current value of the **NUMERIC DIGITS** variable.

● Example

```
ABS('34.56')     returns the value 34.56
ABS(' -3.476')   returns the value 3.476
```

◘ ADDRESS instruction

● General format

```
ADDRESS environment [expression] or
     [VALUE] expression ;
```

● Description

The **ADDRESS** instruction specifies the environment where non-REXX commands are to be executed. The environment can be set temporarily or permanently depending on whether the expression is coded. The setting of the environment is checked with the **ADDRESS** function.

environment is a character string constant; it is one of the following:

EPM   Routes commands to EPM editor
CMD   Routes commands for batch processing

expression is first evaluated by REXX; the result is sent to the host environment as a command to be executed. If *expression* is not specified, the destination is set permanently until the next **ADDRESS** instruction is issued. Subsequent non-EXEC commands will be sent to this new host environment. If *expression* is specified, then the host environment is effective during the execution of this **ADDRESS** instruction.

VALUE is used if the first character of *expression* is a special character.

● Return

The return code from the host environment, after the command is executed, is placed in the special variable RC.

● Example

The following **ADDRESS** instruction sends a file called 'TEST.CMD' to CMD for execution.

```
ADDRESS CMD 'TEST.CMD'
```

◘ ADDRESS function

● General format

```
ADDRESS
```

● Description

The **ADDRESS** function returns the name of the host environment to which non-REXX commands are currently routed.

- Return

The **ADDRESS** function returns the current name of the host environment. It is one of the following:

CMD   EPM   DOS

- Example

```
ADDRESS()   /* returns the current destination of the
             environment */
```

◻ ARG function

- General format

```
ARG([n][,option])
```

- Description

The **ARG** function either returns an argument string or tests the existence of an argument passed to a previously called function or routine.

n is an argument number. If it is specified, the *n*th argument is returned.

option is a character string whose first character is an E or an O. If it is specified, the **ARG** function checks for the presence of the *n*th argument string.

- Return

The **ARG** function returns the following:

- If *n* and *option* are not specified, it returns the number of arguments passed to the function.
- If *option* is E, it returns 1 if argument *n* exists; otherwise it returns 0.
- If *option* is O, it returns 1 if argument *n* is omitted; otherwise it returns 0.

- Example

```
ARG()          /* returns the number of arguments */
               /* passed to the function */
```

```
ARG(3)              /* returns the third argument */
ARG(2,'Omitted')        /* checks whether the 2nd
                        /* argument has been omitted */
```

◘ ARG instruction

● General format

```
ARG template;
```

● Description

The **ARG** instruction parses the arguments passed to a program or subroutine and places them in variables. The parsing is done according to parsing rules of REXX.

template consists of symbols, separated by blanks.

● Return

The **ARG** instrction returns parsed arguments.

● Example

Let's say the function

```
    Mywork: Arg string, num1, num2
```

is called in the following way:

```
    MYWORK('DATA 3', 30, 50).
```

After parsing, the symbols will have the following values:

```
    STRING has 'DATA 3'.
    NUM1 has '30'.
    NUM2 has '50'.
```

◘ BEEP function

● General format

```
BEEP (frequency, duration)
```

● Description

The **BEEP** function sounds the speaker for a limited duration at a given frequency.

frequency is given in hertz, and the range is 37 to 32,767 Hz.

duration is used to limit the length of the sound and the range is 1 to 60,000 ms.

- Return

None.

◘ BITAND function

- General format

```
BITAND(string1[,[string2][,pad]])
```

- Description

The **BITAND** function performs an **AND** operation on two strings bit by bit. The number of bits on which the operation is performed is determined by the longest string. If padding is supplied, the **AND** operation of the shorter input string is extended. If padding is not supplied, the **AND** operation stops when the bits of the shorter string have been exhausted; the remaining bits of the longer string are added to the result.

string1, *string2*, and *pad* are input strings used for the **AND** operation. *string1* is required; *string2* and *pad* are optional.

- Return

The **BITAND** function returns a string which is the result of an **AND** operation on *string1*, *string2*, and *pad*.

- Example

```
BITAND('63'x,'33'x)     /* returns  '23'x */
BITAND('43'x,'4444'x) /* returns  '4044'x */
BITAND('43'x,'4444'x,'70'x)    /*returns  '4440'x */
```

◘ BITOR function

- General format

```
BITOR(string1[,[string2][,pad]])
```

● Description

The **BITOR** function performs an **OR** operation on two strings bit by bit. The number of bits on which the operation is performed is determined by the longest string. If padding is supplied, the **OR** operation on the shorter input string is extended. If padding is not supplied, the **OR** operation stops when the bits of the shorter string have been exhausted; the remaining bits of the longer string are added to the result.

string1, *string2*, and *pad* are input strings used for the **OR** operation. *string1* is required; *string2* and *pad* are optional.

● Return

The **BITOR** function returns a string which is the result of an OR operation on *string1*, *string2*, and *pad*.

● Example

```
BITOR('63'x,'33'x)        /* returns  '73'x */
BITOR('63'x,'3333'x)   /* returns  '7333'x */
BITOR('63'x,'3333'x,'77'x)   /* returns  '7377'x */
```

◘ BITXOR function

● General format

```
BITXOR(string1[,[string2][,pad]])
```

● Description

The **BITXOR** function performs an exclusive OR (**XOR**) operation on two strings bit by bit. The number of bits on which the operation is performed is determined by the longest string. If padding is supplied, the **XOR** operation of the shorter input string is extended. If padding is not supplied, the **XOR** operation stops when the bits of the shorter string have been exhausted; the remaining bits of the longer string are added to the result.

string1, *string2*, and *pad* are input strings used for the **XOR** operation. *string1* is required; *string2* and *pad* are optional.

• Return

The **BITXOR** function returns a string which is the result of an **XOR** operation of *string1*, *string2*, and *pad*.

• Example

```
BITXOR('63'x,'33'x)    /* returns  '40'x */
BITXOR('63'x,'3333'x) /* returns  '4033'x */
BITXOR('63'x,'3333'x,'77'x)    /* returns  '4040'x */
```

◻ B2X function—binary to hexadecimal

• General format

```
B2X(binary-string)
```

• Description

The **B2X** function converts a string in binary format to a string in hexadecimal format.

binary-string is a string that contains 0s and 1s. It is valid to include blanks in boundaries between every four digits. The blanks are ignored during the conversion.

• Return

The **B2X** function returns parsed arguments.

• Example

```
B2X('11000011') /* returns 'C3' */
B2X('10111')    /* returns '17' */
           B2X('1 1111 0000') /* returns '1F0' */
```

◻ CALL instruction

• General format

```
CALL <name [expression,...] or
     OFF condition        or
        ON condition [NAME trapname]> ;
```

● Description

The **CALL** instruction executes a subroutine, a program, a built-in function, or an external routine. Control is passed to the called routine, and after its execution is completed, control is returned to the statement following the **CALL** statement in the calling routine. Or, the **CALL** instruction is used to turn on or off the trapping of certain conditions.

name is the name of the subroutine, program, or function to be invoked.

expression is first evaluated and resolved into parameters to be passed to the invoked routine. The entry of an expression is optional.

condition can be one of the following: **ERROR, FAILURE, HALT,** or **NOTREADY**.

trapname is a routine or label to which control goes when a certain condition occurs.

● Return

After completion of the called routine, any return value is placed in the variable *return*. If no value is returned by the invoked routine, then *return* is initialized to null.

● Example

In the following program fragment a subroutine *square* is called, which calculates the square root of an expression *y*.

```
arg  y              /* parse y */
call square y       /* call the routine to calculate */
                    /* the square root of y */
say 'square root of 'y ' is ' result

square: procedure   /* procedure called square */
    arg n           /* parse y */
    return n*n      /* calculate and return square */
                    /* root */
```

◘ CENTER or CENTRE function

● General format

```
CENTER(string,length[,pad])
   or
CENTRE(string,length[,pad])
```

- Description

The **CENTER** function centers a string within a given area.

string is the string to be centered. If *string* is longer than the specified area, it is truncated on both sides.

length is the number of characters within which *string* is to be centered.

pad is the character to use for padding on both the right and left sides of the centered *string*. If *pad* is not entered, then spaces are used.

- Return

The **CENTER** function returns the centered *string*.

- Example

```
CENTER(ABCD,8,'.')      returns '..ABCD..'
CENTER(ABCD,8)          returns '  ABCD  '
```

◻ CHARIN function—character Input

- General format

```
CHARIN([name][,start][,length])
```

- Description

The **CHARIN** function reads a string from an input stream.

name is used to specify an input stream from which a string is read. The stream can be a file or any other input OS/2 device such as a keyboard. If this parameter is omitted, the string is read from the device called **STDIN. STDIN** is the default stream.

start is used to specify the starting position at which the read operation begins. If this parameter is omitted, the characters are read from the current position of the pointer associated with each stream. After the operation the pointer is moved forward by the number of characters read.

length is used to limit the number of characters read from the input stream. If *length* is 0, then a null string is returned; if it is omitted, only one character is returned.

● Return

The **CHARIN** function returns a string from a default or specific stream.

● Example

```
CHARIN(infile,1,3)  /* returns 'NYC' */
                    /* the first 3 characters */
CHARIN(infile,1,0)  /* returns a null string returns */
CHARIN(infile)      /* 'N' the character position is */
                    /* at 1 because of the previous call */
CHARIN(infile,2)    /* returns 'NY', two characters from */
                    /* position 2 */
CHARIN()            /*  returns 'a', one character from */
                    /* the default input stream  */
```

◻ CHAROUT function—character output

● General format

```
CHAROUT([name][,string][,start])
```

● Description

The **CHAROUT** function sends a string to an output stream.

name is used to specify an output stream to which a string is written. The stream can be a file or any other output OS/2 device such as a screen or a printer. If this parameter is omitted, the string is written to the device called **STDOUT**. The default stream is the screen.

string contains characters to be written to the output stream. If you omit this parameter, then no characters are sent and the function returns 0.

start is used to specify the starting position at which the write operation begins. If this parameter is omitted, the characters are written from the current position of the pointer associated with each stream. After the operation the pointer is moved forward by the number of characters sent.

● Return

The **CHAROUT** function returns the number of characters remaining to be written after attemping to write. This number can be zero to many.

● Example

```
CHAROUT(outfile,'Hi')    /* returns 0, writes 2*/
                         /*  characters */
CHAROUT(outfile,'Hi',5)  /* returns 0, writes */
                         /* 2 characters from */
                         /* from position 5   */
CHAROUT('Hi')            /* returns 0, writes 2 characters  */
                         /* to STDOUT */
```

◻ CHARS function—character remaining

● General format

```
CHARS([name])
```

● Description

The **CHARS** function is used to get the number of characters remaining in an input stream.

name is used to specify a file, and if it is omitted, the number of characters left in the default input stream (**STDIN**) is returned.

● Return

The **CHARS** function returns the number of a character remaining in an input stream.

● Example

```
CHARS(infile)     /* returns 0, may be */
                  /* the first 3 characters */
CHARS(infile)     /* returns 0, may be */
CHARS()           /* returns 2, may be  */
```

◻ COMPARE function

● General format

```
COMPARE(string1,string2[,pad])
```

● Description

The **COMPARE** function compares two strings.

string1 and *string2* are the strings being compared.

pad is an optional padding character; if it is not specified, the default character is blank.

- Return

The function returns

- Zero if both input strings are the same.
- A nonzero value if the input strings are not the same; this value is also the position of the first mismatched characters.

- Example

```
COMPARE('345','345')        returns 0 (exact match)
COMPARE('MOO%% ','MOO','%') returns 6 (1st mismatch after
                            padding character
COMPARE('daa','do')         returns 1 (1st mismatched
                            character).
```

◘ CONDITION function

- General format

```
CONDITION([option])
```

- Description

The **CONDITION** function obtains the information for the currently trapped REXX condition.

option is one of the following: C, D, I, or S. Their meanings are as follows:

C   causes the name of the current trapped condition to be
     returned
D   causes the description of the string to be returned
I   causes the name of the actual instruction that was being executed
     when the condition was trapped to be returned
S   causes the status of the condition trapped to be returned

- Return

The **CONDITION** function returns the information related to the currently trapped condition depending on the option. A null string is returned if no condition trap is in effect.

- Example

```
CONDITION(I) returns the instruction that caused the trap.
```

COPIES function—concatenate string

- General format

```
COPIES(string,n)
```

- Description

The **COPIES** function concatenates or appends a string to itself a certain number of times.

string is the string concatenated to itself.

n is the number of times needed to concatenate *string* to itself.

- Return

The **CONDITION** function returns a concatenated string, or a null string if *n* is zero.

- Example

```
COPIES('Hi',2)      returns   'HiHi'
COPIES('Hi',0)      returns   '' (null string)
```

C2D function—character to decimal

- General format

```
C2D(string[,n])
```

- Description

The **C2D** function converts a string into a decimal number.

string is a string 0 to 250 characters in length.

n is the number of bytes where the signed fixed-number part of *string* is to be stored.

● Return

The **C2D** function returns a decimal number.

● Example

```
C2D('09'x)              returns decimal 9
C2D('E4',2)             returns decimal 288 (positive number in
                        two bytes)
C2D('a')                returns 97 (ASCII)
```

�‍◻ C2X function—character to hexadecimal

● General format

```
C2X(string)
```

● Description

The **C2X** function converts a string into its equivalent ASCII hexadecimal numbers.

string is a character string to be converted to its equivalent ASCII numbers.

● Return

The **C2X** function returns ASCII numbers.

● Example

```
C2X('0456')      returns 'F1F2F3C1C2C3'
```

◻ DATATYPE function—determine data type

● General format

```
DATATYPE(string[,type])
```

● Description

The **DATATYPE** function tests the data type of a string.

string is a character string whose data type is to be tested.

type is the type to be tested for. If *type* is not specified, the default data type to be tested for is **NUM**, if it is numeric; the default type is **CHAR** for all other cases.

- Return

The function returns 1 (TRUE) if *string* is of the specified or default data type; otherwise it returns 0 (FALSE). The following list gives the relationship between the return values and *type*.

Type	Return code
A—alphanumeric	1 if *string* contains only characters in the range a to z, A to Z, or 0 to 9
C—SBCS/DBCS	1 if string is a mixed SBCS/DBCS string
D—DBCS	1 if string is a pure DBCS string
N—numeric	1 if *string* is a valid REXX number
W—whole number	1 if *string* is a valid REXX whole number
L—lowercase	1 if *string* contains only characters in the range a to z
U—uppercase	1 if *string* contains only characters in the range A to Z
M—mixed-case	1 if *string* contains only characters in the range a to z or A to Z
S—symbol	1 if *string* contains only valid REXX symbols
B—bit	1 if *string* contains only 1s and 0s
X—hexadecimal	1 if *string* contains characters in the range a to f, A to F, or 0 to 9, or blank

- Example

```
DATATYPE(' 55 ')           returns NUM (numeric)
DATATYPE('&e55 ')          returns CHAR (character string)
DATATYPE('Bob','M')        returns 1 (mixed case)
DATATYPE('67.89','N')      returns 1 (numeric)
DATATYPE('67.89','X')      returns 0 (not hexadecimal
                           numbers)
DATATYPE('')               returns CHAR (null string)
```

◻ DATE function—get local date

- General format

```
DATE([option])
```

* Description

The **DATE** function obtains the current date.

option is a code specifying the format of the date. The default format is 'dd mmm yyyy', as in 21 July 1992.

* Return

The function returns the current date in a format specified by one of the following options:

Option	Returns date in format
B—base	Number of days into the current century in the form 'ddddd'
D—days	Number of days into the current year in the form 'ddd'
L—language	Date in the format 'dd Month yyyy'.
U—USA	Date in the form 'mm/dd/yy'
E—European	Date in the form 'dd/mm/yy'
J—Julian	Date in the form 'yyddd'
M—month	Full name of current month
O—ordered	Date in the form 'yy/mm/dd'
S—standard	Date in the form 'yyyymmdd'
W—week	Day of the week (e.g., Monday, Tuesday)

* Example

```
DATE()       returns the current date ('23 July 1992')
DATE(J)      returns the date in Julian format (92205)
DATE(D)      returns the number of days into this year
             (205)
```

◘ DELSTR function—delete string

* General format

```
DELSTR(string,n[,length])
```

* Description

The **DELSTR** function deletes a certain number of characters from a string.

string is the string from which characters are deleted.

n is the starting position from which characters are deleted in *string*.

length is the number of characters to delete. If *length* is greater than the total number of characters in *string*, then no action is taken. If *length* is not specified, then all characters from position *n* on are deleted.

● Return

The **DELSTR** function returns the changed string.

● Example

```
DELSTR('ABCDEF',2,1)    deletes 'B', leaving 'ACDEF'
DELSTR('ABCDEF',3,2)    deletes 'CD', leaving 'ABEF'
DELSTR('ABCDEF',9)      no change
```

◘ DELWORD function—delete word

● General format

```
DELWORD(string,n[,length])
```

● Description

The **DELWORD** function deletes a certain number of words from a string.

string is the string from which words are deleted.

n is the starting position from which words are deleted in *string*.

length is the number of words to delete. If *length* is greater than the total number of words in *string*, then no action is taken. If *length* is not specified, then all the words from position *n* on are deleted.

● Return

The **DELWORD** function returns the changed string.

● Example

```
DELWORD('Ten days, two hours, and five minutes',3,2)
         returns  'Ten days, and five minutes'

DELWORD('Ten days, two hours, and five minutes',8)
         returns  'Ten days, two hours, and five minutes'
```

▫ DIGITS function

- General format

```
DIGITS()
```

- Description

The **DIGITS** function retrieves the current setting of the **NUMERIC DIGITS** option.

- Return

The **DIGITS** function returns the current setting of **NUMERIC DIGITS**.

- Example

```
DIGITS()  /* get the current NUMERIC DIGITS */
```

▫ DIRECTORY function—change directory

- General format

```
DIRECTORY([new-directory])
```

- Description

The **DIRECTORY** function is used to change to a new directory, if a directory is supplied and it exists. It also returns the current directory. If a new directory is omitted, the current directory is returned, or a null value is returned if an error occurs.

new-directory is used to specify the name of a valid and existing directory in the OS/2 system.

- Return

The **DIRECTORY** function returns the current directory. The first two characters of the directory name indicate the drive.

- Example

```
DIRECTORY()             /* returns the current directory */
DIRECTORY("C:\OS2\SYSTEM") /* returns  C:\OS2\SYSTEM */
```

◘ DO instruction

● General format

```
DO [expression or variable=start]
   [TO limit][BY increment];
   [FOR expression];
   [WHILE expression];
   [UNTIL expression];
   statement
      .
      .
      .

END [symbol];
```

```
Simple DO:

  DO
     statement
        .
        .
        .

  END;
```

```
Controlled repetitive DO:

  DO variable=start [TO end];
     statement
        .
        .
        .

  END;
```

```
DO-WHILE loop:

  DO variable=start [TO end] WHILE expression;
     statement
        .
        .
        .

  END;
```

```
DO-FOR loop:

  DO variable=start [TO end] FOR expression;
     statement
        .
        .
        .

  END;
```

```
DO-UNTIL loop:

  DO variable=start [TO end] UNTIL expression;
     statement
        .
        .
        .

  END;
```

```
DO-FOREVER loop:

  DO FOREVER ;
     statement
        .
        .
        .
  END;
```

- Description

The **DO** instruction executes a group of REXX statements a number of times depending on an expression. The expression is evaluated every time the **DO** loop is executed. The **DO** instruction can be divided into the following categories:

- Simple **DO**
- Controlled repetitive **DO**
- **DO-WHILE** loop
- **DO-FOR** loop
- **DO-UNTIL** loop
- **DO-FOREVER** loop

expression is any valid REXX expression.

variable is any valid REXX variable name.

start is the value to which *variable* is initialized before the start of the **DO** loop.

end is the limit; when *variable* passes this value, the loop terminates.

increment is the value by which *variable* is incremented.

statement is a valid REXX statement which is executed with the **DO** loop.

The **END** clause marks the end of the **DO** instruction.

- Return
        None.

- Example

In the following program fragment, the variable *start* is initialized to 3.

In the **DO** instruction, the variable is x and its starting value is 3. The variable x is incremented by 2 during every iteration of the **DO** loop. The loop stops when x is 40. During every loop, the statement 'say x' is executed.

```
start=3;                    /* initialize start to 3 */
Do x=start to 40 by 2;      /* starting value of x is 3 */
   say x                    /* statement to be executed */
End;                        /* in the DO loop */
```

◻ DROP instruction

- General format

```
DROP name...
```

- Description

The **DROP** instruction restores one or more variables to their uninitialized state. In other words, such variables no longer have any value.

name is a valid variable name to be freed.

- Return

None.

- Example

```
fruit = 'apple'  /* initialize the variable fruit to */
                 /* 'apple'   */
DROP fruit       /* free the variable fruit  */
                 /* from the stack */
```

◻ D2C function—convert decimal to character

- General format

```
D2C(number[,n])
```

- Description

The **D2C** function converts a decimal number to a character string in binary representation.

number is a whole number to be converted.

n is the number of characters in the result.

● Return

The **D2C** function returns the binary representation of a decimal number.

● Example

```
D2C(8)              returns '08'x
D2C(-127,2)         returns 'FF81'x (-127 = FF81 hex)
```

◘ D2X function—convert decimal to hexadecimal

● General format

```
D2X(number[,n])
```

● Description

The **D2X** function converts a decimal number to a character string in hexadecimal representation.

number is a whole number to be converted.

n is the number of characters in the result.

● Return

The **D2X** function returns the hexadecimal representation of a decimal number.

● Example

```
D2X(8)              returns '08'
D2X(-127,4)         returns 'FF81' (-127 = FF81 hex)
```

◘ ENDLOCAL function—restore variables

● General format

```
ENDLOCAL()
```

● Description

The **ENDLOCAL** function is used to restore the initial environment. It sets the values for drive, directory, and the environment variables to the state they were before the last **SETLOCAL** function was issued.

- Return

The **ENDLOCAL** function returns 1 if the restore operation is successful; 0 if the restore operation fails or no **SETLOCAL** was previously executed.

- Example

```
y = SETLOCAL()           /* save the current environment */
   .
   .
   .
y = ENDLOCAL()           /* restore the initial environment */
```

◘ ERRORTEXT function—return message text

- General format

```
ERRORTEXT(n)
```

- Description

The **ERRORTEXT** function returns a message text associated with an error number.

n is the error number; it is in the range 0 to 99.

- Return

The **ERRORTEXT** function returns the message text or a null string if the error number or message is not defined.

- Example

```
ERRORTEXT(16) returns 'Label not found'
```

◘ EXIT instruction—Terminate program

- General format

```
EXIT [expression];
```

- Description

The **EXIT** instruction ends the execution of a REXX program and returns control to the calling program.

expression is optional; its value is evaluated before termination of the program.

- Return

A value is returned to the calling program depending on whether *expression* is part of the **EXIT** instruction.

- Example

In the following program fragment, the program will terminate returning the value '12'.

```
x = 4
EXIT x*3 /* terminate program */
```

◘ FILESPEC—parse file specification

- General format

```
FILESPEC(option,filespec)
```

- Description

The **FILESPEC** function gives selected information such as drive, path, or name of a file specification.

option is one of the following:

Drive	The drive letter of the given file specification
Path	The directory path of the given file specification
Name	The filename of the given file specification

filespec is the file specification.

- Return

The **FILESPEC** function returns the drive letter, directory path, or filename.

- Example

```
myfile = "C:\BOOK\OS2REF\CHAPTER.11"
      say FILESPEC("Drive",myfile)  /* returns "C:" */

say FILESPEC("Path",myfile) /* returns "\BOOK\OS2REF\" */
say FILESPEC("Name",myfile) /* returns "CHAPTER.11" */

name = "Name"
say FILESPEC(name,myfile) /* returns "CHAPTER.11" */
```

◘ FORM function—get the NUMERIC FORM setting

- General format

```
FORM()
```

- Description

The **FORM** function returns the current setting of **NUMERIC FORM**.

- Return

The **FORM** function returns '**SCIENTIFIC**' or '**ENGINEERING**'.

- Example

```
NUMERIC FORM ENGINEERING
x = FORM()               /* returns ENGINEERING */
```

◘ FORMAT function—format numeric values

- General format

```
FORMAT(number[,before][,after][,expp][,expt])
```

- Description

The **FORMAT** function formats a numeric value; otherwise default formatting is done.

number is the numeric value to be formatted. If only *number* is entered, it is formatted and rounded using the standard REXX rules.

before is the number of digits allowed to the left of the decimal point.

after is the number of digits allowed to the right of the decimal point.

expp is used to set the number of positions for the exponent part.

expt is used to set the trigger point for the exponential notation.

- Return

  The **FORMAT** function returns the formatted numeric value.

- Example

  ```
  x = FORMAT("34567.89",2,2)   /* returns  3.456789E+04 */
  ```

◘ FUZZ function—get the NUMERIC FUZZ setting

- General format

  ```
  FUZZ()
  ```

- Description

  The **FUZZ** function returns the current setting of **NUMERIC FUZZ**.
  The default REXX setting is 0.

- Example

  ```
  NUMERIC FUZZ 1
  x = FUZZ()               returns 1
  ```

◘ IF instruction—condition processing

- General format

  ```
  IF expression [;] THEN [;] statement
              [ELSE [;] statement]
  ```

- Description

  The **IF** instruction executes one or many REXX statements based on the
  result of evaluating an expression.

  expression is a valid REXX expression; after its evaluation, the result is
  either 1 (TRUE) or 0 (FALSE).

THEN is a keyword that marks the statement(s) to be executed if *expression* evaluates to 1 (TRUE).

statement is a valid REXX statement.

ELSE is the keyword that marks the statement(s) to be executed if *expression* evaluates to 0 (FALSE).

(**Note**: The statement of either **THEN** or **ELSE**—never both—is executed.)

● Example

In the following program fragment, the expression in the **IF** instruction is **x < 3**. After the expression is evaluated, depending on whether the result is 1 or 0, the **NOP** or **SAY** instruction is executed.

```
IF x < 3
    THEN NOP
    ELSE
    SAY "x is greater than or equal to 3"
```

◘ INSERT function—insert string

● General format

```
INSERT(ins-string,string[,[n][,[length][,pad]]])
```

● Description

The **INSERT** function inserts a string into another string at a specified position. Padding is done if required.

ins-string is the string inserted into *string*.

string is the string in which *ins-string* is inserted.

n is the character position after which *ins-string* is inserted in *string*. The value of *n* must be nonnegative, and its default value is 0.

length is the length of *ins-string*.

pad is the character for padding if *length* is greater than the length of *ins-string*.

- Return

  The **INSERT** function returns *string* with *ins-string* inserted.

- Example

  ```
  INSERT(' ','GOODBOY',4)        returns 'GOOD BOY'
  INSERT('ABC','abc',5,6,'%') returns 'abc%%ABC%%%'
  ```

◘ INTERPRET instruction—interpret a statement

- General format

  ```
  INTERPRET expression ;
  ```

- Description

  The **INTERPRET** instruction interprets and executes an expression.

  expression contains one or many valid REXX statements. It is first evaluated and then executed by the REXX interpreter as if it were a REXX statement.

- Example

  ```
  ohmy = "SAY 'ohmy'"

  INTERPRET ohmy          /* interpret and execute */
  ```

◘ ITERATE instruction—end current iteration of DO loop

- General format

  ```
  ITERATE[name];
  ```

- Description

  The **ITERATE** instruction stops the current iteration of a **DO** loop and transfers control to the **END** statement. The **DO** loop continues after testing any expression associated with the loop.

  name is a control variable for the **DO** loop.

● Example

The following **DO** loop will display 1, 3, and 4; it skips the display of 2 because of the **ITERATE** instruction with the loop.

```
DO j = 1 TO 4
   IF j = 2 THEN ITERATE
   SAY j
END
```

◘ LASTPOS function—find the last position of a substring

● General format

```
LASTPOS(substring,string[,start])
```

● Description

The **LASTPOS** function finds the last occurrence, starting from position 1, of a substring within a string.

substring is the string searched for in *string*.

string is the string searched for in *substring*.

start is the starting position for the search.

● Return

The **LASTPOS** function returns the position of the last occurrence if *substring* is found in *string*; otherwise it yields 0.

● Example

```
LASTPOS("dogs","All dogs go to heaven") returns 5
LASTPOS("hogs","All dogs go to heaven") returns 0
```

◘ LEAVE instruction—terminate a DO loop

● General format

```
LEAVE[name];
```

● Description

The **LEAVE** instruction stops a **DO** loop and transfers control to the statement following the **END** statement.

name is a control variable for the **DO** loop.

● Example

The following **DO** loop will display 1 and stop when the value of **j** is 2.

```
DO j = 1 TO 4
   IF j = 2 THEN LEAVE
   SAY j
END
```

◻ LEFT function—left-justify text

● General format

```
LEFT(string,length[,pad])
```

● Description

The **LEFT** function left-justifies a text.

string is the text to be justified.

length is the length of the justified text.

pad is the padding character.

● Return

The **LEFT** function returns the left-justified text.

● Example

```
LEFT("All dogs go to heaven",23) returns
    "All dogs go to heaven   "
```

◘ LENGTH function—calculate the length of a string

- General format

```
LENGTH(string)
```

- Description

The **LENGTH** function determines the number of characters in a string.

string is the string for which the length is to be determined.

- Return

The **LENGTH** function returns the length of *string*.

- Example

```
LENGTH("All dogs go to heaven") returns 21.
```

◘ LINEIN function—line input

- General format

```
LINEIN([name][,line][,count])
```

- Description

The **LINEIN** function reads a line of characters from an input stream.

name is the input stream. It may be a file or any other standard device. If this parameter is omitted, the default stream is **STDIN**.

line is optional; if it is used, the read position of the stream is set to the first line. The value for *line* can be only 1. If this parameter is omitted, then **LINEIN** reads one line from the current position.

count is a flag indicating whether to read a line. Its value can be only 0 or 1. If it is 0, the read operation does not take place; otherwise it reads a line of characters from the input stream.

- Return

The **LINEIN** function returns

- One line of string
- A partial line, if a stream has been read by **CHARIN**
- Null, if count is 0

- Example

```
LINEIN()  /* reads a line from the */
          /* default input stream */
infile = 'CHAPTER.11'
LINEIN(infile) /* reads the current line from */
          /* CHAPTER.11 starting at the  */
          /* current read position */
LINEIN(infile,1,1)        /* read the first time,   */
          /* ans sets the read position */
          /* on the second line */
LINEIN(infile,1,0)        /* returns a null character  and */
          /* sets the read position to the first line*/
```

◻ LINEOUT function—line output

- General format

```
LINEOUT([name][,string][,line])
```

- Description

The **LINEOUT** function writes a string of characters to an output stream, which can be a file or a valid device.

name is the output stream. It may be a file or any other standard device. If this parameter is omitted, the string is written to the **STDOUT**, the default output stream.

line, when set to 1, tells **LINEOUT** to set the write position to the first character. This is the only valid value for *line*. If omitted, the line is appended to the output stream.

- Return

The **LINEOUT** function returns 1, if successful; 0, if not successful.

- Example

```
LINEOUT(,'The world of REXX')  /* writes the line to the */
                    /*default output stream */
outfile = 'CHAPTER.11'
LINEOUT(outfile,'chapter 11: rexx') /* appends the string */
                 /* to the CHAPTER.11 file  */
LINEOUT(outfile,'CHAPTER 11: REXX,1)
                    /* overwrites the string, */
                    /* starting from first character */
                 /* position */
```

◘ LINES function—line remaining

- General format

```
LINES([name])
```

- Description

The **LINES** function checks whether the end-of-file is reached in an input stream.

name is the input stream. It may be a file or any other standard device. If this parameter is omitted, the default stream is **STDIN**.

- Return

The **LINES** function returns 1, if there is data between the current read character position and the end of the characters of the input stream; 0, if there is no data.

- Example

```
LINES(infile) /* returns 0, means end-of-file is reached */
LINES()       /* returns 1, means there is data in STDIN */
```

◘ MAX function—determine the maximum value

- General format

```
MAX(number,...)
```

- Description

The **MAX** function returns the maximum numeric value from a list of numeric values. Up to 20 numbers are allowed.

number is a numeric value.

- Return

The **MAX** function returns the maximum value. The size of the returned value depends on the current setting of **NUMERIC DIGITS**.

- Example

```
MAX(22,34,67,100,1,4)    returns 100.
```

◘ MIN function—determine the minimum value

- General format

```
MIN(number,...)
```

- Description

The **MIN** function returns the minimum numeric value from a list of numeric values. Up to 20 numbers are allowed.

number is a numeric value.

- Return

The **MIN** function returns the minimum value. The size of the returned value depends on the current setting of **NUMERIC DIGITS**.

- Example

```
MIN(22,34,67,100,1,4)    returns 1.
```

◘ NOP instruction—no operation

- General format

```
NOP
```

- Description

The **NOP** instruction does nothing.

- Example

In the following program fragment, the expression in the **IF** instruction is **x < 3**. After the expression is evaluated, depending on whether the result is 1 or 0, the **NOP** or **SAY** instruction is executed. The **NOP** instruction does not produce any result, but the **SAY** instruction does.

```
IF x < 3
    THEN NOP
    ELSE
    SAY "x is greater or equal to 3"
```

◘ NUMERIC instruction—set numeric formats

- General format

```
NUMERIC < DIGITS [expression or 9] > or
        < FORM [SCIENTIFIC or ENGINEERING] > or
        < FUZZ [expression or 0] >;
```

- Description

The **NUMERIC** instruction sets the format for evaluating and reporting arithmetic operations.

DIGITS specifies the number of significant digits to use in calculations and reporting. The *expression* after **DIGITS** must resolve to a positive number. The default number is 9.

FORM specifies the expression of arithmetic values in exponential notation. There are two kinds: **SCIENTIFIC** and **ENGINEERING**. **SCIENTIFIC** means that only one nonzero digit appears before the decimal point of the mantissa, e.g., **3.5E+5**. **ENGINEERING** means that the exponent is a power of 3, e.g., **23E+3**.

FUZZ specifies the number of digits to ignore during a numeric comparison. The *expression* after **FUZZ** must resolve to a positive number. The default is 0.

◘ OPTIONS instruction—pass options to the REXX language processor

- General format

```
OPTIONS expression;
```

- Description

The **OPTIONS** instruction passes special parameters to the REXX language processor in the OS/2 environment to set the DBCS environment. This instruction should appear at the beginning of a program.

expression must contain only the following words; any other word is ignored.

ETMODE   Enable support for DBCS characters in strings
NOETMODE   Disable support for DBCS characters in strings
EXMODE   Enable support for DBCS data operations
NOEXMODE   Disable support for DBCS data operations

◘ OVERLAY function—overlay a string

- General format

```
OVERLAY(new-string,string[,[n][,length][,pad]])
```

- Description

The **OVERLAY** function overlays a string with a new string starting at a given position in the target string. Padding is done if either string is to be extended.

new-string is the string that is to overlay the target *string*.

string is the string to be overlaid by *new-string*.

n is the position of the character in *string* from which the overlay is to start. *n* must be a positive number.

length is the length of *new-string*.

pad is the padding character.

- Return

The **OVERLAY** function returns the overlaid string.

- Example

```
x = OVERLAY('123','1yzv3',2,4,'.'          returns '1123.3'
```

◘ PARSE instruction—assign data

- General format

```
PARSE [UPPER] <ARG or
               EXTERNAL or
               NUMERIC or
               PULL or
               SOURCE or
               VALUE [expression] WITH or
               VAR name or
               VERSION>
         [template];
```

- Description

The **PARSE** instruction places data into one or more variables. The source of the data can be a terminal, a data stack, or arguments passed to a function or subroutine.

UPPER means to convert assigned data to uppercase. The case of the source data remains unchanged.

ARG means that the source of the data is arguments passed to a REXX program or routine.

template consists of alternating patterns and variable names.

EXTERNAL means that the input data are from a terminal.

NUMERIC specifies returning the current settings for **NUMERIC** options.

PULL means that the source of the data is REXX data stacks.

SOURCE means that the source of the data is the program.

VALUE specifies evaluation of *expression*.

WITH is a keyword in the context of *expression*.

VAR specifies that *name* contains the source data.

VERSION specifies returning the current version of REXX.

● Example

```
    CALL Mywork('DATA 3', 30, 50).
    EXIT
Mywork: Arg string, num1, num2
    SAY string           /* displays 'DATA 3' */
    SAY num1             /* displays 30 */
    SAY num2             /* displays 50 */
    Return
```

◘ POS function—search for a substring

● General format

```
POS(substring,string[,start-pos])
```

● Description

The **POS** function searches a string for the first occurrence of a substring.

substring is the string to be searched for.

string is the string to be searched for the *substring*.

start-pos is the starting position.

● Return

The **POS** function returns the character position, relative to 1, if *substring* is found; otherwise a zero is returned.

● Example

```
POS("to","All dogs go to heaven") returns 13.
```

◘ PROCEDURE instruction—define a procedure

● General format

```
PROCEDURE [EXPOSE name,...];
```

- Description

  The **PROCEDURE** instruction defines a procedure.

  EXPOSE is the keyword used to define one or more global variables that are used within the procedure.

  name is a global variable name.

- Example

```
x = "Birds"
CALL proc
EXIT
proc: PROCEDURE EXPOSE x
   SAY x           /* displays "Birds" */
   Return
```

◘ PULL instruction—get an element from the top of the data stack

- General format

```
PULL [template];
```

- Description

  The **PULL** instruction reads the top element of a data stack and uses it as source data. If the data stack is empty, then **PULL** will read from the terminal. The **PULL** instruction is the same as the REXX instruction **PARSE UPPER PULL** [*template*].

  template consists of alternating patterns and variable names.

- Example

```
SAY 'Please enter your first name:'
PULL name
```

◘ PUSH instruction—put an element at the top of the data stack

- General format

```
PUSH [expression];
```

- Description

  The **PUSH** instruction places a new element at the top of the data stack.

  expression is the data element to be placed in the data stack.

- Example

```
line = "WallyMagoo"
PUSH line      /* place line at the top of the stack */
```

◻ QUEUE instruction—put an element at the bottom of the data stack

- General format

```
QUEUE [expression];
```

- Description

  The **QUEUE** instruction places a new element at the bottom of the data stack.

  expression is the data element to be placed in the data stack.

- Example

```
line = "WallyMagoo"
QUEUE line /* place line at the bottom of the stack */
```

◻ QUEUED function—get the number of elements in the queue

- General format

```
QUEUED( )
```

- Description

  The **QUEUED** function returns the number of elements remaining in the data stack.

● Return

The **QUEUED** function returns the number of elements in the stack.

● Example

```
x = QUEUED()      /* query number of elements in queue */
SAY x             /* display number of elements */
```

◻ RANDOM function—generate a random number

● General format

```
RANDOM([min][,[max][,seed]])
```

● Description

The **RANDOM** function generates a pseudo-random number with a specified or default minimum and maximum range.

min is the minimum value above which the pseudo-random number is generated. The default is zero.

max is the maximum value below which the pseudo-random number is generated. The default is 999.

seed is a positive value used to start the random number generation process.

● Return

The **RAMDOM** function returns a positive number as the pseudo-random number.

● Example

The following statement will generate a pseudo-random number in the range 10 to 1000 using the value 3 as the seed.

```
y = RANDOM(10,1000,3)
```

◘ RETURN instruction—return from routine

● General format

```
RETURN [expression];
```

● Description

The RETURN instruction passes control back to the calling function or subroutine. Control goes to the statement following the **CALL** statement.

expression is first evaluated and the result is returned to the calling function or subroutine.

● Example

```
    CALL Mywork(30, 50)
    EXIT
Mywork: Arg num1, num2
    y = num1 * num2  /* calculate sum */
    RETURN y;        /* return sum to caller */
```

◘ REVERSE function—reverse the order of characters in a string

● General format

```
REVERSE(string)
```

● Description

The **REVERSE** function reverses the order of all characters in a string, i.e., the first character is placed in the last position.

string is a string whose characters are reversed.

● Return

The **REVERSE** function returns the reversed string.

● Example

```
REVERSE('abcde') returns 'edcba'.
```

◘ RIGHT function—right-justify text

- General format

```
RIGHT(string,length[,pad])
```

- Description

The **RIGHT** function right-justifies text, using padding characters if necessary.

string is the text to be justified.

length is the length of the justified text.

pad is the padding character.

- Return

The RIGHT function returns the right-justified text.

- Example

```
RIGHT("All dogs go to heaven",23) returns
"  All dogs go to heaven".
```

◘ SETLOCAL function—save environment settings

- General format

```
SETLOCAL()
```

- Description

The **SETLOCAL** function saves the environment settings that are local to the current process. The settings are the current working drive and directory as well as the current values of the environment variables of OS/2.

This function is useful for saving the settings before changing the values with the **VALUE** function. To restore the previous saved values, use the **ENDLOCAL** function.

● Return

The **SETLOCAL** function returns 1, if the settings are successfully saved; 0, if the operation failed.

● Example

```
/* The current path is 'C:\BOOK\ */

 n = SETLOCAL( )    /* save all the environment settings */

/* Change the PATH variable with VALUE function */

p = VALUE('Path','C:\BOOK\OS2REF','OS2ENVIRONMENT')

    .
    .
    .

 n = ENDLOCAL() /* Restore the settings;   */
                /* now the value of PATH variable is */
                /* changed to 'C:\BOOK'*/

SAY 'Resume output'
```

◘ SAY instruction—display data

● General format

```
SAY [expression] ;
```

● Description

The **SAY** instruction sends a line of data to a terminal or **SYSTSPRT** **DD** statement in batch mode.

expression is a valid **REXX** expression which is first resolved and then displayed by the **SAY** instruction.

● Example

```
SAY 'SAY what?'
name = 'Joe'
year = 10
SAY name ' is ' year 'old.'
```

◘ SELECT instruction—conditional execution of statements

- General format

```
SELECT
   WHEN expression[;] THEN[;] statement
   [WHEN expression[;] THEN[;] statement]
   [WHEN expression[;] THEN[;] statement]
      .
      .
      .
   [OTHERWISE[;] statement]
END;
```

- Description

The **SELECT** instruction executes only one statement from a group of statements. The selection depends on the result of evaluating an expression placed after the **WHEN** clause. If the result of the evaluation is 1 (TRUE), then the statement associated with this expression, which is placed after the **THEN** clause, is executed. If the result is 0 (FALSE), then the next expression with the **SELECT** instruction is evaluated. This continues until all the expressions with the **WHEN** clause have been evaluated and the associated statements executed if necessary. If none of the expressions with the **WHEN** clause yields 1 and an **OTHERWISE** clause exists, then the statement specified with that clause is executed. There must be at least one expression and statement with the **WHEN** and **THEN** clauses.

WHEN starts the condition clause.

expression is a valid REXX expression which is tested; the associated statement is executed if the result is 1.

The **THEN** clause specifies the statement to be executed.

statement is a valid REXX statement.

OTHERWISE specifies the statement to be executed when none of the above statements are performed.

END indicates the end of the **SELECT** instruction.

- Example

```
SELECT
   WHEN y = 0 THEN SAY 'Y is 0'
   WHEN y = 1 THEN SAY 'Y is 1'
```

```
    WHEN y = 2 THEN SAY 'Y is 2'
    OTHERWISE SAY 'Y < 0 or > 2'
END
```

◘ SIGN function—determine the sign of a number

- General format

```
SIGN(number)
```

- Description

The **SIGN** function determines the sign of a number.

number is the value whose sign is to be determined.

- Return

The **SIGN** function returns the following:

```
-1 if number is negative
 0 if number is equal to zero
+1 if number is positive
```

- Example

```
SIGN('-2.38')        returns -1
SIGN(0.0)            returns 0
SIGN('2.4')          returns +1
```

◘ SIGNAL instruction—exception condition handler

- General format

```
SIGNAL label
   or
SIGNAL [VALUE] expression
   or
SIGNAL OFF < ERROR or
                FAILURE or
                HALT or
                NOVALUE or
                SYNTAX
            >
   or
SIGNAL ON < ERROR or
                FAILURE or
```

```
        HALT or
        NOVALUE or
        SYNTAX
   >  [NAME label]
```

● Description

The **SIGNAL** instruction can be used in one of the following ways:

- To pass program control to a label or routine
- To enable exception condition processing
- To disable exception condition processing

label is the name of a label to which control is passed.

VALUE specifies the expression which is evaluated.

OFF specifies disabling the conditions that follow.

ON specifies enabling the conditions that follow.

ERROR means that there was a nonzero return code after a host command was executed.

HALT means that the terminal attention key has been pressed and an HT command entered.

NOVALUE means that a non-initialized variable has been used in a statement.

SYNTAX means that the REXX interpreter found a syntax error.

FAILURE means that a negative code was returned after an OS/2 command was executed.

● Example

```
SIGNAL ON NOVALUE novalue /* goto novalue */
    .
    .
    .
Attention: SAY 'Variable not initialized'

    EXIT
```

◘ SOURCELINE function—get a program line

● General format

```
SOURCELINE([line-number])
```

● Description

The **SOURCELINE** function retrieves the relative line number of a REXX source program line.

line-number is optional; when it is specified, the program line of the program is returned. If *line-number* is not specified, the function returns the line number of the last line.

◘ SPACE function—insert characters between words

● General format

```
SPACE(string[,[n][,pad]])
```

● Description

The **SPACE** function either inserts or removes padding characters between words in a string.

string is the string to or from which padding characters are added or removed.

n is the number of padding characters to insert between words of *string*.

pad is the padding character.

● Return

The **SPACE** function returns the changed string.

● Example

```
SPACE("All dogs go to heaven",2,'.')
     returns'All..dogs..go..to..heaven".

SPACE('A B C D      E',0)   returns 'ABCDE'.
```

◘ STREAM function—get status or result of a stream

● General format

```
STREAM([name[, State                   or
             Command, stream-command or
             Description ]
```

● Description

The **STREAM** function is used to set the status of a stream or receive the result of a REXX operation acted on a stream. Both of these requests can be performed on either an input or output stream.

name is a required argument and it must indentify a character stream.

State or **S** is used to check the status of a stream. If this state argument is specified, the function returns one of the following strings to indicate the status of a stream:

ERROR	Meaning the operation on an input or output stream has failed. More information can be obtained on the nature of the error by **STREAM** function using the description argument.
NOTREADY	Meaning that the stream is not available for an input or output operation.
READY	Meaning that the stream is available for an input or output operation.
UNKNOWN	Meaning that the stream is not yet opened for operation.

Command or **C** is issued as a command to a specified stream. With this argument you have to include a stream command.

stream-command can be one of the following:

OPEN	To open the specified stream. This is the default command. With this command, you can also add one of two subcommands: **READ** or **WRITE**. This opens a stream for a read or write opration; for example,

```
stream(strout,'C','OPEN WRITE')
            or
stream(strimp,'C','OPEN READ')
```

CLOSE — To close a stream that was previously opened and returns **READY**, if successful.

SEEK *offset* — To set the character position of an input or output stream. To use this command, you have to first open the stream. *offset* is an integer. This number can be preceded by one of the following characters:

= — The position is set to the offset value from the beginning of the stream.

< — The position is set to the offset value from the end of the stream.

+ — The offset value is added to the current read or write position.

- — The offset value is subtracted from the current read or write position.

The following stream commands return information about a stream.

QUERY EXIST — Returns the full pathname of a stream. If the stream does not exist, the function returns a null string.

QUERY SIZE — Returns the size of a stream.

QUERY DATETIME — Returns the date and timestamps of a stream.

Description or **D** gives additional information about the state of a stream. This argument is useful to obtain the description of an **ERROR** or **NOT READY** state of a stream.

● Return

The **STREAM** function returns

- The state of a stream
- The description of an error
- The pathname, size, and date and time of a stream

● Example

```
STREAM('CHAPTER.11','C','CLOSE') /* close the stream */
STREAM('CHAPTER.11','C','SEEK=2')
                  /* set the character position */
                  /* to 2                       */
STREAM('CHAPTER.11','C','SEEK=-9')
                  /* subtract 9 from the current */
```

```
                        /* character position        */
STREAM('CHAPTER.11','S')  /* query status            */
```

◘ STRIP function—remove leading and trailing characters from a string

- General format

```
STRIP(string[,[Both or Leading or Trailing][,char]])
```

- Description

The **STRIP** function removes any leading and trailing characters from a string.

string is the data from which characters are removed.

Both means to remove both leading and trailing characters from *string*.

Leading means to remove leading characters from *string*.

Trailing means to remove trailing characters from *string*.

char is the character to be removed from *string*; the default is a blank.

- Return

The **STRIP** function returns the stripped string.

- Example

```
STRIP(' Heavenly ',L)        returns 'Heavenly '.
STRIP('.Heavenly.',B,'.')    returns 'Heavenly'.
```

◘ SUBSTR function—extract a substring

- General format

```
SUBSTR(string,position[,[length][,pad]])
```

- Description

The **SUBSTR** function extracts a substring from a string starting at a specified character position.

string is the string from which a portion is extracted.

position is the character position in *string* at which the substring is extracted; it is also the first character of the extracted substring.

length is the number of bytes of the substring.

pad is the padding character.

- Return

The **SUBSTR** function returns the substring.

- Example

```
SUBSTR('Hot dog',4) returns ' dog'
```

◘ SUBWORD function—extract a word from a string

- General format

```
SUBWORD(string,word-position[,word-count])
```

- Description

The **SUBWORD** function extracts one or more words from a string starting at a specified word position.

string is the string from which one or more words are extracted.

word-position is a word position in *string* relative to 1; it is also the first position from which words are extracted.

word-count is the number of words to be extracted. The default is all the remaining words.

- Return

The SUBWORD function returns the extracted words.

- Example

```
SUBWORD('Hot dog',2) returns 'dog'
```

◘ SYMBOL function—get the status of a variable name

- General format

```
SYMBOL(name)
```

- Description

The **SYMBOL** function returns the status of a variable name.

name is a valid REXX variable name.

- Return

The **SYMBOL** function returns

VAR   If the variable name has been assigned a value and has not been deleted with a **DROP** function
LIT   If the variable name has not been assigned a value or if it has been deleted with a **DROP** function
BAD   If the variable name is not valid

- Example

```
d = "horses"
x = SYMBOL("d")          /* returns VAR */
y = SYMBOL("f")          /* returns LIT */
```

◘ TIME function—get the current time of day

- General format

```
TIME('Civil' or 'Elapse' or 'Hours' or 'Long' or
   'Minutes' or 'Normal' or 'Reset' or 'Seconds')
```

- Description

The **TIME** function returns the current time of day in different formats.

- Return

The **TIME** function returns the time in the following formats:

Code	Returns	Format
Civil	Time of day	hh:mmxx
Elapse	Elapsed time	sssssss.uuuuuuu
Hours	Hours since midnight	hh
Long	Time of day in the long form	hh:mm:ss.uuuuuuu
Minutes	Minutes since midnight	mmmm
Normal	Time of day	hh:mm:ss
Reset	Time elapsed since the elapsed clock was set or reset; the clock is reset	
Seconds	Seconds since midnight	sssss

● Example

```
x = TIME('H') /* return hours since midnight */
```

◘ TRACE instruction—set REXX debugging options

● General format

```
TRACE [number];
    or
TRACE   [ [? or !] ['All' or
           'Commands' or
           'Error'    or
           'Failure'  or
           'Intermediates' or
           'Labels'   or
           'Normal'   or
           'Off'  or
           'Results'  or
           'Scan' ]];
```

● Description

The **TRACE** instruction enables and disables tracing of execution of REXX statements.

If *number* has a positive value, it is the number of trace pauses to skip over. If *number* is negative, it is the number of trace outputs to suppress.

? is a prefix which means to enable interactive debugging.

! is a prefix which means to turn off execution of host commands.

All means to display all expressions before execution.

Commands means to display the host command before execution.

Error means to display a host command returning a nonzero code.

Failure means to display a host command returning a negative code.

Intermediates means to display all expressions before execution and all intermediate results.

Labels means to display labels when they are encountered.

Normal means to display a host command returning a negative code.

Off means to end tracing.

Results means to display all expressions before execution and displays the results.

Scan means to check the syntax of REXX statements but not to execute them.

- Example

```
TRACE '?C' /* turn on host command tracing */
```

◻ TRACE function—set or return current trace setting

- General format

```
TRACE    ( [? or !] ['All' or
             'Commands' or
             'Error'     or
             'Failure'   or
             'Intermediates' or
             'Labels'    or
             'Normal'    or
             'Off'       or
             'Results'   or
             'Scan'  )
```

- Description

The **TRACE** function either sets or returns the current REXX trace setting. The following options are used: All, Commands, Error, Failure,

Intermediates, Labels, Normal, Off, Results, and Scan. These options were previously described with the **TRACE** instruction. If the option is omitted, the function returns the current setting.

● Return

The **TRACE** function returns the current setting.

● Example

```
y = TRACE()           /* return the current setting */
x = TRACE('?C')       /* turn on tracing for host commands */
```

◘ TRANSLATE function—translate and reorder characters in a string

● General format

```
TRANSLATE(string[,[outtab][,intab][,pad]])
```

● Description

The **TRANSLATE** function translates and reorders the content of a string depending on input and output translation tables. If the first character of the input table is found in the string, then this matching character in the string is replaced with the first character in the output table. The characters in the input table map to characters in the output table. If only the string is specified, with all other arguments omitted, then **TRANSLATE** converts all characters to uppercase.

string is the string to be translated and reordered.

outtab is the output translation table.

intab is the input translation table.

pad is the padding character used to extend the length of *outtab* if required.

● Example

```
TRANSLATE('abcdef')  returns 'ABCDEF'
TRANSLATE('abcdef','1','abcdef','1') returns '111111'
```

◘ TRUNC function—truncate a number

- General format

```
TRUNC(number[,decimal-places])
```

- Description

The **TRUNC** function formats a number to a specified number of decimal places.

number is the numeric value to be formatted.

decimal-places is the number of decimal places. The default value is 0.

- Return

The **TRUNC** function returns the formatted numeric value.

- Example

```
TRUNC("1222.6757") returns '1222'
TRUNC("1222.6757",2) returns '1222.67'
```

◘ VALUE function—get the content of a symbol

- General format

```
VALUE(name)
```

- Description

The **VALUE** function returns the content of a symbol.

name is a valid REXX symbol or variable name.

- Example

```
x = 'My oh my'

y = VALUE(x)

SAY y        /* displays 'My oh my'*/
```

◘ VERIFY function—compare two strings

- General format

```
VERIFY(string1,string2
        [,'Match' or 'Nomatch'][,position])
```

- Description

The **VERIFY** function compares two strings and determines the position of the first matching character in both strings or the position of the first character that does not match in both strings.

string1 is one of the strings.

string2 is the other string.

Match is the option to check for a matching character in both *string1* and *string2*.

Nomatch is the option to check for the first character in *string1* that does not match *string2*.

position is the starting position of the comparison.

- Return

The **VERIFY** function returns the first position in *string1* that has a matching or nonmatching character. It returns zero if the option is '**Match**' and all characters in *string1* and *string2* match. It also returns zero if none of the characters in *string1* and *string2* match, if the option is '**Nomatch**'.

- Example

```
VERIFY("abcd","ccc",'M')      returns 3
VERIFY("abdc","2",'N')        returns 0
```

◘ WORD function—get a word

- General format

```
WORD(string,word-num)
```

- Description

The **WORD** function extracts a word from a string at a given word position.

string is the string from which the word is extracted.

word-num is the word position relative to 1 in *string*.

- Return

The **WORD** function returns the word extracted.

- Example

```
WORD("The world is but one country",2) returns 'world'
```

◻ WORDINDEX function—get a word position in a string

- General format

```
WORDINDEX(string,word-num)
```

- Description

The **WORDINDEX** function returns the character position of a word in a string. It returns zero if the word is not found.

string is the string that is searched for the character position of a word.

word-num is the position relative to 1 in *string* of the word whose character position is determined.

- Example

```
WORDINDEX("The world is but one country",2) returns 5
```

◻ WORDLENGTH function—get a word length in a string

- General format

```
WORDLENGTH(string,word-num)
```

- Description

  The **WORDLENGTH** function returns the length of a word in a string. It returns zero if the word is not found.

  string is the string that is searched for the length of a word.

  word-num is the position relative to 1 in *string* of the word whose length is determined.

- Example

  ```
  WORDLENGTH("The world is but one country",2) returns 5
  ```

◘ WORDPOS function—get a word position in a string

- General format

  ```
  WORDPOS(string-to-find,string-to-search[,word-num])
  ```

- Description

  The **WORDPOS** function returns the position of a specified word in a string. It returns zero if the word is not found.

  string-to-find is the word searched for in a string.

  string-to-search is the string that is searched.

  word-num is the number of the word at which the search starts and is the word position relative to 1 in *string-to-search*.

- Example

  ```
  WORDPOS("The world is but one country","is") returns 3
  ```

◘ WORDS function—get the number of words in a string

- General format

  ```
  WORDS(string)
  ```

- Description

  The **WORDS** function returns the number of words in a string.

string is the string whose words are counted.

- Example

```
WORDS("The world is but one country") returns 6
```

◘ XRANGE function—get a range of hexadecimal numbers

- General format

```
XRANGE([start][,end])
```

- Description

The **XRANGE** function returns a range of hexadecimal numbers given lower and upper limits.

start is the lower limit of the range.

end is the upper limit of the range.

- Example

```
XRANGE('0','3') returns 'F0F1F2F3'x (ASCII)
```

◘ X2C function—convert hexadecimal to character

- General format

```
X2C(hex-string)
```

- Description

The **X2C** function converts a string of hexadecimal values into a character string.

hex-string is one or more hexadecimal digits to be converted.

- Return

The **X2C** function returns the converted character string.

- Example

```
X2C('F0F1F2')   returns 012
```

◼ X2D function—convert hexadecimal to decimal

- General format

```
X2D(hex-string)
```

- Description

The **X2D** function converts a string of hexadecimal values into a decimal string.

hex-string is one or more hexadecimal digits to be converted.

- Return

The **X2D** function returns the converted decimal string.

- Example

```
X2C('F0F0')   returns 61680
```